Evolutionary Algorithms
in Management Applications

Springer
Berlin
Heidelberg
New York
Barcelona
Budapest
Hong Kong
London
Milan
Paris
Santa Clara
Singapore
Tokyo

Jörg Biethahn · Volker Nissen (Eds.)

Evolutionary Algorithms in Management Applications

With 116 Figures

 Springer

Prof. Dr. Jörg Biethahn
Dr. Volker Nissen

Georg-August-Universität
Institut für Wirtschaftsinformatik
Abteilung Wirtschaftsinformatik I
Platz der Göttinger Sieben 5
D-37073 Göttingen
Germany

Cataloging-in-Publication Data applied for

ᴵ   Die Deutsche Bibliothek - CIP-Einheitsaufnahme

Evolutionary algorithms in management applications / Jörg
Biethahn ; Volker Nissen (Hrsg.). - Berlin ; Heidelberg ; New
York ; Barcelona ; Budapest ; Hong Kong ; London ; Milan ;
Paris ; Santa Clara ; Singapore ; Tokyo : Springer, 1995
  ISBN 3-540-60382-4
NE: Biethahn, Jörg [Hrsg.]

ISBN 3-540-60382-4 Springer-Verlag Berlin Heidelberg New York

SPIN: 10517669   42/2202 - 5 4 3 2 1 0 - Printed on acid-free paper

Preface

Evolutionary Algorithms (EA) are powerful search and optimisation techniques inspired by the mechanisms of natural evolution. They imitate, on an abstract level, biological principles such as a population based approach, the inheritance of information, the variation of information via crossover/mutation, and the selection of individuals based on fitness. The most well-known class of EA are Genetic Algorithms (GA), which have received much attention not only in the scientific community lately. Other variants of EA, in particular Genetic Programming, Evolution Strategies, and Evolutionary Programming are less popular, though very powerful too.

Traditionally, most practical applications of EA have appeared in the technical sector. Management problems, for a long time, have been a rather neglected field of EA-research. This is surprising, since the great potential of evolutionary approaches for the business and economics domain was recognised in pioneering publications quite a while ago. John Holland, for instance, in his seminal book *Adaptation in Natural and Artificial Systems* (The University of Michigan Press, 1975) identified economics as one of the prime targets for a theory of adaptation, as formalised in his *reproductive plans* (later called Genetic Algorithms).

Interest in EA has risen considerably over the last five years. We have recently witnessed an increasing number of interesting EA-papers related to management problems, appearing distributed over many conferences and journals. This volume is a collection of innovative papers concerning the application of EA in the domain of management. The focus is on optimisation, thereby looking at EA mainly from the viewpoint of operations research. Some of the contributions describe practical applications in business, while others should be classified application-oriented research. We have grouped the contributions in sections. The first part of this book lays the foundations for a thorough understanding of the other papers by introducing the field of EA. It also gives an overview of the current state of EA-research with respect to management applications. Many references are classified and listed in the paper by *Nissen*.

Parts 2 to 6 of this volume contain applications of EA in various economic sectors, namely industry, trade, financial services, traffic management, and education. In the following, we shall briefly review the contents of these contributions.

Scheduling is an important practical problem in industry that is hard to tackle with traditional optimisation methods, due to conflicting requirements, interrelated constraints, and high computational complexity. Additionally, unexpected events such as delays and machine breakdowns may require prompt changes of schedules in operation. The GA based approach described by *Filipic* in his paper deals with a subclass where the optimality of schedules is related to resource management. An asymmetric crossover operator ensures that newly generated solutions remain valid. Elitism and local improvement of candidate solutions are also included in the algorithm to enhance the results of genetic search. The resulting scheduling system is capable of dealing with highly constrained and complex problem instances. Filipic discusses two practical examples: scheduling a production unit in a textile factory, and resource management in ship repair.

In the paper of *Rixen et al.* the authors are concerned with scheduling jobs on a collator machine which connects nails to strips for professional nailing tools. The general setting is a just-in-time production process of a company that produces specialised fastening tools for the automobile industry, and other fasteners. Minimising the mean absolute lateness of jobs is the objective. The current manual scheduling is very time-consuming. The authors propose an event-driven automated scheduling approach based on a method that generates machine schedules, and a rule which determines when to apply the method. A simulation study establishes the superiority of the discussed GA based methodology. Since scheduling is a dynamic problem, the GA is used on a rolling time basis. The genetic schedule representation is based on two interacting strings, where the first one encodes the job sequence on the given machine, while the second one determines the number of double shifts used to process each of the jobs.

Complex manufacturing systems are frequently characterised by routing flexibility which aims at improving system performance. Manufacturers, though, have been slow to exploit the benefits, a likely reason being the complexity of the resulting scheduling problems. To overcome these limitations, *Bowden and Bullington* present an unsupervised GA based machine learning technique to address control issues for complex manufacturing processes. The technique uses a computer simulation to derive a knowledge base, consisting of a collection of rules as a scheduling and control scheme tailored for the given production system. This procedure requires little *a priori* scheduling and control expertise as input and, thus, can be used to derive control knowledge for a variety of production systems without adjusting the general method.

In the contribution of *Ettl and Schwehm* a just-in-time production line is considered which is composed of a sequence of production stages, where the flow of parts through the overall facility is controlled by a combined push/pull policy which is implemented by means of kanbans. In order to operate such a system effectively, two important plant configuration problems must be solved. First, one must decide on the number of production stages and the number of workstations assigned to individual stages. Second, given a partition of the production line, an optimal number of kanbans should be assigned to each production stage. For these problems Ettl and Schwehm propose to use a general-purpose GA package with adapted solution representation. The evaluation of solutions is done via a queueing network representation of the kanban system and an approximate analytical method, since simulation would be much more computationally expensive. Practical experiments establish that the accuracy of the GA based methodology is quite satisfactory over a wide range of problem instances.

In constrained optimisation it is common practice to use penalty functions which penalise solutions that fail to satisfy all constraints. The general understanding seems to be that well-chosen, graded penalties are better than harsh penalties. In their paper, *Krause and Nissen* compare the effect of different types of penalty functions in the context of abstract facility layout problems of varying complexity. They employ a simple Evolution Strategy as the basic optimisation technique. The empirical results indicate that, for this application, finetuning penalty factors is unnecessary, even when there are only few valid solutions. The authors also compare two multicriteria optimisation techniques on this problem domain where the number of violated constraints becomes a second objective to be minimised. The results establish the superiority of the one multicriteria approach over the other, when finding a large set of pareto-optimal (non-dominated) solutions is the main goal. Both methods are inferior to penalty function approaches, however, when finding a good valid solution is desired.

The Bin Packing Problem underlies many practical optimisation problems, such as the cutting of tubes and rods from a stock of constant length in construction. *Falkenauer* concentrates on developing a tailored GA approach for this problem class that is significantly improved over a more naive standard GA. In particular, he proposes a solution representation that reflects the structure of the problem being optimised, and uses a powerful local optimisation technique, inspired by ideas of Martello and Toth, to improve GA solutions. Extensive experimental comparisons confirm the superiority of Falkenauer's hybrid GA approach over a recent sophisticated branch-and-bound procedure of Martello and Toth, in both the quality of solutions and the speed of their delivery. Both heuristics employ the same local optimisation techniques, but use different global mechanisms for generating candidate solutions. Given the superiority of the GA based approach, this further underlines the power of GA in searching vast solution spaces of difficult problems.

The contribution of *Parada Daza et al.* investigates the use of GA for the two-dimensional guillotine cutting problem (cut of a number of rectangular pieces from a single rectangular plate) with minimum trim loss, also respecting several practical constraints. This cutting problem is represented by a syntactic binary tree which is then encoded as a string suitable for processing by a GA. Experimental results establish the superiority of this technique over the well-known algorithm of Oliveira and Ferreira for large problem instances. A characteristic of the GA used here is the variable string length. Starting with short strings representing individual pieces to cut, the overall approach is quite alike the messy-GA developed by Goldberg and co-workers. Operators include rotation of pieces, a feature that can significantly improve solution quality.

Broekmeulen presents a hierarchical algorithm to solve the facility management problem in large distribution centers for vegetables and fruits in the Netherlands. Adequate storage conditions are a prerequisite to minimise quality loss on these sensitive goods. The system must balance quality loss against utilization of storage capacity. In particular, clusters of product groups must be formed, and optimal cluster storage properties determined. This is a highly complex, non-linear decision problem that can only be solved iteratively for real world instances. Broekmeulen uses a GA to allocate storage capacity and adequate conditions to clusters, while the grouping part of the overall problem is done via Linear Programming. The planning process is performed iteratively, allowing the facility manager to interact with the software system.

Terano et al. present a novel method to analyse data on consumer goods gathered via questionaires. In particular, they extract classification rules from noisy data on oral care products to explain the relationship of product image and product features in order to make decisions for promotion. A GA is developed to extract relevant product features later used by an induction technique to build decision trees. A special part of the GA is the employment of human market specialist's preferences in the evaluation step. This is necessary as the domain involves subjective judgments, and the explicit definition of an evaluation function is difficult. It requires, however, to keep the GA population size small due to the high effort in evaluation. Results are presented for experiments with two selected images ('innovative' and 'effective'). The generated decision tree is based on a relatively small number of features.

Marks et al. in their paper investigate how players in oligopolistic markets respond to their rival's behaviour. They use GA based machine learning to derive improved contingent strategies for such markets, in order to provide insights into the evolution of oligopolistic markets and the patterns of behaviour observed in reality. Using empirical data on the weekly prices and promotional instruments of the four largest and several smaller coffee sellers in a regional U.S. retail market, they model sellers as finite automata with memory of previous weeks' actions. A market model is employed to predict seller's market shares and profits in response to actions of other participants. The authors use a GA to derive automata which are fit, given their environment, as described by their rival's actions in the past and the implicit demand for coffee. Several manegerial implications of this approach are outlined.

Optimising a real system with simulation is frequently a very difficult task. One reason being the often large and complex search space of values for the decision variables, which prohibits the use of more conventional optimisation techniques. Evolutionary Algorithms are particularly well-suited for determining good decision variable settings of a simulation model in the case of a complex search space. For a given setting a fitness value can be calculated by executing the simulation. Fitness values enable the EA to perform a goal-oriented search in the space of parameter settings. *Nissen and Biethahn* look at an example that is further complicated by the stochastic nature of the problem. In particular, using a GA, they determine a good management policy for an inventory simulation in a make-to-stock plant, where demand is stochastic with respect to quantity and intervals, and replenishment times are also of a stochastic nature. In a comparison with two classical optimisation methods the GA produces good results more reliably, and also appears to be more robust when only few evaluations can be performed for each trial solution.

Many financial market participants are affected by fluctuations in foreign exchange rates. The ability to forecast exchange rates is obviously of great potential value. *Bauer* focuses on developing a GA for the purpose of monthly currency allocation decisions that takes into account fundamental economic variables. The author has chosen the problem of how to allocate assets between U.S. dollars and German deutschemarks. He tests the model over the 1984-93 time period. The results show that the GA can find interesting trading rules, although the forecasting potential of these rules may be inconclusive. Another important contribution of the paper is the description of how asset allocation decisions can be modelled using GAs.

The financial services sector is a prime target for the application of data analysis techniques to aid in decision making. A basic problem in credit control is the construction of a scorecard from variables relating to the particular features of the bank/customer relationship. The construction of such scorecards is a time-consuming modelling task that must take into account the quality of the available data. Current statistical techniques are constrained in their efficiacy by various factors. The alternative approach, put forward by *Ireson and Fogarty*, attempts to provide the benefits from both statistical and expert system/machine learning techniques to overcome some of these limitations. They have developed a GA based decision support system for evolving Bayesian classifiers from a set of observed data. The fitness of a given individual in the GA population is calculated by constructing a probabilistic classifier from the representation and evaluating the prediction on a training set of data. In comparison with alternative machine learning techniques, the GA produces significantly better results without the requirement of special statistical knowledge. A detailed evaluation of the system is presently being carried out in conjunction with a bank.

Vere, with his experience at Bank of America, applies in his contribution Genetic Classification Trees to the problem of predicting the prepayment of home mortgages. Individual home mortgage loans have a lifespan. Many people prepay their loan for various reasons. Since the financial return which a lender derives from a loan is a function of the actual lifespan of the loan, it is important for the bank to correctly predict this lifespan in order to set loan parameters so as to maximise profits. In his approach, the author extends and customises the Genetic Programming operators of tree crossover and mutation to advantage for the evolution of classification trees, using the notions of subtree visitations and subtree fitness contributions. Unvisited subtrees can be pruned away, and subtree fitness can be monitored in order to focus crossover and mutation activity. These ideas may also benefit Genetic Programming in general.

In their paper *de la Maza and Yuret* describe a stock market simulation in which stock market participants, characterised by a four parameter model, use a GA to gradually improve their trading strategies over time. Experiments show that, under certain conditions, some participants can make consistent profits over an extended period of time. Although the simulation does not capture all the subtleties and nuances of the market, their findings might help to explain the success of some real-world money makers. Practical experiments investigate questions such as whether market participants still uncover good strategies in the face of noise, and what effect forced liquidations have on profit. The authors are co-founders of a money management firm that applies EA to produce customised trading strategies. Their contribution also includes a discussion of the shortcomings of Neural Networks, the most widely used AI method for financial time series analysis.

McDonnell and co-workers propose a rule-based strategy for ramp metering control of U.S. freeways. The controller determines ramp discharge rules based on sensor data of freeway occupancy levels. Evolutionary Programming is used to adapt rule thresholds, so that this general procedure can be applied to any freeway configuration. The methodology is successfully evaluated with a sophisticated traffic simulation program on a uniform freeway segment. An advantage of the rule-based approach is that it can be implemented in real-time via a look-up table. Moreover, knowledge from traffic control engineers can be directly incorporated into the control strategy.

Air traffic control systems in many countries must cope with rising traffic congestion and, therefore, increasing delay, due to growing air traffic and prescribed standard flight routes. *Gerdes* demonstrates in her contribution the use of a GA in determining conflict-free flight routes for aircraft in the case of free routing. The overall objectives are to decrease the delay of aircraft, and use the airspace more efficiently. The employed GA is a modification of the modGA by Michalewicz (1992). Routing of aircraft is performed interactively with the flight controller.

Baita et al. deal with vehicle scheduling for the mass transportation system of the city of Mestre, Italy. The goal is to assign a fleet of vehicles to a set of trips under constraints. While using a GA with redundant coding to account for incompatibilities of trips they achieve a significant improvement over the currently employed solution. The problem is studied under single as well as multiple objectives. The authors experiment with different selection variants, and finally use tournament and local geographic selection in parallel.

Constructing timetables is a very tough combinatorial optimisation problem that has long been studied. However, no satisfying automated approach exists to date for complex real-world situations. Timetabling is regularly required at universities and high-schools, and, performed manually, a laborious task. *Junginger* in his contribution proposes a GA based automated approach for constructing timetables at German high schools (Gymnasien) where teaching subjects are offered as courses that may vary in duration, and where pupils must choose from a variety of courses. The objective is to find a valid and efficient schedule. Junginger's solution representation is a zero-one matrix matching school hours and courses. Although the application is simplified, results are encouraging to extend this approach, and include further practical constraints.

Finally, we would like to thank Christian Behr, Matthias Krause, Uwe Steinhardt, and Gerald Wissel for the technical support provided in the preparation of this volume. We also thank Springer-Verlag, and especially Dr. Werner Müller, for the good cooperation and support.

Göttingen, June 1995

Jörg Biethahn
Volker Nissen

Contents

Part 1   Foundations

An Introduction to Evolutionary Algorithms 3
Volker Nissen, Jörg Biethahn

An Overview of Evolutionary Algorithms in Management
Applications 44
Volker Nissen

Part 2   Applications in Industry

A Genetic Algorithm Applied to Resource Management in
Production Systems 101
Bogdan Filipic

A Case Study of Operational Just-In-Time Scheduling Using
Genetic Algorithms 112
Ivo Rixen, Christian Bierwirth, Herbert Kopfer

An Evolutionary Algorithm for Discovering Manufacturing Control
Strategies 124
Royce Bowden, Stanley F. Bullington

Determining the Optimal Network Partition and Kanban Allocation
in JIT Production Lines 139
Markus Ettl, Markus Schwehm

On Using Penalty Functions and Multicriteria Optimisation
Techniques in Facility Layout 153
Matthias Krause, Volker Nissen

Tapping the Full Power of Genetic Algorithm through Suitable
Representation and Local Optimization: Application to Bin Packing 167
Emanuel Falkenauer

A Hybrid Genetic Algorithm for the Two-Dimensional Guillotine
Cutting Problem 183
Victor Parada Daza, Ricardo Muñoz, Arlindo Gómes de Alvarenga

XIV

Part 3   Applications in Trade

Facility Management of Distribution Centres for Vegetables and
Fruits 199
Rob A.C.M. Broekmeulen

Integrating Machine Learning and Simulated Breeding Techniques
to Analyze the Characteristics of Consumer Goods 211
Takao Terano, Yoko Ishino, Kazuyuki Yoshinaga

Adaptive Behaviour in an Oligopoly 225
Robert E. Marks, David F. Midgley, Lee G. Cooper

Determining a Good Inventory Policy with a Genetic Algorithm 240
Volker Nissen, Jörg Biethahn

Part 4   Applications in Financial Services

Genetic Algorithms and the Management of Exchange Rate Risk 253
Richard J. Bauer

Evolving Decision Support Models for Credit Control 264
Neil S. Ireson, Terence C. Fogarty

Genetic Classification Trees 277
Steven A. Vere

A Model of Stock Market Participants 290
Michael de la Maza, Deniz Yuret

Part 5   Applications in Traffic Management

Using Evolutionary Programming to Control Metering Rates on
Freeway Ramps 305
*John R. McDonnell, David B. Fogel, Craig R. Rindt, Wilfred W.
Recker, Lawrence J. Fogel*

Application of Genetic Algorithms for Solving Problems Related to
Free Routing for Aircraft 328
Ingrid Gerdes

Genetic Algorithm with Redundancies for the Vehicle Scheduling
Problem 341
Flavio Baita, Francesco Mason, Carlo Poloni, Walter Ukovich

Part 6   Planning in Education

Course Scheduling by Genetic Algorithms 357
Werner Junginger

Appendix

About the Authors 371

Part One
Foundations

To my family   *J.B.*
To my brother Gunter *V.N.*

An Introduction to Evolutionary Algorithms

Volker Nissen, Jörg Biethahn

Abteilung Wirtschaftsinformatik I, Universität Göttingen, Platz der Göttinger Sieben 5, 37073 Göttingen, Germany, {vnissen, jbietha}@gwdg.de

Abstract. We discuss the mainstream directions of Evolutionary Algorithms (EA), a class of stochastic search and optimisation techniques with heuristic character. EA have recently attracted many researchers and practitioners, not only in the management domain, due to their applicability to very complex problems. In this paper, we describe, next to the standard forms of Genetic Algorithms, Genetic Programming, Evolution Strategies and Evolutionary Programming, also Learning Classifier Systems, and some other hybrid approaches that integrate different technologies. Our focus, however, is on Genetic Algorithms as the most prominent and diversified EA-type.

Keywords. genetic algorithms, genetic programming, evolution strategies, evolutionary programming, classifier systems, hybrid systems, optimisation

1   Introduction[*]

Recently, innovative technologies which are based on principles from nature have successfully been applied to a variety of complex problems in optimisation, system identification, data mining and other areas. *Parallel Problem Solving from Nature* (Schwefel and Männer 1991) has been coined as an expression to embrace these technologies, among which Simulated Annealing, artificial neural networks, and Evolutionary Algorithms are perhaps the most prominent branches.

Although global convergence proofs are available for some of these approaches, they must be viewed as heuristics for the purposes of practical optimisation under resource limits and time-constraints. In this paper, we discuss Evolutionary Algorithms (EA) to provide the foundations for the other papers in this volume. Though EA they may be applied in different ways, we mainly look at EA as a promising new class of operations research techniques. For a discussion from a machine learning viewpoint see e.g. Fogel (1995). Due to space limitations, we cannot detail every promising algorithmic variant that has been proposed. By citing the appropriate literature, however, we have tried to provide some paths to follow up for the reader who wants further information.

---

[*] The figures in this paper are taken from Nissen (1994a).

The general organisation of the paper is as follows: In section 2 we introduce EA from a unifying perspective, focussing on the common paradigm of the various mainstream forms. Section 3 highlights Genetic Algorithms, the most popular EA-variant as can be verified by the composition of contributions in this volume. Section 4 outlines Genetic Programming (GP). GP is essentially an important spin-off from the field of Genetic Algorithms, and aims at automatically evolving computer programs to solve problems. Evolution Strategies, as discussed in section 5, are a form of EA that is particularly popular in Germany where this methodology also originated. Evolutionary Programming, described in section 6, is very similar to Evolution Strategies, though independently developed. Section 7 discussed Learning Classifier Systems and, in short form, some other hybrid approaches. In these systems, EA are integrated with various technologies to achieve better overall performance by combining the advantages of the different system components. Finally, we conclude the paper in section 8.

2   Evolutionary Algorithms

Evolutionary Algorithms are search and optimisation techniques based on the principles of natural evolution. The important mainstrean forms of EA are

- Genetic Algorithms (GA)
- Genetic Programming (GP)
- Evolution Strategies (ES)
- Evolutionary Programming (EP).

As will be detailed later, these approaches show some differences, mainly w.r.t. solution representation, overall sequence of operations, selection scheme, implementation and importance of crossover/mutation, and determination of strategy parameters. However, one should rather point to the *common paradigm* underlying all major EA-variants. They imitate, on an abstract level, the basic idea of a population approach and the principles of replication, variation, and selection from evolution theory (figure 1). Besides biologically inspired terminology (explained in table 1), EA differ from conventional search methods in a number of ways:

- With the exception of GP that generates program code, EA in general operate on a string or vector representation of the decision variables.
- They, generally, process a set of solutions, exploring the search space from many different points simultaneously.
- The basic EA-operators imitate processes of replication, variation, and selection as the driving forces of natural evolution. The idea is that favouring the fittest solutions in selection, and a variation of inherited material in the offspring will, over many iterations, lead to particularly good solutions for the given problem.
- For goal-directed search, only information on the quality (fitness) of solutions is required. This fitness information is frequently calculated from

an objective function, but may also be obtained by other measures, e.g. simulation. No auxiliary knowledge such as derivatives is required. However, incorporating available domain knowledge in solution representation, initialisation, operators or decoding scheme may substantially increase the competitiveness of an EA at the cost of a reduced scope of application.

- Stochastic elements are deliberately employed. This means no pure random search, though, but an intelligent exploration of the search space. Information from already discovered good solutions is *exploited* while promising new areas of the search space continue to be *explored*.

One starts with an initial set (population) of alternative solutions (individuals) for the given problem. Frequently, these initial solutions are randomly generated or evenly scattered over the region of interest in search space. Then, the evolutionary operators of replication, variation, and selection are applied. The exact sequence and implementation of these operators varies between the different EA mainstream forms. By performing these steps, new solutions (offspring) are generated which can then be evaluated in terms of solution quality (fitness). The interplay of replication, variation and selection of the fittest leads to solutions of increasing quality over the course of many (sometimes thousands) of iterations (generations). When finally a termination criterion is met, such as a maximum number of generations, the search process is terminated and the final solution output. A nice feature of EA is their ability to continue the optimisation as long as resources are available. An overview of major advantages and disadvantages of EA as optimisation techniques are given in table 2.

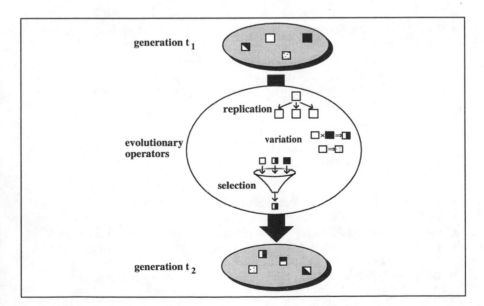

Fig. 1. Basic EA-cycle.

individual	structure (contains the adequately represented elements of a solution to the given problem)
population	set of individuals
parents	individuals selected for reproduction
children, offspring	new solutions generated from the parents
fitness	solution quality w.r.t. the given objectives
crossover	search operator that mixes elements from different individuals
mutation	search operator that modifies a given single individual
generation	EA-iteration

Mainly in the GA-context:

chromosome (composed of genes)	basically identical with individual; occasionally an individual is composed of several chromosomes; common form: string
gene	bit (assuming binary coding)
allele	value of a gene (binary: 0 or 1)
genotype	coded solution
phenotype	decoded solution

Table 1. Some basic EA-terminology.

Advantages:
- basic EA-forms are broadly applicable though may generate only mediocre solutions
- flexible customising is possible to better suit the needs of the given application and produce high quality solutions
- well suited for high dimensional complex search spaces
- reliable (in general)
- no restrictive assumptions about the objective function (need not be continuous or differentiable, for instance)
- applicable even in cases where not much domain knowledge is available
- allow for multiple criteria optimisation
- easily combined with other techniques (initialisation heuristics, local search etc.)
- efficient use of parallel hardware (inherently parallel algorithms)

Disadvantages:
- heuristic character (no guarantee to reach *global* optimum in limited time)
- theory of EA is still in its infancy
- comparatively high CPU-requirements (alleviated by rapid progress in hardware)
- often ineffective in fine-tuning final solution (hybridising with local search is a useful countermeasure)
- finding good settings for strategy parameters (e.g. population size and structure, crossover rate) can be difficult and requires some experience

Table 2. Main advantages and disadvantages of EA for parameter optimisation.

EA proved robust in solving very diverse complex optimisation and adaptation tasks. Table 3 gives an overview of some published applications of EA in management science and other domains. To summarise, EA are innovative and promising techniques, applicable to many complex problems (high-dimensional, multimodal, ill-defined, stochastic perturbations) where more traditional methods (such as gradient-based hillclimbers) cannot be applied. When the given problem has a structure that permits the application of an efficient solution technique (such as Linear Programming), though, EA are likely to be inferior. However, such dedicated solution techniques are not available for many practical problems in operations research and other domains.

- path planning for mobile robots
- optimising structure and parameters of an Artificial Neural Net
- data mining
- system identification and optimal control
- design applications in engineering and telecommunication
- task allocation in multiprocessor systems
- line balancing in industry
- production scheduling
- vehicle routing
- personnel scheduling

Table 3. Some published applications of EA.

3 Genetic Algorithms

3.1 An Elementary GA

Genetic Algorithms were originally developed by Holland (1975, 1992), and later refined by De Jong (1975), Goldberg (1989), and many others. They imitate evolutionary processes with a particular focus on genetic mechanisms. The standard GA operates on a population of bitstrings (figure 2). Each individual represents a solution, coding all the decision variables. GA individuals are characterised by a duality of bitstring-code (genotype) and the decoded solution (phenotype), roughly imitating the natural model. Real numbers can, with limited accuracy, be binary coded as well.

Example: We want to binary code a real variable x which is defined over

$$-1 \leq x \leq 2 \quad x \in R .$$

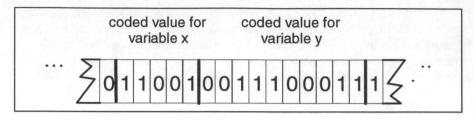

Fig. 2. Coding in standard GAs.

First, we must decide the required precision for coding x. Assuming the first digit after the decimal point is sufficient, we can think of the defined domain for x as divided in 30 intervals of 0.1 width each. To binary code this precision at least 5 bits are necessary, because $16=2^4<30<2^5=32$. We define a decoding function D where

$$D(00000) = -1 \quad \text{(lower bound } I_{min})$$

$$D(11111) = 2 \quad \text{(upper bound } I_{max})$$

All other possible bitstrings $(b_4b_3b_2b_1b_0)$ are linarly mapped to real values in the interval $[I_{min}, I_{max}]$. First, the strings are converted from base 2 to base 10:

$$x' = \sum_{i=0}^{4} b_i \cdot 2^i$$

Then, the decoded real number is given by:

$$x = I_{min} + \frac{I_{max} - I_{min}}{2^5 - 1} \cdot x'$$

For instance, the string *10000* would be decoded as follows:

$$x' = 16$$

$$x = -1 + \frac{3}{31} \cdot 16 = 0{,}5483856 \approx 0{,}5.$$

It is obvious that such a discrete coding of real numbers can lead to problems, since the mapping of bitstrings to real numbers may not be unequivocal. (The string 01111 decodes to a value $x=0.5$, too.) Especially for combinatorial problems, one frequently uses non-binary solution representations in GAs, since they often better preserve structural characteristics of the application (see section 3.2).

A GA population constists of *n* individuals (generally between 30 and 500). The initial population is frequently generated at random, and consecutive generations are evolved by applying the operators of selection, crossover, and mutation. Additional operators may be used, and many variations of the GA-scheme have been proposed in the literature. In the following, we describe the algorithmic steps of a rather elementary GA, with some resemblance to Goldberg's *Simple GA* (Goldberg 1989). Some important extensions are given in section 3.2 .

Step 1: Initialisation

As mentioned above, the standard procedure would be to randomly generate the initial population. If prior domain knowledge is available, it may be used, e.g. by restricting the initialisation to a region of interest, or by applying an initialisation heuristic. However, it is important to ensure a high degree of diversity among solutions, in order for the crossover operator to work effectively ('grist for the genetic mill').

Step 2: Evaluation

During evaluation a fitness value is determined for all solutions in the current population. The fitness Φ_i of an individual i ($i=1,2...n$) is frequently calculated by transforming the corresponding objective function value F_i. However, one may also determine the quality of a solution by experiment or simulation, if required. For now, we assume a maximisation problem, and fitness to be positive and identical to the objective function value.

Step3: Fitness-proportional selection

In our elemenatary GA we apply fitness-proportional selection. The idea is to give good solutions a higher chance of passing their 'genes' to the following generation than bad ones. One may think of the individuals in the current population as segments on a wheel of fortune with segment-size according to fitness (figure 3). The selection probability $P_s(i)$ of an individual i is given by:

$$P_s(i) = \frac{\Phi_i}{\sum_{j=1}^{n} \Phi_j}$$

The wheel is spun twice to determine two mating partners for the next step.

Step 4: Crossover.

Crossover is the main search operator in GAs, mixing elements of different solutions. The most simple form is one-point crossover as depicted in figure 4. Based on a crossover rate P_c (recommended $P_c \geq 0{,}6$), we first determine whether or not a crossover of the two mating partners should take place. If this is not the case, then both individuals are further processed as described in step 5. Else, we randomly determine a common crossover point on both strings, without caring for boundaries between different coded decision variables.

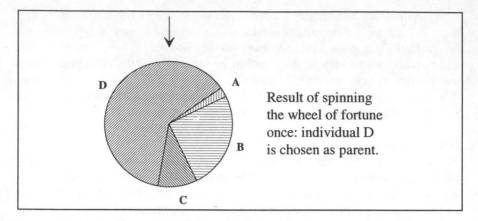

Result of spinning
the wheel of fortune
once: individual D
is chosen as parent.

Fig. 3. Visualisation of fitness-proportional selection in Genetic Algorithms.

Now segments are exchanged between both strings as is illustrated in figure 4. Thereby, the mating partners are recombined to produce two offspring. The children are not exact copies of their parents, but they do inherit certain characteristics from both parents. One further step is necessary, before the offspring are in their final form.

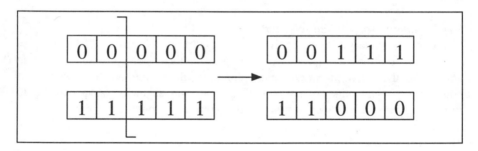

Fig. 4. One-point crossover of two bitstrings.

Step 5: Mutation.

Mutation is a background operator in GAs. Its main purpose is to reintroduce lost alleles (bit values) into the population. Without this mechanism, a GA might, by chance, unintentionally exclude promising areas of the search space due to premature convergence of certain genes in the whole population to a common bit value. Mutation is generally implemented in the following way. Each bit of an individual is flipped with a predetermined probability P_m. Common values for the mutation rate are in the interval [0.01 , 0.001]. It can be useful to vary the mutation rate during the course of a GA-run. Particularly in the final phase of optimisation, when crossover loses effectiveness due to declining diversity in the population, the importance of mutation increases and a higher mutation rate may be useful.

Step 6: Add both offspring to the new population
Initially, at the beginning of the generational cycle, the new population is empty, and it is now successively filled with new individuals created from the parents.

Step 7: Repeat steps 3 to 6 until the new population is filled

Step 8: Check termination criteria
If a termination criterion holds, the process is stopped and results are communicated to the user. Possible criteria are related to solution quality (aspiration level), or used resources (such as a maximum number of iterations). If no termination criterion holds, the process is iterated from step 2.

We shall now look at a (tailored) example to better understand the working of our elementary GA (table 4). This intuitive approach is close to Goldberg (1989).

Example: Let our objective function be

$F(x) = 2x$ Max ! $0 \leq x \leq 63$; x is integer

Objective function and fitness function are assumed to be identical. The initial population consists of the four individuals given in table 4. Fitness-proportional selection is implemented by repeatedly spinning a wheel of fortune (often refered to as *roulette wheel selection*) Since only whole units can be selected, a difference between expected and actual number of offspring per individual occurs. It is, nevertheless, obvious that the good individual #3 has a stronger influence on the successor generation than the rather bad individual #2. While #3 produces two offspring #2 'dies out'.
After crossover and mutation some interesting observations can be made:

1. By recombining individuals #3 and #4 a new best solution has emerged that is quite close to the global optimum *111111*.

2. Crossover is rather ineffective for individuals #1 and #2 which are identical w.r.t. many genes.

3. Compared to the initial population, where alleles were evenly distributed, now certain alleles (mostly 1s) have become predominant at many string positions.

4. Not only the population average fitness value but also the currently best solution found have improved as compared to the prior generation.

individual i	string (genotype)	decoded x-value	Φ_i	P_s $\Phi_i / \Sigma\Phi_j$	expected offspring	actual offspring	offspring before crossover
1	0 1 0 1 0 0	20	40	0,16	0,64	1	0 1 0|1 0 0
2	0 0 1 0 1 1	11	22	0,09	0,36	0	1 1 0|1 0 0
3	1 1 0 1 0 0	52	104	0,41	1,64	2	1 1|0 1 0 0
4	1 0 1 0 1 1	43	86	0,34	1,36	1	1 0|1 0 1 1
predominant alleles:	* * * * * *	$\Sigma = 252$ $\varnothing = 63$		$\Sigma = 1$	$\Sigma = 4$	$\Sigma = 4$	

crossover-partner	crossover-point	offspring after crossover	offspring after mutation	decoded x-value	Φ_i
2	3	0 1 0 1 $\boxed{0}$ 0	0 1 0 1 $\boxed{1}$ 0	22	44
1	3	1 1 0 1 0 0	1 1 0 1 0 0	52	104
4	2	1 1 1 0 1 1	1 1 1 0 1 1	59	118
3	2	1 0 0 1 0 0	1 0 0 1 0 0	36	72
		predominant alleles:	1 1 0 1 * 0		$\Sigma = 338$ $\varnothing = 84,5$

Table 4. Simulation of an elementary GA with a population size of four individuals, fitness-proportional selection, and one-point crossover. The fitness function to be maximised is $\Phi = 2x$ (x must be integer and in the range [0, 63]). See also explanations in the main text.

The first and last point illustrates the power of crossover when combined with selection. Crossover can mix useful elements of the parents to produce even better children. Good individuals are favoured during selection. Population diversity declines in the course of the optimisation, though (point 3). When a gene is converged to a common value in all strings of the population, then only a random mutation can reintroduce the lost allele. As individuals become more and more homogeneous, crossover loses effectivity (point 2), and the selection pressure decreases. This is why GAs are usually not very efficient at fine-tuning solutions in the final phase of optimisation. Various measures have been proposed to keep up diversity (e.g. dividing the population in subpopulations that occasionally exchange individuals). Post-processing GA-individuals with a quick local hillclimbing technique has often proved useful to increase GA-efficiency.

The steps of our elementary GA are listed in figure 5 in pseudo code.

```
5       start
10      generate initial population of binary coded individuals at random
15      repeat
20              evaluate all individuals using some fitness function
25              new population = { }
30              while new population not full do
35                      select two individuals for mating proportional to their
                        fitness
40                      recombine individuals according to $p_c$ to form two
                        offspring
45                      mutate each bit of offspring with probability $p_m$
50                      insert offspring into new population
55              end of while
60              old population = new population
65      until termination criterion holds
70      print results
75      stop
```

Fig. 5. Elementary GA in pseudo-code.

3.2   Selected Extensions

More than other EA-forms, the field of Genetic Algorithms is characterised by high dynamics. Modifications and extensions of the technology are continuously being developed. We can only mention some selected aspects here, which appear particularly useful in practice. A far more complete and detailed discussion can be found in Nissen (1994a).

3.2.1   Population Concept

The elementary GA assumes *generational replacement*, i.e. all inidviduals of a population are replaced in each GA-cycle. Syswerda (1989, 1991) and Whitley (1989) proposed a modification where just a few individuals are replaced during a cycle. Davis (1991) developed this approach further that has the following characteristics:

- the number of individuals to be replaced becomes a strategy parameter (usually the one or two worst solutions are replaced)

- offspring may only enter the population when they are sufficiently different from individuals already present in the population (no duplicates).

This variant is termed *Steady-State GA*. It allows fit individuals to survive for an extended period of time, while also diversity is being maintained. Higher crossover and mutation rates may be used to increase the explorative character of the GA. Steady-State approaches are not applicable when the fitness function includes stochastic perturbations, since mediocre individuals which, by chance, have gained a positive evaluation may manifest themselves in the population.

So far, we have assumed a GA that operates on a single large population where individuals may recombine freely. This is unrealistic in terms of the natural model one tries to imitate. Two approaches that better fit the example of nature are the *migration model* and the *diffusion or neighbourhood model*. In the migration model, one structures the overall population in a number of seperated demes (subpopulations) which occasionally exchange some individuals. For an early example of this approach see Tanese (1989). The diffusion model, on the other hand, stays with the concept of a single population but defines a neighbourhood for each individual. Selection is done locally and all interactions between individuals are restricted to the defined neighbourhood. However, the neighbourhoods of different individuals may overlap, so that good individuals can spread through the population over time. An early example can be found in Mühlenbein (1989). Both models tend to better preserve diversity in the population than the standard approach. They can, moreover, make efficient use of parallel hardware such as transputer systems.

3.2.2 Crossover

As mentioned before, crossover is the dominating search operator in GAs. Much effort has been devoted to devise very efficient forms of crossover. In experiments, traditional one-point crossover is frequently inferior to other crossover variants (see e.g. Syswerda 1989 and Eshelman et al. 1989). Two important crossover types are *n-point crossover* and *uniform crossover*.

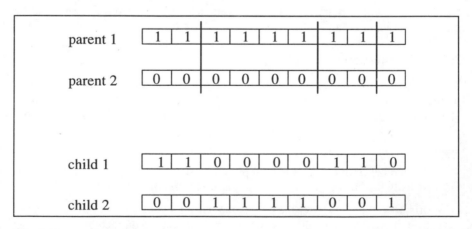

Fig. 6. Three-point crossover

N-point crossover is a straightforward extension of traditional one-point crossover as can be seen from the example in figure 6. Here, three crossover points are chosen randomly (but identical for both individuals) and fragments are exchanged between the strings. The adequate number of crossing points will usually depend on the length of the strings.

Uniform crossover (Syswerda 1989) is different (figure 7). A child is created by copying bits from the one or other parent following a so called crossover mask. A crossover mask is itself a string of bits with length identical to the strings to be crossed. It is created randomly anew for every crossover. A zero (one) in the mask indicates that for this bit position the bit value of parent 1 (parent 2) must be copied into the corresponding position of child 1. It is possible to assign different probabilities of occurence to zeros and ones in the crossover mask, thereby influencing the disruptive effect of uniform crossover. By using the inverse crossover mask one can simultaneously create a second child.

parent 1	0	0	1	1	1	1
parent 2	1	1	1	1	0	0
mask	0	1	0	1	0	1
inverse mask	1	0	1	0	1	0
child 1	0	1	1	1	1	0
child 2	1	0	1	1	0	1

Fig. 7. Uniform Crossover

3.2.3   Coding

Instead of standard binary coding one nowadays frequently uses *Gray code*, which is also bit-based. The basic idea is that small changes in the coded structures (genotypes) should also cause only small changes in the decoded phenotypes. Otherwise, one would unnecessarily complicate the search. This mapping characteristic is not guaranteed with standard binary coding as is demonstrated in table 5. Decimal numbers 3 and 4 are neighbours in variable space, but when standard binary coded (with 3 bits) virtually every bit is different. The distance of two strings can be measured by the sum of differing bits, or *Hamming distance*.

decimal number	standard binary code	Hamming distance (n, n-1) binary code	Gray code	Hamming distance (n, n-1) Gray code
0	000	-	000	-
1	001	1	001	1
2	010	2	011	1
3	011	1	010	1
4	100	3	110	1
5	101	1	111	1
6	110	2	101	1
7	111	1	100	1

Table 5. Differences in hamming distance when using standard binary code or Gray code. Hamming distance here means the number of differing binary digits for two neighbouring decimal numbers.

Gray code ensures that neighbouring values in decimal space are binary coded in such a way that they differ by exactly one bit. To convert standard binary code in Gray code and vice versa the following formulas are applicable:

a) standard binary code to Gray code

$$\gamma_k = \begin{cases} \beta_1 & \text{for } k = 1 \\ \beta_{k-1} \oplus \beta_k & \text{else} \end{cases}$$

where

γ_k: k'th bit in Gray Code (from left)
β_k: k'th bit in standard binary code (from left)
$\oplus$:   addition modulo 2

b) Gray code to standard binary code

$$\beta_k = \oplus_{i=1}^{k} \gamma_i$$

Gray code is generally preferable over standard binary code. There are many applications, however, where other forms of solution representation seem more adequate since they better preserve characteristics of the application domain that can then be exploited by tailored search operators. Incorporating available domain-knowledge in representation and search operators can greatly impove the efficiency of a GA. This is particularly true for combinatorial optimisation problems such as the Travelling Salesman Problem (TSP). The TSP can be represented in binary form. However, a *permuation coding* appears much more natural for this type of application.

3.2.4 Sequence Operators

Traditional forms of crossover fail when permutation codings are used. As can be seen from figure 8, they may lead to the creation of invalid solutions.

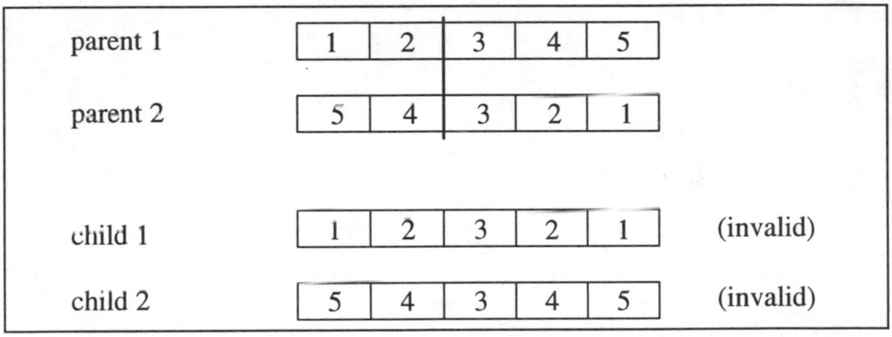

parent 1	1	2	3	4	5
parent 2	5	4	3	2	1
child 1	1	2	3	2	1	(invalid)
child 2	5	4	3	4	5	(invalid)

Fig. 8. Traditional one-point crossover leading to invalid solutions for a small Travelling Salesman Problem with 5 nodes.

For sequencing problems, such as the TSP, specialised *sequence operators* have been devised. They can be differentiated in unary and binary sequence operators (Fox and McMahon 1991). Unary operators take an initial sequence and reorder a part of it. Binary operators are closer to crossover, drawing information from two parent individuals to produce offspring.

Figure 9 demonstrates the recombination process in uniform order-based crossover (Davis 1991). This operator is analogous with uniform crossover, also using a binary mask, and combines *relative* orderings of sequence elements from the parent strings in the children. Some other sequence operators, such as partially-mapped crossover (Goldberg and Lingle 1985) tend to preserve the *absolute* orderings in the children, while edge recombination (Whitley et al.1989) preserves *edge* (neighbourhood) *information*. An overview and empirical comparison of sequence operators is given in Fox and McMahon (1991).

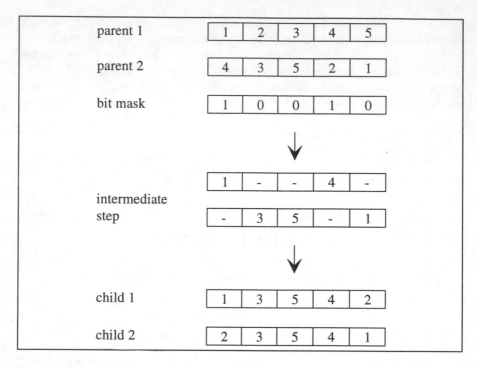

Fig. 9. Uniform Order-Based Crossover

Uniform order-based crossover proceeds as follows: First, a bit mask of the same length as the parent strings is randomly generated. Wherever the mask contains a one (zero) the corresponding element of parent 1 (parent 2) is copied into child 1 (child 2). Now a list of all elements from parent 1 (parent 2) is generated associated with a zero (one) in the crossover mask. The list is then permutated so that the elements appear in the same relative order as in parent 2 (parent 1). From left to right one then fills with this permutated list the gaps on child 1 (child 2).

An overview of some important unary operators is given in figure 10.

3.2.5   Selection Scheme and Fitness Scaling

Selection can be divided into two steps. First, each individual is assigned a selection probability. Then, individuals are sampled based on their selection probabilities. The standard approach, outlined in our elementary GA, assumes fitness-proportional selection probabilities. Without further measures, two negative consequences can arise from this choice:

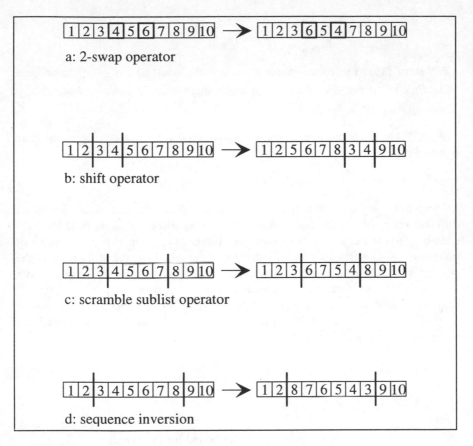

Fig. 10. Unary sequence operators

On the one hand, rather fit (but non-optimal) individuals can quickly dominate the population and lead to a premature stagnation of the search process. On the other hand, individuals tend to be very similar in later phases of the search process due to the influence of selection. Then, fitness values in the population will become rather uniform as well, selection pressure rapidly declines, and the search loses goal-orientation and effectivity.

A countermeasure to keep up and control selective pressure is the introduction of a *scaling function* that transforms the objective function value F_i of individuals i ($i=1,2...n$). Scaling can be required for other reasons as well, for instance, when negative objective function values occur. Some scaling functions are presented in Goldberg (1989) and Grefenstette and Baker (1989). The most simple form is *linear scaling*. With Φ_i as the fitness value of individual i, F_i as the corresponding objective function value, and α and β as parameters, it takes the form:

$$\Phi_i = \alpha \cdot F_i + \beta$$

$$\text{s.t.} \quad \overline{\Phi} = \overline{F}, \quad \Phi_{max} = c \cdot \overline{F} \quad c \in R^+, \quad \Phi_i \geq 0$$

Goldberg (1989) recommends for small populations $(50 \leq n \leq 100)$ to chose a value for c in the range $1.2 \leq c \leq 2$. Quite common is *linear dynamic scaling*:

$$\Phi_i = \alpha \cdot F_i + \beta(t)$$

With P(t) as the population at time t, and assuming a maximisation problem, one possible definition for $\beta(t)$ is:

$$\beta(t) = -\min\{F_j | j \in P(t)\}$$

Dynamical scaling better preserves selection pressure than static forms. A different selection scheme that avoids scaling is based on a ranking of individuals according to their objective function value (Baker 1985). The expected number of offspring associated with a given individual is now a function of its rank in the population. Thereby, a constant selective pressure is kept over the entire GA-run since only relative differences in solution quality matter in the selection process. Ranking produced good results on multimodal functions in experiments performed by Hoffmeister and Bäck (1992), using the following *linear ranking* scheme ($P_s(i)$ is the selection probability of individual i):

$$P_s(i) = \frac{1}{n} \cdot (max - (max - min) \cdot \frac{r(i) - 1}{n - 1})$$

$$\text{s.t.} \quad P_s(i) \geq 0, \quad \sum_{i=1}^{n} P_s(i) = 1$$

where: max :   userdefined upper bound for the expected number of children of an individual

              min :   lower bound for the expected number of children of an individual

              r(i) :   rank of individual i in the population sorted from best to worst based on fitness

Due to the contraints it is also required that $min = 2 - max$ and $1 \leq max \leq 2$. Baker suggests a value $max = 1.1$.

Whether selection probabilities are assigned fitness-proportional or based on ranking, we still must sample the mating partners in a further step. A simple spinning wheel approach (roulette wheel selection) was suggested in the elementary GA for this purpose. However, this approach suffers from a drawback. As Baker (1987) has pointed out, because of the stochastic character of sampling any individual with positive selection probability could fill the entire next population. This is undesirable since it undermines the purpose of selection. Baker proposed a sampling algorithm with desirable characteristics: *stochastic universal sampling*. It is illustrated by a wheel of fortune in figure 11. The important difference to the simple spinning wheel approach (stochastic sampling with replacement) in the elementary GA is that a complete pool of mating partners for the following generation is determined in one step. Stochastic universal sampling is analogous to a wheel of fortune with n equally spaced pointers.

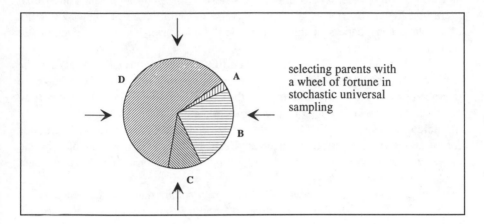

selecting parents with a wheel of fortune in stochastic universal sampling

Fig. 11. Illustration of stochastic universal sampling (population size = 4).

Another popular selection scheme is tournament selection, based on an unpublished concept by Wetzel and described e.g. in Goldberg and Deb (1990). It avoids scaling, too. The basic idea is to choose a group of n_{ts} elements (frequently $n_{ts}=2$) from the population with or without replacement. The best solution from this group is kept deterministically or with a certain probability (stochastic variant) and chosen to become a parent. The process is repeated as often as required for generating the next population.

Goldberg and Deb (1990) have compared the different selection schemes under idealised assumptions and seem to favour ranking and tournament selection over fitness-proportional selection. In practice, all three selection schemes are used, but fitness-proportional selection is probably most widespread.

In many applications variations of the *elitist model*, originally proposed by De Jong (1975), are employed. Elitist selection modifies the basic selection scheme in such a way that a copy of the best solution in the current population is always copied to the next generation. However, this may lead to premature convergence of the population, when the search becomes trapped in a local optimum.

A totally different approach to selection was put forward by Hillis (1990), who implemented a scheme of *co-evolving parasites* in an experiment to evolve general sorting networks. He allowed test cases to evolve independently of the sorting networks, creating a kind of host-parasite relationship. This approach does not require the specification of a fitness function, and is, thus, very useful for ill-defined problems in practice. For an application of this idea in Job Shop Scheduling see Holmes et al. (1995).

3.2.6 Constraints

The handling of constraints is a major research area in evolutionary computation due to its great practical importance. Numerous approaches have been proposed, and we can only give a very brief overview here, while pointing to some additional literature. Recent overviews are given in Nissen (1994a) and Michalewicz (1995). Moreover, many papers in this volume deal with various forms of constrained optimisation problems.

Constraints may be viewed as application-specific information that can be exploited by chosing a *tailored solution representation and search operators* to guarantee valid solutions. This is also the most common approach of handling constraints. It is very consequently implemented in the GENOCOP-system of Michalewicz (1992). GENOCOP is, so far, restricted to linear constraints. Bounds for variables and integer requirements can also be satisfied via representation and operators. The system is currently being extended to include non-linear constraints.

Intelligent *decoding functions* and *repair algorithms* that also guarantee valid solutions are frequently found in scheduling applications. Syswerda and Palmucci (1991), for instance, address the problem of scheduling resources and tasks in a development laboratory of the U.S. Navy. Each GA-solution consists of a ordering of tasks that in then processed by an automised schedule builder to construct a legal schedule, satisfying various constraints. Finally, the schedule is evaluated to produce fitness information for the GA. Nakano (1991) presents a repair algorithm termed 'forcing'. In contrast to decoding functions, repair algorithms work on the genotype level (string). Nakano applies a binary coded GA to a Job Shop Scheduling Problem. Invalid strings are converted to the nearest legal string. Whether or not such repaired strings should be fed back into the population is still a theme of scientific dispute (see, for instance, Orvosh and Davis 1993).

Paredis proposed a general approach for handling constraints in Genetic Algorithms (Paredis 1992, 1993): *constraint propagation*. The basic idea is a constraint-directed search, i.e. constraints are used to successively reduce the search space. Paredis describes an algorithm which operates on a state-space representation, where a state represents a set of potential solutions. Whenever the search algorithm makes a choice, a splitting operator creates a new state which contains only those potential solutions of the previous state that are consistent with the choice made.

While the constraint handling techniques described so far aim at producing only legal solutions, the next two methods tolerate illegal solutions, and try to exploit useful information contained in them. *Penalty function* approaches degrade the fitness value of an illegal solution according to the extent of constraint violation. The general understanding seems to be that tailored graded penalties are preferable over harsh penalties (Richardson et al. 1989). For a critical perspective on this recommendation see Krause and Nissen (1995). One should also note that with a penalty approach, in complex optimisation problems, much effort goes into generating illegal solutions.

One can also apply *multicriteria optimisation techniques* to handle constraints. The number of violated constraints becomes an additional goal to be minimised. Besides, the constraints may be weighted or each taken as an individual objective. Liepins et al. (1990) use this methodology for a set covering problem. Krause and Nissen (1995) apply two different multicriteria approaches in evolutionary facility layout.

Many of the constraint handling techniques outlined for GA here actually carry over well to other types of Evolutionary Algorithms described in later sections of this paper.

3.3 GA-Theory: The Schema Theorem and Some Criticism

When presenting our elementary GA, we tried to create an intuitive understanding of the working and success of a GA. Holland (1975, 1992) more formally analysed GA-behaviour, leading to the development of his famous Schema Theorem. A schema is a 'generalization of an interacting, coadapted set of genes' (Holland). From an algorithmic viewpoint, schemata are similarity templates describing a set of strings with common values at certain string positions. The unspecified string positions of strings from such a set are represented in the schema by a don't care symbol such as '*'. The following explanations assume binary coding, though the schema concept extends to alphabets of higher cardinality as well. We follow the notation in Goldberg (1989).

Example: The schema $H_1 = 101**$ describes a set of binary strings of length L=5, where the first three positions are fixed as 101, and the last two positions can take on a value of either 1 or 0. This set is given by

   {10100, 10101, 10110, 10111}.

All these strings are instances of the schema H_1. However, they are also instances of other schemata such as $H_2 = 1****$. This schema is more general than H_1 since it contains fewer fixed bits. One also says that H_1 is of a higher order than H_2. The order o(H) is defined as the number of fixed positions in the template. Hence, the order of schema H_1 is o(H_1)=3, and the order of schema H_2 is o(H_2)=1. The distance between the first and the last fixed position is called the defining length δ of the schema. In our example it is given by $\delta(H_1)$=3-1=2 and for schema H_2 as $\delta(H_2)$=1-1=0. Geometrically, schemata may be characterised as hyperplanes in search space (see Goldberg 1989 for details). Each binary string is a member of 2^L schemata. Depending on its diversity, a population of binary strings therefore contains between 2^L and $n \cdot 2^L$ schemata. The number of possible schemata for binary coded strings of length L is given as 3^L. More general, the number of possible schemata for alphabets of cardinality k is given by $(k+1)^L$. The lower the cardinality of the alphabet used the higher the number of available schemata. Binary coding offers the maximum number of schemata per bit of information of any coding (Goldberg 1989). This has traditionally been used as an argument to favour binary coding in GAs.

Holland has shown that a GA with fitness-proportional reproduction, while only acting on *n* individuals in a generational cycle, actually processes order $O(n^3)$ schemata. This is known as the intrinsic or *implicit parallelism* of these so called *canonical GAs*. Only schemata with a certain minimum probability of survival are considered. The survival probability of a schema is mainly influenced by the disruptive effect of crossover.

A randomly created initial population will contain a quite even distribution of schemata. In later stages of the optimisation process the diversity of individuals in the population will have declined, and certain schemata have become dominant. This is due to the influence of selection that favours fit individuals and concentrates the search on promising regions. Holland has formalised this for canonical GAs in his Schema Theorem. Let $m(H,t+1)$ be the expected number of instances of a schema H in generation *t+1*. Based on the actual number $m(H,t)$ of instances of schema H in the current population in generation *t*, the Schema Theorem gives a lower bound for $m(H,t+1)$. Let $\Phi(H,t)$ be the observed mean fitness of all instances of schema H in generation *t*, and $\overline{\Phi}(t)$ be the observed mean fitness of the population in generation *t*. With P_m as mutation rate and P_c as crossover rate the Schema Theorem is:

$$m(H,t+1) \geq m(H,t) \cdot \frac{\Phi(H,t)}{\overline{\Phi}(t)} \cdot [1 - P_c \frac{\delta(H)}{L-1} - P_m o(H)]$$

The Schema Theorem states that short, low-order schemata associated with (observed) above-average fitness values (so called *building blocks*) will be allocated exponentially increasing trials in subsequent generations. At the same time, below-average schemata will receive exponentially fewer trials.

A more intuitive but simplifying view on the working of a GA is given by the *Building Block Hypothesis* (BBH) that is derived from the Schema Theorem:

> *(...) instead of building high-performance strings by trying every conceivable combination, we construct better and better strings from the best partial solutions of past samplings. (...), so does a genetic algorithm seek near optimal performance through the juxtaposition of short, low-order, high performance schemata, or building blocks.* (Goldberg 1989, p. 41)

The BBH is strongly inspired by optimisation, while Holland viewed GAs as models of adaptive systems (see also De Jong 1993). Stated in this simple form, the BBH, for instance, ignores possible non-linear interdependencies beween different solution elements (or genes). However, such interdependencies typically occur in GA applications.

Lately, there has been much scientific dispute about the significance of the Schema Theorem. While Holland and his school have build further theory on it, other researchers doubt its significance in practical applications with finite population sizes. The main objection is that with finite population sizes massive *sampling errors* w.r.t. the observed fitness of schemata will occur due to the fitness variance of instances of the same schema.

> *The estimate of the fitness of a schema is equal to the exact fitness in very simple applications only. (...) But if the estimated fitness is used in this interpretation, then the schema theorem is almost a tautology, only describing proportional selection.* (Mühlenbein 1991, p. 324)

> *The effect of fitness variance within schemas is that, in populations of realistic size, the observed fitness of a schema may be arbitrarily far from the static average fitness, even in the initial population.* (Grefenstette 1993, p. 80)

Another objection is that samples from two intersecting schemata are not longer independent when the population converges to these schemata at different rates (*collateral convergence*). For more details see Grefenstette (1993).

A different approach to describing the dynamics of GAs starts from a Markov chain perspective (see e.g. Suzuki 1993, Horn 1993). Many publications under this paradigm suffer from simplifying assumptions, though. Others are only applicable in special cases.

In our view, a paradigm shift in GA-theory can be expected in the near future. For now, it is fair to state that a generally accepted theoretical basis for GAs is still ahead of us.

4 Genetic Programming

Genetic Programming (GP) is essentially a GA-variant with a different solution representation. Koza (Koza 1992a,b, 1994) started from the observation that representation is a key issue in GAs, because it is actually the coding of the underlying problem that a GA can manipulate.

> 'For many problems in machine learning and artificial intelligence, the most natural known representation for a solution is a hierarchical computer program of indeterminate size and shape, as opposed to character strings whose size has been determined in advance.' (Koza 1992a, p. 210)

GP implements this approach by automatically evolving computer programs to solve a given problem, starting the evolutionary process with an initial population of randomly generated programs of functions and terminals appropriate to the problem domain. Each program is evaluated in terms of fitness by running it on a number of representative testproblems and averaging the results. Due to space limitations, we can only outline the basic approach of GP here. Further details and extensions can be found in the cited literature.

Earlier evolutionary approaches to the generation of program code are, for instance, due to Friedberg (1958, 1959), Cramer (1985), Fujiki and Dickinson (1987) and De Jong (1987), but it were Koza and Rice to mature this technology and demonstrate its potential in a number of interesting studies. Applications include forecasting, data mining, generation of random numbers, and optimal control to name just a few.

GP starts with a set (e.g. 500) of randomly generated computer programs, consisting of elements from a set of functions (arithmetic, mathematical, boolean functions, loop operators, domain-specific functions etc.) and a set of terminals (constants, variables). Both sets must be predetermined by the user, and influence the efficiency of the search process and generated programs. The terminal and function set should be selected to satisfy the requirements of closure and sufficiency. *Closure* means that each function in the function set should be well defined for any conceiveable combination of arguments. *Sufficiency* demands the set of functions and terminals to be capable of solving the given problem.

Programs can be represented and manipulated as rooted, point-labeled trees with ordered branches. Koza codes his programs in LISP using only atoms and lists, although his approach is not limited to this programming language. However, LISP is syntactically simple, and it is a particularly convenient language to apply a customised form of genetic crossover-operator to the program trees. Other programming languages frequently used with GP are C and C^{++}.

To generate an individual for the initial population one randomly determines a function from the function set to be the label for the root of the tree. Arguments for the chosen function are randomly determined from the union of function set and terminal set. If another function is chosen as an argument, then the generating process continues recursively. When a terminal is chosen to be the label for a given point, this position becomes an end point of the tree and the generating process is terminated for that point. For more details on this initialisation procedure see Koza (1992 a,b).

Next, the fitness of each generated program tree must be determined. This is usually achieved by running the program on a representative set of testproblems, measuring some error term and averaging the results (*raw fitness*). Frequently, raw fitness is then *normalised* to lie in the interval [0,1], with higher fitness values indicating a better solution, while the sum of the normalised fitness values in the population is unity.

In the next step, a new population of computer programs is created by applying the two primary operations reproduction and crossover with defined probabilities P_r and P_c (not unusual is $P_r=0.1$, $P_c=0.9$). During reproduction a computer program is selected based on its fitness value and copied into the new population without modification. Fitness proportionate reproduction, as described for GAs, is a popular selection rule. Note, that the copied program also remains in the old population.

Crossover creates new solutions by exchanging randomly chosen subtrees of two existing programs. In general, selection for crossover is also based on fitness as outlined above. The number of nodes in the parents as well as the positions of crossover points in parental programs are typically not equal. The maximal depth of a newly produced trees may be restricted to avoid excessively complex programs that are hard to interpret. Note that the crossover operation is well defined and syntactically legal for any two program trees and crossover points. Figure 12 illustrates the overall crossover process.

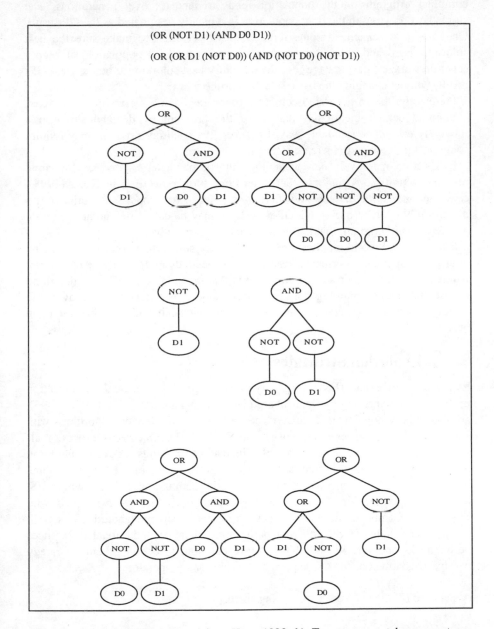

Fig. 12. Crossover in GP (adapted from Koza 1992a,b). Top: two parental program trees. Middle: the two crossover fragments to be exchanged between the parents. Bottom: the resulting new programs.

The steps of reproduction/crossover and solution evaluation are iteratively performed until a termination criterion holds. As should have become clear, there are strong similarities to the basic GA-cycle. By these mechanisms, the fitness of computer programs in the population tends to increase over generations. The single best program in the final population is typically designated as the GP-result. One may also implement some form of elitist selection to make sure the best solution discovered in the entire run is present in the final population, or keep a seperate storage ('golden cage') for the currently best solution (to be the final GP-result) without changing the basic selection process.

Frequently, the so generated computer programs have a hierarchical character, containing default hierarchies that solve the problem by decomposition in a relatively easy understandable way. However, the resulting program may require some post-processing to increase efficiency.

GP is a comperatively new technology that is characterised by very dynamic research activities. A major recent extension, further detailed in Koza (1994), concerns *automatically defined functions*. Here, functions (subroutines) are dynamically evolved during the GP-run. They may be called by another program part (e.g. main program) that is simultaneously being evolved.

Practical real-world applications of GP are still rather scarce, but many interesting application-oriented research has been done (see e.g. Koza 1994, Kinnear 1994). A major advantage of GP is that it can be applied even though no expert knowledge regarding the application domain is available. Moreover, the GP-algorithm may generate highly efficient solutions that nobody has hit upon before.

5   Evolution Strategies

Evolution Strategies (ES), originally developed for practical optimisation problems in engineering by Rechenberg (1973, 1994) and Schwefel (1977, 1995), are particularly popular in Germany. They are similar to Genetic Algorithms with some notable differences (Hoffmeister and Bäck 1991). ES directly process real-valued vectors of the objective variables instead of bitstrings. GA rely mainly on recombination to explore the search space with mutation serving as some background operator. In contrast, mutation is the dominating operator within ES, implementing some kind of hill-climbing search procedure when coupled with selection. Recombination, though, takes a prominent part in standard ES as well. As will be detailed in the follwing paragraphs, there are additional differences between ES and GA w.r.t. solution representation, selection scheme, strategy parameter adaptation, and the sequence of evolutionary operators.

A standard ES-cycle takes the following form:

Step 1: Initialisation

A population of μ individuals is generated. If no prior information about the location of a global optimum in solution space is available, the individuals should be evenly distributed over the whole region of interest. Each individual i ($i=1,2...μ$) is a vector that consists of values x_j ($j=1,2...m$) for all decision variables of the given application, and between 1 and m so called '(average) mutation step sizes' $σ_s$ ($s = 1,2...m'$; $m' ≤ m$). The mutation step sizes are strategy parameters of the ES that are self-adaptively modified, parallel to the optimisation of decision variable values, during the course of the search process. One can, therefore, speak of a two-level optimisation in ES. Initial values for the $σ_s$ should be equal and fairly large to avoid premature convergence.

Step 2: Evaluation

Each individual is now evaluated according to the given fitnesss function. In general, fitness and objective function value are identical.

Step 3: Reproduction

From the μ parents λ children (Schwefel recommends $μ/λ ≈ 1/7$) are created by iteratively performing the following steps:

Step 3.1: Selection and recombination

To determine values for decision variables as well as strategy parameters of a child C, corresponding values of two randomly selected parents A and B are recombined and the result mutated. All individuals in the current population have equal selection probabilities. Empirically, using different types of recombination for decision variables and strategy parameters has shown the best results. *Discrete recombination* is used to determine the decision variable values of the child. Here, values are copied into the child from the first or the second parent. The decision which parent to choose from is randomly made anew for every variable. Usually, each parent has an equal chance to pass on its values. *Intermediate recombination* is applied to the strategy parameters, leading to the following formula for the mutation step sizes $σ_s$ of the child C:

$$σ_S(C) = 0.5 \cdot (σ_S(A) + σ_S(B)) \qquad s = 1,2...m', \quad m' ≤ m$$

Recombination is important for the self-adaptation of strategy parameters in ES (Schwefel 1995).

Step 3.2: Mutation of the child

Now, the generated child is mutated by first modifying its $σ_s$, and then applying these step sizes to mutate the decision variables. The mutation of the $σ_s$ is based on the Log-normal distribution:

$$\sigma'_s(C) = \sigma_s(C) \cdot \exp(\tau' \cdot N(0,1) + \tau \cdot N_s(0,1))$$

$$\tau' \propto (\sqrt{2 \cdot m})^{-1}$$
$$\tau \propto (\sqrt{2\sqrt{m}})^{-1}$$

where $N(0,1)$ is a standard-normally distributed random variable, and τ' as well as τ are exogeneous parameters. $\tau' \cdot N(0,1)$ is a global factor that allows for an overall change of the mutability, while $\tau \cdot N_s(0,1)$ allows for individual changes of the step sizes σ_s. Frequently one sets $\tau' = \tau = 1$. By taking the Log-normal distribution it is secured that the σ_s stay positive. The self-adaptation of strategy parameters according to the topological requirements of the fitness landscape gives the ES great flexibility.

Now the decision variables are mutated using the modified step sizes σ_s', interpreted as standard deviations of normally distributed random variables. If $m' < m$, then several decision variables are mutated with the same standard deviation. Formally:

$$x_j'(C) = x_j(C) + N_j(0, \sigma_j'(C))$$

where $N_j(\mu, \sigma)$ is again a normally distributed random variable, determined anew for each decision variable of the child C. By using this type of mutation, one tries to imitate the observation that in nature parents and children share many characteristics, and small deviations are much more frequent than strong mutations.

Step 3.3: Evaluation of the child
The fitness of the child is determined as described in step 2.

Step 4: Selection
With *extinctive selection*, ES employ a deterministic selection scheme. There are two general methods for maintaining a population of solutions in ES. In the first, λ offsprings are generated from μ parents and all $\mu + \lambda$ solutions are placed in competition. Only the μ best individuals survive to form the next generation. This is denoted by the term $(\mu + \lambda)$-ES. In the second, the parents are eliminated after each generation, and only the children compete for survival. The μ best children survive to form the next generation, and this is called a (μ, λ)-ES. In general, (μ, λ)-selection is preferable, since it allows for a temporal deterioration of the population's best solution. This in turn might be necessary to overcome local optima and avoid premature convergence. In contrast, the $(\mu + \lambda)$-selection scheme is *elitist* since it always preserves the best solution found so far.

Step 5: Repeat steps 3 and 4 until termination criterion holds

Figure 13 gives an overview of the standard ES-procedure. There are some variations of this basic scheme, described in Schwefel (1995) and Rechenberg (1994). A concise overview can also be found in Bäck and Schwefel (1993). Perhaps most notable is the ES-variant with self-adaptive correlated mutations to more efficiently guide the search process. Deviations from the standard scheme for combinatorial optimisation problems are presented in Ablay (1991) and Nissen (1994b).

Several authors (e.g. Born 1978, Beyer 1993) have developed global convergence proofs for simplified versions of the ES procedure presented here. However, global convergence with probability 1 for an ES with recombination and self-adaptation of strategy parameters has not been proved, yet. For practical puroposes it would also be important to know how closely the global optimum can be approximated by an ES under time-constraints, thereby dropping the unrealistic assumption of an infinite time-horizon for optimisation.

5	start
10	generate initial population of μ individuals
15	evaluate all initial individuals according to some fitness function
20	repeat
25	intermediate population = { };
30	for i=1 to λ do
35	select two individuals for mating with equal probability
40	discrete recombination to determine values for decision variables of offspring
45	intermediate recombination to determine 'mutation step sizes' for offspring
50	mutate offspring's mutation step sizes using log-normally distributed random variables
55	mutate offspring's decision variable values using normally distributed random variables
60	insert ith offspring into intermediate population
65	endfor
65	evaluate all individuals in intermediate population
70	select μ best individuals of intermediate population (assuming (μ,λ)-selection), or select μ best individuals from set of parents and children (assuming $(\mu+\lambda)$-selection) as new generation
75	until termination criterion holds
80	print results
85	stop

Fig. 13. Standard Evolution Strategy in pseudo code.

6   Evolutionary Programming

Evolutionary Programming (EP) is another mainstream form of EA. EP is quite similar to ES, though independently developed by L.J. Fogel and co-workers in the sixties (Fogel et al. 1966). The current state of the technology and some applications are presented in detail in Fogel (1995). EP has no restrictions on the solution representation. Instead, the representation should follow naturally from the given application domain. We focus on EP for parameter optimisation problems. Here, an individual is a vector of values for all decision variables.

Opposite to GA, EP employs mutation as the only search operator. No crossover or inversion operators are used. This is justified by looking at evolution from a higher level of abstraction.

The basic EP-cycle is similar to a strictly mutation-based $(\mu+\mu)$-ES, though a stochastic selection scheme is applied instead of deterministic selection in ES. Moreover, mutation step sizes are adapted differently. The basic EP steps are as follows:

Step 1: Initialisation

A population of μ individuals is randomly generated, where the initial values of all decision variables x_j (j= 1,2...m) are uniformly distributed between an upper bound a_m and a lower bound b_m in each of the m dimensions.

Step2: Evaluation of the initial population

Each individual i (i=1,2...μ) is assigned a fitness value Φ_i. The fitness value is essentially the objective function value, possibly transformed by a scaling function to secure $\Phi_i \geq 0$. The fitness can, moreover, be modified by a random variation v_i, so that, more formally, holds:

$$\Phi_i = G(F(\vec{x}_i), v_i) \quad (i = 1,2...\mu)$$

The functions G and F can be as complex as required so that, for instance, the fitness can be a function of the other population members, simulating the formation of ecological niches or co-evolutionary mechanisms.

Step 3: Reproduction and evaluation of offspring

Each parent produces one offspring by duplication. Thereafter, the offspring are mutated by adding normally distributed random variables $N(\mu,\sigma)$ with expectation 0 and dynamically adapted standard deviations to the current decision variable values in each of the m dimensions. Contrary to ES, standard deviation ('mutation step size') is a function of the parent's fitness. To accelerate the search process, one reduces the mutation step sizes when approaching the optimum. This implicitly assumes a minimisation task, and the globally optimal fitness value to be zero - possibly achievable by a transformation of the objective function. However, the global optimum may be unknown, so that a different procedure may be required.

More formally we have (j=1,2...m ; i=1,2...μ):

$$x_j(i+\mu) = x_j(i) + N(0, \sqrt{k_j \cdot \Phi_i + z_j})$$

where k_j is a scaling constant and z_j represents an offset, i.e. a minimum amount of variance. Frequently, one choses $k_j=1$ and $z_j=0$ for all j to reduce the number of EP strategy-parameters. Following mutation, all children are evaluated as described in step 2.

Step 4: Stochastic selection (tournament)

Now a stochastic tournament takes place where parents and children compete for survival. Each of them has its fitness value compared to W randomly determined opponents. Assuming a minimisation problem, the number of wins w_i of an individual i is determined according to

$$w_i = \sum_{g=1}^{W} w_g \quad \text{where} \quad w_g = \begin{cases} 1 & \text{for} \quad \Phi_i \le \Phi_r \quad r \ne i \\ 0 & \text{else} \end{cases}$$

r is an integer uniform random number in the interval $[1, 2\mu]$.

Now, all parents and children are ranked according to their respective numbers of wins w_i. The μ best individuals based on this ranking are chosen as new parents. Note that in EP selection is a stochastic process, as in nature, where even bad individuals have a certain chance of survival and reproduction. The more competitions an individual faces, the harder the selection becomes. Thus, we have a very flexible opportunity to determine selection intensity in EP. However, the tournament causes higher CPU-requirements as deterministic selection.

Step 5: Repeat steps 3 and 4 until termination criterion holds

Figure 14 gives an overview of the standard EP approach in pseudo code. This basic form of EP has been extended and varied in different directions. We cannot detail these variants here and refer the interested reader to Fogel (1995). A modification of EP for combinatorial optimisation problems can be found in Nissen (1994a, 1995).

Theoretical results for EP are rather scarce. Fogel (1995) proves basic asymptotic convergence properties, using a Markov chain approach and imposing some simplifications. He assumes an infinite time-horizon for optimisation. This assumption, of course, greatly reduces the relevance of his convergence results in practical optimisation under resource constraints.

```
5     start
10    generate initial population of μ individuals randomly using some adequate
      solution representation
15    evaluate initial individuals according to some fitness function
20    current population = initial population
25    repeat
30              intermediate population = current population
35              for i=1 to μ do
40                      generate ith offspring by duplicating ith parent
45                      mutate ith offspring using normally distributed random
                        variables
50                      evaluate ith offspring;
55                      insert ith offspring into intermediate population;
60              endfor;
65              for j=1 to 2μ do
70                      hold sequential competitions between jth individual and W
                        randomly determined opponents using their respective
                        fitness values to determine wins
75              rank individuals of the intermediate population in descending order
                according to no. of wins
80              select μ highest ranking individuals as new current population;
85    until termination criterion holds
90    print results
95    stop
```

Fig. 14. Standard Evolutionary Programming in pseudo code.

7   Hybrid Systems

7.1   Learning Classifier Systems

Machine learning is a central theme of Artificial Intelligence research. Learning Classifier Systems (CS) (Holland and Reitman 1978; Holland et al. 1986; Goldberg 1989; Holland 1992) are rule-based inductive machine-learning systems capable of learning by feedback. They rely on Genetic Algorithms as one of two employed learning techniques. The standard components of a CS are (figure 15):

- rule base (knowledge base)
- message list
- conflict resolution component
- credit allocation component (learning component #1)
- Genetic Algorithm (learning component #2)
- input interface (detectors)
- output interface (effectors)

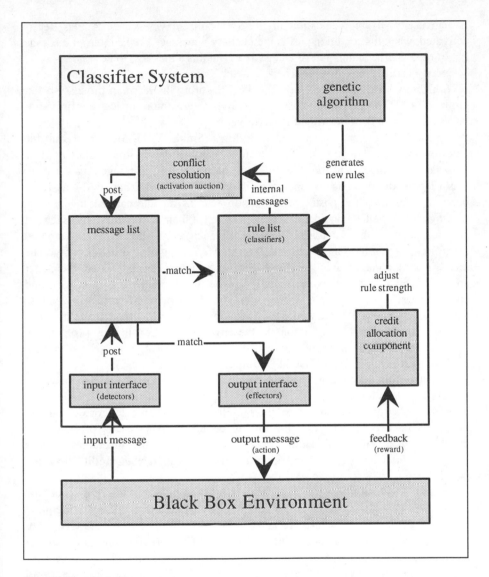

Fig. 15. Standard CS

CS are an active area of research, and only the basic methodolgy can be outlined in the context of this volume. Knowledge, or more exactly, hypothetical knowledge is stored in a CS in the form of simple production rules. They are refered to as 'classifiers' and consist of a condition-part (if-clause) and an action part (then-clause). Knowledge is generally coded in binary form (plus a wildcard symbol) to ease processing by a Genetic Algorithm, but may also be stored at a higher (symbolic) representation level, more expressive and understandable for the human user. All communication in a CS is done via messages. A classifer is activated, when his condition part is matched by a message on the internal message list of the CS. The action part of a classifier contains a message to be send.

Every classifier has assigned a parameter (*strength*) that signals its average usefulness or level of confirmation for the CS during the learning process so far. Holland (1992) characterises classifiers as hypotheses, more or less confirmed as is documented in their individual strength value.

A basic CS-cycle can be outlined as follows (Smith 1991): Messages from the environment enter the system via detectors which code environmental input as messages for placement on the internal message list. Messages can satisfy classifiers in the rule base by matching their condition parts. Satisfied classifiers become candidates for posting their action part as an internal message to the message list. Whether candidate classifiers can post their action to the message list is determined by the outcome of a stochastic activation auction. Each satisfied classifier makes a bid based upon ist importance (strength) and its specifity. The more specific a classifier is, and the higher its assigned strength value, the better are its chances in the activation auction. Now the message list is purged and chosen classifiers place their messages on the list. Effectors (fixed rules whose action affects the environment of the CS) that are matched by the current message list are allowed to post their actions to the environment. Consistency problems at the effectors, when different, simultaneous messages urge to take mutually exclusive actions, are again solved by competition (Holland 1992).

Feedback from the environment, following an output of the CS, is distributed by the credit allocation component. It varies the relative importance (strength) of individual classifiers according to their ability to contribute to correct output. Holland´s bucket brigade, though showing certain weaknesses, is probably the most prominent credit allocation algorithm. It sets up the mechanisms of a competitive service economy and links conflict resolution with credit allocation (see Goldberg 1989 for further details).

From time to time a Genetic Algorithm is invoked to search the rule space and replace weak classifiers by new rules generated by recombining and mutating good classifiers. The strength values are taken as fitness information by the GA. Over time, the CS should build up an internal model of its environment, and learn to produce correct output from a given input. CS were originally designed for learning situations where feedback is rather scarce, and chains of classifiers must be build to react on a given input, executing some form of internal reasoning process. Building and maintaining such chains of classifiers, however, is frequently still a problem with the available CS-technology today. Related areas where technological advances are necessary for CS to mature are, for instance, the design and complex interaction of the two learning components, stable convergence to an optimal rule base, and the dispute about the most adequate knowledge representation.

An important feature of CS is the emergence of default hierarchies. They consist of different levels of classifiers with increasing specifity. Less specific basic classifiers are overruled by more specific ones to handle exception situations. This results in a very efficient form of knowledge representation, and allows for transfer and generalisation of the learned material.

The functional similarity of CS to artificial neural networks (NN) is obvious. This has been formally shown by transforming a CS into an equivalent NN, and vice versa (Davis 1989 a,b; Belew and Gherrity 1989). The functional similarity of CS and NN has important implications for possible future applications of CS in management (and elsewhere). When the remaining technological difficulties of todays CS are solved, we can expect them to compete with NN, which have been established in a wide spectrum of applications (mainly forecasting, optimisation and classification), in management as well as other domains. Note that classifiers (rules) exhibit some advantages over neural nodes with respect to semantic content, inclusion of available domain knowledge and scalability of the rule base.

There is a growing interest in applying CS within explanatory models of economics. The basic idea is to simulate institutions, markets or economies and study their behaviour. Also common to these approaches is a concern with artificial adaptive agents - consumers, firms, government agencies, banks etc. - that face and rank alternative actions which impinge upon one another, often in a setting of constrained resources (Arthur 1989). Artificial agents may be designed with CS or the Echo model (Holland 1992), another recent development in the area of EA.

These agents may interact with one another and their simulated environment following and adapting local rules, thereby creating a complex, global system behaviour that mirrors aspects of economic reality. Varying the experimental design gives rise to different system evolutions, which may be helpful in understanding real-world phenomenons. Computational systems where interesting global behaviour emerges from local interactions are generally referred to as emergent computations (see Forrest 1990, Forrest and Miller 1990 for further details).

7.2   Other Hybrid Approaches

When different technologies are merged, one can hope for some sort of symbiosis that leads to a particularly good performance of the hybrid system by combining the respective strengths' of the individual components. The number of publications where EA have been hybridised with other innovative technologies is growing rapidly, and we can only sketch some mainstream directions here. A much more extensive and systematic overview, containing many references to relevant literature, is given in Nissen (1994a).

For instance, one has used EA, with varying success, to optimise the architecture and connection weights of artificial NN. EA have also been employed to solve the feature selection problem in NN-applications with many possible input variables. A wide spectrum of such combinations is e.g. given in Whitley and Schaffer (1992) and Pearson et al. (1995). Occasionally, integration follows the opposite direction, as in the XROUTE-system that assists in vehicle routing problems

(Kadaba et al. 1991). Here, a NN partially initialises a GA to reduce the computational effort.

Combining EA and fuzzy set theory, pioneered by Karr (1991 a,b), has proved useful in determining critical system parameters of fuzzy controllers, such as shape and position of membership functions, and for the optimisation of a fuzzy rule base. Since control, forecasting and classification are quite similar in principle, these developments are also of distinct importance for future applications of this hybrid technology in the business domain.

There are various alternatives to combine EA with the versatile simulation method (Biethahn and Nissen 1994). These concern decision models as well as explanatory models. Using EA as a means to determine good values for the decision variables of a simulation model can turn simulation into a powerful optimisation tool for complex economic problems. Moreover, techniques from the field of EA can be used for evolving the most adequate simulation model structure and for the experimental analysis of emerging patterns in complex, nonlinear systems (see also section 7.1).

Besides, there are many useful combinations of conventional optimisation techniques and EA. Many authors have used quick hillclimbing algorithms, for instance, to locally optimise GA-individuals, thereby significantly improving overall system performance. Others have relied on heuristics to initialise their GA startpopulation. In highly constrained applications, like job shop scheduling, a traditional technique may be employed to transform a coded GA-individual into a valid solution. Occasionally (see e.g. Lee and Takagi 1993), one has attempted to solve the problem of finding appropriate GA strategy-parameter settings by employing a rule-based system for this purpose.

8 Conclusions

Evolutionary Algorithms are promising and broadly applicable search and optimisation techniques, based on the mechanisms of natural evolution. We have presented the various mainstream forms of EA, with a particular focus on Genetic Algorithms as the most prominent and diversified type. Interest in EA has risen dramatically over the last decade, and they have been applied with fair success to a large variety of complex problems. We are still far from a unifying theory of EA, though, and progress in this respect is rather slow as compared to applied research.

Moreover, different EA-approaches have rather seldom been systematically compared in practical applications or on testproblems in order to determine their relative strength. We have also seen relatively few publications attempting to evaluate EA in comparison with other modern heuristics like Simulated Annealing (Kirkpatrick et al. 1983), Tabu Search (Glover 1989, 1990), artificial neural nets or Threshold Accepting (Dueck and Scheuer 1990). It would be of great practical importance to know which type of heuristic works best for which class of problems. This implies that adequate measures to classify practical problems must be developed. One possible starting point are the works by Kauffman (1989),

Manderick et al. (1991) and others on the characterisation of fitness landscapes. Here are fruitful areas for further research.

Additional potential for practical applications results from the various possible combinations and integrations of EA with other innovative technologies like fuzzy set theory, simulation, neural nets and knowledge-based systems. Although the development of such hybrid systems requires much expertise and resources, one can rightfully hope for excellent overall performance by combining the respective strengths of different approaches in one integrated system.

With the appearence of professional EA-tools, the further spreading of parallel computers where EA can be efficiently implemented, and the integration of EA in hybrid approaches, we expect an even greater interest in this innovative technology in the near future.

References

Ablay, P. (1991): Ten Theses Regarding the Design of Controlled Evolutionary Strategies. In: Becker, J.D.; Eisele, I.; Mündemann, F.W. (eds.): Parallelism, Learning, Evolution. Proceedings of the Workshops on Evolutionary Models and Strategies, and on Parallel Processing 1989. Springer, Berlin: 457-481

Arthur, W.B. (1989): The Economy and Complexity. In: Stein, D.L. (ed.): Lectures in the Sciences of Complexity, Vol. 1. Addison Wesley, Redwood City/CA: 713-740

Bäck, T.; Schwefel, H.-P. (1993): An Overview of Evolutionary Algorithms for Parameter Optimization. Evolutionary Computation 1: 1-23

Baker, J.E. (1985): Adaptive Selection Methods for Genetic Algorithms. In Grefenstette, J.J. (ed.): Proceedings of an International Conference on Genetic Algorithms and Their Applications. Lawrence Erlbaum, Hillsdale/NJ: 101-111

Baker, J.E. (1987): Reducing Bias and Inefficiency in the Selection Algorithm. In: Grefenstette, J.J. (ed.): Genetic Algorithms and Their Applications. Proceedings of the Second International Conference on Genetic Algorithms. Lawrence Erlbaum, Hillsdale/NJ: 14-21

Belew, R.K.; Gherrity, M. (1989): Back Propagation for the Classifier System. In: Schaffer, J.D. (ed.): Proceedings of the Third International Conference on Genetic Algorithms. Morgan Kaufmann, San Mateo/CA : 275-281

Beyer, H.-G. (1993): Toward a Theory of Evolution Strategies: Some Asymptotical Results from the $(1,+\lambda)$-Theory. Evolutionary Computation 1: 165-188

Biethahn, J.; Nissen, V. (1994): Combinations of Simulation and Evolutionary Algorithms in Management Science and Economics. Annals of OR 52: 183-208

Born, J. (1978): Evolutionsstrategien zur numerischen Lösung von Adaptationsaufgaben. Doctoral Dissertation, Humboldt University, Berlin

Cramer, N.L. (1985): A Representation for the Adaptive Generation of Simple Sequential Programs. In: Grefenstette, J.J. (ed.): Proceedings of an International Conference on Genetic Algorithms and Their Applications. Lawrence Erlbaum, Hillsdale/NJ:183-187

Davis, L. (1989a): Mapping Neural Networks into Classifier Systems. In: Schaffer, J.D. (ed.): Proceedings of the Third International Conference on Genetic Algorithms. Morgan Kaufmann, San Mateo/CA : 375-378

40

Davis, L. (1989b): Mapping Classifier Systems into Neural Networks. In: Touretzky, D.S. (ed.): Advances in Neural Information Processing 1. Morgan Kaufmann, San Mateo/CA: 49-56

Davis, L. (1991): A Genetic Algorithms Tutorial. In: Davis, L. (ed.): Handbook of Genetic Algorithms. Van Nostrand Reinhold, New York: 1-101

De Jong, K. (1975): An Analysis of the Behavior of a Class of Genetic Adaptive Systems. Doctoral Dissertation, University of Michigan, Ann Arbor

De Jong, K. (1987): On Using Genetic Algorithms to Search Program Spaces. In: Grefenstette, J.J. (ed.): Genetic Algorithms and Their Applications. Proceedings of the Second International Conference on Genetic Algorithms: 210-216

De Jong, K. (1993): Genetic Algorithms are NOT Function Optimizers. In: Whitley, L.D. (ed.): Foundations of Genetic Algorithms 2. Morgan Kaufmann, San Mateo/CA: 5-17

Dueck, G.; Scheuer, T. (1990): Threshold Accepting: A General Purpose Optimization Algorithm Appearing Superior to Simulated Annealing. Journal of Computational Physics 90: 161-175

Eshelman, L.J.; Caruana, R.A.; Schaffer, J.D. (1989): Biases in the Crossover Landscape. In: Schaffer, J.D. (ed): Proceedings of the Third International Conference on Genetic Algorithms. Morgan Kaufmann, San Mateo/CA: 10-19

Fogel, D.B. (1995): Evolutionary Computation. Toward a New Philosophy of Machine Intelligence. IEEE Press, Piscataway/NJ

Fogel, L.J.; Owens, A.J.; Walsh, M.J. (1966): Artificial Intelligence Through Simulated Evolution. John Wiley/NY

Forrest, S. (1990): Emergent Computation: Self Organizing, Collective, and Cooperative Phenomena in Natural and Artificial Computing Networks. Physica D 42: 1-11

Forrest, S.; Miller, J.H. (1990): Emergent Behavior in Classifier Systems. Physica D 42: 213-227

Fox, B.R.; McMahon, M.B. (1991): Genetic Operators for Sequencing Problems. In: Rawlins, G.J.E. (ed.): Foundations of Genetic Algorithms. Morgan Kaufmann, San Mateo/CA: 284-300

Friedberg, R.M. (1958): A Learning Machine: Part I. IBM Journal of Research and Development 2: 2-13

Friedberg, R.M., Dunham, B.; North, J.H. (1959): A Learning Machine: Part II. IBM Journal on Research and Development 3: 282-287

Fujiki, C.; Dickinson, J. (1987): Using the Genetic Algorithm to Generate LISP Source Code to Solve the Prisoner's Dilemma. In: Grefenstette, J.J. (ed.): Genetic Algorithms and Their Applications. Proceedings of the Second International Conference on Genetic Algorithms: 236-245

Glover, F. (1989): Tabu Search - Part I. ORSA Journal on Computing 1: 190-206

Glover, F. (1990): Tabu Search - Part II. ORSA Journal on Computing 2: 4-32

Goldberg, D.E. (1989): Genetic Algorithms in Search, Optimization, and Machine Learning. Addison-Wesley, Reading/MA

Goldberg, D.E.; Lingle Jr., R. (1985): Alleles, Loci, and the Travelling Salesman Problem. In: Grefenstette, J.J. (ed.): Proceedings of an International Conference on Genetic Algorithms and Their Applications. Lawrence Erlbaum, Hillsdale/NJ: 154-159

Goldberg, D.E.; Deb, K. (1990): A Comparative Analysis of Selection Schemes Used in Genetic Algorithms. TCGA Report 90007, University of Alabama, The Clearinghouse for Genetic Algorithms, Tuscaloosa

Grefenstette, J.J.; Baker, J.E. (1989): How Genetic Algorithms Work. A Critical Look at Implicit Parallelism. In: Schaffer, J.D. (ed): Proceedings of the Third International Conference on Genetic Algorithms. Morgan Kaufmann, San Mateo/CA: 20-27

Grefenstette, J.J. (1993): Deception Considered Harmful. In: Whitley, L.D. (ed.): Foundations of Genetic Algorithms 2. Morgan Kaufmann, San Mateo/CA: 75-91

Hillis, W.D. (1990): Co-Evolving Parasites Improve Simulated Evolution as an Optimisation Procedure. Physica D 42: 228-234

Hoffmeister, F.; Bäck, T. (1991): Genetic Algorithms and Evolution Strategies: Similarities and Differences. In: Schwefel, H.-P.; Männer, R. (eds.): Parallel Problem Solving from Nature. Springer, Berlin: 455-469

Hoffmeister, F.; Bäck, T. (1992): Genetic Algorithms and Evolution Strategies. Similarities and Differences. Technical Report SYS-1/92, University of Dortmund, Germany

Holland, J.H. (1992, 1975): Adaptation in Natural and Artificial Systems, 2. ed. MIT Press, Cambridge/MA, (1. ed. 1975, The University of Michigan Press, Ann Arbor)

Holland, J.H.; Reitman, J.S. (1978): Cognitive Systems Based on Adaptive Algorithms. In: Waterman, D.A.; Hayes-Roth, F. (eds.): Pattern-Directed Inference Systems. Academic Press, New York

Holland; J.H.; Holyoak, K. J.; Nisbett, R.E.; Thagard, P.R. (1986): Induction: Processes of Inference, Learning, and Discovery. MIT Press, Cambridge/MA

Holmes, J; Routen, T.W.; Czarnecki, C.A. (1995): Heterogeneous Co-Evolving Parasites. In: Pearson, D.W.; Steele, N.C.; Albrecht, R.F. (eds.): Artificial Neural Nets and Genetic Algorithms. Proceedings of the International Conference in Alés, France. Springer, Wien: 156-159

Horn, J. (1993): Finite Markov Chain Analysis of Genetic Algorithms with Niching. In: Forrest, S. (ed.): Proceedings of the Fifth International Conference on Genetic Algorithms. Morgan Kaufmann, San Mateo/CA: 110-117

Kadaba, N. ; Nygard, K.E.; Juell, P.L. (1991): Integration of Adaptive Machine Learning and Knowledge-Based Systems for Routing and Scheduling Applications. Expert Systems With Applications 2: 15-27

Karr, C. (1991a): Genetic Algorithms for Fuzzy Controllers. AI Expert 6 (2): 26-33

Karr, C. (1991b): Applying Genetics to Fuzzy Logic. AI Expert 6 (3): 38-43

Kauffman, S.A. (1989): Adaptation on Rugged Fitness Landscapes. In: Stein, D.L. (ed.) Lectures in the Sciences of Complexity, Vol. 1. Addison Wesley, Redwood City/CA: 527-618

Kinnear, K.E. (ed.) (1994): Advances in Genetic Programming. MIT Press, Cambridge/MA

Kirkpatrick, S.; Gelatt, C.D.; Vecchi, M.P. (1983): Optimization by Simulated Annealing. Science 220: 671-680

Koza, J.R. (1992a): The Genetic Programming Paradigm: Genetically Breeding Populations of Computer Programs to Solve Problems. In: Soucek, B. and the IRIS Group (eds.): Dynamic, Genetic, and Chaotic Programming. The Sixth Generation. John Wiley, New York: 203-321

Koza, J.R. (1992b): Genetic Programming. MIT Press, Cambridge/MA

Koza, J.R. (1994): Genetic Programming II. MIT Press, Cambridge/MA

Krause, M.; Nissen, V. (1995): On Using Penalty Functions and Multicriteria Optimisation Techniques in Facility Layout. In this volume

Lee, M.; Takagi, H. (1993): Dynamic Control of Genetic Algorithms Using Fuzzy Logic Techniques. In: Forrest, S. (ed.): Proceedings of the Fifth International Conference on Genetic Algorithms. Morgan Kaufmann, San Mateo/CA: 76- 83

Liepins, G.E.; Hilliard, M.R.; Richardson, J.; Palmer, M. (1990): Genetic Algorithms Applications to Set Covering and Travelling Salesman Problems. In: Brown, D.E.; White, C.C. (eds.): Operations Research and Artificial Intelligence: The Integration of Problem-Solving Strategies. Kluwer, Boston: 29-57

Manderick, B.; de Weger, M.; Spiessens, P. (1991): The Genetic Algorithm and the Structure of the Fitness Landscape. In: Belew, R.K.; Booker, L.B. (eds.): Proceedings of the Fourth International Conference on Genetic Algorithms. Morgan Kaufmann, San Mateo/CA: 143-150

Michalewicz, Z. (1992): Genetic Algorithms + Data Structures = Evolution Programs. Springer, Berlin

Michalewicz, Z. (1995): Constraint Handling Techniques in Evolutionary Computation Methods. To appear in: Proceedings of the Fourth Annual Conference on Evolutionary Programming, San Diego

Mühlenbein, H. (1989): Parallel Genetic Algorithms, Population Genetics and Combinatorial Optimization. In: Schaffer, J.D. (ed): Proceedings of the Third International Conference on Genetic Algorithms. Morgan Kaufmann, San Mateo/CA: 416-421

Mühlenbein, H. (1991): Evolution in Time and Space- The Parallel Genetic Algorithm. In: Rawlins, G.J.E. (ed.): Foundations of Genetic Algorithms. Morgan Kaufmann, San Mateo/CA: 316-337

Nakano, R. (1991): Conventional Genetic Algorithms for Job Shop Problems. In: Belew, R.K.; Booker, L.B. (eds.): Proceedings of the Fourth International Conference on Genetic Algorithms. Morgan Kaufmann, San Mateo: 474-479

Nissen, V. (1994a): Evolutionäre Algorithmen. Darstellung, Beispiele, betriebswirtschaftliche Anwendungsmöglichkeiten. DUV Deutscher Universitätsverlag, Wiesbaden

Nissen, V. (1994b): Solving the Quadratic Assignment Problem with Clues from Nature. IEEE Transactions on Neural Networks 5: 66-72

Nissen, V. (1995): Evolutionary Algorithms for the Quadratic Assignment Problem: An Empirical Comparison. To appear in Bäck, T.; Fogel, D.; Michalewicz, Z. (eds.): Handbook of Evolutionary Computation. Oxford University Press, New York

Orvosh, D.; Davis, L. (1993): Shall We Repair? Genetic Algorithms, Combinatorial Optimization, and Feasibility Constraints. In: Forrest, S. (ed.): Proceedings of the Fifth International Conference on Genetic Algorithms. Morgan Kaufmann, San Mateo/CA: 650

Paredis, J. (1992): Exploiting Constraints as Background Knowledge for Genetic Algorithms: A Case-Study for Scheduling. In: Männer, R.; Manderick, B. (eds.): Parallel Problem Solving from Nature, 2. Proceedings of the Second Conference. North Holland, Amsterdam : 229-238

Paredis, J. (1993): Genetic State-Space Search for Constrained Optimization Problems. In: Proceedings of the International Joint Conference on Artificial Intelligence, Chambery/France: 967-972

Pearson, D.W.; Steele, N.C.; Albrecht, R.F. (eds.) (1995): Artificial Neural Nets and Genetic Algorithms. Proceedings of the International Conference in Alès, France. Springer, Wien

Rechenberg, I. (1973): Evolutionsstrategie. Optimierung technischer Systeme nach Prinzipien der biologischen Evolution. Frommann-Holzboog, Stuttgart

Rechenberg, I. (1994): Evolutionsstrategie'94. Frommann-Holzboog, Stuttgart

Richardson, J.T.; Palmer, M.R.; Liepins, G.E.; Hilliard, M. (1989): Some Guidelines for Genetic Algorithms with Penalty Functions. In: Schaffer, J.D. (ed): Proceedings of the Third International Conference on Genetic Algorithms. Morgan Kaufmann, San Mateo/CA: 191-197

Schwefel, H.-P. (1977): Numerische Optimierung von Computer-Modellen mittels der Evolutionsstrategie. Birkhäuser, Basel

Schwefel, H.-P. (1995): Evolution and Optimum Seeking. John Wiley, New York

Schwefel, H.-P.; Männer, R. (eds.) (1991): Parallel Problem Solving from Nature. Proceedings of the First Workshop Dortmund 1990. Springer, Berlin

Smith, R.E. (1991): Default Hierarchy Formation and Memory Exploitation in Learning Classifier Systems. Doctoral Dissertation, TCGA Report 91003, University of Alabama, The Clearinghouse for Genetic Algorithms, Tuscaloosa

Starkweather, T.; McDaniel, S.; Mathias, K.; Whitley, D. (1991): A Comparison of Genetic Sequencing Operators. In: Belew, R.K.; Booker, L.B. (eds.): Proceedings of the Fourth International Conference on Genetic Algorithms. Morgan Kaufmann, San Mateo: 69-73

Suzuki, J. (1993): A Markov Chain Analysis on a Genetic Algorithm. In: Forrest, S. (ed.): Proceedings of the Fifth International Conference on Genetic Algorithms. Morgan Kaufmann, San Mateo/CA: 146-153

Syswerda, G. (1989): Uniform Crossover in Genetic Algorithms. In: Schaffer, J.D. (ed.): Proceedings of the Third International Conference on Genetic Algorithms. Morgan Kaufmann, San Mateo: 2-9

Syswerda, G. (1991): A Study of Reproduction in Generational and Steady-State Genetic Algorithms. In: Rawlins, G.J.E. (ed.):Foundations of Genetic Algorithms. Morgan Kaufmann, San Mateo/CA: 94-101

Syswerda, G.; Palmucci, J. (1991): The Application of Genetic Algorithms to Resource Scheduling. In: Belew, R.K.; Booker, L.B. (eds.): Proceedings of the Fourth International Conference on Genetic Algorithms. Morgan Kaufmann, San Mateo: 502-508

Tanese, R. (1989): Distributed Genetic Algoritms. In: Schaffer, J.D. (ed): Proceedings of the Third International Conference on Genetic Algorithms. Morgan Kaufmann, San Mateo/CA: 434-439

Whitley, D. (1989): The GENITOR Algorithm and Selection Pressure: Why Rank-Based Allocation of Reproductive Trials is Best. In: Schaffer, J.D. (ed.): Proceedings of the Third International Conference on Genetic Algorithms. Morgan Kaufmann, San Mateo/CA: 116-121

Whitley, D.; Starkweather, T.; Fuquay, D. (1989): Scheduling Problems and Travelling Salesmen: The Genetic Edge Recombination Operator. In: Schaffer, J.D. (ed.): Proceedings of the Third International Conference on Genetic Algorithms. Morgan Kaufmann, San Mateo: 133-140

Whitley, L.D.; Schaffer, J.D. (eds.) (1992): COGANN-92 International Workshop on Combinations of Genetic Algorithms and Neural Networks. IEEE Computer Society Press, Los Alamitos/CA

An Overview of Evolutionary Algorithms in Management Applications

Volker Nissen

Abteilung Wirtschaftsinformatik I, Universität Göttingen, Platz der Göttinger Sieben 5, 37073 Göttingen, Germany, vnissen@gwdg.de

Abstract. In this paper an evaluation of the current situation regarding Evolutionary Algorithms (EA) in management applications is given. While assembling as many references as possible, the overview is, of course, not complete, but should give a representative account of current focuses of research and practical applications. EA-references are divided in three major categories: practical applications in business, applications-oriented research (mainly at universities), and abstract standard operations research problems with relevance beyond the domain of management.

Keywords. genetic algorithms, genetic programming, evolution strategies, evolutionary programming, classifier systems, hybrid systems, management problems

1 Introduction

Evolutionary Algorithms (EA) are a rapidly increasing field of research. This has been most visibly documented in a number of conference proceedings: [GREF85a; GREF87a; SCHA89; BELE91; SCHW91; MÄNN92; FOGE92b; FOGE93b; SEBA94; DAVI94a, PEAR95]. Moreover, a sizable number of monographs on EA have appeared in various languages, and e-mail discussion lists serve as a medium for quick information exchange. Numerous journal articles, proceedings papers, research reports and working papers have been published that deal with the subject of EA. Much of this research is not widely known, even not in the EA-community, as the field becomes increasingly diversified and complex.

In an attempt to structure one important area of applied EA-research, this paper gives an overview of EA in management applications. The dominant field of EA-applications still seems to be the technical sector. Many references to purely technical applications are given in [BÄCK92]. Applications of EA in management science and closely related fields like organisational ecology have been covered by fewer EA researchers - with a strong bias towards scheduling and production planning problems. I believe that EA have considerable potential for applications outside the rather narrow domain of scheduling and related combinatorial problems.

This was the initial incentive to start collecting references about the status quo of EA-applications in management science. This paper intends to make available my findings to other researchers in the field. It classifies and lists some 500 references to current as well as finished research projects and practical applications. Although much effort has been devoted to collect as many references as possible, the list is certainly not complete. However, it should give a representative account of the current emphasis in research and practice. This paper is an update of a technical report published in 1993, containing roughly 230 references [NISS93b]. The underlying database is continuously being updated.

2 Technical Remarks

A few technical remarks seem to be necessary. This overview is based on a detailed evaluation of the literature and information posted to the relevant e-mail discussion lists Genetic Algorithms (GA) Digest (GA-List-Request@AIC.NRL. NAVY.MIL), Evolutionary Programming (EP) Digest (EP-List-Request@ magenta.me.fau.edu), Genetic Programming (GP) List (genetic-programming-REQUEST@cs.stanford. edu), the EMSS-list (dduane@gmu.edu) on evolutionary models in the social sciences, and two other specialised lists on timetabling (ttp-request@cs.nott.ac.uk) and scheduling (gasched-owner@acse.sheffield.ac.uk) with EA. Additional information was gathered by private communication with fellow researchers, consultants and users of EA in business. A request for information posted in the GA Digest and other e-mail lists also produced some useful response.

It is not easy to draw a strict border line between applications in management and technical applications. Layout problems may serve as an example where economic aspects mix with technical considerations. When economic aspects appeared to play an important role the application was included in the reference list. The distinction will always be vague, though. This also in principle applies to the distinction between management science and economics. Areas of interest to both domains, such as research in organisations, speculative markets or game theory are part of the list.

Sometimes it was also rather difficult to decide, on the basis of the literature reviewed, whether papers actually discussed a practical application in business (section 3.1) or 'just' application-oriented research (section 3.2). When only test problems were discussed without reference to a practical project then no immediate practical background was assumed. This also applies to projects using historical real data. Application-oriented research and general standard problems (section 3.3) are two evaluations that refer to projects not linked to practical applications in business. While projects in section 3.2 are restricted to management problems, general standard problems may concern management as well as other (e.g. technical) domains. A well known example for a general standard problem with applicability in different domains is the traveling salesman problem (TSP).

Multiple publications on the same project count as one application, but all known references are given in the tables. The year of earliest presentation of an application, as given in the tables of section 3, generally refers to the earliest source found. Note that when an application was, for instance, presented at a workshop in 1989 while the proceedings volume was published in 1991, then the application´s earliest presentation date will be 1989 in the tables of section 3. In some cases authors (e.g. Koza, Michalewicz) have included all previously published material in easily accessible books or larger papers. Here, only the overall references are cited in the reference list.

It is common practice to modify the standard-EA to better suit a given application. Occasionally, this results in various forms of hybridising with conventional algorithms. The EA-type listed in the tables of section 3, therefore, refers to the underlying basic variant of EA that was used. Only in the case of Classifier Systems or EA-hybrids with neural networks or knowledge-based systems this has been included as additional information in the tables.

For the majority of all cited references the original papers were available for investigation. In some cases, however, secondary literature had to be used, because it was impossible or too difficult to obtain the original sources.

3 Applications in Management Science and Related Fields

3.1 Practical Applications in Business

An overview of practical EA-applications is given in table 1. To date the quantity and diversity of applications is still moderate if one compares with the huge variety of optimisation problems faced in management. Besides, many systems referenced in table 1 must be considered prototypes. Although this information is hard to extract from the given data, the number of running systems actually applied routinely in daily practice is likely to be rather small.

Combinatorial optimisation with a focus on scheduling is dominant. Most applications appear in an industrial setting with emphasis on production (figure 1). This is not surprising, since production can be viewed as one large and complex optimisation task that determines a companies competitive strength and success in business. Other business functions such as strategic planning, inventory, and marketing have not received much attention by the EA-community so far, although some pioneering publications (see also table 2) have demonstrated the relevance of EA to these fields.

The energy sector is another strong area of application where mainly Evolution Strategies (ES) are applied. ES are dominant here, because this EA-variant originated in the engineering field and has traditionally been strong in technical applications. The GA-community still lacks behind, but, in general, the GA-methodology would fit these types of applications, too.

The financial services sector has traditionally been very progressive in its EDP-applications, but publications in the scientific press are rather scarce. A focus on credit control and identification of good investment strategies is visible, though. The actual number of EA-applications in this sector is likely to be much higher than the figures make believe. This might also hold for business-oriented applications in the military sector. In these unpublished applications GA are the most likely EA-variant employed, since their research community is by far the largest.

Interest in ES, EP and GP is growing, so that a rise in the number of their respective applications can be expected in the near future. One should note, however, that ES are already quite frequently applied in practice. Originally developed as an optimisation tool for engineering, there has traditionally been a tendency to overcome the status of pure academic exercise in the ES-community. EP and GP do not seem to have been applied much in management. The small EP-community appears to focus on military and technical applications. GP is a very recent technique that has caught some attraction mainly from practitioners in the financial sector, while GP-researchers are still working to reach the level of practical applicability in other domains.

A few hybrid systems integrating EA with artificial neural networks and production systems exist. Since they are expensive to develop and may yield considerable strategic advantage over competitors, it can be assumed that much work in hybrid systems is actually kept secret and does not appear in the figures. This also holds for applications developed by commercial EA suppliers, sometimes with the aid of professional and semi-professional EA-tools.

If one considers the publication dates of practical EA-applications (figure 2), a sharp rise in publications since the late 1980s is obvious. This movement can almost solely be attributed to an increased interest in GA where the number of researchers has risen dramatically. To infer that GA are superior over other EA-techniques can not be justified by these figures, though. It is rather the good 'infrastructure' of the GA-community that fuels this trend: regular GA-conferences since 1985, the availability of an introductory text book [GOLD89], (semi-)professional GA-tools, a well-organised and widely distributed newslist (GA-digest), and cumulative effects following successful pilot applications.

All in all, it seems fair to say that we have not seen the big breakthrough of EA in management practice, yet. Interest in these new techniques, however, has risen considerably over the last five years and will lead to a further increase in practical applications in the near future.

Economic Sector/Functional Unit of Enterprise	Practical Application in Business	EA-Type	References	Date of Earliest Known Presentation
1. Industry	Line balancing in the metal industry	GA	[FALK92]	1992
1.1 Production	Line balancing in the metal industry	GA	[FULK93b]	1993
	Simultaneous planning of production program, lot-sizes and production sequence in the wallpaper industry	ES	[ZIMM85]	1984
	Grouping orders into lots in a foundry	GA	[FALK91b]	1991
	Multi-objective production planning in the metal industry	ES	[BUSC91]	1991
	Multi-objective production planning	ES	[NOCH90]	1990
	Deciding on buffer capacity and # of system pallets in chained production	ES	[NOCH90]	1990
	Production planning in the chemical industry	GA	[BRUN93]	1993
	Lotsizing and sequencing in the car industry	ES	[ABLA91], [ABLA95a]	1989
	Flow shop scheduling for the production of integrated circuits	GA	[WHIT91], [STAR92]	1991
	Sector release scheduling at a computer board assembly and test facility	GA	[CLEV89]	1989
	Sequencing orders in the electrical ind.	ES	[ABLA90]	1989
	Sequencing orders in the paper industry	ES	[ABLA90]	1989
	Scheduling for a foundry of core-pour-mold operations	GA	[FULK93a]	1993
	Sequencing orders for the production of engines	ES	[SCHÖ90], [SCHÖ91], [SCHÖ92], [SCHÖ94]	1990
	Process planning for a complex part of a multi-spindle machine	GA	[VÁNC91]	1991
	Stacking of aluminium plates onto pallets	GA	[PROS88]	1988
	Production planning with dominant setup-costs	GA	[SCHÜ94]	1994
	Scheduling (assumed: production scheduling) at Daimler-Benz*	ES	[FOGA95a], [FOGA95b]	1995
	Scheduling (assumed: production scheduling) at Rolls Royce*	GA	[FOGA95a], [FOGA95b]	1995
	Sequencing and lotsizing in the pharmaceutical industry	GA	[SCHU94]	1994
	Forge scheduling	GA	[SIRA95]	1995
	Sequencing in a hot-rolling process	GA	[SCHU92], [SCHU93b	1992
	Slab design (kind of bin packing)	GA	[HIRA95]	1995

* Applications not confirmed by companies involved

Table 1. Practical applications.

Economic Sector/Functional Unit of Enterprise	Practical Application in Business	EA-Type	References	Date of Earliest Known Presentation
1.1 Production	Scheduling and resource management in ship repair	GA	[FILI94], [FILI95]	1994
	JIT-scheduling of a collator machine	GA	[RIXE95]	1995
1.2 Personnel	Scheduling personnel in textile industry	ES	[SCHÄ93]	1993
	Crew-scheduling in an industrial plant	GA	[MOCC95]	1995
1.3 Distribution	Siting of retail outlets	GA	[HUGH90]	1990
	Allocation of orders to loading docks in a brewery	GA	[STAR91b], [STAR92], [STAR93]	1991
	Multi-commodity transshipment problem	GA	[THAN92b]	1992
2. Financial Services	Assessing insurance risks	GA	[HUGH90]	1990
	Developing rules for dealing in currency markets	GA	[HUGH90]	1990
	Modelling trading behavior in financial markets (Citibank)	CS	[SCHU93a]	1993
	Trading strategy search	GA	[NOBL90]	1990
	Security selection and portfolio optimisation	GA	[NOBL90]	1990
	Risk management (search for suitable positions in securities)	GA	[NOBL90]	1990
	Credit scoring	GA	[NOBL90],	1990
	Credit scoring	GA	[WALK94]	1994
	Time series analysis	GA	[NOBL90]	1990
	Credit card application scoring	GA	[FOGA91], [FOGA92]	1991
	Credit card account performance scoring	GA	[FOGA91], [FOGA92]	1991
	Credit card transaction fraud detection	GA	[FOGA91], [FOGA92]	1991
	Financial trading rule generation	GP	[KERS94]	1994
	Fraud detection at Bank of America	GP	[VERE95b]	1995
	Building financial trading models	GP	[ROGN94]	1994
	Improving trading strategies over time in a stock market simulation	GA	[MAZA95]	1995
	Prediction of prepayment rates for adjustable rate home mortgage loans	GP	[VERE95a]	1995
	Constructing scorecards for credit control	GA	[FOGA94b], [IRES94], [IRES95]	1994

Table 1 (continued). Practical applications (CS = Learning Classifier System - a machine learning system that uses GA).

Economic Sector/Functional Unit of Enterprise	Practical Application in Business	EA-Type	References	Date of Earliest Known Presentation
3. Traffic	Routing and scheduling of freight trains	GA	[GABB91]	1991
	Scheduling trains on single-track lines	GA	[MILL93], [ABRA93b], [ABRA94]	1993
	Vehicle routing (UPS)	GA-XN	[KADA90a], [KADA90b], [KADA91]	1990
	School bus routing	GA	[THAN92a]	1992
	Determining rail-track reconstruction sites to minimise traffic disturbance	ES	[ABLA92], [ABLA95a]	1992
	Scheduling cleaning personnel for trains	ES	[ABLA92], [ABLA95a]	1992
	Scheduling aircraft landing times to minimise cost	GA	[ABRA93a]	1993
	Elevator dispatching	GA	[SIRA95]	1995
	Vehicle scheduling problem of the mass transportation company of Mestre	GA	[BAIT95]	1995
4. Energy	Optimal load management in a network of power plants	ES	[ADER85], [WAGN85]	1985
	Optimised power flow in electrical energy supply networks	ES	[MÜLL83a], [MÜLL83b], [MÜLL86]	1983
	Optimised power flow in electrical energy supply networks	ES	[FUCH83]	1983
	Core optimisation of fast breeder reactors w.r.t. cost of fuel and economic efficiency	ES	[HEUS70]	1970
	Optimising a chain of hydro-electric power plants	GA	[HÜLS94]	1994
	Scheduling planned maintenance of the UK electricity transmission network	GA	[LANG95]	1995
	Network pipe-sizing for British Gas	GA	[SURR94]	1994
	Scheduling in a liquid petroleum pipeline	GA	[SCHA94]	1994
	Achieving maximum efficiency in power station cycles	ES	[SONN82]	1981
5. Education	School timetable problem	GA	[COLO91a], [COLO91b], [COLO92a]	1990
	Scheduling student presentations	GA	[PAEC94b]	1994

Table 1 (continued). Practical applications (GAXN = GA-hybrid with neural network and knowledge-based system)

Economic Sector/Functional Unit of Enterprise	Practical Application in Business	EA-Type	References	Date of Earliest Known Presentation
5. Education	Integrating a Prolog assignment program with GA as a hybrid solution for a polytechnic timetable problem	GA	[LING92a]	1992
	Timetabling of exams and classes	GA	[ERGU95]	1995
	Exam scheduling problem	GA	[CORN93], [CORN94], [ROSS94a], [ROSS94b]]	1993
	School timetable problem	GA	[LING92b]	1992
6. Tele-communication	Designing low cost sets of packet switching communication network links	GA	[DAVI87], [COOM87], [DAVI89]	1987
	Anticipatory routing and scheduling of call requests	GA	[COX91]	1991
	Designing a cost-efficient telecommunication network with a guaranteed level of survivability	GA	[DAVI93b]	1993
	Local and wide area network design to maximise performance on different goals	GA	[KEAR95]	1995
	TSP for several system installers under multiple constraints	GA	[KEAR95]	1995
	Optimising telecommunication network layout in developing countries	GA	[KEIJ95]	1995
7. Health Care	Scheduling patients in a hospital	ES	[ABLA92], [ABLA95a]	1992
	Allocating investments to various health-service programs	ES	[SCHW72]	1972
8. Disposal systems	Optimal siting of local waste disposal systems	ES	[FALK80]	1980
	Vehicle routing and location planning for waste disposal systems	ES	[DEPP92]	1992
9. Trade	Determining cluster storage properties for product clusters in a distribution centre for vegetables and fruits	GA	[BROE95a], [BROE95b]	1995
	Determining the correct quantity of new book's first editions	ES	[ABLA95a]	1995
10. Military Sector	Scheduling a F-14 flight simulator to pilots	GA	[SYSW91a], [SYSW91b]	1991
11. Government	Optimising budgeting rules by data analysis	GA	[PACK90]	1990

Table 1 (continued). Practical applications.

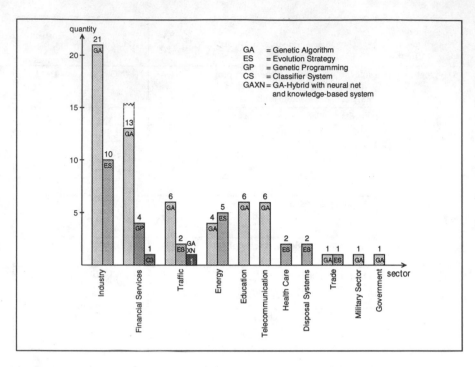

Fig. 1. Practical applications ordered by economic sectors.

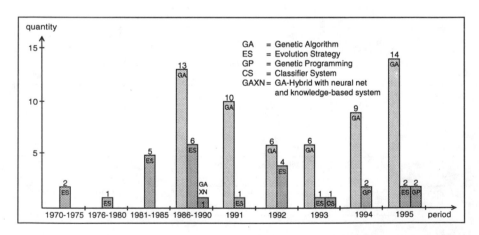

Fig. 2. Practical applications ordered by earliest year of presentation.

3.2   Application-Oriented Research

This evaluation (table 2) focussed on research in management science that was not linked to some practical project in business. GA-research is even more dominant here than in practical applications. The overall picture with respect to major fields of interest and used EA-variants is similar to the previous section. However, the quantity and diversity of projects is larger than in practical applications. Research interest in production planning and financial services is particularly high.

Notable is the strong bias of research towards job shop and flow shop scheduling. Production planning is an important problem in practice, of course. However, the standard testproblems used by many authors (including me, in a different domain) frequently lack many of the practical constraints faced in production. Research on standard operations research problems like job shop scheduling sometimes has become some sort of tournament where practical relevance of the approach comes second to minimal improvements of some published benchmark results on simplifying testproblems. Moreover, the considerable versatility of EA has, in my view, not been adequately appreciated in the domain of management science so far.

General Topic	Research Application	# of Pro-jects	EA Type	References	Date of Earliest Known Presen-tation
Location problems	Facility layout/Location planning	4	GA	[KHUR90], [TAM92], [SMIT93], [NISS94b], [KRAU95]	1990-1994
		1	ES	[NISS94a]	
	Layout design	1	GA	[STAW95]	1995
	Locational and sectoral model.	1	GA	[STEN94b]	1994
	Location planning in distribut.	1	GA	[DEMM92]	1992
R & D	Learning models of consumer choice	2	GA, CS	[GREE87], [OLIV93]	1987, 1993
Inventory	Optimising a Wagner-Whitin model	1	ES	[SCHO76]	1976
	Optimising decision variables of a stochastic inventory simulation	1	GA, ES,EP	[BIET94], [NISS94a], [NISS95a], [NISS95b], [NISS95c]	1994
	Multicriteria Inventory Classification	1	GA	[GÜVE95]	1995
	Scheduling transportation vehicles in large warehouses	1	GA	[SCHÖ94]	1994

Table 2. Application-oriented research (CS = Learning Classifier System - a machine learning system that uses GA).

General Topic	Research Application	# of Projects	EA Type	References	Date of Earliest Known Presentation
Production	Dynamic multi-product, multi-stage lot-sizing problem	1	GA	[HELB93]	1992
	Minimising total intercell and intracell moves in cellular manufacturing	1	GA	[GUPT92]	1992
	Line balancing	3	GA	[ANDE90], [SCHÜ92], [BRÄH92], [WEBE93], [GEHR94], [TSUJ95]	1990, 1992, 1995
	Knowledge base refinement and rule-based simulation for automated transportation system steel manufacturing	1	CS	[TERA94]	1994
	Short term production scheduling	2	GA	[MICH95], [KURB95a], [KURB95b]	1995
	Lotsizing and scheduling	1	GA	[GRÜN95]	1995
	Production planning tool containing GA as automised scheduling component	1	GA	[HANS95]	1995
	Parameter optimisation of a simulation model for production planning	1	GA	[CLAU95]	1995
	Flexible optimisation tools for intelligent manufacturing systems	1	GA	[WELL94]	1994
	Production planning under real-world constraints	1	GA	[STAC94]	1994
	Discovering manufacturing control strategies	1	GA	[BOWD92], [BOWD95]	1992
	Two-stage production scheduling problem	1	GA	[QUIN95]	1995
	Production scheduling (various GA-approaches)	1	GA	[PESC94]	1994
	Evolutionary parameterisation of a lotsizing heuristic under capacity constraints	1	GA	[SCHW94]	1994
	Determining the optimal network partition and Kanban allocation in JIT production lines	1	GA	[ETTL95], [SCHW95]	1995
	Optimising a material-flow system	1	ES	[NOCH86], [NOCH90]	1986

Table 2 (continued). Application-oriented research.

General Topic	Research Application	# of Pro-jects	EA Type	References	Date of Earliest Known Presen-tation
Production	Flow shop scheduling	8	GA	[CART91], [RUBI92], [REEV92], [STÖP92], [BIER92a], [BAC93], [CART93b],[REEV93b], [BIER94], [CART94], [HADI95], [SANG95], [STAW95]	1991-1995
		2	ES	[ABLA79], [ABLA87], [WERN84], [WERN88]	1979, 1984
		1	CS	[BADA91]	1991
	Job shop scheduling	32	GA	[DAVI85], [LIEP87], [BIEG90], [KHUR90], [BAGC91], [FALK91a], [HUSB91a], [HUSB91b], [KANE91], [NAKA91], [NISH91], [BEAN92a], [BRUN92], [DORN92], [HUSB92],[PARE92a], [PARE92b], [PESC92], [STOR92], [TAMA92], [YAMA92], [ATLA93], [BIER93a], [BIER93b], [CLAU93], [DAVI93a], [DORN93a], [DORN93b], [FANG93], [GEUR93], [HUSB93], [JONE93], [KOPF93a], [PESC93], [STOR93], [UCKU93], [VOLT93], [APPE94], [BRUN94a], [BRUN94b], [HUSB94], [MATT94], [NAKA94], [PALM94b], [TUSO94a], [TUSO94b], [HADI95], [HOLM95], [JÓZE95], [NORM95], [PARK95], [ROGN95], [SZAK95]	1985-1995
		1	CS	[HILL87], [HILL89a], [HILL89b], [HILL90]	1987
		1	ES	[HÖNE90]	1990
	Design of cost-minimal cable networks to connect production appliances	1	ES	[SCHI81]	1981
	Grouping parts	1	GA	[STAW95]	1995
	Job Sched. in Elect. Assembly	1	GA	[DEO95]	1995

Table 2 (continued). Application-oriented research.

General Topic	Research Application	# of Projects	EA Type	References	Date of Earliest Known Presentation
Production	Routing in manufacturing	1	GA	[STAW95]	1995
	Scheduling and resource management in a textile factory	1	GA	[FILI92], [FILI93], [FILI95]	1992
	Sequencing jobs in car industry	1	GA	[DEGE95]	1995
	Scheduling maintenance tasks	1	GA, ES	[GREE94]	1994
	Scheduling problem in a plastics forming plant	1	GA	[TAMA93]	1993
	Scheduling problem in hot rolling process	1	GA	[TAMA94a]	1994
	Parallel machine tool schedul.	1	GA	[NORM95]	1995
	Open shop scheduling	1	GA	[FANG93]	1993
	Simultaneous lotsizing and sequencing of jobs in printed circuit board manufacturing	1	GA	[LEE93]	1993
	Production scheduling	1	GA	[WEIN93]	1993
	Machine component grouping	1	GA	[VENU92]	1992
	Scheduling solvent production	1	GAX	[IGNI91], [IGNI93]	1991
	Classification of engineering design for later reuse	1	GAN	[CAUD92]	1992
	Industrial bin packing problems	1	GA	[FALK92],[FALK94a], [FALK94b], [FALK95]	1992
	Two-dimensional guillotine cutting problem	1	GA	[PARA95]	1995
	Best cut bar problem to minimise waste material	1	GA, ES	[ORDI95]	1995
Distribution	Vehicle routing	5	GA	[THAN91a], [THAN91b], [THAN93a], [THAN93b], [THAN93c], [LONT92], [MAZI92], [MAZI93], [BLAN93], [HIRZ92], [PANK93], [KOPF93b], [KOPF94]	1991-1993
	Vehicle Fleet Scheduling	1	GA	[STEF95]	1995
	Linear and nonlinear transportation problems	1	GA	[MICH92]	1989
	Multicriteria Solid Transportation Problems	1	GA	[IDA95]	1995

Table 2 (continued). Application-oriented research (GAN, GAX = GA-hybrids with neural net and knowledge-based system respectively)

General Topic	Research Application	# of Pro-jects	EA Type	References	Date of Earliest Known Presen-tation
Distribution	Minimisation of freight rate in commercial road transportation	1	GA	[KOPF92]	1992
	Pallet packing/ stacking in trucks	1	GA	[JULI92], [JULI93]	1992
	Assigning customer tours to trucks	1	GA	[SCHR91], [BORK92], [BORK93]	1991
	Solving a two-stage distribution problem	1	GA	[BRAU93]	1993
Strategic Managemt., Controlling , Organisation	Forecasting of company profit	1	GA	[THOM86]	1986
	Top-down calculation of budget models	1	ES	[SPUT84]	1984
	Evolution of organisational forms under environmental selection	1	GA	[BRUD92a], [BRUD93]	1992
	Portfolio-optimisation , deciding between projects of different requirements and expected cash-flows	1	ES	[ABLA95b]	1995
	Business System Planning	1	GA	[KNOL93]	1993
	Dynamic solutions to a strategic market game	1	GA	[BOND94]	1994
	Relationship between organisational structure of the firm and its capability to learn and adapt to changes	1	CS	[MARE92a], [MARE92b]	1992
Timetabling	Timetable problems	12	GA	[ABRA91], [FANG92], [PAEC93], [BURK94], [KINN94], [PAEC94a], [ROSS94c], [BURK95a], [BURK95b], [FUKU95], [JACK95], [JUNG95], [MACD95], [AVIL95], [ERBE95], [QUEI95]	1991-1995
		1	ES	[HENS86]	1986
Trade	Sales forecasting for a newspaper publisher	1	GA	[SCHÖ93]	1993
	Selecting competitive products as part of product-market development analysis	1	GA	[BALA92]	1992

Table 2 (continued). Application-oriented research.

General Topic	Research Application	# of Projects	EA Type	References	Date of Earliest Known Presentation
Trade	Market segmentation (deriving product-market structures)	1	GA	[HURL94], [HURL95]	1994
	Feature selection in the context of analysing the characteristics of consumer goods	1	GA	[TERA95]	1995
	Emergence of corporate routines for price and quantity decisions in oligopolistic markets	1	GP	[DOSI93]	1993
	Site location of retail stores	1	GA	[HURL94], [HURL95]	1994
	Solving multi-stage location problems	1	GA	[SCHÜ95]	1995
	Evolution of trade strategies	1	GA, GP	[LENT94]	1994
	Determining good pricing strategies in an oligopolistic market (U.S. coffee market)	1	GA	[MARK89], [MARK92a], [MARK92b], [MARK95]	1989
Financial Services	Bankruptcy prediction	1	GA	[SIKO92], [SIKO93a]	1992
	Loan default prediction	1	GA	[SIKO92], [SIKO93a]	1992
	Time series prediction of financial data	1	GP	[GERR93]	1993
	Financial forecasting	1	GA	[BORA95]	1995
	Predicting horse races	1	GP	[PERR94]	1994
	Financial analysis	1	GP	[SING94]	1994
	Stock market forecaster	1	GA	[MOOR94]	1994
	Stock price time series prediction	1	GP	[WARR94]	1994
	Trend prediction in financial time series	1	GP	[EGLI94]	1994
	Bond rating	1	GA	[SIKO93b]	1993
	Commercial loan risk classification	1	GA	[SIKO92], [SIKO93a]	1992
	Building classification rules for credit scoring	1	GA	[MACK94], [MACK95]	1994
	Credit card attrition problem	1	GP	[TUFT93]	1993
	Filtering insurance applications	1	GA	[GAMM91]	1991
	Investment portfolio selection	1	GA	[LORA95]	1995
	Stock market simulation	1	GA	[ARTH91b]	1991

Table 2 (continued). Application-oriented research.

General Topic	Research Application	# of Projects	EA Type	References	Date of Earliest Known Presentation
Financial Services	Economic modelling of money markets by adaptive agents	1	CS	[BOEH94]	1994
	Learning strategies in a multi-agent stock market simulation	1	GA	[LEBA94]	1994
	Behavior of trading automata in a computerised double auction market	3	CS	[ANDR91], [ARTH91a], [ARTH92], [HOLL92b], [NOTT92]	1990
	Modeling traders in a stock market	1	GAN	[MARG91], [MARG92]	1991
	Acquisition of double auction market strategies	1	GP	[ANDR94]	1993
	Optimised stock investment	1	GA	[EDDE95]	1995
	Evolutionary simulation of asset trading strategies	1	GA, ES	[RIEC94]	1994
	Genetic rule induction for financial decision making	1	GA	[GOON94]	1994
	Discovering good investment strategies	1	GA	[BAUE92], [BAUE94a], [BAUE94b], [BAUE95]	1992
	Analysing the currency market	1	CS	[BELT93]	1993
	DSS for negotiation support in apartment rental	1	GA	[MATW91]	1991
Energy Management	Finding multiple load flow solutions in electrical power networks	1	GA	[YIN91], [YIN94]	1991
	Clustering of power networks	1	GA	[DING92]	1992
	Forecasting natural gas demand for an energy supplier	1	GA	[SCHO93]	1993
	Unit commitment problem	2	GA	[DASG93], [KAZA95]	1993
	Optimal arrangement of fresh and burnt fuel in nuclear fuel management	1	GA	[HEIS94a], [HEIS94b]	1994
	Fuel cycle optimisation	1	GA	[POON90], [POON92]	1990
Water Supply Systems	Designing water distribution networks	3	GA	[CEMB92], [MURP92], [LOHB93], [MURP93], [WALT93a], [WALT93b], [WALT93c], [WALT93d], [DAVI94b], [SIMP94a], [SIMP94b], [WALT94], [SAVI94a], [SAVI94b], [SAVI95a], [SAVI95b]	1992, 1994
	Optimisation of regional water supply systems	1	ES	[CEMB77]	1977

Table 2 (continued). Application-oriented research.

General Topic	Research Application	# of Pro-jects	EA Type	References	Date of Earliest Known Presen-tation
Traffic Management	Optimising train schedules to minimise passenger change-times	1	GA	[NACH93], [NACH95]	1993
	Improv. of railway timetables	1	GA	[WEZE94]]	1994
	Scheduling underground trains	1	ES	[HAMP81]	1981
	Elevator group control	1	GA	[ALAN95]	1995
	Free routing for aircraft	1	GA	[GERD94a], [GERD94b], [GERD94c], [GERD95]	1994
	Airline crew scheduling	1	GA	[CHU95]	1995
	Control of metering rates on freeway ramps	1	EP	[MCDO95]	1995
Personnel Management	Employee staffing and scheduling	2	GA	[EAST93], [LEVI93a], [LEVI93b], [LEVI95]	1993
	Medium-to short-term audit-staff scheduling	1	GA	[SALE94]	1994
Miscel-laneous	General resource allocation problems	1	GA	[BEAN92a]	1992
		1	ES	[SCHO76]	1976
	Forecasting time series data in economic systems	1	GP	[LEE95]	1995
	Adapting agricultural models to fit different regions	1	GA	[JACU95]	1995
	Analysis of call and service processing in telecomm.	1	GA	[SINK95]	1995
	Design of communication networks	1	GAX	[CLIT89]	1989

Table 2 (continued). Application-oriented research (GAX = GA-hybrids with knowledge-based system).

3.3 General Standard Problems

Table 3 lists EA-applications on abstract operations research problems with relevance not only to management science but other domains as well. Many of them refer to randomly generated data or testproblems given in the literature. The interested reader will find some applications from evolutionary economics under the heading 'Iterated Games'.

Besides GA (dominant) and ES, some applications of EP and GP as well as CS are found in the area of game theory, and for some combinatorial problems such as the traveling salesman problem (TSP). The TSP is a particularly well-studied problem that has led to the creation of a number of specialised recombination operators for GA. The potential of GA for the field of combinatorial optimisation is generally considered to be high, but there has been some scientific dispute on this theme (see GA Digest 7 (1993) 6 and following issues).

Standard Problem	EA-Type	References
Traveling salesman problem	GA	[BRAD85], [GOLD85], [GREF85b], [GREF87b], [JOG87], [LIEP87], [MÜHL87], [OLIV87], [SIRA87], [SUH87a], [SUH87b], [WHIT87], [MÜHL88], [GORG89], [NAPI89], [BRAU90], [JOHN90], [LIEP90], [BIER91], [BRAU91], [ESHE91], [FOX91], [GORG91a], [GORG91b], [GORG91c], [LIDD91], [MAND91], [MÜHL91b], [STAR91a], [STAR91b], [ULDE91], [WHIT91], [BIER92b], [DAVI92], [KOLE92], [MATH92], [MOSC92a], [MOSC92b], [MÜHL92], [STAR92], [BAC93], HOMA93a], [HOMA93b], [KIDO93], [STAN93], [SYSW93], [TSUT93], [CHEN94], [DARW94], [DZUB94], [EIBE94], [TAMA94b], [TANG94], [VALE94], [YOSH94], [BIAN95], [COTT95], [ROBB95]
	GAN	[NYGA90]
	ES	[ABLA79], [BRAD85], [HENS86], [ABLA87], [HERD88], [GROO91], [HERD91], [HOFF91b], [RUDO91], [BEYE92],
	EP	[FOGE88], [FOGE90], [AMBA91], [AMBA92]
Iterated games (freq. Prisoner's Dilemma)	GA	[ADAC87], [AXEL87], [AXEL88], [MARK89], [MATS90], [ADAC91], [LIND91], [MÜHL91c], [CHAT92], [MICH92], [STAN93], [DAWI95], [SIEG95], [BURN95], [HART95], [HAO95]
	EP	[FOGE91], [FOGE92a], [FOGE93a], [FOGE94], [FOGE95]
	GP	[FUJI87], [KOZA92a], [KOZA92b]
	CS	[MILL89], [BRUD92b]
Steiner problems	GA	[HESS89], [GERR91], [HESS91], [JULS93], [KAPS93], KAPS94]
	ES	[OSTE92], [OSTE94]
Set covering	GA	[LIEP87], [LIEP90], [LIEP91], [SEN93], [SEKH93], [BEAS94]
	ES	[REPP85]
Quadratic assignment problem	GA	[COHO86], [BROW89], [MÜHL89], [MÜHL90], [HUNT91], [MANI91], [MÜHL91a], [BEAN92a], [COLO92b], [NISS92],[POON92], [TATE93a], [TATE93b], [FLEU94], [MARE94a], [MARE94b], [NISS94a], [NISS94c], [NISS94d]
	ES	[MANI91], [COLO92b], [NISS92], [NISS93a], [NISS94a], [NISS94c], [NISS94d], [NISS94e]
	EP	[NISS94a], [NISS94c], [NISS94d]
Assignment prob.	GA	[CART93a], [LEVI93c]
Orthogonal packing	GA	[JAKO94a], [JAKO94h]
Bin packing	GA	[FOUR85], [SMIT85], [DAVI90], [KRÖG91], [DAVI92], [FALK92], [KRÖG92], [SMIT92b], [REEV93a], [FALK94a], FALK94b], [HINT94], [FALK95], [KHUR95]
	ES	[KHUR95]

Table 3. Standard management-science problems (GAN = GA-hybrid with neural net, CS = Learning Classifier System).

Standard Problem	EA-Type	References
Knapsack	GA	[GOLD87], [SMIT87], [DASG92], [SMIT92a], [GORD93], [THIE93], KHUR94a]
	ES	[HENS86]
Partitioning problems	GA	[LASZ90], [COHO91a], [COHO91b], [COLL91], [HULI91], [JONE91], [LASZ91], [DRIE92], [HULI92], [MARU92], [MÜHL92], [LEVI93a], [MARU93], [INAY94], [HÖHN95], [SAVI95c]
Graph coloring	GA	[DAVI90], [DAVI91], [EIBE94], [FLEU95a], [FLEU95b]
Min. vertex cover	GA	[KHUR94b], [KHUR94c]
Graph theoretic problems	GP	[PALM94a]
Mapping	GA	[MANS91], [NEUH91], [ANSA92]
Maximum clique	GA	[BAZG95], [FLEU95b]
Maximum flow problem	GA	[MUNA93]
General Integer	GA	[BEAN92b], [HADJ92]
Programming	ES	[ABLA79]
Satisfiability Prob.	GA	[JONG89], [FLEU95b], [HAO95]
Scheduling (general)	GA	[HOU92], [LAWT92], [KIDW93], [ADIT94a], [ADIT94b], [ANDE94], [HOU94], [SCHW94], [SEIB94]
	CS	[SANN88]
Routing	GA	[LIEN94a], [LIEN94b], [MARI94]
Query optimisation	GA	[YANG93]
Task allocation	GA	[FALC95]
Load balancing in databases	GA	[ALBA95]

Table 3 (continued). Standard management-science problems.

4   Conclusions

Over the last five years, interest in EA has risen considerably amongst researchers and practitioners in the management domain, although we have not seen the major breakthrough of EA in practical applications, yet. Most people have been attracted by GA, while ES, EP and GP are not so widely known. GP is the newest technique and is just reaching the level of practical applicability, particularly in the financial sector. EP and ES are very similar, so that they could actually compete on the same types of application. However, EP lacks behind ES in terms of practical applications or application-oriented research in the management domain. The dominance of GA should not be interpreted as superiority of this approach. It rather seems to be a good 'infrastructure' that contributes to the trend for GA.

Most applications in management science concern GA in combinatorial optimisation. In contrast to the common trend, our research at Göttingen seems to indicate that strictly mutation based search might actually be more successful for certain combinatorial problems than recombination-based GAs. This is in good agreement with the findings of other researchers (e.g. [FOGE88]).

Most researchers focus on standard problems to test the quality of their algorithms. Practical applications are often characterised by conflicting objectives and constraints that are not covered by most testproblems. Nevertheless, EA have already produced many impressive results, and the current efforts to develop professional EA-tools and parallelise EA-applications are fueling the positive trend. These factors and the exponentially growing number of EA-researchers will lead to more practical applications in the future and a better understanding of the relative advantages and weaknesses of the approach.

EA are more and more integrated as an optimisation module in large software products (e.g. for production planning). Thereby, the end-user will often be unaware that an evolutionary approach to problem solving is employed.

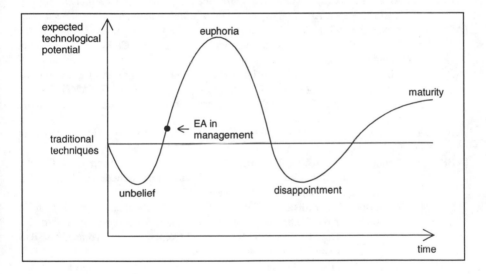

Fig. 3. Estimation of the current state of EA in management applications.

Finally, I have tried to assess the current position of EA in management applications w.r.t. the technological life-cycle (see figure 3). Future applications should attempt to further broaden the focus of today's applied EA-research in management, and assess as well as exploit the considerable versatility of these techniques in the light of the vast variety of operations research related problems. Hybrid systems, which combine the relative advantages of different problem solving techniques, will prove particularly useful and form powerful tools for practical applications in business.

64

References

[ABLA79]   Ablay, P. (1979): Optimieren mit Evolutionsstrategien. Reihenfolgeprobleme, nichtlineare und ganzzahlige Optimierung. Doctoral Dissertation, University of Heidelberg, Germany

[ABLA87]   Ablay, P. (1987): Optimieren mit Evolutionsstrategien. Spektrum der Wissenschaft 7: 104-115

[ABLA90]   Ablay, P. (1990): Konstruktion kontrollierter Evolutionsstrategien zur Lösung schwieriger Optimierungsprobleme der Wirtschaft. In: Albertz, J. (ed.): Evolution und Evolutionsstrategien in Biologie, Technik und Gesellschaft, 2nd ed. Freie Akademie, Wiesbaden: 73-106

[ABLA91]   Ablay, P. (1991): Ten Theses Regarding the Design of Controlled Evolutionary Strategies. In: [BECK91]: 457-481

[ABLA92]   Ablay, P. (1992): 1. Optimal Placement of Railtrack Reconstruction Sites. 2. Scheduling of Patients in a Hospital 3. Scheduling Cleaning Personnel for Trains. Personal Communication

[ABLA95a] Ablay, P. (1995): Evolutionäre Strategien im marktwirtschaftlichen Einsatz. Business Paper, Ablay Optimierung Inc., Gräfelfing/Munich

[ABLA95b] Ablay, P. (1995): Portfolio-Optimization in the Context of Deciding Between Projects of Different Requirements and Expected Cash-Flows. Personal Communication

[ABRA91]   Abramson, D.; Abela, J. (1991): A Parallel Genetic Algorithm for Solving the School Timetabling Problem. Technical Report TR-DB-91-02 (RMIT TR 118 105 R), North Ryde NSW, Macquarie Centre, Division of Information Technology, Australia

[ABRA93a] Abramson, D. (1993): Scheduling Aircraft Landing Times. Personal Communication

[ABRA93b] Abramson, D.; Mills, G.; Perkins, S. (1993): Parallelisation of a Genetic Algorithm for the Computation of Efficient Train Schedules. In: Parallel Computing and Transputers Conference: 1-11

[ABRA94]   Abramson, D.; Mills, G.; Perkins, S. (1994): Parallelism of a Genetic Algorithm for the Computation of Efficient Train Schedules. In: Arnold, D.; Christie, R.; Day, J.; Roe, P. (eds.): Parallel Computing and Transputers. IOS Press, Amsterdam: 139-149

[ADAC87]   Adachi, N. (1987): Framework of Mutation Model for Evolution in the Ecological Model Game World. IIAS-SIS Research Report No. 74, Numazu, Japan

[ADAC91]   Adachi, N.; Matsuo, K. (1991): Ecological Dynamics under Different Selection Rules in Distributed and Iterated Prisoner's Dilemma Game. In: [SCHW91]: 388-394

[ADER85]   Adermann, H.-J. (1985): Treatment of Integral Contingent Conditions in Optimum Power Plant Commitment. In: Wacker, H.J. (ed.): Applied Optimization Techniques in Energy Problems. Teubner, Stuttgart: 1-18

[ADIT94a] Aditya, S.-K.; Bayoumi, M.; Lursinap, C. (1994): Genetic Algorithm for Near Optimal Scheduling and Allocation in High Level Synthesis. In: [KUNZ94]: 85-86

[ADIT94b] Aditya, S.-K.; Bayoumi, M.; Lursinap, C. (1994): Genetic Algorithm for Near Optimal Scheduling and Allocation in High Level Synthesis. In: [HOPF94]: 91-97

[ALAN95] Alander, J.; Ylinen, J.; Tyni, T. (1995): Elevator Group Control Using Distributed Genetic Algorithms. In: [PEAR95]: 400-403

[ALBA95] Alba, E.; Aldana, J.F.; Troya, J.M. (1995): A Genetic Algorithm for Load Balancing in Parallel Query Evaluation for Deductive Relational Databases. In: [PEAR95]: 479-482

[AMBA91] Ambati, B.K.; Ambati, J.; Mokhtar, M.M. (1991): Heuristic Combinatorial Optimization by Simulated Darwinian Evolution: a Polynomial Time Algorithm for the Traveling Salesman Problem. Biological Cybernetics 65: 31-35

[AMBA92] Ambati, B.K.; Ambati, J.; Mokhtar, M.M. (1992): An O(n log n)-time Genetic Algorithm for the Traveling Salesman Problem. In: [FOGE92b]: 134-140

[ANDE90] Anderson, E.J.; Ferris, M.C. (1990): A Genetic Algorithm for the Assembly Line Balancing Problem. In: Proceedings of the Integer Programming/Combinatorial Optimization Conference. University of Waterloo Press, Ontario: 7-18

[ANDE94] Andersen, B. (1994): Tuning Computer CPU Scheduling Algorithms. In: [SEBA94]: 316 -323

[ANDR91] Andreoni, J.; Miller, J.H. (1991): Auctions with Adaptive Artificially Intelligent Agents. Working Paper 91-01-004, Santa Fe Institute

[ANDR94] Andrews, M.; Prager, R. (1994): Genetic Programming for the Acquisition of Double Auction Market Strategies. In: Kinnear Jr., K.E. (ed.): Advances in Genetic Programming. MIT Press, Cambridge: 355-368

[ANSA92] Ansari, N.; Chen, M.-H.; Hou, E.S.H. (1992): A Genetic Algorithm for Point Pattern Matching. In: [SOUC92]: 353-371

[APPE94] Appelrath, H.-J.; Bruns, R. (1994): Genetische Algorithmen zur Lösung von Ablaufplanungsproblemen. In: Reusch, B. (ed.): Fuzzy Logik. Theorie und Praxis. Springer, Berlin: 25-32

[ARTH91a] Arthur, B.W. (1991): Designing Economic Agents that Act Like Human Agents: A Behavioral Approach to Bounded Rationality. The American Economic Review 81: 353-359

[ARTH91b] Arthur, B.; Holland, J.; Palmer, R.; Tayler, P. (1991): Using Genetic Algorithms to Model the Stock Market. In: Proceedings of the Forecasting and Optimization in Financial Services Conference. IBC Technical Services Ltd., London

[ARTH92] Arthur, B.W. (1992): On Learning and Adaption in the Economy. Working Paper 92-07-038, Santa Fe Institute, U.S.A.

[ATLA93] Atlan, L.; Bonnet, J.; Naillon, M. (1993): Learning Distributed Reactive Strategies by Genetic Programming for the General Job Shop Problem. Research Paper, later published in: Proceedings of the Seventh Annual Florida Artificial Intelligence Research Symposium

[ATMA92] Atmar, W. (1992): On the Rules and Nature of Simulated Evolutionary Programming. In: [FOGE92b]: 17-26

[AVIL95] Avila, I. (1995): GA to Construct School Timetables. Genetic Algorithms in Production Scheduling List (E-Mail List), 15.6.1995

[AXEL87]   Axelrod, R. (1987): The Evolution of Strategies in the Iterated Prisoner's Dilemma. In: Davis, L. (ed.): Genetic Algorithms and Simulated Annealing. Morgan Kaufmann, Los Altos/CA.: 32-41

[AXEL88]   Axelrod, R.; Dion, D. (1988): The Further Evolution of Cooperation. Science 242: 1385-1390

[BAC93]   Bac, F.Q.; Perov, V.L. (1993): New Evolutionary Genetic Algorithms for NP-Complete Combinatorial Optimization Problems. Biological Cybernetics 69: 229-234

[BÄCK92]   Bäck, T.; Hoffmeister, F.; Schwefel, H.-P. (eds.) (1992): Applications of Evolutionary Algorithms. Technical Report No. SYS-2/92, University of Dortmund, Computer Science Department, Germany

[BADA91]   Badami, V.S.; Parks, C.M. (1991): A Classifier Based Approach to Flow Shop Scheduling. Computers & Industrial Engineering 21: 329-333

[BAGC91]   Bagchi, S.; Uckun, S.; Miyabe, Y.; Kawamura, K. (1991): Exploring Problem-Specific Recombination Operators for Job Shop Scheduling. In: [BELE91]: 10-17

[BAIT95]   Baita, F.; Mason, F.; Poloni, C.; Ukovich, W. (1995): Genetic Algorithm with Redundancies for the Vehicle Scheduling Problem. In this volume

[BAKE91]   Baker, E.K.; Schaffer, J.R. (1991): Solution Improvement Heuristics for the Vehicle Routing Problems with Time Window Constraints. American Journal of Mathematics and Management Sciences 6: 261-300

[BALA92]   Balakrishman, P.V.S.; Jacob, V.S. (1992): A Genetic Algorithm Based Decision Support System for Optional Product Design. Paper presented at the T.I.M.S. Annual Conference, London Business School, July 15-17, London

[BAUE92]   Bauer, R.J.; Liepins, G.L. (1992): Genetic Algorithms and Computerized Trading Strategies. In: O'Leary, D.E.; Watkins, P.R. (eds.): Expert Systems in Finance. Elsevier Science, Amsterdam: 89-100

[BAUE94a] Bauer, R.J. (1994): Genetic Algorithms and Investment Strategies. John Wiley & Sons, New York

[BAUE94b] Bauer, R.J. (1994): An Introduction to Genetic Algorithms: A Mutual Fund Screening Example. Neurove$t Journal 4: 16-19

[BAUE95]   Bauer, R.J. (1995): Genetic Algorithms and the Management of Exchange Rate Risk. In this volume

[BAZG95]   Bazgan, C.; Lucian, H. (1995):A Genetic Algorithm for the Maximal Clique Problem. In: [PEAR95]: 499-502

[BEAN92a] Bean, J.C. (1992): Genetics and Random Keys for Sequencing and Optimization. Technical Report 92-43, The University of Michigan, Department of Industrial and Operations Engineering

[BEAN92b] Bean, J.C.; Hadj-Alouane, A.B. (1992): A Dual Genetic Algorithm for Bounded Integer Programs. Technical Report 92-53, The University of Michigan, College of Engineering, Department of Industrial and Operations Research

[BEAS94]   Beasley, J.E.; Chu, P.C. (1994): A Genetic Algorithm for the Set Covering Problem. Genetic Algorithms Digest (E-Mail List) 8 (38), 5.10.1994

[BECK91]   Becker, J.D.; Eisele, I.; Mündemann, F.W. (eds.) (1991): Parallelism, Learning, Evolution. Proceedings of the Workshop on Evolutionary Models and Strategies, Neubiberg, Germany, March 10-11, 1989, and the Workshop on Parallel Processing: Logic, Organization, and Technology - WOPPLOT 89, Wildbad Kreuth, Germany, July 24-28, 1989. Springer, Berlin

[BELE91]   Belew, R.K.; Becker, L.B. (eds.) (1991): Proceedings of the Fourth International Conference on Genetic Algorithms.UCSD, San Diego, July 13-16. Morgan Kaufmann, San Mateo/CA.

[BELT93]   Beltrametti, L.; Marengo, L.; Tamborini, R. (1993): A Learning Experiment with Classifier System: The Determinants of the Dollar-Mark Exchange Rate. Discussion Paper No. 5/93, University of Trento, Department of Economics, Italy

[BEYE92]   Beyer, H.-G. (1992): Some Aspects of the 'Evolution Strategy' for Solving TSP-Like Optimization Problems Appearing at the Design Studies of a 0.5 TeV e^+e^--Linear Collider. In: [MÄNN92]: 361-370

[BIAN95]   Bianchini, R.; Brown, C.M.; Cierniak, M.; Meira, W. (1995): Combining Distributed Populations and Periodic Centralized Selections in Coarse-Grain Parallel Genetic Algorithms. In: [PEAR95]: 483-486

[BIEG90]   Biegel, J.E.; Davern, J.J. (1990): Genetic Algorithms and Job Shop Scheduling. Computers & Industrial Engineering 19: 81-91

[BIER91]   Bierwirth, C.; Mattfeld, D.C.; Stöppler, S. (1991): Pseudo-Parallelity and Distributed Programming under UNIX-System V. In: Grauer, M.; Pressmar, D.B. (eds.): Proceedings of the Conference on Parallel Algorithms and Transputers for Optimization. Springer, Berlin: 35-44

[BIER92a] Bierwirth, C. (1992): Optimierung der Ablaufplanung einer Fließfertigung mit Parallelen Genetischen Algorithmen. Doctoral Dissertation, University of Bremen, Department of Economics, Germany

[BIER92b] Bierwirth, C.; Mattfeld, D.C. (1992): Implementierung eines Parallelen Genetischen Algorithmus in einem verteilten System. Paper presented at the PECOR Workshop of the DGOR, Dec. 4, Düsseldorf

[BIER93a] Bierwirth, C. (1993): A Generalized Permutation Approach to Jobshop Scheduling with Genetic Algorithms. To appear in OR Spektrum, Special Issue Local Search

[BIER93b] Bierwirth, C.; Kopfer, H.; Mattfeld, D.; Utecht, T. (1993): Genetische Algorithmen und das Problem der Maschinenbelegung. Eine Übersicht und ein neuer Ansatz. Technical Report No. 3, University of Bremen, Department of Economics, Germany

[BIER94]   Bierwirth, C. (1994): Flowshop Scheduling mit Parallelen Genetischen Algorithmen - Eine Problemorientierte Analyse genetischer Suchstrategien. Vieweg/DUV, Wiesbaden

[BIET94]   Biethahn, J.; Nissen, V. (1994): Combinations of Simulation and Evolutionary Algorithms in Management Science and Economics. Annals of OR 52: 183-208

[BIET95]   Biethahn, J. (ed.) (1995): Simulation als betriebliche Entscheidungshilfe: Neuere Werkzeuge und Anwendungen aus der Praxis. Proceedings of the 5th Simulation Symposium, March 13-15 1995, Braunlage

[BLAN93]   Blanton, J.L.; Wainwright, R.L. (1993): Multiple Vehicle Routing with Time and Capacity Constraints Using Genetic Algorithms. In: [FORR93]: 452-459.

[BOEH94]   Boehme, F. (1994): Adaptive Coordination Mechanism in the Economic Modelling of Money Markets. In: [STEN94a]: 179-199

68

[BOND94]   Bond, G.; Liu, J.; Shubik, M. (1994): Dynamic Solutions to a Strategic Market Game: Analysis, Programming and a Genetic Algorithm Approach. In: [STEN94a]: 84-111

[BORA95]   Borasky, M.E. (1995): Financial Forecasting. Personal Communication

[BORK92]   Borkowski, V. (1992): Entwicklung eines Genetischen Algorithmus zur Fahrzeugeinsatzplanung im Werksverkehr. Diploma Thesis, University of Hagen, Department of Economics, Germany

[BORK93]   Borkowski, V. (1993): Vergleich zwischen einem Expertensystem und alternativen Entscheidungsunterstützungs-Methoden in der Vertriebslogistik, Doctoral Dissertation, University of Erlangen-Nürnberg, Technical Reports of the Computer Science Department Vol. 26, No. 6, Erlangen, Germany

[BOWD92]   Bowden, R.O. (1992): Genetic Algorithm Based Machine Learning Applied to the Dynamic Routing of Discrete Parts. Doctoral Dissertation, Mississippi State University, Department of Industrial Engineering, U.S.A.

[BOWD95]   Bowden, R.; Bullington, S.F. (1995): An Evolutionary Algorithm for Discovering Manufacturing Control Strategies. In this volume

[BRAD85]   Brady, R.M. (1985): Optimization Strategies Gleaned from Biological Evolution. Nature 317: 804-806

[BRÄH92]   Brähler, U. (1992): Abstimmung von Montagelinien mit einem Genetischen Algorithmus. Diploma Thesis, University of Hagen, Department of Economics, Germany

[BRAN95]   Branke, J.; Kohlmorgen, U.; Schmeck, H.; Veith, H. (1995): Steuerung einer Heuristik zur Losgrößenplanung unter Kapazitätsrestriktionen mit Hilfe eines parallelen genetischen Algorithmus. In: [KUHL95]: 21-31

[BRAU90]   Braun, H. (1990): Massiv parallele Algorithmen für kombinatorische Optimierungsprobleme und ihre Implementierung auf einem Parallelrechner. Doctoral Dissertation, University of Karlsruhe (TH), Germany

[BRAU91]   Braun, H. (1991): On Solving Travelling Salesman Problems by Genetic Algorithms. In: [SCHW91]: 129-133

[BRAU93]   Braun, J. (1993): Entwicklung eines Genetischen Algorithmus zur Lösung eines zweistufigen Distributionsproblems. Diploma Thesis, University of Hagen, Department of Economics, Germany

[BROE95a]   Broekmeulen, R.A.C.M. (1995): Facility Management of Distribution Centres for Vegetables and Fruits. In: [KUHL95]: 32-39

[BROE95b]   Broekmeulen, R.A.C.M. (1995): Facility Management of Distribution Centres for Vegetables and Fruits. In this volume

[BROW89]   Brown, D.E.; Huntley, C.L.; Spillane, A.R. (1989): A Parallel Genetic Heuristic for the Quadratic Assignment Problem. In: [SCHA89]: 406-415

[BRUD92a]   Bruderer, E. (1992): How Organizational Learning Guides Environmental Selection. Working Paper, The University of Michigan, School of Business Administration, U.S.A.

[BRUD92b]   Bruderer, E. (1992): Strategic Learning. Working Paper, The University of Michigan, U.S.A.

[BRUD93]   Bruderer, E. (1993): How Strategies are Learned. Doctoral Dissertation, University of Michigan, Ann Arbor, U.S.A.

[BRUN92]   Bruns, R. (1992): Incorporation of a Knowledge-Based Scheduling System into a Genetic Algorithm. In: Proceedings of the 'GI-Jahrestagung' 1992, Karlsruhe

[BRUN93] Bruns, R. (1993): Direct Chromosome Representation and Advanced Genetic Operators for Production Scheduling. In: [FORR93]: 352-359

[BRUN94a] Bruns, R. (1994): GAP - A Knowledge-Augmented Genetic Algorithm for Industrial Production Scheduling Problems. In: [KUNZ94]: 87-88

[BRUN94b] Bruns, R. (1994): GAP - A Knowledge-Augmented Genetic Algorithm for Industrial Production Scheduling Problems. In: [HOPF94]: 98-99

[BURK94] Burke, E.; Elliman, D.; Weare, R. (1994): A Genetic Algorithm Based University Timetabling System. In: Proceedings of the 2nd East-West International Conference on Computer Technologies in Education, Sep. 19-23, Crimea, Ukraine, Vol. I: 35-40

[BURK95a] Burke, E.K.; Elliman, D.G.; Weare, R.F. (1995): The Automated Timetabling of University Examinations in Higher Education (in Russian). To appear in East-West Journal on Computers in Education

[BURK95b] Burke, E.K.; Elliman, D.G.; Weare, R.F. (1995): Automated Timetabling in Higher Education. Invited for IEE Journal of Engineering Science and Education (in preparation)

[BURN95] Burns, T.D. (1995): GA to Solve Simple Game Theory Problems. Genetic Algorithms Digest (E-Mail List) 9 (36), 22.6.1995

[BUSC91] Busch, M. (1991): Paretooptimale Strategien für ein PPS-System mittels Simulation. Diploma Thesis, University of Dortmund, Department of Computer Science, Germany

[CART91] Cartwright, H.M.; Mott, G.F. (1991): Looking Around: Using Clues from Data Space to Guide Genetic Algorithm Searches. In: [BELE91]: 108-114

[CART93a] Cartwright, H.M.; Harris, S.P. (1993): The Application of the Genetic Algorithm to Two-Dimensional Strings: The Source Apportionment Problem. In: [FORR93]: 631

[CART93b] Cartwright, H.M.; Long, R.A. (1993): Simultaneous Optimisation of Chemical Flowshop Sequencing and Topology Using Genetic Algorithms. Ind. Eng. Chem. Res. 32: 2706-2713

[CART94] Cartwright, H.M.; Tuson, A.L. (1994): Genetic Algorithms and Flowshop Scheduling: Towards the Development of a Real-Time Process Control System. In: [FOGA94a]: 277-290

[CAUD92] Caudell, T.P. (1992): Genetic Algorithms as a Tool for the Analysis of Adaptive Resonance Theory Network Training Sets. In: Whitley, L.D.; Schaffer, J.D. (eds.): COGANN-92 International Workshop on Combinations of Genetic Algorithms and Neural Networks. IEEE Computer Society Press, Los Alamitos/CA: 184-200

[CEMB77] Cembrowicz, R.G.; Krauter, G.E. (1977): Optimization of Urban and Regional Water Supply Systems. In: Proceedings of the Conference on Systems Approach for Development. Kairo: 449-454

[CEMB92]: Cembrowicz, R.G. (1992): Water Supply Systems Optimisation for Developing Countries. In: Coulbeck, B.; Evans, E. (eds.): Pipeline Systems. Kluwer Academic Publishers, Norwell/MA: 59-76

[CHAT92] Chattoe, E. (1992): Evolutionary Models of Economic Agency. Personal Communicatio

[CHEN94] Chen, H.; Flann, N.S. (1994): Parallel Simulated Annealing and Genetic Algorithms: A Space of Hybrid Methods. In: [DAVI94a]: 428-438

70

[CHU95]   Chu, P.C.; Beasley, J.E. (1995): A Genetic Algorithm for the Set Partitioning Problem. Research Paper, Imperial College, The Management School, London, U.K.

[CLAU93]   Claus, T. (1993): Genetische Simulation. Paper presented at the 4th Symposium „Simulation als betriebliche Entscheidungshilfe", March 15-17, Braunlage

[CLAU95]   Claus, T. (1995): Objektorientierte Simulation und evolutionäre Parameteroptimierung. In: [BIET95]: 87-96

[CLEV89]   Cleveland, G.A.; Smith, S.F. (1989): Using Genetic Algorithms to Schedule Flow Shop Releases. In: [SCHA89]: 160-169

[CLIT89]   Clitherow, P.; Fisher, G. (1989): Knowledge Based Assistance of Genetic Search in Large Design Spaces. In: Ali, M. (ed.): Proceedings of the Second International Conference on Industrial & Engineering Applications of Artificial Intelligence & Expert Systems IEA/AIE 89. ACM, New York: 729-734

[COHO86]   Cohoon, J.P.; Paris, W.D. (1986): Genetic Placement. In: Proceedings of the IEEE International Conference on Computer Aided Design. Digest of Technical Papers: 422-425

[COHO91a]   Cohoon, J.P.; Martin, W.N.; Richards, D.S. (1991): Genetic Algorithms and Punctuated Equilibria. In: [SCHW91]: 134-144

[COHO91b]   Cohoon, J.P.; Martin, W.N.; Richards, D.S. (1991): A Multi-population Genetic Algorithm for Solving the K-Partition Problem on Hyper-Cubes. In: [BELE91]: 244-248

[COLL91]   Collins, R.J.; Jefferson, D.R. (1991): Selection in Massively Parallel Genetic Algorithms. In: [BELE91]: 249-256

[COLO91a]   Colorni, A.; Dorigo, M.; Maniezzo, V. (1991): Genetic Algorithms and Highly Constrained Problems: The Time-Table Case. In: [SCHW91]: 55-59

[COLO91b]   Colorni, A.; Dorigo, M.; Maniezzo, V. (1991): Gli algoritmi genetici e il problema dell'orario (Genetic Algorithms and the Problem of Timetables) (Italian). Ricerca Operativa 60: 5-31

[COLO92a]   Colorni, A.; Dorigo, M.; Maniezzo, V. (1992): Genetic Algorithms: A New Approach to the Timetable Problem. In: Akgül, M.; Hamacher, H.W.; Tüfekci, S. (eds.): Combinatorial Optimization. New Frontiers in Theory and Practice. Springer, Berlin: 235-239

[COLO92b]   Colorni, A.; Dorigo, M.; Maniezzo, V. (1992): ALGODESK: an Experimental Comparison of Eight Evolutionary Heuristics applied to the QAP Problem. Report No. 92-052, Milano Polytechnic, Department of Electronics, Italy

[COOM87]   Coombs, S.; Davis, L. (1987): Genetic Algorithms and Communication Link Speed Design: Constraints and Operators. In: [GREF87a]: 257-260

[CORN93]   Corne, D.; Fang, H.-L.; Mellish, C. (1993): Solving the Module Exam Scheduling Problem with Genetic Algorithms. In: Chung; Lovegrove; Ali (eds.): Proceedings of the Sixth International Conference in Industrial and Engineering Applications of Artificial Intelligence and Expert Systems: 370-373

[CORN94]   Corne, D.; Ross, P.; Fang, H.-L. (1994): Fast Practical Evolutionary Timetabling. In: [FOGA94a]: 250-263

[COTT95]   Cotta, C.; Aldana, J.F.; Nebro, A.J.; Troya, J.M. (1995): Hybridizing Genetic
            Algorithms with Branch and Bound Techniques for teh Resolution of the TSP.
            In: [PEAR95]: 277-280

[COX91]   Cox Jr., L.A.; Davis, L.; Qiu, Y. (1991): Dynamic Anticipatory Routing in
            Circuit-Switched Telecommunications Networks. In: [DAVI91]: 124-143

[DARW94]   Darwen, P.J.; Yao, X. (1994): On Evolving Robust Strategies for Iterated
            Prisoner's Dilema. Technical Report, Australian Defence Force Academy,
            University of New South Wales, University College, Department of Computer
            Science, Canberra

[DASG92]   Dasgupta, D.; McGregor, D. R. (1992): Nonstationary Function Optimization
            using the Structured Genetic Algorithm. In: [MÄNN92]: 145-154

[DASG93]   Dasgupta, D. (1993): Unit Commitment in Thermal Power Generation Using
            Genetic Algorithms. In: Chung, P.W.H.; Lovegrove, G.; Ali, M. (eds.):
            Industrial and Engineering Applications of Artificial Intelligence and Expert
            Systems. Proceedings of the Sixth International Conference. Gordon and
            Breach Science Publishers

[DAVI85]   Davis, I. (1985): Job Shop Scheduling with Genetic Algorithms. In:
            [GREF85a]: 136-140

[DAVI87]   Davis, L.; Coombs, S. (1987): Genetic Algorithms and Communication Link
            Speed Design: Theoretical Considerations. In: [GREF87a]: 252-256

[DAVI89]   Davis, L.; Coombs, S. (1989): Optimizing Network Link Sizes with Genetic
            Algorithms. In: Elzas, M.S.; Ören, T.I.; Zeigler, B.P. (eds.): Modelling and
            Simulation Methodology. North-Holland, Amsterdam: 317-331

[DAVI90]   Davis, L. (1990): Applying Adaptive Algorithms to Epistatic Domains. In:
            Mirchandani, P.B.; Francis, R.L. (eds.): Proceedings of the Ninth International
            Joint Conference on Artificial Intelligence, Vol. 1. John Wiley & Sons, New
            York: 162-164

[DAVI91]   Davis, L. (1991): Handbook of Genetic Algorithms. Van Nostrand Reinhold,
            New York

[DAVI92]   Davidor, Y.; Ben-Kiki, O. (1992): The Interplay among the Genetic Algorithm
            Operators: Information Theory Tools Used in a Holistic Way. In: [MÄNN92]:
            75-84

[DAVI93a]   Davidor, Y.; Yamada, T.; Nakano, R. (1993): The ECOlogical Framework II:
            Improving GA Performance at Virtually Zero Cost. In: [FORR93]: 171-176

[DAVI93b]   Davis, L.; Orvosh, D.; Cox, A.; Qiu, Y. (1993): A Genetic Algorithm for
            Survivable Network Design. In: [FORR93]: 408-415

[DAVI94a]   Davidor, Y.; Schwefel, H.-P.; Männer, R. (eds.) (1994): Parallel Problem
            Solving from Nature - PPSN III. International Conference on Evolutionary
            Computation. The Third Conference on Parallel Problem Solving from Nature,
            Oct. 1994, Jerusalem. Springer, Berlin

[DAVI94b]   Davidson, J.W.; Goulter, I.C. (1994): Genetic Algorithm for the Design of
            Branched Distribution Systems. ASCE Journal of Computing in Civil
            Engineering (accepted)

[DAWI95]   Dawid, H. (1995): Learning by Genetic Algorithms in Evolutionary Games. In:
            Derigs, U.; Bachem, A.; Drexl, A. (eds.): Operations Research Proceedings
            1994. Selected Papers of the International Conference on Operations Research,
            Berlin, Aug. 30 - Sep. 2 1994. Springer, Berlin: 261-266

[DEGE95] Dege, V. (1995): Sequencing Jobs in the Car Industry (Skoda). Personal Communication

[DEMM92] Demmel, A. (1992): Entwurf und Realisierung eines Genetischen Algorithmus zur Standortplanung im Distributionsbereich. Diploma Thesis, University of Hagen, Department of Economics, Germany

[DEO95] Deo, S. (1995): GA for Scheduling of Jobs for Electronics Assmbly. Personal Communication

[DEPP92] Depping, J. (1992): Kombinierte Touren- und Standortplanung bei der Hausmüllentsorgung mit einem evolutionsstrategischen Ansatz. Diploma Thesis, University of Dortmund, Department of Computer Science, Germany

[DING92] Ding, H.; El-Keib, A.A.; Smith, R.E. (1992): Optimal Clustering of Power Networks Using Genetic Algorithms. TCGA Report No. 92001, University of Illinois, Urbana-Champaign, U.S.A.

[DORN92] Dorndorf, U.; Pesch, E. (1992): Evolution Based Learning in a Job Shop Scheduling Environment. Research Memorandum 92-019, University of Limburg, Belgium

[DORN93a] Dorndorf, U.; Pesch, E. (1993): Genetic Algorithms for Job Shop Scheduling. In: Operations Research Proceedings. Papers of the 21st Annual Meeting of DGOR in Cooperation with ÖGOR 1992, Aachen, September 9-11, 1992. Springer, Berlin: 243-250

[DORN93b] Dorndorf, U.; Pesch, E. (1993): Combining Genetic and Local Search for Solving the Job Shop Problem. Preprints of the APMOD93 Conference Budapest 1993: 142-149

[DOSI93] Dosi, G.; Marengo, L.; Bassanini, A.; Valente, M. (1993): Microbehaviours and Dynamical Systems: Economic Routines as Emergent Properties of Adaptive Learning. Research Paper, Rom 1993. In: Antonelli, C.; David, P.A. (eds.): Path-Dependent Economics. Kluwer Academic Publishers

[DRIE92] Driessche, R. V.; Piessens, R. (1992): Load Balancing with Genetic Algorithms. In: [MÄNN92]: 341-350

[DZUB94] Dzubera, J.; Whitley, D. (1994): Advanced Correlation Analysis of Operators for the Traveling Salesman Problem. In: [DAVI94a]: 68-77

[EAST93] Easton, F.F.; Mansour, N. (1993): A Distributed Genetic Algorithm for Employee Staffing and Scheduling Problems. In: [FORR93]: 360-367

[EBEL90] Ebeling, W. (1990): Applications of Evolutionary Strategies. System Analysis Modeling Simulation 7: 3-16

[EDDE95] Eddelbüttel, D. (1995): Optimized Stock Investment. Personal Communication

[EGLI94] Eglit, J.T. (1994): Trend Prediction in Financial Time Series. In: [KOZA94b]: 31-40

[EIBE94] Eiben, A.E.; Raué, P.-E.; Ruttkay, Z. (1994): Genetic Algorithms with Multi-parent Recombination. In: [DAVI94a]: 78-87

[ERBE95] Erben, W. (1995): Timetabling Using Genetic Algorithms. In: [PEAR95]: 30-32

[ERGU95] Ergul, A. (1995): Timetabling of Exams and Classes. Genetic Algorithms in Production Scheduling List (E-Mail List), 31.1.1995

[ESHE91] Eshelman, L.J. (1991): The CHC Adaptive Search Algorithm: How to Have Safe Search when Engaging in Nontraditional Genetic Recombination. In: [RAWL91]: 265-283

[ETTL95]   Ettl, M.; Schwehm, M. (1995): Determining the Optimal Network Partition and Kanban Allocation in JIT Production Lines. In this volume

[FALC95]   De Falco, I.; Del Balio, R.; Tarantino, E. (1995): Comparing Parallel Tabu Search and Parallel Genetic Algorithms on the Task Allocation Problem. In: [PEAR95]: 380-383

[FALK80]   von Falkenhausen, K. (1980): Optimierung regionaler Entsorgungssysteme mit der Evolutionsstrategie. In: Schwarze, J. et al. (eds.): Proceedings in Operations Research 9. Physica, Würzburg: 46-51

[FALK91a]   Falkenauer, E.; Bouffouix, S. (1991): A Genetic Algorithm for Job Shop. In: Proceedings of the 1991 IEEE International Conference on Robotics and Automation, Sacramento, California - April 1991: 824-829

[FALK91b]   Falkenauer, E. (1991): A Genetic Algorithm for Grouping. In: Proceedings of the Fifth Intern. Symposium on Applied Stochastic Models and Data Analysis, April 23-26, Granada. World Scientific Publishing, Granada: 198-206

[FALK92]   Falkenauer, E.; Delchambre, A. (1992): A Genetic Algorithm for Bin Packing and Line Balancing. In: Proceedings of the 1992 IEEE International Conference on Robotics and Automation, May 1992. Nice: 1186-1192

[FALK94a]   Falkenauer, E. (1994): A Hybrid Grouping Genetic Algorithm for Bin Packing. Research Paper, CRIF Industrial Management and Automation, Brussels, Belgium

[FALK94b]   Falkenauer, E. (1994): A New Representation and Operators for Genetic Algorithms Applied to Grouping Problems. Evolutionary Computation 2: 123-144

[FALK95]   Falkenauer, E. (1995): Tapping the Full Power of Genetic Algorithm through Suitable Representation and Local Optimization: Application to Bin Packing. In this volume

[FAND92]   Fandel, G.; Gulledge, T.; Jones, A. (eds.) (1992): New Directions for Operations Research in Manufacturing. Proceedings of a Joint US/German Conference, July 30-31 1991, Gaithersburg, Maryland. Springer, Berlin

[FAND93]   Fandel, G.; Gulledge, T.; Jones, A. (eds.) (1993): Operations Research in Production Planning and Control. Proceedings of a Joint German/US-Conference 1992. Springer, Berlin

[FANG92]   Fang, H.L. (1992): Investigating GAs for Scheduling. MSc Dissertation, University of Edinburgh, Department of Artificial Intelligence, Edinburgh, U.K.

[FANG93]   Fang, H.-L.; Ross, P; Corne, D. (1993): A Promising Genetic Algorithm Approach to Job-Shop Scheduling, Rescheduling, and Open-Shop Scheduling Problems. In: [FORR93]: 375-382

[FILI92]   Filipic, B. (1992): Enhancing Genetic Search to Schedule a Production Unit. In: Neumann, B. (ed.): ECAI 92. Proceedings of the 10th European Conference on Artificial Intelligence, August 3-7, Vienna, Austria. John Wiley & Sons, Chichester: 603-607

[FILI93]   Filipic, B. (1993): Enhancing Genetic Search to Schedule a Production Unit. In: Dorn, J.; Froeschl, K.A. (eds.): Scheduling of Production Processes. Ellis Horwood, Chichester: 61-69

[FILI94]   Filipic, B.; Srdoc, A. (1994): Task Scheduling and Resource Management in Ship Repair Using a Genetic Algorithm. In: Brodda, J.; Johansson, K. (eds.):

Proceedings of the 8th International Conference on Computer Applications in Shipbuilding, Vol. 2, Bremen: 15.17-15.28

[FILI95] Filipic, B. (1995): A Genetic Algorithm Applied to Resource Management in Production Systems. In this volume

[FLEU94] Fleurent, C.; Ferland, J.A. (1994): Genetic Hybrids for the Quadratic Assigment Problem. In: Pardalos, P.M.; Wolkowicz, H. (eds.): DIMACS Series in Discrete Mathematics and Theoretical Computer Science 16: 173-188

[FLEU95a] Fleurent, C.; Ferland, J.A. (1995): Genetic and Hybrid Algorithms for Graph Coloring. To appear in: Laporte, G.; Osman, I.H.; Hammer, P.L. (eds.): Annals of Operations Research, Special Issue Metaheuristics in Combinatorial Optimization

[FLEU95b] Fleurent, C.; Ferland, J.A. (1995): Object-Oriented Implementation of Heuristic Search Methods for Graph Coloring, Maximum Clique and Satisfiability. To appear in: Trick, M.A.; Johnson, D.S. (eds.): The Second DIMACS Challenge, Special Issue

[FOGA91] Fogarty, T.C. (1991): Credit Scoring and Control Applications of the Genetic Algorithm. In: Parallel Problem Solving form Nature - Applications in Statistics and Economics, PASE Workshop Proceedings Zürich 1991: 147-148

[FOGA92] Fogarty, T.C. (1992): Developing Rule-Based Systems for Credit Card Applications from Data with the Genetic Algorithm. IMA Journal of Mathematics Applied in Business and Industry 4: 53-59

[FOGA94a] Fogarty, T.C. (ed.) (1994): Evolutionary Computing. AISB Workshop, Leeds, U.K., April 11-13. Selected Papers. LNCS 865. Springer, Berlin

[FOGA94b] Fogarty, T.C.; Ireson, N.S. (1994): Evolving Bayesian Classifiers for Credit Control - a Comparison with Other Machine Learning Methods. IMA Journal of Mathematics Applied in Business and Industry 5: 63-75

[FOGA95a] Fogarty, T.C. (1995): Proposal for a Network of Excellence in Evolutionary Computing (EvoNet). Part 2. University of the West of England, Bristol, U.K.

[FOGA95b] Fogarty, T.C. (1995): Scheduling at Daimler-Benz and Rolls Royce. Personal Communication

[FOGE66] Fogel, L.J.; Owens, A.J.; Walsh, M.J. (1966): Artificial Intelligence through Simulated Evolution. John Wiley & Sons, New York

[FOGE88] Fogel, D.B. (1988): An Evolutionary Approach to the Traveling Salesman Problem. Biological Cybernetics 60: 139-144

[FOGE90] Fogel, D.B. (1990): A Parallel Processing Approach to a Multiple Traveling Salesman Problem Using Evolutionary Programming. In: Proceedings of the Fourth Annual Symposium on Parallel Processing, Fullerton, Cal.: 318-326

[FOGE91] Fogel, D.B. (1991): The Evolution of Intelligent Decision Making in Gaming. Cybernetics and Systems: 223-236

[FOGE92a] Fogel, D.B. (1992): Evolving Artificial Intelligence. Doctoral Dissertation, University of California at San Diego, U.S.A.

[FOGE92b] Fogel, D.B.; Atmar, W. (eds.) (1992): Proceedings of the First Annual Conference on Evolutionary Programming. La Jolla, Cal.; February 21-22. Evolutionary Programming Society, San Diego, Cal.

[FOGE93a] Fogel, D.B. (1993): Evolving Behaviors in the Iterated Prisoner's Dilemma. Evolutionary Computation 1: 77-97

[FOGE93b] Fogel, D.B.; Atmar, W. (eds.) (1993): Proceedings of the Second Annual Conference on Evolutionary Programming. Evolutionary Programming Society, San Diego/CA

[FOGE94] Fogel, D.B. (1994): Evolving Continuous Behaviors in the Iterated Prisoner's Dilemma. In: [SEBA94]: 119-130

[FOGE95] Fogel, D.B. (1995): Evolutionary Computation. Toward a New Philosophy of Machine Intelligence. IEEE Press, New York

[FORR93] Forrest, S. (ed.) (1993): Proceedings of the Fifth International Conference on Genetic Algorithms. Morgan Kaufmann, San Mateo/CA

[FOUR85] Fourman, M.P. (1985): Compaction of Symbolic Layout Using Genetic Algorithms. In: [GREF85a]: 141-153

[FOX91] Fox, B.R.; McMahon, M.B. (1991): Genetic Operators for Sequencing Problems. In: [RAWL91]: 284-300

[FUCH83] Fuchs, F.; Maier, H.A. (1983): Optimierung des Lastflusses in elektrischen Energieversorgungsnetzen mittels Zufallszahlen. Archiv für Elektrotechnik 66: 85-94

[FUJI87] Fujiki, C.; Dickinson, J. (1987): Using the Genetic Algorithm to Generate LISP Source Code to Solve the Prisoner's Dilemma. In: [GREF87a]: 236-245

[FUKU95] Fukushima, M. (1995): Generating Class Timetable. Timetabling Problems List (E-Mail List), 24.2.1995

[FULK93a] Fulkerson, W. (1993): Scheduling in a Foundry. Personal Communication

[FULK93b] Fulkerson, W. (1993): Scheduling Assembly Lines. Personal Communication

[GABB91] Gabbert, P.S. et al. (1991): A System for Learning Routes and Schedules with Genetic Algorithms. In: [BELE91]: 430-436

[GAMM91] Gammack, J.G.; Fogarty, T.C.; Battle, S.A.; Miles, R.G. (1991): Management Decision Support from Large Databases: the IDIOMS Project. In: Proceedings of the AMSE International Conference on Signals and Systems, Vol. 1. Warsaw 1991: 213-219

[GARI91] de Garis, H. (1991): Genetic Programming: Building Artificial Nervous Systems with Genetically Programmed Neural Network Modules. In: Soucek, B. and the IRIS Group (eds.): Neural and Intelligent Systems Integration. John Wiley & Sons, New York: 207-234

[GEHR94] Gehring, H.; Schütz, G. (1994): Zwei Genetische Algorithmen zur Lösung des Bandabgleichproblems. In: Werners, B.; Gabriel, R. (eds.): Operations Research. Reflexionen aus Theorie und Praxis. Springer, Berlin

[GERD94a] Gerdes, I.S. (1994): Application of Genetic Algorithms to the Problem of Free-Routing of Aircraft. IEEE: ICEC'94, Vol. II, Orlando: 536-541

[GERD94b] Gerdes, I. (1994): Construction of Conflict-Free Routes for Aircraft in Case of Free-Routing with Genetic Algorithms. In: [KUNZ94]: 97-98

[GERD94c] Gerdes, I. (1994): Construction of Conflict-Free Routes for Aircraft in Case of Free-Routing with Genetic Algorithms. In: [HOPF94]: 143-149

[GERD95] Gerdes, I. (1995): Application of Genetic Algorithms for Solving Problems Related to Free Routing for Aircraft. In this volume

[GERR91] Gerrits, M.; Hogeweg, P. (1991): Redundant Coding of an NP-Complete Problem Allows Effective Genetic Algorithm Search. In: [SCHW91]: 70-74

[GERR93] Gerrets, M.; Walker, R.; Haasdijk, E. (1993): Time Series Prediction of Financial Data. Personal Communication

[GEUR93] Geurts, M. (1993): Job Shop Scheduling. Personal Communication

76

[GOLD85] Goldberg, D.E.; Lingle Jr., R. (1985): Alleles, Loci, and the Traveling Salesman Problem. In: [GREF85a]: 154-159

[GOLD87] Goldberg, D.E.; Smith, R.E. (1987): Nonstationary Function Optimization Using Genetic Algorithms with Dominance and Diploidy. In: [GREF87a]: 59-68

[GOLD89] Goldberg, D.E. (1989): Genetic Algorithms in Search, Optimization, and Machine Learning. Addison-Wesley, Reading, Mass.

[GOON94] Goonatilake, S.; Feldman, K. (1994): Genetic Rule Induction for Financial Decision Making. In: Stender, J.; Hillebrand, E.; Kingdon, J. (eds.): Genetic Algorithms in Optimisation, Simulation and Modelling. Frontiers in Artificial Intelligence and Applications, Vol. 23, IOS Press, Amsterdam

[GORD93] Gordon, V.S.; Whitley, D. (1993): Serial and Parallel Genetic Algorithms as Function Optimizers. In: [FORR93]: 177-183

[GORG89] Gorges-Schleuter, M. (1989): ASPARAGOS An Asynchronous Parallel Genetic Optimization Strategy. In: [SCHA89]: 422-427

[GORG91a] Gorges-Schleuter, M. (1991): Explicit Parallelism of Genetic Algorithms through Population Structures. In: [SCHW91]: 150-159

[GORG91b] Gorges-Schleuter, M. (1991): ASPARAGOS A Parallel Genetic Algorithm and Population Genetics. In: [BECK91]: 407-418

[GORG91c] Gorges-Schleuter, M. (1991): Genetic Algorithms and Population Structures. A Massively Parallel Algorithm. Doctoral Dissertation, University of Dortmund, Department of Computer Science, Germany

[GREE87] Greene, D.P.; Smith, S.F. (1987): A Genetic System for Learning Models of Consumer Choice. In: [GREF87a]: 217-223

[GREE94] Greenwood, G. (1994): Preventative Maintenance Tasks. Genetic Algorithms Digest (E-Mail List) 8 (15), 10.5.1994

[GREF85a] Grefenstette, J.J. (ed.) (1985): Proceedings of an International Conference on Genetic Algorithms and Their Applications. July 24-26, Pittsburgh. Lawrence Erlbaum, Hillsdale/N.J.

[GREF85b] Grefenstette, J.; Gopal, R.; Rosmaita, B.; Gucht, D.V. (1985): Genetic Algorithms for the Traveling Salesman Problem. In: [GREF85a]: 160-168

[GREF87a] Grefenstette, J.J. (ed.) (1987): Genetic Algorithms and Their Applications. Proceedings of the Second International Conference on Genetic Algorithms, MIT, Cambridge, July 28-31. Lawrence Erlbaum, Hillsdale, N.J.

[GREF87b] Grefenstette, J.J. (1987): Incorporating Problem Specific Knowledge into Genetic Algorithms. In: Davis, L. (ed.): Genetic Algorithms and Simulated Annealing. Morgan Kaufmann, Los Altos, California: 42-59

[GROO91] de Groot, C.; Würtz, D.; Hoffmann, K.H. (1991): Optimizing Complex Problems by Nature's Algorithms: Simulated Annealing und Evolution Strategy - a Comparative Study. In: [SCHW91]: 445-454

[GRÜN95] Grünert, T. (1995): Lotsizing and Scheduling. Genetic Algorithms in Production Scheduling List (E-Mail List), 26.1.1995

[GUPT92] Gupta, Y.P.; Sundaram, C.; Gupta, M.C.; Kumar, A. (1992): Minimizing Total Intercell and Intracell Moves in Cellular Manufacturing: a Genetic Algorithm Approach. In: Proceedings of the Annual Meeting of the Decision Science Institute, Nov. 22-24, San Francisco: 1523-1525

[GÜVE95] Güvenir, H.A. (1995): A Genetic Algorithm for Multicriteria Inventory Classification. In: [PEAR95]: 6-9

[HADI95]   Hadinoto, D. (1995): Single Machine Scheduling Problems and Permutation
            Flow Shop Problems. Genetic Algorithms in Production Scheduling List (E-
            Mail List), 15.3.1995

[HADJ92]   Ben Hadj-Alouane, A.; Bean, J.C. (1992): A Genetic Algorithm for the
            Multiple-Choice Integer Program. Technical Report 92-50, The University of
            Michigan, College of Engineering, Department of Industrial and Operations
            Research, U.S.A.

[HAMP81]   Hampel, C. (1981): Ein Vergleich von Optimierungsverfahren für die
            zeitdiskrete Simulation. Doctoral Dissertation, Technical University of Berlin,
            Germany

[HANN89]   Hannan, M.T.; Freeman, J. (1989): Organizational Ecology. Harvard
            University Press, Cambridge, Mass.

[HANS95]   Hansen, S. (1995): PROFIT, Software für die Prognose, Planung und
            Steuerung der Produktion. In: [BIET95]: 175-180

[HAO95]   Hao, J.K. (1995): A Clausal Genetic Representation and its Related
            Evolutionary Procedures for Satisfiability Problems. In: [PEAR95]: 289-292

[HART95]   Hartley, S.J. (1995): GA to Solve the Boolean Satisfiability Problem. Genetic
            Algorithms Digest (E-Mail List) 9 (36), 22.6.1995

[HEIS94a]   Heistermann, J. (1994): Genetic Algorithms at Siemens. In: [KUNZ94]: 100-
            101

[HEIS94b]   Heistermann, J. (1994): Genetic Algorithms at Siemens. In: [HOPF94]: 150-
            159

[HELB93]   Helber, S. (1993): Lösung dynamischer mehrstufiger Mehrprodukt-Losgrößen-
            probleme unter Kapazitätsrestriktionen durch lokale Suchverfahren. In:
            Operations Research Proceedings. Papers of the 21st Annual Meeting of
            DGOR in Cooperation with ÖGOR 1992, Sep. 9-11, Aachen. Springer, Berlin:
            133

[HENS86]   Hense, A.V. (1986): Adaptionsstrategien zur Lösung schwieriger
            Optimierungsaufgaben. Diploma Thesis, University of Dortmund, Department
            of Computer Science, Germany

[HERD88]   Herdy, M. (1988): Anwendung der Evolutionsstrategie auf das Travelling
            Salesman Problem. Thesis, Technical University of Berlin, Department of
            Bionics, Germany

[HERD91]   Herdy, M. (1991): Application of the Evolutionsstrategie to Discrete
            Optimization Problems. In: [SCHW91]: 188-192

[HESS89]   Hesser, J.; Männer, R.; Stucky, O. (1989): Optimization of Steiner Trees using
            Genetic Algorithms. In: [SCHA89]: 231-236

[HESS91]   Hesser, J.; Männer, R.; Stucky, O. (1991): On Steiner Trees and Genetic
            Algorithms. In: [BECK91]: 509-525

[HEUS70]   Heusener, G. (1970): Optimierung natrium-gekühlter schneller Brutreaktoren
            mit Methoden der nicht-linearen Programmierung. Doctoral Dissertation,
            University of Karlsruhe, Germany

[HILL87]   Hilliard, M.R.; Liepins, G.E.; Palmer, M.; Morrow, M.; Richardson, J. (1987):
            A Classifier-Based System for Discovering Scheduling Heuristics. In:
            [GREF87a]: 231-235

[HILL89a]   Hilliard, M.R.; Liepins, G.; Rangarajan, G.; Palmer, M. (1989): Learning
            Decision Rules for Scheduling Problems: A Classifier Hybrid Approach. In:

78

Proceedings of the Sixth International Workshop on Machine Learning: 188-190

[HILL89b] Hilliard, M.R.; Liepins, G.E.; Palmer, M.; Rangarajan, G. (1989): The Computer as a Partner in Algorithmic Design: Automated Discovery of Parameters for a Multi-Objective Scheduling Heuristic. In: Sharda, R.; Golden, B.; Wasil, E.; Balci, O.; Steward, W. (eds.): Impacts of Recent Computer Advances on Operations Research. North-Holland, New York: 321-331

[HILL90] Hilliard, M.R.; Liepins, G.E.; Palmer, M. (1990): Discovering and Refining Algorithms through Machine Learning. In: Brown, D.E.; White, C.C. (eds.): Operations Research and Artificial Intelligence: The Integration of Problem-Solving Strategies. Kluwer Academic Publishers, Boston: 59-78

[HINT94] Hinterding, R. (1994): A New Way of Solving the Bin Packing Problem Using GAs. Genetic Algorithms Digest (E-Mail List) 8 (15), 10.5.1994

[HIRA95] Hirayama, K. (1995): Slab Design Problem in Steel Production (involves sequencing order plates, deciding slab sizes and total number of slabs). Genetic Algorithms Digest (E-Mail List) 9 (37), 28.6.1995

[HIRZ92] Hirzer, J. (1992): Lösung des Standard-Tourenplanungsproblems mit einem Genetischen Algorithmus. Diploma Thesis, University of Hagen, Department of Economics, Germany

[HOFF91a] Hoffmeister, F.; Bäck, T. (1991): Genetic Algorithms and Evolution Strategies: Similarities and Differences. In: [SCHW91]: 455-469

[HOFF91b] Hoffmeister, F. (1991): Scalable Parallelism by Evolutionary Algorithms. In: Grauer, M.; Pressmar, D.B. (eds.): Parallel Computing and Mathematical Optimization. Springer, Berlin: 177-198

[HÖHN95] Höhn, C.; Reeves, C. (1995): Incorporating Neighbourhood Search Operators into Genetic Algorithms. In: [PEAR95]: 214-217

[HOLL86] Holland, J.H.; Holyoak, K.J.; Nisbett, R.E.; Thagard, P.R. (1986): Induction: Processes of Inference, Learning, and Discovery. MIT Press, Cambridge, Mass.

[HOLL92a] Holland, J.H. (1992): Adaptation in Natural and Artificial Systems. 2nd ed. MIT Press, Cambridge/MA.

[HOLL92b] Holland, J.H. (1992): Genetische Algorithmen. Spektrum der Wissenschaft 9: 44-51

[HOLM95] Holmes, J.; Routen, T.W.; Czarnecki, C.A. (1995): Heterogeneous Co-Evolving Parasites. In: [PEAR95]: 156-159

[HOMA93a] Homaifar, A.; Guan, S.; Liepins, G.E. (1993): A New Approach on the Traveling Salesman Problem by Genetic Algorithms. In: [FORR93]: 460-466

[HOMA93b] Homaifar, A.; Guan, S.; Liepins, G.E. (1993): Schema Analysis of a New Approach to the Traveling Salesman Problem by Genetic Algorithms. To appear in Complex Systems

[HÖNE90] Hönerloh, A. (1990): Der Einsatz von Evolutionsstrategien zur Entscheidungsvorbereitung in der betrieblichen Ablaufplanung. Diploma Thesis, University of Göttingen, Department of Economics, Germany

[HOPF94] Hopf, J. (ed.) (1994): Genetic Algorithms within the Framework of Evolutionary Computation. Proceedings of the KI-94 Workshop. Max-Planck-Institut für Informatik, Technical Report MPI-I-94-241, Saarbrücken

[HOU92] Hou, E.S.H.; Ren, H.; Ansari, N. (1992): Efficient Multiprocessor Scheduling Based on Genetic Algorithms. In: [SOUC92]: 339-352

[HOU94]   Hou, E.S.H.; Ansari, N.; Ren, H.A. (1994): A Genetic Algorithm for Multiprocessor Scheduling. IEEE Transactions on Parallel and Distributed Systems 5: 113-120

[HUGH90]   Hughes, M. (1990): Improving Products and Process - Nature's Way. Industrial Management & Data Systems 6: 22-25

[HULI91]   Hulin, M. (1991): Circuit Partitioning with Genetic Algorithms Using a Coding Scheme to Preserve the Structure of a Circuit. In: [SCHW91]: 75-79

[HULI92]   Hulin, M. (1992): Evolution Strategies for Circuit Partitioning. In: [SOUC92]: 413-437

[HÜLS94]   Hülsemann, M. (1994): Schwellkettenoptimierung bei Wasserkraftwerken. Paper presented at the International Conference on Operations Research, TU Berlin. Aug. 30 - Sept. 2, Berlin

[HUNT91]   Huntley, C.L.; Brown, D.E. (1991): A Parallel Heuristic for Quadratic Assignment Problems. Computers & Operations Research 18: 275-289

[HURL94]   Hurley, S.M.L.; Stephens, N.M. (1994): Applying Genetic Algorithms to Problems in Marketing. In: Bloemer, J.; Lemmink, J.; Kasper, H. (eds.): Proceedings of the 23rd EMAC Conference, Marketing: Its Dynamics and Challenges. European Marketing Academy, Maastricht

[HURL95]   Hurley, S.; Moutinho, L.; Stephens, N.M. (1995): Solving Marketing Optimization Problems using Genetic Algorithms. Research Paper, University of Cardiff, U.K.

[HUSB91a] Husbands, P.; Mill, F. (1991): Simulated Co-Evolution as The Mechanism for Emergent Planning and Scheduling. In: [BELF91]: 264-270

[HUSB91b] Husbands, P.; Mill, F.; Warrington, S. (1991): Genetic Algorithms, Production Plan Optimisation and Scheduling. In: [SCHW92]: 80-84

[HUSB92]   Husbands, P. (1992): Genetic Algorithms in Optimisation and Adaption. In: Kronsjo, L.; Shumsheruddin, D. (eds.): Advances in Parallel Algorithms. Blackwell Scientific Publishing, Oxford: 227-277

[HUSB93]   Husbands, P. (1993): An Ecosystem Model for Integrated Production Planning. Intl. Journal of Computer Integrated Manufacturing 6: 74-86

[HUSB94]   Husbands, P. (1994): Distributed Coevolutionary Genetic Algorithms for Multi-Criteria and Multi-Constraint Optimisation. In: [FOGA94a]: 150-165

[IDA95]   Ida, K.; Gen, M.; Li, Y. (1995): Solving Multicriteria Solid Transportation Problem with Fuzzy Numbers by Genetic Algorithms. Paper to be presented at EUFIT 1995, European Conference on Fuzzy and Intelligent Technologies, Aachen/Germany (Aug. 29-31)

[IGNI91]   Ignizio, J.P. (1991): Introduction to Expert Systems. McGraw-Hill, New York

[IGNI93]   Ignizio, J.P. (1993): A Hybrid Expert System for Process Scheduling. Paper presented at the Workshop on Genetic Algorithms in the Petroleum Industry, Aberdeen 1993

[INAY94]   Inayoshi, H.; Manderick, B. (1994): The Weighted Graph Bi-Partitioning Problem: A Look at GA. In: [DAVI94a]: 617-625

[IRES94]   Ireson, N.S. (1994): Evolving a Classifier for the TSB Loan Application Data. Research Paper, University of the West of England (UWE), Bristol, U.K.

[IRES95]   Ireson, N.S.; Fogarty, T.C. (1995): Evolving Decision Support Models for Credit Control. In this volume

[JACK95]   Jackson, K.; Weare, R. (1995): Generating Exam Timetables. Personal Communication

80

[JACU95]   Jacucci, G.; Foy, M.; Uhrik, C. (1995): Genetic Algorithms (Gas) in the Role of Intelligent Regional Adaptation Agents for Agricultural Decision Support Systems. In: [PEAR95]: 428-431

[JAKO94a] Jakobs, S. (1994): On Genetic Algorithms for the Packing of Polygons. In: [KUNZ94]: 81-82

[JAKO94b] Jakobs, S. (1994): On Genetic Algorithms for the Packing of Polygons. In: [HOPF94]: 84-85

[JOG87]   Jog, P.; Gucht, D.V. (1987): Parallelisation of Probabilistic Sequential Search Algorithms. In: [GREF87a]: 170-176

[JOHN90]   Johnson, D.S. (1990): Local Optimization and the Traveling Salesman Problem. In: Proceedings of the 17th Colloquium on Automata, Languages, and Programming. Springer, Berlin: 446-461

[JONE91]   Jones, D.R.; Beltramo, M.A. (1991): Solving Partitioning Problems with Genetic Algorithms. In: [BELE91]: 442-449

[JONE93]   Jones, A.; Rabelo, L. (1993): Integrating Neural Nets, Simulation, and Genetic Algorithms for Real-Time Scheduling. In: [FAND93]: 550-566

[JONG89]   De Jong, K.A.; Spears, W.M. (1989): Using Genetic Algorithms to Solve NP-Complete Problems. In: [SCHA89]: 124-132

[JÓZE95]   Józefowska, J.; Rózycki, R.; Weglarz, J. (1995): A Genetic Algorithm for Some Discrete-Continuous Scheduling Problems. In: [PEAR95]: 273-276

[JULI92]   Juliff, K. (1992): Using a Multi Chromosome Genetic Algorithm to Pack a Truck. Technical Report (RMIT CS TR 92-2) Version 1.0, August 1992, Royal Melbourne Institute of Technology, Department of Computer Science, Australia

[JULI93]   Juliff, K. (1993): A Multi-Chromosome Genetic Algorithm for Pallet Loading. In: [FORR93]: 467-473

[JULS93]   Julstrom, B.A. (1993): A Genetic Algorithm for the Rectilinear Steiner Problem. In: [FORR93]: 474-480

[JUNG95]   Junginger, W. (1995): Course Scheduling by Genetic Algorithms. In this volume

[KADA90a] Kadaba, N. (1990): XROUTE: A Knowledge-Based Routing System Using Neural Networks and Genetic Algorithms. Ph.D. Dissertation, North Dakota State University, Fargo/ND, U.S.A.

[KADA90b] Kadaba, N.; Nygard, K.E. (1990): Improving the Performance of Genetic Algorithms in Automated Discovery of Parameters. In: Porter, B.W.; Mooney, R.J. (eds.): Proceedings of the Seventh International Conference on Machine Learning. Morgan Kaufmann, San Mateo, Cal.: 140-148

[KADA91]   Kadaba, N.; Mygard, K.E.; Juell, P.L. (1991): Integration of Adaptive Machine Learning and Knowledge-Based Systems for Routing and Scheduling Applications. Expert Systems With Applications 2: 15-27

[KANE91]   Kanet, J.J.; Sridharan, V. (1991): PROGENITOR: A Genetic Algorithm for Production Scheduling. Wirtschaftsinformatik 33: 332-336

[KAPS93]   Kapsalis, A.; Rayward-Smith, V.J.; Smith, G.D. (1993): Solving the Graphical Steiner Tree Problem using Genetic Algorithms. Journal of the Operations Research Society 44: 397-406

[KAPS94]   Kapsalis, A.; Smith, G.D.; Rayward-Smith, V.J. (1994): A Unified Paradigm for Parallel Genetic Algorithms. In: [FOGA94a]: 131-149

[KAZA95] Kazarlis, S.A. (1995): A Genetic Algorithm Solution to the Unit Commitment Problem. Paper presented at the IEEE PES (Power Engineering Society) Winter Meeting, Jan. 1995, New York

[KEAR95] Kearns, B. (1995): 1. A Real-Life Variation of the Travelling Salesperson Problem for Several System Installers under Multiple Constraints. 2. Local and Wide Area Network Design to Maximize Performance on Three Different Goals. Genetic Programming List (E-Mail List), 8.3.1995

[KEIJ95] Keijzer, M. (1995): Optimizing the Layout for Telecommunication Networks in Developing Countries. Genetic Programming List (E-Mail List), 13.4.1995

[KERS94] Kershaw, P.S.; Edmonds, A.N. (1994): Genetic Programming of Fuzzy Logic Production Rules with Application to Financial Trading Rule Generation. Paper presented at the ECAI94 Workshop on Applied GAs

[KHUR90] Khuri, S.; Batarekh, A. (1990): Genetic Algorithms and Discrete Optimization. In: Abstracts of the „Operations Research 1990" International Conference on Operations Research, Aug. 28-31, Vienna: A 147

[KHUR94a] Khuri, S.; Bäck, T.; Heitkötter, J. (1994): The Zero/One Multiple Knapsack Problem and Genetic Algorithms. In: Deaton, E.; Oppenheim, D.; Urban, J.; Berghel, H. (eds.): Proceedings of the 1994 ACM Symposium on Applied Computing. ACM Press, New York: 188-193

[KHUR94b] Khuri, S.; Bäck, T. (1994): An Evolutionary Heuristic for the Minimum Vertex Cover Problem. In: [KUNZ94]: 83-84

[KHUR94c] Khuri, S.; Bäck, T. (1994): An Evolutionary Heuristic for the Minimum Vertex Cover Problem. In: [HOPF94]: 86-90

[KHUR95] Khuri, S.; Schütz, M.; Heitkötter, J. (1995): Evolutionary Heuristics for the Bin Packing Problem. In: [PEAR95]: 285-288

[KIDO93] Kido, T.; Kitano, H.; Nakanishi, M. (1993): A Hybrid Search for Genetic Algorithms: Combining Genetic Algorithms, TABU Search, and Simulated Annealing. In: [FORR93]: 641

[KIDW93] Kidwell, M.D. (1993): Using Genetic Algorithms to Schedule Distributed Tasks on a Bus-Based System. In: [FORR93]: 368-374

[KINN94] Kinnebrock, W. (1994): Optimierung mit Genetischen und Selektiven Algorithmen. R. Oldenbourg, München/Wien

[KNOL93] Knolmayer, G.; Spahni, D. (1993): Darstellung und Vergleich ausgewählter Methoden zur Bestimmung von IS-Architekturen. In: Reicher, H. (ed.): Informatik - Wirtschaft - Gesellschaft. 23. GI-Jahrestagung Dresden, Sep. 27 - Oct. 1. Springer, Berlin

[KOLE92] Kolen, A.; Pesch, E. (1992): Genetic Local Search in Combinatorial Optimization. In: Discrete Applied Mathematics

[KOPF92] Kopfer, H. (1992): Konzepte genetischer Algorithmen und ihre Anwendung auf das Frachtoptimierungsproblem im gewerblichen Güterfernverkchr. OR Spektrum: 137-147

[KOPF93a] Kopfer, H.; Rixen, I. (1993): Genetische Algorithmen für das Job-Shop Scheduling Problem. Technical Report No. 4, University of Bremen, Department of Economics, Chair of Logistics, Germany

[KOPF93b] Kopfer, H.; Erkens, E.; Pankratz, G. (1993): Ein Genetischer Algorithmus für das Tourenplanungsproblem. Paper presented at 'Jahrestagung der DGOR und NSOR', Amsterdam 1993

82

[KOPF94]   Kopfer, H.; Pankratz, G.; Erkens, E. (1994): Entwicklung eines hybriden Genetischen Algorithmus zur Tourenplanung. OR Spektrum 16: 21-31

[KOZA92a]   Koza, J.R. (1992): The Genetic Programming Paradigm: Genetically Breeding Populations of Computer Programs to Solve Problems. In: [SOUC92]: 203-321

[KOZA92b]   Koza, J.R. (1994): Genetic Programming. On the Programming of Computers by Means of Natural Selection. MIT Press, Cambridge/MA.

[KOZA94a]   Koza, J.R. (1994): Genetic Programming II. Automatic Discovery of Reusable Programs. MIT Press, Cambridge/MA.

[KOZA94b]   Koza, J.R. (ed.) (1994): Genetic Algorithms at Stanford 1994. Stanford Bookstore, Stanford University, Stanford, U.S.A.

[KRAU95]   Nissen, V.; Krause, M. (1995): On Using Penalty Functions and Multicriteria Optimisation in Facility Layout. In this volume

[KRÖG91]   Kröger, B.; Schwenderling, P.; Vornberger, O. (1991): Parallel Genetic Packing of Rectangles. In: [SCHW91]: 160-164

[KRÖG92]   Kröger, B.; Schwenderling, P.; Vornberger, O. (1992): Parallel Genetic Packing on Transputers. Technical Report, Osnabrücker Schriften zur Mathematik, Vol I 29, University of Osnabrück, Department of Mathematics/Computer Science, Germany

[KUHL95]   Kuhl, J.; Nissen, V. (eds.) (1995): Evolutionäre Algorithmen in Management-Anwendungen. Proceedings of a Workshop on EA in Management Applications, Feb. 23 1995, Göttingen

[KUNZ94]   Kunze, J.; Stoyan, H. (eds.): KI-94 Workshops. 18. Deutsche Jahrestagung für Künstliche Intelligenz, KI-94, Saarbrücken, Sep. 18-23 1994, Extended Abstracts. Gesellschaft für Informatik, Bonn

[KURB95a]   Kurbel, K.; Schneider, B.; Singh, K. (1995): Parallelization of Hybrid Simulated Annealing and Genetic Algorithm for Short-Term Production Scheduling. In: Zhong, B. (ed.): Proceedings of the International Symposium on Intelligence, Knowledge and Integration for Manufacturing March 28-31, Southeast University, Nanjing, P.R. China. Southeast University Press: 321-326

[KURB95b]   Kurbel, K.; Rohmann, T. (1995): Ein Vergleich von Verfahren zum Problem der Maschinenbelegungsplanung: Simulated Annealing, Genetische Algorithmen. Mathematische Optimierung (to appear)

[LANE92]   Lane, D.A. (1992): Artificial Worlds and Economics. Working Paper 92-09-048, Santa Fe Institute, U.S.A.

[LANG95]   Langdon, W.B. (1995): Scheduling Planned Maintenance of the UK Electricity Transmission Network. Genetic Programming List (E-Mail List), 26.3.1995

[LASZ90]   von Laszewski, G. (1990): A Parallel Genetic Algorithm for the Graph Partitioning Problem. In: Fielding, D.L. (ed.): Transputer Research and Applications 4. Proceedings of the 4th Conference of the North-American Transputers Users Group. IOS Press, Ithaca: 164-172

[LASZ91]   von Laszewski, G.; Mühlenbein, H. (1991): Partitioning a Graph with a Parallel Genetic Algorithm. In: [SCHW91]: 165-169

[LAWT92]   Lawton, G. (1992): Genetic Algorithms for Schedule Optimization. AI Expert 7: 23-27

[LEBA94]   LeBaron, B. (1994): An Artificial Stock Market. MIT AI Vision Seminar Colloquium, Stanford

[LEE93]   Lee, I.; Sikora, R.; Shaw, M.J. (1993): Joint Lot Sizing and Sequencing With
             Genetic Algorithms for Scheduling: Evolving the Chromosome Structure. In:
             [FORR93]: 383-389
[LEE95]   Lee, G.Y. (1995): Forecasting Time Series Data in Economic Systems. Genetic
             Programming List (E-Mail List), 14.3.1995
[LENT94]   Lent, B. (1994): Evolution of Trade Strategies Using Genetic Algorithms and
             Genetic Programming. In: [KOZA94b]: 87-98
[LEVI93a]   Levine, D.M. (1993): A Genetic Algorithm For The Set Partitioning Problem.
             In: [FORR93]: 481-487
[LEVI93b]   Levine, D.M. (1993): A Parallel Genetic Algorithm for the Set Partitioning
             Problem. Doctoral Dissertation, Illinois Institute of Technology, U.S.A.
[LEVI93c]   Levitin, G.; Rubinovitz, J. (1993): Genetic Algorithm for Linear and Cyclic
             Assignment Problem. Computers & Operations Research 20: 575-586
[LEVI95]   Levine, D. (1995): A Parallel Genetic Algorithm for the Set Partitioning
             Problem. Submitted for publication
[LIDD91]   Lidd, M.L. (1991): Traveling Salesman Problem Domain Application of a
             Fundamentally New Approach to Utilizing Genetic Algorithms.
[LIEN94a]   Lienig, J; Brandt, H. (1994): An Evolutionary Algorithm for the Routing of
             Multi-Chip Modules. In: [DAVI94a]: 588-597
[LIEN94b]   Lienig, J.; Thulasiraman, K. (1994): A Genetic Algorithm for Channel Routing
             in VLSI Circuits. Evolutionary Computation 1: 293-311
[LIEP87]   Liepins, G.E.; Hilliard, M.R.; Palmer, M.; Morrow, M. (1987): Greedy
             Genetics. In: [GREF87a]: 90-99
[LIEP90]   Liepins, G.E.; Hilliard, M.R. (1990): Genetic Algorithms Applications to Set
             Covering and Traveling Salesman Problems. In: Brown, D.E.; White, C.C.
             (eds.): Operations Research and Artificial Intelligence: The Integration of
             Problem-Solving Strategies. Kluwer Academic Publishers, Boston: 29-57
[LIEP91]   Liepins, G.E.; Potter, W.D. (1991): A Genetic Algorithm Approach to
             Multiple-Fault Diagnosis. In: [DAVI91]: 237-250
[LIND91]   Lindgren, K. (1991): Evolutionary Phenomena in Simple Dynamics. In:
             Langton, C.; Taylor, C.; Farmer, J.D.; Rasmussen, S. (eds.): Artificial Life II,
             Santa Fe Institute Studies in the Sciences of Complexity, Vol. X, Addison
             Wesley, Reading/MA
[LING92a]   Ling, S.E. (1992): Integrating a Prolog Assignment Program with Genetic
             Algorithms as a Hybrid Solution for a Polytechnic Timetable Problem. MSc
             Dissertation, University of Sussex, School of Cognitive and Computing
             Sciences, U.K.
[LING92b]   Ling, S.-E. (1992): Integrating Genetic Algorithms with a PROLOG
             Assignment Program as a Hybrid Solution for a Polytechnic Timetable
             Problem. In: [MÄNN92]: 321-329
[LOHB93]   Lohbeck, T.K. (1993): Genetic Algorithms in Layout Selection for Tree-like
             Pipe Networks. M.Phil. Thesis, University of Exeter, U.K.
[LONT92]   Lontke, M. (1992): Genetischer Algorithmus zur Ein-Depot-Tourenplanung.
             Paper presented at the „PECOR-Tagung der DGOR", Dec. 4, Düsseldorf
[LORA95]   Loraschi, A.; Tettamanzi, A.; Tomassini, M.; Verda, P. (1995): Distributed
             Genetic Algorithms with an Application to Portfolio Selection Problems. In:
             [PEAR95]: 384-387

84

[MACD95] MacDonald, C.C.J. (1995): University Timetabling Problems. Timetabling Problems List (E-Mail List), 11.4.1995

[MACK94] Mack, D. (1994): Genetische Algorithmen zur Lösung des Klassifikationsproblems. Implementierung eines neuen Genetischen Algorithmus zur Klassifikation (GAK) unter Verwendung des Prototyp-Gedankens. Diploma Thesis, University of Karlsruhe, Germany

[MACK95] Mack, D. (1995): Ein Genetischer Algorithmus zur Lösung des Klassifikationsproblems. In: [KUHL95]: 50-62

[MAND91] Manderick, B.; Weger, M.D.; Spiessens, P. (1991): The Genetic Algorithm and the Structure of the Fitness Landscape. In: [BELE91]: 143-150

[MANI91] Maniezzo, V. (1991): The Rudes and the Shrewds: an Experimental comparison of Several Evolutionary heuristics applied to the QAP problem. Report No. 91-042, Milano Polytechnic, Department of Electronics

[MÄNN92] Männer, R.; Manderick, B. (eds.) (1992): Parallel Problem Solving from Nature. Proceedings of the Second Conference on Parallel Problem Solving from Nature, Brussels, Sep. 28-30. North-Holland, Amsterdam

[MANS91] Mansour, N.; Fox, G.C. (1991): A Hybrid Genetic Algorithm for Task Allocation in Multicomputers. In: [BELE91]: 466-473

[MARE92a] Marengo, L. (1992): Structure, Competence and Learning in an Adaptive Model of the Firm. European Study Group for Evolutionary Economics (ed.): Papers on Economics & Evolution No. 9203, Freiburg

[MARE92b] Marengo, L. (1992): Coordination and Organizational Learning in the Firm. Journal of Evolutionary Economics 2: 313-326

[MARE94a] Maresky, J.; Davidor, Y.; Gitler, D.; Aharoni, G.; Barak, A. (1994): Selectively Destructive Restart. In:[KUNZ94]: 71-72

[MARE94b] Maresky, J.; Davidor, Y.; Gitler, D.; Aharoni, G.; Barak, A. (1994): Selectively Destructive Restart. In: [HOPF94]: 50-55

[MARG91] Margarita, S. (1991): Neural Networks, Genetic Algorithms and Stock Trading. In: Kohonen, T. (ed.): Artificial Neural Networks. Proceedings of the 1991 International Conference in Artificial Neural Networks (ICANN-91): Espoo, Finland, June 24-28. Amsterdam: 1763-1766

[MARG92] Margarita, S. (1992): Genetic Neural Networks For Financial Markets: Some Results. In: Neumann, B. (ed.): Proceedings of the 10th European Conference on Artificial Intelligence, Aug. 3-7, Vienna. John Wiley & Sons, Chichester: 211-213

[MARI94] Marin, F.J.; Trelles-Salazar, O.; Sandoval, F. (1994): Genetic Algorithms on LAN-Message Passing Architectures Using PVM: Application to the Routing Problem. In: [DAVI94a]: 534-543

[MARK89] Marks, R.E. (1989): Breeding Hybrid Strategies: Optimal Behavior for Oligopolists. In: [SCHA89]: 198-207

[MARK92a] Marks, R.E. (1992): Repeated Games and Finite Automata. In: Creedy, J.; Eichberger, J.; Borland, J. (eds.): Recent Advances in Game Theory. Edward Arnold, London: 43-64

[MARK92b] Marks, R.E. (1992): Breeding Optimal Strategies: Optimal Behaviour for Oligopolists. Journal of Evolutionary Economics 2: 17-38

[MARK95] Marks, R.E.; Midgley, D.F.; Cooper, L.G. (1995): Adaptive Behaviour in an Oligopoly. In this volume

[MARU92]   Maruyama, T.; Konagaya, A.; Konishi, K. (1992): An Asynchronous Fine-Grained Parallel Genetic Algorithm. In: [MÄNN92]: 563-572

[MARU93]   Maruyama, T.; Hirose, T.; Konagaya, A. (1993): A Fine-Grained Parallel Genetic Algorithm for Distributed Parallel Systems. In: [FORR93]: 184-190

[MATH92]   Mathias, K.; Whitley, D. (1992): Genetic Operators, the Fitness Landscape and the Traveling Salesman Problem. In: [MÄNN92]: 219-228

[MATS90]   Matsuo, K.; Adachi, N. (1990): Metastable Antagonistic Equilibrium and Stable Cooperative Equilibrium in Distributed Prisoner's Dilemma Game. In: Lasker, G.E. (ed.): Advances in Support Systems Research: 483-487

[MATT94]   Mattfeld, D.C.; Kopfer, H.; Bierwirth, C. (1994): Control of Parallel Population Dynamics by Social-Like Behavior of GA-Individuals. In: [DAVI94a]: 16-25

[MATW91]   Matwin, S.; Szapiro, S.; Haigh, K. (1991): Genetic Algorithms Approach to Negotiation Support System. IEEE Transactions on Systems, Man, and Cybernetics 21 (1): 102-114

[MAZA93]   de la Maza, M.; Tidor, B. (1993): An Analysis of Selection Procedures with Particular Attention Paid to Proportional and Boltzmann Selection. In: [FORR93]: 124-131

[MAZA95]   de la Maza, M.; Yuret, D. (1995): A Model of Stock Market Participants. In this volume

[MAZI92]   Maziejewski, S. (1992): The Vehicle Routing and Scheduling Problem with Time Window Constraints Using Genetic Algorithms. Diploma Thesis, University of Karlsruhe (TH), Department of Logic, Complexity and Deduction, Germany. Also   Norges Tekniske Høgskole, Institutt for Dateteknikk og Telematik, Norway

[MAZI93]   Maziejewski, S. (1993): Ein Genetischer Ansatz für die Tourenplanung mit Kundenzeitschranken. Paper presented at 'Jahrestagung der DGOR und NSOR', Amsterdam

[MCDO95]   McDonnell, J.R.; Fogel, D.B.; Rindt, C.R.; Recker, W.W.; Fogel, L.J. (1995): Using Evolutionary Programming to Control Metering Rates on Freeway Ramps. In this volume

[MICH92]   Michalewicz, Z. (1992): Genetic Algorithms + Data Structures = Evolution Programs. Springer, Berlin

[MICH95]   Micheletti, A. (1995): Short Term Production Scheduling. Genetic Algorithms in Production Scheduling List (E-Mail List), 27.4.1995

[MILL89]   Miller, J. (1989): The Coevolution of Automata in the Repeated Prisoner's Dilemma. Working Paper 89-003, Santa Fe Institute, U.S.A.

[MILL93]   Mills, G. (1993): Scheduling Trains. Personal Communication

[MOCC95]   Mocci, F. (1995): Crew-Scheduling in an Industrial Plant. Timetabling Problems List (E-Mail List), 29.3.1995

[MOOR94]   Moore, B. (1994): Effect of Population Replacement Strategy on Accuracy of Genetic Algorithm Market Forecaster. In: [STEN94a]: 169-178

[MOSC92a]   Moscato, P.; Norman, M.G. (1992): A 'Memetic' Approach for the Traveling Salesman Problem. Implementation of a Computational Ecology for Combinatorial Optimization on Message-Passing Systems. In: Proceedings of PACTA '92 - International Conference on Parallel Computing and Transputer Applications, Sep. 21-25, Barcelona

[MOSC92b] Moscato, P.; Tinetti, F. (1992): Blending Heuristics with a Population-Based Approach: A 'Memetic' Algorithm for the Traveling Salesman Problem. Submitted to Discrete Applied Mathematics

[MÜHL87] Mühlenbein, H.; Gorges-Schleuter, M.; Krämer, O. (1987): New Solutions to the mapping problem of parallel systems: The Evolution Approach. Parallel Computing 4: 269-279

[MÜHL88] Mühlenbein, H.; Gorges-Schleuter, M.; Krämer, O. (1988): Evolution Algorithms in Combinatorial Optimization. Parallel Computing 7: 65-85

[MÜHL89] Mühlenbein, H. (1989): Parallel Genetic Algorithms, Population Genetics and Combinatorial Optimization. In: [SCHA89]: 416-421

[MÜHL90] Mühlenbein, H. (1990): Parallel Genetic Algorithms, Population Genetics and Combinatorial Optimization. In: Voigt, H.-M.; Mühlenbein, H.; Schwefel, H.-P. (eds.): Evolution and Optimization '89. Selected Papers on Evolution Theory, Combinatorial Optimization, and Related Topics. Akademie-Verlag, Berlin: 79-85

[MÜHL91a] Mühlenbein, H. (1991): Parallel Genetic Algorithms, Population Genetics and Combinatorial Optimization. In: [BECK91]: 398-406

[MÜHL91b] Mühlenbein, H. (1991): Evolution in Time and Space - The Parallel Genetic Algorithm. In: [RAWL91]: 316-337

[MÜHL91c] Mühlenbein, H. (1991): Darwin's Continent Cycle Theory and Its Simulation by the Prisoner's Dilemma. Complex Systems 5: 459-478

[MÜHL92] Mühlenbein, H. (1992): Parallel Genetic Algorithms and Combinatorial Optimization. In: Proceedings of Computer Science and Operations Research - New Developments in their Interfaces. ORSA, Pergamon Press

[MÜLL83a] Müller, H.; Pollhammer, G. (1983): Evolutionsstrategische Lastflußoptimierung. Technical Report p5068, Technical University of Berlin, Department for Electrics and High Voltage Technology, Germany

[MÜLL83b] Müller, H. (1983): Power Flow Optimization in Electric Networks by Evolutionary Strategic Search. In: Proceedings of the 6th European Congress on Operations Research, July 1983, Vienna: 107

[MÜLL86] Müller, H.; Theil, G.; Waldmann, W. (1986): Results of Evolutional Random Search Procedure for Load Flow Optimization in Electric Networks. In: Prekopa, A.; Szelezsan, J.; Strazicky, B. (eds.): System Modelling and Optimization. Proceedings of the Twelfth IFIP Conference 1985. Springer, Berlin: 628-636

[MUNA93] Munakata, T.; Hashier, D.J. (1993): A Genetic Algorithm Applied to the Maximum Flow Problem. In: [FORR93]: 488-493

[MURP92] Murphy, L.J.; Simpson, A.R. (1992): Genetic Algorithms in Pipe Network Optimization. Research Report No. R93, University of Adelaide, Department of Civil and Environmental Engineering, Australia

[MURP93] Murphy, L.J.; Simpson, A.R.; Dandy, G.C. (1993): Pipe Network Optimization Using an Improved Genetic Algorithm. Research Report No. R109, University of Adelaide, Department of Civil and Environmental Engineering, Australia

[NACH93] Nachtigall, K.; Voget, S. (1993): A Genetic Algorithm Approach to Periodic Programs. Technical Report. Hildesheimer Informatik-Berichte 16/93, University of Hildesheim, Department of Mathematics, Germany

[NACH95] Nachtigall, K.; Voget, S. (1995): Optimierung von periodischen Netzplänen mit Genetischen Algorithmen. In: [KUHL95]: 41-49

[NAKA91]   Nakano, R.; Yamada, T. (1991): Conventional Genetic Algorithm for Job Shop Problems. In: [BELE91]: 474-479

[NAKA94]   Nakano, R.; Davidor, Y.; Yamada, T. (1994): Optimal Population Size under Constant Computation Cost. In: [DAVI94a]: 130-138

[NAPI89]   Napierala, G. (1989): Ein paralleler Ansatz zur Lösung des TSP. Diploma Thesis, University of Bonn, Germany

[NEUH91]   Neuhaus, P. (1991): Solving the Mapping-Problem - Experiences with a Genetic Algorithm. In: [SCHW91]: 170-175

[NISH91]   Nishikawa, Y.; Tamaki, H. (1991): A Genetic Algorithm as Applied to the Jobshop Scheduling. Transactions of the Society of Instrument and Control Engineers (Japan) 27: 593-599 (in Japanese)

[NISS92]   Nissen, V. (1992): Evolutionary Algorithms for the Quadratic Assignment Problem. Technical Report, University of Göttingen, Computer Science Department, Germany

[NISS93a] Nissen, V. (1993): A New Efficient Evolutionary Algorithm for the Quadratic Assignment Problem. In: Operations Research Proceedings. Papers of the 21st Annual Meeting of DGOR in Cooperation with ÖGOR 1992, Aachen, Sep. 9-11, 1992. Springer, Berlin: 259-267

[NISS93b] Nissen, V. (1993): Evolutionary Algorithms in Management Science. An Overview and List of References. European Study Group for Evolutionary Economics (eds.): Papers on Economics & Evolution No. 9303, Freiburg

[NISS94a] Nissen, V. (1994): Evolutionäre Algorithmen. Darstellung, Beispiele, betriebswirtschaftliche Anwendungsmöglichkeiten. DUV, Wiesbaden

[NISS94b] Nissen, V.; Krause, M. (1994): Constrained Combinatorial Optimization with an Evolution Strategy. In: Reusch, B. (ed.): Fuzzy Logik. Theorie und Praxis. Springer, Berlin: 33-40

[NISS94c] Nissen, V. (1994): A Comparison of Different Evolutionary Algorithms on the Quadratic Assignment Problem. In: [KUNZ94]: 75-76

[NISS94d] Nissen, V. (1994): Comparing Different Evolutionary Algorithms on the Quadratic Assignment Problem. In: [HOPF94]: 55-72

[NISS94e] Nissen, V. (1994): Solving the Quadratic Assignment Problem with Clues from Nature. IEEE Transactions on Neural Networks: Special Issue on Evolutionary Computation 5: 66-72

[NISS95a] Nissen, V. (1995): Evolutionary Optimisation of a Stochastic Inventory Simulation. In: Derigs, U.; Bachem, A.; Drexl, A. (eds.): Operations Research Proceedings 1994. Selected Papers of the International Conference on Operations Research, Berlin, Aug. 30 - Sep. 2 1994. Springer, Berlin: 466-471

[NISS95b] Nissen, V.; Biethahn, J. (1995): Determining a Good Inventory Policy With a Genetic Algorithm. In this volume

[NISS95c] Nissen, V.; Biethahn, J. (1995): Zur Robustheit Genetischer Algorithmen bei der Stochastischen Optimierung am Beispiel der Simulation. In: [BIET95]: 113-131

[NOBL90]   Noble, A. (1990): Using Genetic Algorithms in Financial Services. In: Proceedings of the Two Day International Conference on Forecasting & Optimisation in Financial Services, Oct. 3-4. IBC Ltd, Technical Services (Organiser), London

[NOCH86]   Noche, B.; Kottkamp, R.; Lücke, G.; Peters, E. (1986): Optimizing Simulators within Material Flow Systems. In: Proceedings of the Second European Simulation Congress Simulation Councils: 651-657

[NOCH90]   Noche, B. (1990): Simulation in Produktion und Materialfluß. Entscheidungsorientierte Simulationsumgebung. Verlag TÜV Rheinland, Köln

[NORM95]   Norman, B.A. (1995): Job Shop Scheduling. Genetic Algorithms Digest (E-Mail List) 9 (26), 1.5.1995

[NOTT92]   Nottola, C.; Leroy, F.; Davalo, F. (1992): Dynamics of Artificial Markets. In: Varela, F.J.; Bourgine, P. (eds.): Toward a Practice of Autonomous Systems. Proceedings of the First European Conference on Artificial Life. MIT Press, Cambridge, Mass.: 185-194

[NYGA90]   Nygard, K.E.; Kadaba, N. (1990): Modular Neural Networks and Distributed Adaptive Search for Traveling Salesman Algorithms. In: Applications of Artificial Neural Networks. Proceedings of the SPIE 1294: 442-451

[OLIV87]   Oliver, I.M.; Smith, D.J.; Holland, J.R.C. (1987): A Study of Permutation Crossover Operators on the Traveling Salesman Problem. In: [GREF87a]: 224-225

[OLIV93]   Oliver, J.R.(1993): Discovering Individual Decision Rules: an Application of Genetic Algorithms. In: [FORR93]: 216-222

[ORDI95]   Ordieres Mere, J.B. (1995): Best Cut Bar Problem to Minimize Waste Material. Genetic Algorithms in Production Scheduling List (E-Mail List), 30.1.195

[OSTE92]   Ostermeier, A. (1992): An Evolution Strategy with Momentum Adaption of the Random Number Distribution. In: [MÄNN92]: 197-206

[OSTE94]   Ostermeier, A.; Gawelczyk, A.; Hansen, N. (1994): Step-size Adaptation Based on Non-local Use of Selection Information. In: [DAVI94a]: 189-198

[PACK90]   Packard, N. H. (1990): A Genetic Learning Algorithm for the Analysis of Complex Data. Complex Systems 4: 543-572

[PAEC93]   Paechter, B.; Lucian, H.; Cumming, A. (1993): An Evolutionary Approach to the General Timetable Problem. The Scientific Annals of the Al I Cuza University of Iasi (Romania), Special Issue for the ROSYCS Symposium

[PAEC94a]   Paechter, B.; Cumming, A.; Luchian, H.; Petriuc, M. (1994): Two Solutions to the General Timetable Problem Using Evolutionary Methods. To appear in IEEE WCCI

[PAEC94b]   Paechter, B. (1994): Optimising a Presentation Timetable Using Evolutionary Algorithms. In: [FOGA94a]: 264-276

[PALM94a]   Palmer, C.C. (1994): Application of GP Techniques to Various Graph Theoretic Problems. Genetic Programming List (E-Mail List), 5.8.1994

[PALM94b]   Palmer, G. (1994): An Integrated Approach to Manufacturing Planning. PhD Thesis, University of Huddersfield, U.K.

[PANK93]   Pankratz, G. (1993): Entwicklung, Realisierung und Konfigurierung eines Genetischen Algorithmus für das Standard-Tourenplanungsproblem. Diploma Thesis, University of Siegen, Germany

[PARA95]   Parada Daza, V.; Muñoz, R.; Gómes de Alvarenga, A. (1995): A Hybrid Genetic Algorithm for the Two-Dimensional Guillotine Cutting Problem. In this volume

[PARE92a]   Paredis, J. (1992): Exploiting Constraints as Background Knowledge for Genetic Algorithms: a Case-study for Scheduling. In: [MÄNN92]: 229-238

[PARE92b] Paredis, J.; Van Rij, T. (1992): Intelligent Modelling, Simulation and Scheduling of Discrete Production Processes. In: Proceedings of Computer Science and Operations Research - New Developments in their Interfaces. Pergamon Press

[PARK95] Park, L.-J. (1995): Job Shop Scheduling. Genetic Algorithms in Production Scheduling List (E-Mail List), 20.4.1995

[PEAR95] Pearson, D.W.; Steele, N.C.; Albrecht, R.F. (eds.) (1995): Artificial Neural Nets and Genetic Algorithms. Proceedings of the International Conference in Alès/France. Springer, Wien

[PERR94] Perry, J.E. (1994): The Effect of Population Enrichment in Genetic Programming. In: Proceedings of the IEEE World Congress on Computational Intelligence. IEEE Press, New York

[PESC92] Pesch, E.; Dorndorf, U. (1992): Job Shop Scheduling mittels Genetischer Algorithmen. Paper presented at the 'Jahrestagung der DGOR/ÖGOR', Sep. 9-11, Aachen

[PESC93] Pesch, E. (1993): Machine Learning by Schedule Decomposition. Research Memorandum 93-045, Limburg University, Belgium

[PESC94] Pesch, E. (1994): Learning in Automated Manufacturing. Physica, Heidelberg

[POON90] Poon, P.W. (1990): Genetic Algorithms and Fuel Cycle Optimization. The Nuclear Engineer 31 (6): 173-177

[POON92] Poon, P.W.; Parks, G.T. (1992): Optimising PWR Reload Core Designs. In: [MÄNN92]: 371-380

[PROS88] Prosser, P. (1988): A Hybrid Genetic Algorithm for Pallet Loading. In: Proceedings of the European Conference on AI, Munich: 159-164

[QUEI95] Queiros, F. (1995): GA to solve Timetabling Problem. Timetabling Problems List (E-Mail List), 26.6.1995

[QUIN95] Quinn, G.R. (1995): Two-Stage Production Scheduling Problem. Personal Communication

[RAWL91] Rawlins, G.J.E. (ed.): Foundations of Genetic Algorithms. Morgan Kaufmann, San Mateo/CA

[RECH73] Rechenberg, I. (1973): Evolutionsstrategie. Optimierung technischer Systeme nach Prinzipien der biologischen Evolution. Frommann-Holzboog, Stuttgart

[REEV92] Reeves, C.R. (1992): A Genetic Algorithm Approach to Stochastic Flowshop Sequencing. In: Proceedings of the IEE Colloquium on Genetic Algorithms for Control and Systems Engineering, London 1992

[REEV93a] Reeves, C.R. (1993): Bin packing, Personal Communication

[REEV93b] Reeves, C.R. (1993): A Genetic Algorithm for Flowshop Sequencing. Submitted to: Computers and Operations Research

[REPP85] Reppenhagen, R. (1985): Adaptive Suchalgorithmen. Diploma Thesis, University of Paderborn, Department of Mathematics/Computer Science, Germany

[RIEC94] Rieck, C. (1994): Evolutionary Simulation of Asset Trading Strategies. In: [STEN94a]: 112-136

[RIXE95] Rixen, I.; Bierwirth, C.; Kopfer, H. (1995): A Case Study of Operational Just-In-Time Scheduling Using Genetic Algorithms. In this volume

[ROBB95] Robbins, P. (1995): The Use of a Variable Length Chromosome for Permutation Manipulation in Genetic Algorithms. In: [PEAR95]: 144-147

90

[ROGN94]   Rognerud, N. (1994): Building Financial Trading Models. Personal
             Communication
[ROGN95]   Rognoni, R. (1995): Job Shop Scheduling. Genetic Algorithms in Production
             Scheduling List (E-Mail List), 9.3.1995
[ROSS94a]   Ross, P.; Corne, D.; Fang, H.-L. (1994): Successful Lecture Timetabling with
             Evolutionary Algorithms. In: Eiben, A.E.; Manderick, B.; Ruttkay, Z. (eds.):
             Workshop Notes, ECAI'94 Workshop W17: Applied Genetic and other
             Evolutionary Algorithms
[ROSS94b]   Ross, P.; Corne, D.; Fang, H.-L. (1994): Improving Evolutionary Timetabling
             with Delta Evaluation and Directed Mutation. In: Research Paper 707,
             University of Edinburgh, Department of Artificial Intelligence, U.K.
[ROSS94c]   Ross, P.; Corne, D.; Fang, H.-L. (1994): Improving Evolutionary Timetabling
             with Delta Evaluation and Directed Mutation. In: [DAVI94a]: 556-565
[RUBI92]   Rubin, P.A.; Ragatz, G.L. (1992): Scheduling in a Sequence Dependent Setup
             Environment with Genetic Search. In: Proceedings of the Annual Meeting of
             the Decision Science Institute, Nov. 22-24, San Francisco: 1029-1031
[RUDO91]   Rudolph, G. (1991): Global Optimization by Means of Distributed Evolution
             Strategies. In: [SCHW91]: 209-213
[SALE94]   Salewski, R.; Bartsch, T. (1994): A Comparison of Genetic and Greedy
             Randomized Algorithms for Medium-to Short-Term Audit-Staff Scheduling.
             Working Paper, University of Kiel, Germany
[SANG95]   Sanagalli, M.; Semeraro, Q.; Tolio, T. (1995): Performance of Genetic
             Algorithms in the Solution of Permutation Flowshop Problems. In: [PEAR95]:
             495-498
[SANN88]   Sannier, A.V.; Goodman, E.D. (1988): Midgard: A Genetic Approach to
             Adaptive Load Balancing for Distributed Systems. In: Laird, J. (ed.):
             Proceedings of the Fifth International Conference on Machine Leraning, June
             12-14, University of Michigan, Ann Arbor. Morgan Kaufmann, San
             Mateo/CA: 174-180
[SAVI94a]   Savic, D.A.; Walters, G.A. (1994): Genetic Algorithms and Evolution Program
             Decision Support. In: Knezevic, J. (ed.): Proceedings of an International
             Symposium on Advances in Logistics. University of Exeter, U.K.: 72
[SAVI94b]   Savic, D.A.; Walters, G.A. (1994): Evolution Programs in Optimal Design of
             Hydraulic Networks. In: Parmee, I.C. (ed.): Adaptive Computing in
             Engineering Design and Control. University of Plymouth, U.K.: 146-150
[SAVI95a]   Savic, D.A.; Walters, G.A. (1995): Genetic Operators and Constraint Handling
             Pipe Network Optimization. Paper accepted for presentation at the 1995 AISB
             Workshop On Evolutionary Computing, April 3-4, University of Sheffield,
             U.K.
[SAVI95b]   Savic, D.A.; Walters, G.A. (1995): Place of Evolution Programs in Pipe
             Network Optimization. Paper accepted for presentation at the ASCE National
             Conference on Water Resources Planning and Management, May 7-10,
             Boston/MA, U.S.A.
[SAVI95c]   Savic, D. (1995): Partitioning Problems for Part Replacement. Personal
             Communication
[SCHA89]   Schaffer, J.D. (ed.) (1989): Proceedings of the Third International Conference
             on Genetic Algorithms, George Mason University, June 4-7. Morgan
             Kaufmann, San Mateo/CA

[SCHÄ93]   Schäfer, U. (1993): Personnel Scheduling. Personal Communication

[SCHA94]   Schack, B. (1994): Scheduling in a Liquid Petroleum Pipeline. Personal Communication

[SCHI81]   Schiemangk, C. (1981): Anwendung einer Evolutionsstrategie zum Auffinden eines optimalen Subgraphen. In: Zingert (ed.): Numerische Realisierung mathematischer Modelle. Akademie der Wissenschaften der DDR: 167-181

[SCHO76]   Schoebel, R. (1976): Anwendung der Evolutionsstrategie auf deterministische Modelle der Operations Research. Working Paper, Technical University of Berlin, Department of Bionics, Germany

[SCHÖ90]   Schöneburg, E.; Heinzmann, F.; Dörrich, T. (1990): Produktionsplanung mit Methoden der Künstlichen Intelligenz und Genetischen Algorithmen. CHIP Professional 9: 68-75

[SCHÖ91]   Schöneburg, E.; Heinzmann, F.; Dörrich, T. (1991): Industrielle Planung mit Methoden der künstlichen Intelligenz. DV-Management 1: 26-29

[SCHÖ92]   Schöneburg, E.; Heinzmann, F. (1992): PERPLEX: Produktionsplanung nach dem Vorbild der Evolution. Wirtschaftsinformatik 34: 224-232

[SCHO93]   Schoenauer, M.; Xanthakis, S. (1993): Constrained GA Optimization. In: [FORR93]: 573-580

[SCHÖ93]   Schöneburg, E. (1993): Zeitreihenanalyse und -prognose mit Evolutionsalgorithmen. Working Paper, Expert Informatik GmbH, Berlin, Germany

[SCHÖ94]   Schöneburg, E.; Heinzmann, F.; Feddersen, S. (1994): Genetische Algorithmen und Evolutionsstrategien. Eine Einführung in Theorie und Praxis der simulierten Evolution. Addison-Wesley, Bonn

[SCHR91]   Schroetter, M. (1991): Planung des Werkfernverkehrs mit Genetischen Algorithmen. Diploma Thesis, University of Erlangen-Nürnberg, Department of Computer Science, Germany

[SCHU92]   Schulte, J.; Becker, B. (1992): Production Using Genetic Algorithms. In: Zaremba, M.B. (ed.): Proceedings of IFAC-Conference INCOM'92. International Federation of Automatic Control (IFAC)

[SCHÜ92]   Schütz, G. (1992): Ein genetischer Algorithmus zum Bandabgleich. Paper presented at the „PECOR-Tagung der DGOR", Dec. 4, Düsseldorf,

[SCHU93a] Schuh, H.; von Randow, G. (1993): Gut erforscht ist halb erfunden. Die Zeit 9, Feb. 26. 1993: 42

[SCHU93b] Schulte, J.; Becker, B.-D. (1993): Optimierung in der Werkstattsteuerung: Simulation und Genetische Algorithmen. In: Proceedings of 8. Symposium Simulationstechnik, ASIM, Berlin, Sept. 1993: 599-602

[SCHÜ94]   Schüler, T.; Uthmann, T. (1994): Erzeugung realitätsnaher Produktionspläne durch Einsatz Genetischer Algorithmen (GAs). In: [KUNZ94]: 230-231

[SCHU94]   Schulte, J.; Frank, A. (1994): Optimierung von Losgröße und Reihenfolge einer Serienfertigung: Gegenüberstellung einer Heuristik mit den Genetischen Algorithmen. In: Jahrbuch Fraunhofer-Institut für Produktionstechnik und Automatisierung. Stuttgart

[SCHÜ95]   Schütz, G. (1995): Parallele Suche zur Lösung mehrstufiger Standortprobleme (abstract). In: [KUHL95]: 40

[SCHW72]   Schwefel, D. (1972): Gesundheitsplanung im Departamento del Valle del Cauca. Report of the German Development Institute, Berlin. German Development Institute, Berlin

92

[SCHW81]   Schwefel, H.-P. (1981): Numerical Optimization of Computer Models. John Wiley & Sons, Chichester

[SCHW91]   Schwefel, H.-P.; Männer, R. (eds.) (1991): Parallel Problem Solving from Nature. Proceedings of the First Workshop PPSN I, Dortmund, Oct.1-3. Springer, Berlin

[SCHW94]   Schwehm, M.; Walter, T. (1994): Mapping and Scheduling by Genetic Algorithms. In: Buchberger, B; Volkert, J. (eds.): Parallel Processing: CONPAR 94 - VAPP VI. Third Joint International Conference on Vector and Parallel Processing in Linz, Austria, Sep. 1994, LNCS 854. Springer, Berlin: 69-74

[SCHW95]   Schwehm, M. (1995): Optimierung der Partitionierung und Kanban-Zuordnung bei JIT-Fertigungsstraßen. In: [KUHL95]: 11-20

[SEBA94]   Sebald, A.V.; Fogel. L.J. (eds.) (1994): Proceedings of the Third Annual Conference on Evolutionary Programming. Feb. 24-26, San Diego/CA. World Scientific Press, Singapore

[SEIB94]   Seibulescu, A. (1994): Instruction Scheduling on Multiprocessors Using a Genetic Algorithm. In: [KOZA94b]: 130-139

[SEKH93]   Sekharan, A.; Wainwright, R.L. (1993): Manipulating Subpopulations of Feasible and Infeasible Solutions in Genetic Algorithms. In: Procceddings of the 1993 ACM/SIGAPP Symposium on Applied Computing: 118-125

[SEN93]   Sen, S. (1993): Minimal Cost Set Covering Using Probabilistic Methods. In: Proceedings of the 1993 ACM/SIGAPP Symposium on Applied Computing: 157-164

[SIEG95]   Sieg, G. (1995): Genetische Algorithmen zum Design erfolgreicher Wettbewerbsstrategien. In: [KUHL95]: 63-72

[SIKO92]   Sikora, R. (1992): Learning Control Strategies for a Chemical Process: A Distributed Approach. IEEE Expert 7 (3): 35-43

[SIKO93a]   Sikora, R. (1993): A Double Layered Learning Approach for Acquiring Classification Rules: Integrating Genetic Algorithms with Similarity-Based Learning. ORSA Journal of Computing (accepted)

[SIKO93b]   Sikora, R.; Shaw, M. (1993): The Evolutionary Model of Group Problem Solving: A Computational Study of Distributed Rule Learning. To appear in Information Systems Research

[SIMP94a]   Simpson, A.R.; Dandy, G.C.; Murphy, L.J. (1994): Genetic Algorithms Compared to Other Techniques for Pipe Optimization. ASCE Journal of Water Resources Planning and Management 120 (4)

[SIMP94b]   Simpson, A.R.; Goldberg, D.E. (1994): Pipeline Optimisation via Genetic Algorithms: From Theory to Practice. In: Miller, D.S. (ed.): Water Pipeline Systems. Mechanical Engineering Publications Ltd., London: 309-320

[SING94]   Singleton, A. (1994): Genetic Programming with C++. Byte 19: 171-176

[SINK95]   Sinkovic, V.; Lovrek, I. (1995): Performance of Genetic Algorithm Used for Analysis of Call and Service Processing in Telecommunications. In: [PEAR95]: 281-284

[SIRA87]   Sirag, D.J.; Weisser, P.T. (1987): Toward a Unified Thermodynamic Genetic Operator. In: [GREF87a]: 116-122

[SIRA95]   Sirag, D. (1995): Forge Scheduling and Elevator Dispatching (Scheduling). Genetic Algorithms in Production Scheduling List (E-Mail List), 21.2.1995

[SMIT85]   Smith, D. (1985): Bin Packing with Adaptive Search. In: [GREF85a]: 202-206a

[SMIT87]   Smith, R.E. (1987): Diploid Genetic Algorithms for Search in Time Varying Environments. In: Proceedings of the Annual Southeast Regional Conference of the ACM: 175-179

[SMIT92a]   Smith, R.E.; Goldberg, D.E. (1992): Diploidy and Dominance in Artificial Genetic Search. Complex Systems 6: 251-285

[SMIT92b]   Smith, W. (1992): Bin Packing. Personal Communication

[SMIT93]   Smith, A.E.; Tate, D.M. (1993): Genetic Optimization Using a Penalty Function. In: [FORR93]: 499-503

[SONN82]   Sonnenschein, H. (1982): A Modular Optimization Calculation Method of Power Station Energy balance and Plant Efficiency. Journal of Engineering for Power 104: 255-259

[SOUC92]   Soucek, B. (ed.) (1992): Dynamic, Genetic, and Chaotic Programming. The Sixth-Generation. John Wiley & Sons, New York

[SPUT84]   Sputek, K. (1984): Anwendung evolutorischer Suchstrategien zur Top-Down-Rechnung von Budgetierungsmodellen. Diploma Thesis, Technical University of Berlin, Department of Economics, Germany

[STAC94]   Stache, U. (1994): Untersuchung der Eignung von Genetischen Algorithmen in der simultanen Termin- und Kapazitätsplanung. Doctoral Dissertation, University of Dortmund, Department of Computer Science, Germany

[STAN93]   Stanley, A.; Ashlock, D. (1993): Iterated Prisoner's Dilemma with Choice and Refusal of Partners. In: Langton, C. (ed.): Artificial Life III. Proceedings, Santa Fe Institute Studies in the Sciences of Complexity, Vol. 16: 131-176

[STAR91a]   Starkweather, T.; Whitley, D.; Mathias, K. (1991): Optimization Using Distributed Genetic Algorithms. In: [SCHW91]: 176-185

[STAR91b]   Starkweather, T.; McDaniel, S.; Mathias, K.; Whitley, D.; Whitley, C. (1991): A Comparison of Genetic Sequencing Operators. In: [BELE91]: 69-76

[STAR92]   Starkweather, T.; Whitley, D.; Mathias, K.; McDaniel, S. (1992): Sequence Scheduling with Genetic Algorithms. In: [FAND92]:129-148

[STAR93]   Starkweather, T.; Whitley, D. (1993): A Genetic Algorithm for Scheduling with Resource Consumption. In:[FAND93]: 567-583

[STAW95]   Stawowy, A. (1995): Scheduling, Routing, Layout and Grouping. Genetic Algorithms in Production Scheduling List (E-Mail List), 21.4.1995

[STEF95]   Stefanitsis, E.; Christodoulou, N.; Psarras, J. (1995): Combination of Genetic Algorithms and CLP in the Vehicle-Fleet Scheduling Problem. In: [PEAR95]: 22-29

[STEN94a]   Stender, J.; Hillebrand, E. (eds.) (1994): Many-Agent Simulation and Artificial Life. Frontiers in Artificial Intelligence and Applications Vol. 25, IOS Press, Amsterdam

[STEN94b]   Stender, J. (1994): Locational and Sectoral Modelling using Genetic Algorithms. In: [STEN94a]: 218-235

[STÖP92]   Stöppler, S.; Bierwirth, C. (1992): The Application of a Parallel Genetic Algorithm to the n/m/P/C_{max} Flowshop Problem. In: [FAND92]: 161-175

[STOR92]   Storer, R. H.; Wu, S.D.; Vaccari, R. (1992): Local Search in Problem and Heuristic Space for Job Shop Scheduling Genetic Algorithms. In: [FAND92]: 150-160

[STOR93]   Storer, R.H.; Wu, S.D.; Park, I. (1993): Genetic Algorithms in Problem Space for Sequencing Problems. In: [FAND93]: 584-597

[SUH87a]   Suh, J.Y.; Gucht, D.V. (1987): Distributed Genetic Algorithms. Technical Report No. 225, Indiana University, Computer Science Department, U.S.A.

[SUH87b]   Suh, J.Y.; Gucht, D.V. (1987): Incorporating Heuristic Information into Genetic Search. In: [GREF87a]: 100-107

[SURR94]   Surry, P. (1994): Gas Network Pipe Sizing with GAs. Technical Report EPCC-TR94-11, Edinburgh Parallel Computing Centre, U.K..

[SYSW91a] Syswerda, G.; Palmucci, J. (1991): The Application of Genetic Algorithms to Resource Scheduling. In: [BELE91]: 502-508

[SYSW91b] Syswerda, G. (1991): Schedule Optimization Using Genetic Algorithms. In: [DAVI91b]: 332-349

[SYSW93]   Syswerda, G. (1993): Simulated Crossover in Genetic Algorithms. In: [WHIT93]: 239-255

[SZAK95]   Szakal, L. (1995): Job Shop Scheduling. Genetic Algorithms in Production Scheduling List (E-Mail List), 15.3.1995

[TAM92]   Tam, K.Y. (1992): Genetic Algorithms, Function Optimization, and Facility Layout Design. European Journal of Operations Research 63: 322-346

[TAMA92]   Tamaki, H.; Nishikawa, Y. (1992): A Parallel Genetic Algorithm based on a Neighborhood Model and Its Application to the Jobshop Scheduling. In: [MÄNN92]: 573-582

[TAMA93]   Tamaki, H.; Hasegawa, Y.; Kozasa, J. Araki, M. (1993): Application of Search Methods to Schedulung Problem in Plastics Forming Plant: A Binary Representation Approach. In: Proceedings of the 32nt IEEE Conference on Decision and Control (32nd CDC): 3845-3850

[TAMA94a] Tamaki, H.; Mori, M.; Araki, M.; Mishima, Y.; Ogai, H. (1994): Multi-Criteria Optimization by Genetic Algorithms: A Case of Scheduling in Hot Rolling Process. In: Proc. of the 3rd Conference of the Association of Asian-Pacific Operational Research Societies within IFORS (APORS'94), to be published. Also Technical Report of the Automatic Control Engineering Group, Department of Electrical Engineering II, Kyoto University, Japan

[TAMA94b] Tamaki, H.; Kita, H.; Shimizu, N.; Maekawa, K.; Nishikawa, Y. (1994): A Comparison Study of Genetic Codings for the Traveling Salesman Problem. In: Proceedings of the 1st IEEE Conference on Evolutionary Computation (ICEC'94): 1-6

[TANG94]   Tang, A.Y.-C.; Leung, K.-S. (1994): A Modified Edge Recombination Operator for the Traveling Salesman Problem. In: [DAVI94a]: 180-188

[TATE93a] Tate, D.M.; Smith, A.E. (1993): A Genetic Approach to the Quadratic Assignment Problem. Computers & Operations Research (accepted)

[TATE93b] Tate, D.M.; Smith, A.E. (1993): Unequal Area Facility Layout Using Genetic Search. Submitted to IIE Transactions

[TERA94]   Terano, T.; Muro, Z. (1994): On-the-Fly Knowledge Base Refinement by a Classifier System. AICOM 7: 86-97

[TERA95]   Terano, T.; Yoshinaga, K. (1995): Integrating Machine Learning and Simulated Breeding Techniques to Analyze the Characteristics of Consumer Goods. In this volume

[THAN91a] Thangiah, S.R. (1991): GIDEON: A Genetic Algorithm System for Vehicle Routing with Time Windows. Doctoral Dissertation, North Dakota State University, Fargo/ND, U.S.A.

[THAN91b] Thangiah, S.R.; Nygard, K.E.; Juell, P.L. (1991): GIDEON: A Genetic Algorithm System for Vehicle Routing with Time Windows. In: Proceedings of the IEEE Conference on Artificial Intelligence Applications, Miami: 322-328

[THAN92a] Thangiah, S.R.; Nygard, K.E. (1992): School Bus Routing Using Genetic Algorithms. In: Proceedings of the SPIE Conference on Applications of Artificial Intelligence X: Knowledge Based Systems, Orlando: 387-389

[THAN92b] Thangiah, S.R.; Nygard, K.E. (1992): MICAH: A Genetic Algorithm System for Multi-Commodity Transshipment Problems. In: Proceedings of the Eigth IEEE Conference on Artificial Intelligence for Applications, Monterey/CA 1992: 322-328

[THAN93a] Thangiah, S.R. (1993): Vehicle Routing with Time Windows Using Genetic Algorithms. Technical Report SRU-CpSc-TR-93-23, Slippery Rock University, Computer Science Department, U.S.A.

[THAN93b] Thangiah, S.R.; Vinayagamoorthy, R.; Gubbi, A.V. (1993): Vehicle Routing with Time Deadlines Using Genetic and Local Algorithms. In: [FORR93]: 506-513

[THAN93c] Thangiah, S.R.; Gubbi, A.V. (1993): Effect of Genetic Sectoring on Vehicle Routing Problems with Time Windows. Technical Report SRU-CpSc-TR-92-13, Slippery Rock University, AI and Robotics Laboratory, Slippery Rock/PA

[THIE93] Thiel, J.T.; Voß, S. (1993): Some Experiences on Solving Multiconstraint Zero-One Knapsack Problems with Genetic Algorithms. Working Paper, TH Darmstadt. To appear in INFOR

[THOM86] Thompson, B.; Thompson, B. (1986): Evolving Knowledge from Data. Computer Language 11: 23-26

[TSUJ95] Tsujimura, Y.; Gen, M.; Li, Y.; Kubota, E. (1995): An Efficient Method for Solving Fuzzy Assembly-line Balancing Problems Using Genetic Algorithms. Paper to be presented at EUFIT 1995, European Conference on Fuzzy and Intelligent Technologies, Aachen/Germany (Aug. 29-31)

[TSUT93] Tsutsui, S.; Fujimoto, Y. (1993): Forking Genetic Algorithm with Blocking and Shrinking Modes (fGA). In: [FORR93]: 206-213

[TUFT93] Tufts, P. (1993): Parallel Case Evaluation for Genetic Programming. In: Stein, D.L.; Nadel, L. (eds.): 1993 Lectures in Complex Systems. Santa Fe Institute Studies in the Science of Complexity Vol. 10. Addison-Wesley, Reading/MA

[TUSO94a] Tuson, A.L. (1994): The Use of Genetic Algorithms To Optimise Chemical Flowshops of Unrestricted Topology. Chemistry Part II Thesis, Oxford University, U.K.

[TUSO94b] Tuson, A.L. (1994): The Implementation of a Genetic Algorithm for the Scheduling and Topology Optimisation of Chemical Flowshops. Technical Report TRGA94-01, Oxford University, U.K.

[UCKU93] Uckun, S.; Bagchi, S.; Kawamura, K.; Miyabe, Y. (1993): Managing Genetic Search in Job Shop Scheduling. IEEE Expert 8: 15-24

[ULDE91] Ulder, N.L.J. et al. (1991): Genetic Local Search Algorithms for the Traveling Salesman Problem. In: [SCHW91]: 109-116

[VALE94]   Valenzuela, C.L.; Jones, A.J. (1994): Evolutionary Divide and Conquer (I): A Novel Genetic Approach to the TSP. Evolutionary Computation 1: 313-333

[VÁNC91]   Váncza, J.; Márkus, A. (1991): Genetic Algorithms in Process Planning. Computers in Industry 17: 181-194

[VENU92]   Venugopal, V; Narendran, T.T. (1992): A Genetic Algorithm Approach to the Machine-Component Grouping Problem with Multiple Objectives. Computers and Industrial Engineering 22 (4): 469-480

[VERE95a]   Vere, S.A. (1995): Genetic Classification Trees. In this volume

[VERE95b]   Vere, S.A. (1995): Fraud Detection at Bank of America. Personal Communication

[VOIG89]   Voigt, H.-M. (1989): Evolution and Optimization. An Introduction to Solving Complex Problems by Replicator Networks. Akademie, Berlin

[VOLT93]   Volta, G. (1993): Job Shop Scheduling. Personal Communication

[WAGN85]   Wagner, H. (1985): Procedures for the Solution of the Unit Commitment Problem. In: Wacker, H.J. (ed.): Applied Optimization Techniques in Energy Problems. Teubner, Stuttgart: 449-470

[WALK94]   Walker, R.F.; Haasdijk, E.W.; Gerrets, M.C. (1994): Sex Between Models. Credit Scoring using a Genetic Algorithm. Research Paper, CAP VOLMAC Corp., Huis ter Heide

[WALT93a]   Walters, G.A.; Smith, D.K. (1993): An Evolutionary Design Algorithm for the Optimal Layout of Tree Networks. Engineering Optimization (accepted)

[WALT93b]   Walters, G.A.; Cembrowicz, R.G. (1993): Optimal Design of Water Distribution Networks. In: Cabrera, E.; Martinez, F. (eds.): Water Supply Systems, State of the Art and Future Trends. Computational Mechanics Publications: 91-117

[WALT93c]   Walters, G.A.; Lohbeck, T.K. (1993): Optimal Layout of Tree Networks Using Genetic Algorithms. Engineering Optimization 22: 27-48

[WALT93d]   Walters, G.A. (1993): Evolutionary Design for the Optimal Layout of Tree Networks. Report 93/11, University of Exeter, Centre for Systems and Control Engineering, U.K.

[WALT94]   Walters, G.A.; Savic, D.A. (1994): Optimal Design of Water Systems Using Genetic Algorithms and Other Evolution Programs. In: Blain, W.R.; Katsifarakis, K.L. (eds.): Hydraulic Engineering Software, Vol. 1: Water Resources and Distribution. Computational Mechanics Publications: 19-26

[WARR94]   Warren, M.A. (1994): Stock Price Time Series Prediction Using Genetic Programming. In: [KOZA94b]: 180-183

[WEBE93]   Weber, H. (1993): Entwicklung eines genetischen Verfahrens zum Bandabgleich unter Berücksichtigung praxisrelevanter Restriktionen. Diploma Thesis, University of Hagen, Department of Economics, Germany

[WEIN93]   Weingarten, U. (1993): Ein Ansatz zur Anwendung Genetischer Algorithmen auf das Problem der Grobterminierung. Paper presented at the 'Jahrestagung von DGOR und NSOR', Amsterdam

[WELL94]   Weller, R.; Schulte, J.W. (1994): Flexible Optimisation Tools for Intelligent Manufacturing Systems. In: Proceedings Preprints of the 2nd IFAC IFIO/IFORS Workshop IMS '94 in Vienna: 557-562

[WERN84]   Werner, F. (1984): Zur Lösung spezieller Reihenfolgeprobleme, Doctoral Dissertation, Technical University Magdeburg, Germany

[WERN88] Werner, F. (1988): Ein adaptives stochastisches Suchverfahren für spezielle Reihenfolgeprobleme. Ekonomicko-Matematicky Obzor 24: 50-67

[WEZE94] van Wezel, M.C.; Kok, J.N.; von den Berg, J.; van Kampen, W. (1994): Genetic Improvement of Railway Timetables. In: [DAVI94a]: 566-575

[WHIT87] Whitley, D. (1987): Using Reproductive Evaluation to Improve Genetic Search and Heuristic Discovery. In: [GREF87a]: 108-115

[WHIT91] Whitley, D.; Starkweather, T.; Shaner, D. (1991): The Traveling Salesman and Sequence Scheduling: Quality Solutions Using Genetic Edge Recombination. In: [DAVI91]: 350-372

[WITT91] Witt, U. (1991): Evolutionary Economics - an Interpretative Survey. European Study Group for Evolutionary Economics (eds.), Papers on Economics & Evolution No. 9104, Freiburg

[YAMA92] Yamada, T.; Nakano, R. (1992): A Genetic Algorithm Applicable to Large-Scale Job-Shop Problems. In: [MÄNN92]: 281-290

[YANG93] Yang, J.-J.; Korfhage, R.R. (1993): Query Optimization in Information Retrieval Using Genetic Algorithms. In: [FORR93]: 603-611

[YIN91] Yin, X.; Germay, N. (1991): Investigations on Solving the Load Flow Problem by Genetic Algorithms. Electric Power Systems Research 22: 151-163

[YIN94] Yin, X. (1994): Investigation on the Application of Genetic Algorithms to the Load Flow Problem in Electrical Power Systems. Doctoral Thesis, Universite Catholiques de Louvain, Electrotechnics and Instrumentation Laboratory, Louvain-La-Neuve

[YOSH94] Yoshida, Y.; Adachi, N. (1994): A Diploid Genetic Algorithm for Preserving Population Diversity - pseudo-Meiosis GA. In: [DAVI94a]: 36-45

[ZIMM85] Zimmermann, A. (1985): Evolutionsstrategische Modelle bei einstufiger, losweiser Produktion. Peter Lang, Frankfurt/M.

Part Two
Applications in Industry

A Genetic Algorithm Applied to Resource Management in Production Systems

Bogdan Filipič[1,2]

[1] Artificial Intelligence Laboratory, Jožef Stefan Institute
Jamova 39, 61000 Ljubljana, Slovenia
E-mail: *Bogdan.Filipic@ijs.si*
[2] LFDT, Faculty of Mechanical Engineering, University of Ljubljana
Aškerčeva 6, 61000 Ljubljana, Slovenia

Abstract. This chapter presents an Evolutionary Computation approach to scheduling in industrial environments where schedule cost is related to resource management. To construct production schedules with near-optimal resource exploitation, a genetic-algorithm-based system was developed, utilising a direct string representation of schedules, problem-specific initialisation and recombination procedures, elitism and local improvement of solutions. The scheduler was originally evaluated on a problem of optimal energy consumption in a textile factory. It was subsequently upgraded and installed as a resource management tool in the ship repair division of a shipyard, where large numbers of activities have to be scheduled so that optimal work load is provided for workers of different trades. Employing the scheduler, significant savings in resource management were made possible in both production systems.

Keywords. Genetic algorithm, production scheduling, resource management, energy consumption, work force allocation, textile industry, ship repair

1   Introduction

Evolutionary Computation, a field that has emerged from computer modelling of biological evolution, offers a means of effectively searching vast problem spaces and optimising ill-structured domains. Evolutionary Algorithms, and among them particularly Genetic Algorithms, have shown their practical potential in a variety of applications [Davis 1991]. In management, most employments to date have been in production scheduling [Nissen 1993] (see also the overview in this volume). This is not surprising, since scheduling is an important practical problem which is hard to tackle with traditional methods. This is not only due to high computational complexity but also due to interrelated constraints and conflicting requirements to be considered in schedule construction. In addition, unanticipated events in production processes, such as priority changes and machine breakdowns, may require prompt changes of schedules in operation. For these reasons, Operations Research methods are rarely applied in practice, while Evolutionary Algorithms represent a means of generating near-optimal schedules with reasonable computational effort, and adapting to changes in the environment.

This chapter describes a genetic-algorithm-based scheduling system devised to deal with a subclass of problems where the optimality of schedules is related to resource management. The system accepts as input a list of tasks to be executed, resource requirements for each task, time constraints, and (possibly time dependent) quantities of available resources, and generates a schedule with near-optimal resource exploitation. The employed genetic algorithm applies a direct string representation of schedules and is an upgrade of the Simple Genetic Algorithm [Goldberg 1989]. The recombination step is performed by an asymmetric crossover operator which assures that newly created offspring represent valid schedules. Elitism and local improvement of candidate solutions are included in the algorithm to enhance the results of genetic search. The resulting scheduling system is capable of dealing with highly constrained and complex problem instances.

Two applications of the genetic scheduler are presented. Developed in application-oriented research, the program was originally evaluated in optimising schedules for a production unit of a textile factory. The objective was to achieve optimal distribution of energy consumption for a group of machines. Afterwards, the algorithm was upgraded and installed as a resource management tool in ship repair. Here, large numbers of activities are to be scheduled so that optimal work load is provided for the involved workers of different trades. The scheduler covers different hierarchical levels within the production process, ranging from subsystems, such as ship engine repair and docking, to the repair of entire vessels.

The rest of this chapter consists of a presentation of the two resource management problems approached with the genetic scheduler, a description of the scheduler focusing on customisation of the Simple Genetic Algorithm, an overview of the results, and concluding remarks.

2   Two Resource Management Problems

2.1   Distribution of Energy Consumption in a Textile Factory

The problem is from a textile factory, where potential savings in energy costs have been demonstrated using a genetic algorithm [Filipič 1992]. A particular unit of the factory consists of 15 machines performing a specific operation within the production process. Power demand is equal for all machines. However, due to different performance levels, eight machines execute the job in 10 hours, four in 6.5 hours, and three in 5.5 hours. According to the production plan, a specified number of jobs is to be executed daily on each machine. The production plan typically remains unchanged over a number of days. An example of a daily production plan requiring 33 jobs is shown in Table 1 together with the overview of the unit configuration and machine performance.

Table 1. Configuration, machine performance and a daily production plan for the production unit of a textile factory

Machine numbers	Performance in hours	Jobs required per machine
1–6	10.0	2
7–8	10.0	1
9–10	5.5	3
11	5.5	2
12–14	6.5	3
15	6.5	2

Prior to execution, a setup procedure must be accomplished for each job, taking half an hour. Workers arranging the jobs are present from 6 a.m. to 10 p.m. and can prepare at most two jobs at a time. The preparation of a job is immediately followed by its startup. Hence, the earliest possible startup time is 6:30 a.m. and the latest 10 p.m. Jobs prepared towards the end of a working day are left to run overnight. Their execution requires no presence of staff.

Execution of jobs is to be scheduled so that the daily production plan is accomplished, time and personnel constraints are satisfied, and interrelations among jobs are taken into account. The latter includes the treatment of a special case of 10 hour jobs started after 8 p.m. These still run at the beginning of the next working day, so the morning job on the same machine must be delayed.

The resource to be managed through scheduling is energy. The overall energy consumption in the factory consists of the consumption on the considered machines and *background consumption*. Background consumers are the remaining machines and devices in the factory whose operation is not subject to scheduling. The profile of their instantaneous power is known. On the other hand, there is a maximum demand profile, also called *target load*, prescribed for the entire factory. This should be exceeded as little as possible since the excess has to be paid at a higher rate. The objective is therefore to minimise the contribution of the production unit to the target load excess, or, in other words, to schedule the execution of jobs in the unit out of the critical periods during which the background consumption itself exceeds the target load.

Formally, the target load excess caused by the machines in the unit can be defined as follows. Let $P_m(t)$ denote the power demand of the machines running at time t, $P_b(t)$ the demand of the background consumers, and $P(t)$ the total demand of the factory, i.e. $P(t) = P_m(t) + P_b(t)$. Further let $P_{\max}(t)$ be the target load. Then the target load excess contributed by the machines at time t is

$$\Delta P_m(t) = \begin{cases} P_m(t); & P_b(t) \geq P_{\max}(t) \\ P(t) - P_{\max}(t); & P_b(t) < P_{\max}(t) \ \& \ P(t) > P_{\max}(t) \\ 0; & \text{otherwise.} \end{cases}$$

Finally, the cost of a schedule can be expressed in terms of energy consumption resulting from $\Delta P_m(t)$ as

$$C = \int_{t_S}^{t_F} \Delta P_m(t)\, dt,$$

where t_S is the starting time and t_F finishing time of schedule execution. The goal is to minimise the cost over all possible schedules.

2.2 Work Force Allocation in Ship Repair

Ship repair is a complex and dynamic production process which needs to be treated on different levels. Tendering and production planning are done globally for the vessels to be repaired. Work on the vessels already undergoing repair is coordinated at the level of subsystems, such as docking, engine repair, etc. Finally, to realise a repair project, a detailed breakdown of activities needs to be done for every ship module, and each activity specified in terms of resource requirements, duration, time constraints, and interactions with other activities. Similarly, production scheduling in ship repair addresses the construction of global as well as very detailed schedules of activities. The number of activities appearing in the detailed schedules is usually very high.

In the shipyard, where the genetic scheduler is being tested in ship repair [Filipič and Srdoč 1994], scheduling of repair activities is a multi-stage process. It starts with the so-called general diagram of activities and expert estimation of resources, continues with time analysis of the activities and ends with schedule construction and optimisation.

General diagrams of activities are the basis for schedule construction. They have been developed in the company for different sorts of repair projects and cover various types of vessels and ship subsystems. A diagram prescribes the repair activities that have to be carried out, and precedence relations among the activities. For a concrete repair project, each prescribed activity is further specified in terms of its duration and the required resources, i.e. workers of an appropriate trade. This stage is utilised by an expert system, which uses production rules acquired from experienced production planners to assign the type and quantity of a resource to each activity, as well as to calculate its duration.

In the next stage, the generated data is analysed using a project planning software package. Activity precedences and durations are considered to obtain time constraints for the execution of activities. The earliest and the latest possible starting time are calculated for each activity. The critical path is also determined, representing the sequence of activities that determine the overall duration of a project. Critical path activities have to be executed one after another with no delays, while the remaining activities can be scheduled within calculated time intervals.

In the last stage, schedules of ship repair activities are constructed and optimised. A feasible schedule must satisfy time constraints, and, as strictly as possible, account for resource limitations. If the number of workers required for some activity exceeds the number of workers of that trade employed in the shipyard, the company is forced to hire additional staff. The objective is therefore to schedule repair activities in such a way that the employees have regular work loads and the needs for hiring additional workers are minimal.

Similarly to the excess of energy consumption addressed in the textile factory problem, the excess of work load for the workers of trade i at time t is given by

$$\Delta W_i(t) = \begin{cases} W_i(t) - W_i^*; & W_i(t) > W_i^* \\ 0; & \text{otherwise} \end{cases}$$

where $W_i(t)$ is the number of workers of trade i required at time t, and W_i^* the number of employees of this profession. The sum over all k professions involved, integrated over the period of project duration

$$C = \int_{t_S}^{t_F} \sum_{i=1}^{k} \Delta W_i(t) \, dt$$

is treated as schedule cost and employed to guide the search for good schedules.

3   The Employed Genetic Algorithm

3.1   Schedule Representation

Genetic algorithms require candidate solutions to be encoded in a way that ensures the emergence of useful building blocks through recombination and selection. Most often, a string representation is used, where string positions can hold either binary or symbolic values. In the genetic scheduler, schedules are represented as strings of length N, where N is the number of tasks to be scheduled. For the textile factory problem, N is equal to the number of jobs specified by a daily production plan, and for the ship repair application N is equal to the number of non-critical activities.

String elements are integer values denoting starting times of tasks. Tasks are enumerated according to some arbitrary, but fixed enumeration scheme, so that the value at the i-th position in a string denotes the starting time of the i-th task. The range of values appearing in a string depends on time discretisation and on the length of the time period covered by the schedule. In scheduling jobs in the textile factory, half-hour intervals are used as time units, and the period covered is 24 hours. In ship repair projects, time is discretised into four-hour units, while the duration of projects treated to the present is up to 44 days.

The actual starting time of a task can only be selected from the interval between the earliest and the latest starting time. Precedence relations among tasks and other constraints have to be satisfied by schedules as well. In other words, the scheduler only maintains strings representing valid schedules. The genetic algorithm does not need to distinguish valid schedules from the ones violating the constraints, but directly searches for the best among valid schedules. An advantage of this approach is that no penalty functions need to be involved in defining the quality of schedules. On the other hand, the approach requires an adjustment of the algorithm steps where new schedules are created. These are schedule initialisation and recombination.

3.2   Population Initialisation

Genetic search for low-cost schedules starts from a random population of candidate solutions. Initial population schedules are generated by randomly assigning starting times to tasks. For each task, the scheduler maintains the bounds of the time interval valid for starting the task execution. At the beginning of schedule construction, valid time intervals are determined by the earliest and latest starting times, presented as input to the scheduler. In ship repair problems they are obtained in the aforementioned data analysis stage, whereas for the textile factory they are calculated from job durations and production plan requirements.

During schedule construction, starting times of tasks are picked from the intervals uniformly at random. Simultaneously, constraints are checked and valid time intervals updated for tasks not yet scheduled. Updating time intervals includes tightening interval bounds due to interrelations among tasks and disabling particular values due to constraints. If, for example, task T_i is scheduled at its latest starting time, this requires the delayed start of the tasks immediately following T_i. Specifically for the textile factory scheduling, where at most two jobs can be prepared simultaneously, times for which this limit is reached are excluded from time intervals for pending jobs.

The initialisation procedure may however fail to create a complete and valid schedule. When this occurs, the partially built schedule is abandoned and the construction restarted. While this is not critical in ship repair scheduling, where initialisation on average failed on less than 2% of the trials on testing problems, it calls for further improvement in the case of highly constrained problems. In textile factory scheduling, for example, between 20 and 30 trials are needed on average to generate a valid schedule. We plan to upgrade the initialisation procedure with backtracking.

3.3 Recombination of Schedules

Traditional 'blind' recombination operators do not account for constraints while producing new solutions from existing ones. In the genetic scheduler this would very likely result in illegal schedules, hence a straightforward application of traditional operators is not suitable. For this reason, a new problem-specific recombinaton operator was developed. It joins characteristics of the multiple-point crossover and mutation operators. For its specific operation we call it an *asymmetric crossover*.

From two randomly selected parent strings that represent valid schedules, the asymmetric crossover produces an offspring also representing a valid schedule. The offspring is created in three steps. Like with the multiple-point crossover, the crossing sites are determined first, splitting the parent strings into substrings. In addition, one of the parents is randomly chosen to play the dominant role in mating. Second, half of the substrings are copied from the dominant parent to the offspring. Finally, the remaining substring positions are filled in the offspring. The genes to be contributed by the non-dominant parent are checked for schedule validity. If a gene value retains the partially built schedule legal, it is copied to the offspring, otherwise a value is picked at random from starting times still available for the task. Random selection of some gene values contributes the mutation component to the recombination operator. Similarly to the initialisation procedure, the asymmetric crossover may fail to create a valid schedule. In such cases attempts are repeated until recombination succeeds.

3.4 Fitness Function

In the genetic algorithm, the cost of a schedule is mapped to a fitness value that serves to rank population members at the reproduction stage. Let x be a schedule and $C(x)$ its cost as defined for our problems in Subsections 2.1 and 2.2. Fitness of the string representing schedule x is then given by

$$F(x) = C_{\max} - C(x)$$

where $C_{\max}$ is the upper bound for schedule cost. It is equal to the total employment of resources for the execution of all scheduled tasks. The lower the schedule cost $C(x)$, the higher the fitness value $F(x)$.

To avoid premature convergence of the population caused by highly fit individuals possibly emerging in the early period of evolution, fitness is scaled. For this purpose the linear scaling mechanism is used as described by Goldberg [1989].

3.5   Performance Enhancements

Genetic algorithms are known to be successful in locating regions with near-optimal solutions in complex problem spaces, but may have difficulties in converging to the very best among solutions. In the genetic scheduler, two additional mechanisms were implemented to improve scheduler performance: elitism and local optimisation of schedules.

Elitism is aimed at preserving the best individuals that would otherwise be disrupted due to genetic variation. The elitist principle is implemented in a very straightforward manner. If the fittest member of a newly created population is worse than the best individual found so far, the worst individual in the current population is replaced by the best-so-far individual.

Local optimisation of schedules is done using the hill-climbing method. It is applied to schedules after the recombination phase. For each schedule, random changes in starting times of tasks are tested and implemented in the schedule if they reduce the schedule cost. Local optimisation stops after making no further improvement in l_{max} consecutive trials, where l_{max} is an algorithm parameter.

4   Evaluation and Results

4.1   Energy Management in the Textile Factory

The scheduler was first evaluated on the textile factory scheduling problem. Data from Table 1 was used in combination with various target load profiles. Initially, the complexity of the search space for the problem was estimated by multiplying the numbers of possible starting time assignments over all 33 jobs from the daily plan. Using half-hour slots as time units, the calculated order of magnitude was 10^{31}. However, this figure is a rough estimate, since it also includes the schedules where more than two jobs are being prepared at a time. In a more detailed analysis, the actual number of valid schedules was found to be of the order of 10^{26} [Zupanič 1994].

With regard to solution quality, the genetic scheduler was compared to iterated hill-climbing and random schedule generation. For the sake of comparison, the cost of the manually created schedules was provided as well. Finally, for a problem instance with selected target load and background consumption profiles, the optimal solution was also found using the Constraint Logic Programming (CLP) approach, which allowed for further reduction of the search space to a size amenable to enumerative search [Zupanič 1994]. Schedule optimisation results for this particular problem instance are shown in Table 2.

Experiments with random scheduling and iterated hill-climbing as separate methods were performed using the same algorithms as implemented in the genetic scheduler. Each of the three stochastic methods was allowed to eval-

Table 2. Results of schedule optimisation for the textile factory

Method	Schedule cost in kWh	Percent above optimum
Manual scheduling	801.5	39.4
Random schedule generation	765.8±49.6	33.2
Iterated hill climbing	649.3±20.1	12.9
Genetic scheduler	598.3± 7.5	4.1
CLP, enumerative search	575.0	0.0

uate 1000 valid schedules per run. Ten runs were carried out and their best results averaged. They are presented in Table 2 together with their standard deviations. A single run of the genetic scheduler consisted of 50 generations, the population size was 20 individuals, crossover probability 0.7, and the number of crossing sites 3.

Two important conclusions follow from the results. First, manually created schedules can be significantly improved. They are at the level of random assignment of starting times to jobs. In addition to the results in Table 2, it was found that the average cost of all randomly created schedules almost perfectly matches the cost of the manually created schedule. Second, the genetic scheduler consistently finds near-optimal solutions to the problem. Moreover, while the CLP approach used to find the optimal schedule needs to be reprogrammed for each particular problem instance, the genetic scheduler is ready for application on different production unit configurations, daily production plans and energy consumption profiles.

4.2 Scheduling and Resource Management in Ship Repair

A prototype version of the scheduler was installed in the ship repair division of a shipyard, where it is currently under evaluation. At present it supports scheduling and resource management in ship engine repairs, docking, and repairs of a special sort of cargo ships, called bulk carriers.

By now the scheduler has been tested on a series of hypothetical scheduling problems, taking data from real-world examples. The most complex testing problems have included the repair of five ship engines, work on two vessels in docks, and the repair of two bulk carriers. Compared to the job scheduling in the textile factory, these problems are far more demanding. Table 3 summarises their characteristics.

The most detailed evaluation was done on the engine repair problem. The engines undergoing repair were of different types and the number of activities to be carried out varied slightly among the engines. From the total of 130 activities, 67 were not on the critical path and were therefore subject to

Table 3. Characteristics of ship repair scheduling problems

Characteristic	Repair of 5 ship engines	Docking of 2 ships	Repair of 2 bulk carriers
Resources to be optimised	8	5	9
Activities to be scheduled	67	122	162
Repair duration in days	42	27	44
Size of the search space	10^{105}	10^{195}	10^{247}

optimisation. In addition to assigning starting times to these activities, the beginning of the repair had to be determined for each engine as well. As a consequence, 72 starting times were to be defined altogether. The number of possible schedules was again estimated by multiplying the numbers of possible starting times over all activities.

Solving this problem, the genetic algorithm typically converged after 100–200 generations. The population size was 50 individuals, crossover probability 0.7, and the number of crossing sites 5. The obtained schedules exhibited almost perfect resource allocation with a very small excess of work load. For the most critical group of workers, for example, the excess was 104 man-hours for the entire project. The average cost of random schedules for the project was 936 man-hours, and the cost of the schedule in which all activities were assigned the earliest starting time, 1572 man-hours. In realising similar projects in the past, the company had to hire additional work force for several hundred man-hours.

Results of similar quality were obtained in preliminary experiments on docking and bulk carrier repairs. However, the number of schedule evaluations needed was higher as the problems are more complex.

5   Concluding Remarks

The genetic-algorithm-based scheduling system produced high-quality results in production scheduling and resource management in two industrial settings. The system performs well in comparison with other computational approaches and significantly outperforms the manual scheduling techniques used until recently. Most important, its results allow for savings in resource management.

The energy management problem from the textile factory was used as a benchmark in developing the scheduler. In spite of the potential benefits, the system is not in regular use. This is due to the current organisational changes in the factory, and due to the fact that, although impressive in relative terms, the potential savings are not very high in absolute figures. For these reasons, current priorities are on more significant improvements of the production process.

The situation is however different in ship repair, where advantages of the new approach to work force allocation have been clearly shown in the testing phase. The scheduler is now being further developed and prepared for regular use. The focus is on incorporating activity diagrams for additional modules and vessel types, and on treating more complex search spaces. Also, attention will be paid to reactivity, a necessary capability for the system to be of practical use. Finally, closer integration of the scheduler with relevant software systems in the company is foreseen as the next development step.

Acknowledgements

The work presented in this chapter was supported in part by the Slovenian Ministry of Science and Technology under contract No. P2-1266-106. The author wishes to thank to Professors Ivan Bratko and Vladimir Batagelj, and colleagues Matevž Kovačič and Alira Srdoč for their help and cooperation during various stages of the work. Thanks also to the editors for their patience and valuable suggestions.

References

Davis, L. (ed.) (1991): Handbook of Genetic Algorithms. Van Nostrand Reinhold, New York

Filipič, B. (1992): Enhancing Genetic Search to Schedule a Production Unit. In: Neumann, B. (ed.): Proceedings of the 10th European Conference on Artificial Intelligence ECAI-92. John Wiley & Sons, Chichester: 603–607. Also in: Dorn, J.; Froeschl, K. A. (eds.) (1993): Scheduling of Production Processes. Ellis Horwood, Chichester: 61–69

Filipič, B.; Srdoč, A. (1994): Task Scheduling and Resource Management in Ship Repair Using a Genetic Algorithm. In: Brodda, J.; Johansson, K. (eds.): Proceedings of the 8th International Conference on Computer Applications in Shipbuilding, Vol. 2. Bremen: 15.17–15.28

Goldberg, D. E. (1989): Genetic Algorithms in Search, Optimization and Machine Learning. Addison-Wesley, Reading/Mass.

Nissen, V. (1993): Evolutionary Algorithms in Management Science. An Overview and List of References. University of Göttingen, Interdisziplinäres Graduiertenkolleg, Göttingen

Zupanič, D. (1994): Solving a Job Scheduling Problem with CLP. In: Zajc, B.; Solina, F. (eds.): Proceedings of the Third Electrotechnical and Computer Science Conference ERK '94, Vol. B. Portorož, Slovenia: 67–70

A Case Study of Operational Just-In-Time Scheduling Using Genetic Algorithms

Ivo Rixen, Christian Bierwirth and Herbert Kopfer

Department of Economics, University of Bremen

Abstract. Genetic Algorithms (GAs) have shown to fit the complex needs arising from many tasks of academic optimization for almost 20 years. This paper investigates the application of a GA to a real-world scheduling problem. The objective under consideration is just-in-time completion of jobs. First, the strategic concept of just-in-time production is operationalized according to the applicational demands. Using an extract of real-world dynamic data the proposed GA then serves as a schedule builder. A simulation study shows that the GA clearly outperforms the former way of production scheduling in this application area.

Keywords. Genetic Algorithm, just-in-time, dynamic machine scheduling

1 Introduction

Modern concepts for industrial production like *Lean* and *Just-in-Time* have shown a world-wide impact in the last decade, compare e.g. Womack et al. [1990]. One basic idea of the general philosophy emphasizes on-time delivery of subassemblies and final products. But the transfer of this claim to a practical implementation often remains an open challenge for present research. In many sectors of industrial production a variety of technical as well as organizational difficulties prevent an easy realization of new concepts.

On this background the paper transforms the strategic objective of just-in-time production towards an operational goal for machine scheduling in an existing firm. Here, the objective pronounced by just-in-time leads to a function of minimizing the mean absolute lateness, i.e. the sum of earliness and tardiness of released jobs. A bief review on literature dealing with absolute job lateness is given by Fry et al. [1990]. Fry et al. propose a heuristic based on adjacent job exchange in combination with a linear programming approach in order to solve one-machine scheduling problems. Following this line of research we present an automated approach for generating machine schedules with respect to a measure of just-in-time completion of jobs. A GA capable to handle general job shop problems is involved as the basic component of the automated scheduling system. The GA solves a series of static problems which are created by the occurrence of certain events. Since e.g. job release times are unknown in advance, job scheduling appears as a dynamic problem. For this reason the GA has to act on a rolling time basis as proposed by Raman et al. [1989]. A comparison of the proposed automated scheduling approach with traditional scheduling is outlined by an extract of jobs actually processed in the workcenter in 1994.

2 The Application Case Study

2.1 Description of a Job Scheduling Environment

Throughout this paper we consider a firm that acts in the fastening sector. It produces specialized fastening tools for the motor-vehicle industry as well as different kinds of fasteners such as nails, staples and glue.

In the following we study a collator machine which connects certain types of nails to strips of collated nails fitting professional nailing tools. Jobs are given to the collator by specifying a lot-size and a certain nail type. The processing of different jobs may require changeover times which are regarded as a setup for the collator. In order to serve the market the sales department of the firm passes the demand to the manufacturing workcenter. On-time delivery of products, i.e. nailstrips, appears to be the most desirable goal in the workcenter. Early or tardy deliveries are highly discouraged, because they may lead to penalty costs. For this reason the sales department declares a due date for each job which ensures a security time span between job completion and delivery date. The workcenter schedules jobs with respect to the given time constraints only, i.e. without taking aspects of costs into account. As soon as a demand reaches the workcenter the needed raw material is ordered. The material arrives at the workcenter about two weeks after ordering. This point in time is the earliest possible starting time of the corresponding job and is usually called *ready time* of the job.

Job id	Nail type	Request date	Ready time	Setup (hours)	Lot-size	Duration (hours)	Due date
N320	MC62	20.10.93	13.01.94	3	1200	0.0592	26.01.94
N321a	QC70	20.10.93	13.01.94	3	325	0.1606	09.02.94
N321b	QC70	20.10.93	02.02.94	3	325	0.1606	09.02.94
N322a	MC64	20.10.93	02.02.94	3	1107	0.0638	23.02.94
N322b	MC64	20.10.93	16.02.94	3	93	0.0638	23.02.94
N323a	MC65	20.10.93	18.02.94	3	1672	0.0688	23.03.94
N323b	MC65	20.10.93	11.03.94	3	528	0.0688	23.03.94
N324	MC61	20.10.93	11.03.94	3	800	0.0839	06.04.94
N333	QC70	10.12.93	27.12.93	3	34	0.1606	13.12.93
N334	QC70	10.12.93	02.02.94	3	40	0.1606	13.12.93

Table 1. Jobs on *Collator* 3 (part I).

The table above shows all queuing jobs related to *Collator* 3 which were not started within the year 1993. As shown by the table different nail types are processed by this machine. The setup of the collator takes about three hours if processing changes over to another nail type. Sometimes, jobs of the same nail type and request date appear in the Table 1, e.g. N322a, N322b. This happens when ordered raw material arrives in fractions at different dates, also enforcing different ready times of the jobs. Obviously, if a job succeeds another job of the same nail type no time for setup is necessary. The product of the lot-size and the duration defines the processing time of a job in units of industrial working hours.

From time to time, special jobs are released by the research department of the firm. These prototype jobs are processed for innovative purpose only. Although the research department declares a due date for these jobs, they have no definite date of delivery. Table 2 shows the prototype jobs N397 and N405, both characterized by a long setup and a small lot-size.

Let us now consider how scheduling of jobs is actually performed by the workcenter. Fastener products are usually produced by a single dedicated machine. Thus the workcenter is confronted with a number of one-machine scheduling problems. Let us continue to focus on *Collator* 3. For this machine a new schedule, containing all released and not started jobs, is built up from 6 to 7 times a year. The building of a new schedule is triggered by the desire to estimate the work load of machines within the near future. Next to that it can be forced by important events, e.g. a machine breakdown. Scheduling itself is made by hand. Hence it is less inspired by ideas of optimization than by expert knowledge. For example, if a job risks delay its completion may be accelerated by using double shifts. Nevertheless, wage-expensive double shifts should be introduced in urgent situations only.

2.2 An Automated Scheduling Approach

Let us summarize the dynamic scheduling environment of the manufacturing workcenter. Jobs are processed on a single machine without preemption, i.e. each job, once started, must be completed before another job may be started on that machine. They are occasionally released at unspecified points of time. Finally, there is a changeover time between jobs of different types. The primary measure of schedule performance responds to just-in-time completion of jobs. Secondary, double shifts should be avoided whenever possible.

In the following, we propose an automated scheduling approach which introduces two features of optimization into the daily course of the workcenter. First, a method which automatically generates machine schedules based on just-in-time performance, and second, a rule which determines when to use the method. Presently, the point in time when schedule building is done in the workcenter is not event driven. It is performed simultaneously for the whole workcenter about every two months because manual scheduling of a large number of machines is very time consuming. In contrast, a fast computer based method permits the scheduling authority to follow the course of events in the workcenter (e.g. new job releases, machine breakdowns).

Concerning *Collator* 3, Table 2 shows the chronology of such events in the workcenter. Whenever a new event occurs, time has come to generate a new schedule, i.e. to determine starting times of new jobs and to update starting times of waiting jobs. Notice that for those jobs being ready but not yet started a new ready time is defined by the expected completion time of the job currently processed. Handled this way, the dynamic scheduling problem is treated as a series of static problems which are solved on a rolling horizon basis. Obviously, the choice of a method solving this series of problems has an important impact on the quality of the schedule that is actually implemented in the workcenter.

Job id	Nail type	Request date	Ready time	Setup (hours)	Lot-size	Duration (hours)	Due date
Event I at 3.1.94: Job transfer from 1993							
...see Table 1							
Event II at 8.2.94: New job releases							
N377a	MC65	08.02.94	08.04.94	3	1496	0.0688	01.06.94
N377b	MC65	08.02.94	14.04.94	3	176	0.0688	01.06.94
N377c	MC65	08.02.94	11.05.94	3	528	0.0688	01.06.94
N378	MC62	08.02.94	11.05.94	3	1130	0.0592	15.06.94
N384	MC64	08.02.94	11.05.94	3	800	0.0638	29.06.94
Event III at 11.5.94: New job releases							
N391	QC70	11.05.94	14.06.94	3	750	0.1606	20.07.94
N392	QC65	11.05.94	18.05.94	3	500	0.0943	29.07.94
N393	MC65	11.05.94	18.05.94	3	2200	0.0688	15.08.94
N394	MC64	11.05.94	18.05.94	3	1570	0.0638	16.09.94
N395	QC70	11.05.94	18.05.94	3	330	0.1606	30.09.94
N397	RE58	11.05.94	26.05.94	14,5	10	0.1898	24.06.94
Event IV at 11.7.94: New job releases							
N405	RE58	11.07.94	20.07.94	14,5	50	0.1898	27.07.94
N406	MC61	11.07.94	22.07.94	3	680	0.0839	28.09.94
N412	MC65	11.07.94	22.07.94	3	2570	0.0688	23.11.94
N413	QC70	11.07.94	22.07.94	3	620	0.1606	19.10.94
N416	MC62	11.07.94	22.07.94	3	1030	0.0592	30.11.94
N419	MC64	11.07.94	22.07.94	3	740	0.0638	21.12.94
Event V at 16.8.94: Machine breakdown until 5.9.94							
Event VI at 28.9.94: New job release							
N420	QC65	28.09.94	12.10.94	3	500	0.0943	21.12.94

Table 2. Jobs for *Collator* 3 (continued).

On this background the use of a GA offers an interesting opportunity as outlined by Bierwirth and Kopfer [1994]. At the end of a GA-run the generated schedules may contain jobs which will not be started until the next event occurs. The corresponding partial solutions can be used during the initialization of the new GA population in order to solve the scheduling problem resulting from the new event. In a situation where events follow close after each other, or where even real-time scheduling is required, this strategy can enormously enhance the runtime performance of genetic search.

In the presented application runtime performance is of subordinate interest in favor of effectivity because events occur rarely. Thus, it seems suitable to use randomly initialized populations, run the GA several times on the same static problem, and finally implement the best of all generated schedules in the workcenter. Using a GA for schedule generation offers an important advantage. For related or even more complex scheduling problems a suitable GA is available, see Rixen and Kopfer [1994]. We can adapt it to the needs of our application problem by only modifying the schedule building procedure. The adaptation of schedule evaluation according to just-in-time completion of jobs is a theme of the next section.

3 Incorporating Genetic Algorithms

3.1 Just-in-Time Evaluation of Schedules

In order to model the overall goal of the workcenter, i.e. just-in-time completion of jobs with respect to a minimal number of double shifts, the following standard notations are used:

J_j Variables for job id's ($j = 1, 2 ... n$),

r_j Ready time of J_j,

s_{ij} Setup time, changing over from J_i to J_j,

p_j Processing time of J_j in working hours (Lot-size x duration),

d_j Due date of J_j,

α_j Weight factor between earliness and tardiness of J_j ($0 < \alpha_j < 1$),

h Industrial working hours per shift ($h = 7.5$).

In a first step scheduling of tasks on the collator machine requires to sequence n jobs. Assume such a sequence to be given, e.g. $S = J_1, J_2 ... J_n$. Within our approach job sequences like S are generated by a GA. For evaluation the GA needs access to a procedure building a feasible schedule from a sequence and returning its measure of performance.

The question arising is how to calculate starting times for sequenced jobs on the collator Usually machine idle times are inserted between the processing of adjacent jobs if this helps to avoid finishing jobs too early, compare Fry et al. [1990]. For the problem considered this strategy may lead to an increasing number of double shifts if several jobs have a similar due date.

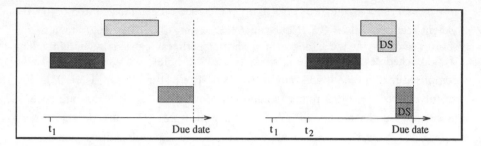

Fig. 1. Two alternative schedule charts for 3 jobs with identical due date
(DS = double shifts).

Figure 1 shows the alternative between starting a job at t_1 or inserting an idle time of $t_2 - t_1$. Although the job is less early in the right chart it enforces double shifts for the following jobs not to become tardy. However, double shifts are discouraged because they increase the costs of a working hour by about 20%. They appear to be reasonable only if a job risks to be tardy. Thus, we are confronted with a situation where minimizing double shifts is in conflict with minimizing absolute job lateness. Since costs arising from earliness of jobs cannot be quantified by the workcenter we focus on minimizing the number of double shifts. Therefore, we refrain from introducing idle times to the collator, i.e. we consider left-shifted schedules of jobs. Hence, the starting times t_j of jobs given in a sequence S are iteratively calculated by

$$t_j = \max\left(\left(t_{pred(j)} + p_{pred(j)} - h \cdot N_{pred(j)} + s_{pred(j),j}\right), r_j\right)$$

Here, N_i denotes the number of double shifts used to process job J_i where $i = pred(j)$ refers to the predecessor of J_j in S, if it exists. Otherwise J_j is the first job of S and t_j is given by the maximum of the machine setup and the ready time only. Both, the sequence of jobs and the number of double shifts for each job are encoded in the genetic representation scheme of schedules. Notice that the term hN_i gives the sum of working hours which are projected for double shifts in order to accelerate job J_i. Since J_i precedes J_j the product hN_i has to be subtracted in order to determine the actual starting time of J_j.

Given the starting time of J_j its completion time simply results from $C_j = t_j + p_j - hN_j$. Thus earliness and tardiness of jobs are calculated by $E_j = \max(d_j - C_j, 0)$ and $T_j = \max(C_j - d_j, 0)$. For some jobs it may be very important not to be late, some other jobs should not be completed too early. Therefore, a job-specific weight factor α_j may be useful to express a preference for early or tardy completion. Hence, we measure the just-in-time performance of a job by $JIT_j = \alpha_j E_j + (1-\alpha_j)T_j$. If no preferences are indicated for a job the weight factor is set to 0.5. Notice that this setting implicitly tends to prefer a shorter tardiness at the expense of a shorter earliness caused by building left-shifted schedules. Nevertheless, since $0 < \alpha_j < 1$ holds, we can state J_j to be completed just in time if and only if $JIT_j = 0$. The just-in-time measure JIT_j of a prototype job J_j is often rather unimportant. In order to neglect the influence of these jobs on the quality of solutions their measure JIT_j may be set to zero beforehand. Now, the overall goal of optimization in the workcenter is stated as

$$\text{minimize } \overline{JIT} = \frac{1}{n^*} \sum_{j=1}^{n} JIT_j ,$$

where n^* denotes the number of non-prototype jobs. This objective function operationalizes the concept of just-in-time production with respect to the details of the application considered. Of course, the details are partly hidden in the genetic representation of the application itself instead of the fitness function. But this apparent drawback, compare Syswerda [1991], is known to be a common feature of successful genetic search in scheduling, compare e.g. the various GA approaches proposed by Pesch [1994].

3.2 Genetic Schedule Representation and Operators

We are looking for a genetic schedule representation which depicts the presented one-machine scheduling problem in the workcenter right down to its important decision details. As outlined in the previous section schedule building requires at least two kinds of decisions. First of all, a schedule is constructed with respect to a sequence representing the order of processing jobs on a machine. Second, a schedule is constructed by means of some integer values representing the number of double shifts for each job. Other variables used in the previous section such as completion times, earliness, and tardiness of jobs can be expressed in terms of both of these decisions. For this reason we propose a genetic schedule representation of two interacting chromosomes.

Chromosome 1 encodes the processing sequence of jobs by use of a permutation scheme of length n. Thus, each item of the permutation represents one job identifier. Reading a permutation from left to right directly decodes a processing sequence. Thereby a natural representation is given which covers each feasible job sequence exactly once. An important advantage of this representation is that a wide range of genetic operators is available for permutation schemes. Nevertheless, the choice of any of these operators should take the properties of the application problem into account. Most of all permutation operators have been designed to serve as a crossover in traveling salesman applications. In this problem class the relative order of cities represented by a permutation is of dominating importance. A given city should be visited together with neighboring cities. Whether this happens, for example, somewhere in the beginning of a tour or at a later stage is of subordinate interest. Quite to the opposite, scheduling requires a somehow position based ordering of jobs. Consider a job which has to be processed early because of an early due date. Then it should occur - independently from the relative order of other jobs - somewhere in the beginning of a permutation. Thus we use *Position-Based Crossover* as proposed by Syswerda [1991] which strongly supports the inheritance of position characteristics. Mutation of Chromosome 1 is performed by swapping of two arbitrary jobs.

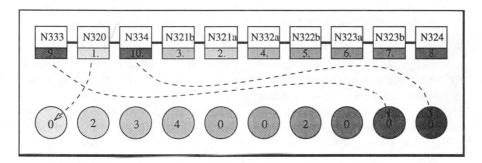

Fig. 2. Schedule decoding of an arbitrary genotype.

Chromosome 2 encodes the number of double shifts used to process each of the n jobs. Consider again the sequence of job identifiers represented in Chromosome 1. Each job identifier J_j can be used as an index that clearly points to a field of Chromosome 2 carrying its N_j value, i.e. the number of double shifts. Hence Chromosome 2 is handled as an array of size n. Figure 2 illustrates the procedure of decoding a bichromosomal genotype. The upper chromosome shows an arbitrary sequence of the 10 jobs sketched in Table 1. The grey scale of items refers to indexes of jobs. As indicated by the three dashed arcs each index references a field of the lower chromosome.

The integer values of Chromosome 2 range from 0 to a maximal number of double shifts of the corresponding job. The maximal number of double shifts is bounded by the integer part of $p_j/2$ for job J_j. The use of integers is motivated by the idea that a double shift is introduced only if its capacity is fully exploited. If $N_j = 0$ the job J_j will be processed without double shifts. Consider job N324 mentioned in Table 1. It occupies *Collator* 3 with a total of 800 × 0.0839 = 67.17 industrial working hours. Notice that a single shift counts 7.5 industrial working hours. Hence N324 can be processed by inserting at most 4 double shifts leading to an entire processing of approximately 5 working days. Without any double shifts N324 occupies the collator machine for about 9 days.

Initial array instantiations of Chromosome 2 are randomly generated using an integer valued uniform distribution over the interval $[0, p_j/2]$ for index j. Since

Chromosome 2 is of an array type *Two-Point Crossover* performs a valid genetic operation. Furthermore, mutations are achieved by randomly selecting a field of the array and increasing or decreasing its value by 1 with respect to the feasible bounds.

To summarize recombination, two offspring are generated from the genotypes of two parents by applying *Position-Based Crossover* and *Two-Point Crossover* to Chromosome 1 and 2 respectively. Mutation of genotypes is achieved in an appropriate manner. The probability of crossover is set to 0.5 and the mutation rate to 0.001. Both parameters appear to follow an often used standard setting.

4 Simulation Study of Automated Scheduling

Following the data of Table 2 we perform an event-driven and GA-based job scheduling for *Collator* 3. The entire simulation run is divided by the six events I-VI. Whenever an event occurs there is a given state of the collator machine which is transformed into a static scheduling problem. Consider e.g. *Event I*. Any decision of how to schedule the 10 jobs N320-N334 determines one part of the scheduling problem we are facing at *Event II*. The other part of this new problem results from the currently released five jobs N377a-N384. Thus, we are faced with a total of six scheduling problems, but only the first of them is determined in the beginning.

Throughout our simulation the GA runs on each of the six static problems for a total of 30 iterations. Using the evaluation and recombination techniques described in the previous section, the population size of the GA is set to 128 individuals and termination occurs after 100 generations. For evaluation a constant weight factor $\alpha_j = 0.5$ is used. Further implementation details of the GA can be found in Rixen and Kopfer [1994]. Although runtime performance is of subordinate interest we would like to mention that a single GA run requires an average runtime of 17 seconds measured on a Sun10 workstation. For each run the best generated schedule is stored. Finally, after 30 iterations the best of all schedules is implemented on *Collator* 3.

The simulation results are shown in Table 3. The jobs listed in the first column appear in the suggested order of processing. Each event is reported by a subtable giving the best GA-generated schedule of the corresponding static problem. The three columns of a subtable refer to the obtained completion time of jobs, the machine setups, and the numbers of used double shifts. A symbol "x" denotes that a machine setup is required. Notice that values representing a date are given in accumulated units of industrial working hours. The entry date 3.1.94 of *Event I* refers to the virtual starting time 0 of the simulation. In order to avoid negative time values the due date of jobs transferred from 1993 is calculated by the maximum of 0 and the original due date.

It can be seen from Table 3 that most of the jobs are subject of several static problems arising from different events. This is the case for those jobs that have not been started before the next event. Consider e.g. the jobs N323b and N323a.

Job id	Due date	C_j	s	N_j	II	s	N_j	III	s	N_j	IV	s	N_j	V	s	N_j	VI	s	N_j	E_j	T_j
		Event I																		**Just-in-Time**	
N333	0	9	x	0																	9
N320	127	131	x	0																2	4
N334	0	171	x	0																	171
N321b	202	200		3																	36
N321a	202	238		2																	10
N322a	277	281	x	4	281	x	4													23	
N322b	277	287		0	287		0														
N323b	277	427	x	0	404	x	0														69
N323a	427	405		2	496		3														72
N324	495	497	x	0	567	x	0														
N377a	780				673	x	0	734	x	0										107	5
N384	930				847	x	0	773	M	0										196	
N377c	780				781	x	1	785	x	0										7	
N377b	780				793		0	855	x	0										*	*
N378	855				749	x	0	871	x	0										44	
N397	915							995	x	0										47	
N391	1042							1045	x	0										50	
N392	1095							1184	x	2	1045	x	0							23	
N405	1080							1287	x	0	1057	M	0								4
N393	1185							1343	x	0	1189	x	3	1296	x	4				2	6
N394	1290										1272	x	0	1348	x	1				1	
N406	1350										1338	x	2	1382	x	3					17
N395	1365										1371	x	3	1459	x	3	1454	x	3		4
N413	1455										1456	x	2	1639	x	0	1639	x	0		31
N412	1635										1635	x	0	1703	x	0	1703	x	0	32	3
N416	1672										1681	x	2	1752	x	0	1753	x	0		
N419	1785										1735	x	0				1788	x	2		
N420	1785																				
Double shifts:		5			7			0			3			8			5			534	445

Table 3. GA suggestion of scheduling on a rolling time basis.

Within the period after *Event I* they are scheduled for completion at 427and 405 respectively, i.e. N323a precedes N323b. But in the following period the processing order changes as shown by the new completion times of 404 and 496. Within this period both jobs are actually processed since they do not appear in the back part of the table again. Very important is the behavior of automated scheduling in case of such unpleasant events as machine breakdowns. Have a look on *Event V* at 16.8.94. The date corresponds to a virtual time of 1191, i.e. the breakdown occurred while setting up the collator for Job N394. Since the machine was repaired until 5.9.94 it could not be used for a total of 32 working hours. The seemingly larger difference between both dates results from a two week vacation in the firm which is not expressed by the virtual simulation time. Notice that the processing order of the following 7 jobs does not change after the breakdown whereas the number of double shifts increases drastically.

Let us now investigate how the objectives of scheduling are satisfied in the simulation run. The bottom row of Table 3 accumulates the number of double shifts which are actually used within one period. Consider Job N377c which is first scheduled at *Event II* using a single double shift. Since its processing is not started in that period we count a total of 7 instead of 8 double shifts. Furthermore we notice that starting this job in the next period does not require a double shift at all. The right column of the table shows the just-in-time performance of each job in terms of earliness and tardiness. The only job which exactly completes at the due date is N378. For most of the other jobs an acceptable deviation of a few hours is reached. Nevertheless, at least some jobs appear to be critical with respect to the due date. Consider e.g. N334. Its completion has a delay of 171 hours, since a due date of 0 hits the beginning of the simulation run. So, why should job N320 precede N334 as suggested by the GA? The answer is given by the ready times of both jobs in Table 3. The sales department arranged a due date at 13.12.93 for N334. Later it turned out that the needed raw material does not reach the workcenter before 2.2.94. Thus, it is obvious that N334 cannot be completed in time.

To summarize, we count 534 hours of earliness and a slightly smaller number of 445 hours of tardiness. These values are achieved by inserting a total of 28 double shifts and lead to the quantity $\overline{JIT} = 17.5$ in terms of our mean just-in-time measure. In comparison, the manually developed schedule really implemented on *Collator* 3 in 1994 is measured with a corresponding value of 33.3 by use of 38 double shifts.

5   Final Remarks

Within this paper we have developed an automated job scheduling system for an existing firm. The promising simulation results reveal the amount of unex- ploited machine capacity in the considered workcenter. There can be no doubt that this capacity has to be utilized in order to realize advanced concepts of production. In case of our workcenter the desired goal of just-in-time completion is approached by a good compromise between interdependent decisions which can be made by a GA. In other scheduling environments we will face different constellations of interacting dependencies but it appears to be likely that a GA will again successfully compromise.

From an academic point of view the constraints and the size of the application considered appear to be still moderate. Nevertheless, an expert could hardly improve the given solution. Thus, it seems worthwhile to investigate the power of general-purpose optimization techniques like GAs in the context of real-world problems. From the firm's point of view the achieved results are so much encouraging that it intends to use the GA for machine scheduling in the near future.

References

Fry, T.D.; Armstrong, R.D.; Rosen L.D.(1990): Single Machine Scheduling to Minimize Mean Absolute Lateness: A heuristic solution. Computers Operational Research 17: 105-112

Bierwirth, C.; Kopfer, H.(1994): Dynamic Task Scheduling with Genetic Algorithm in Manufacturing Systems. Technical Report, University of Bremen, Chair of Logistics, Bremen

Pesch, E.(1994): Learning in Automated Manufacturing. Physica Verlag, Heidelberg

Raman, N.; Rachamadugu, R.; Talbot, F.B.(1989): Real-Time Scheduling of an Automated Manufacturing Center. European Journal of OR 40: 222-242

Rixen, I.; Kopfer, H.(1994): Ein Genetischer Algorithmus für das Job Shop Scheduling Problem. Technical Report, University of Bremen, Chair of Logistics, Bremen

Syswerda, G.(1991): Schedule Optimization using Genetic Algorithms. Davis, L.(ed.): Handbook of Genetic Algorithms. Van Nostrand Reinhold, New York: 332-349

Womack, J.P.; Jones, D.T.; Roos, D.(1990): The Machine that Changed the World. Macmillian Publishing Company, New York

An Evolutionary Algorithm for Discovering Manufacturing Control Strategies

Royce Bowden, Ph.D. and Stanley F. Bullington, Ph.D.

Department of Industrial Engineering, Post Office Drawer U
Mississippi State University, MS 39762 USA

Abstract. This paper presents an unsupervised, genetic algorithm based machine learning technique that has been developed to address control issues for complex manufacturing systems. The machine learning technique supports the co-evolution of control strategies for multiple (and often competing) decision makers without providing them with a great deal of *a priori* control information. Results are presented where competing parts learn appropriate strategies for routing themselves through a simulated cellular manufacturing system.

Keywords. Machine Learning, Manufacturing Control Knowledge

1   Introduction

Recent research in the area of concurrent engineering has focused on reducing the time to plan and manufacture quality products. One result of concurrent engineering is the development of flexible manufacturing process plans [Srihari and Greene 1988]. Flexible process plans not only outline the preferred method of producing a product, but also specify alternative methods (alternative routings and processing steps) that can be used. Coupled with flexibly automated manufacturing facilities, these plans can help shorten the production cycle. Alternative methods or machines can be used, for example, when preferred machines break down or when bottlenecks occur, thereby giving the scheduler an extra degree of flexibility to meet job due dates and better utilize the manufacturing system.

Although this routing flexibility exists and has been shown to improve system performance, manufacturers have been slow to exploit its benefits [Chandra and Talavage 1991]. This is perhaps because scheduling problems are combinatorial problems, and consideration of alternative routes further complicates the situation. Several optimization techniques have been proposed for solving the dynamic routing problem. However, most of these techniques are not useful in practice because the simplifying assumptions necessary to implement them render them ineffective [McKay, et al. 1988]. Therefore, common industrial practice is to adhere to a fixed predetermined route and apply simplistic queue dispatch rules such as the shortest processing time rule [Ben-Arieh, et al. 1988].

In order to capture the production benefits of today's flexibly automated manufacturing facilities, new control methods must be developed. The behavior of these systems is so dynamic that traditional scheduling techniques are outdated. Existing scheduling and control techniques were designed with generality in mind to be applicable to a variety of production systems. This imposed generality decreases the scheduling and control technique's ability to capitalize on a specific system's capability to increase production. What is needed is a robust method for deriving scheduling and control schemes which are tailored for a specific production system. In other words, the method should require little *a priori* scheduling and control expertise as input so that it can be used to derive control knowledge for a variety of production systems without adjusting the method.

To begin addressing these issues, a machine learning technique called the genetic algorithm rule discovery system (GARDS) has been developed [Bowden 1992]. This unsupervised learning process uses a computer simulation model of the manufacturing system, and is guided by the specification of management objectives (e.g., minimize the number of late jobs). In this way, the control scheme is tailored to the specific system. Since GARDS requires little *a priori* domain information it is applicable to many manufacturing system.

2 Genetic Algorithm Rule Discovery System

GARDS differs substantially from other machine learning systems reported in the manufacturing literature. It is related to Shaw's [1989] work in that it uses a form of machine learning to develop a knowledge base consisting of a collection of rules. However, GARDS' genetic algorithm learning process requires no direct supervision and can be used to develop central or distributed control strategies. Although GARDS could be applied to many sequential decision tasks, it is the control of manufacturing systems that support routing flexibility that is currently of interest. The decision-making agents are the part types being processed. GARDS provides a method for part types to evolve strategies for selecting the best route through the manufacturing system based on the current state of the system.

The development of GARDS was influenced by a system called SAMUEL [Grefenstette 1990]. However, GARDS is designed to ultimately handle multiple decision-makers in a complex environment, as opposed to a single decision-maker in a simplistic environment. GARDS' broadly consists of two components: the Unsupervised Learner and the Plan Manager/Evaluator. The system is complete when linked with an application domain (Figure 1). A brief discussion of GARDS follows.

126

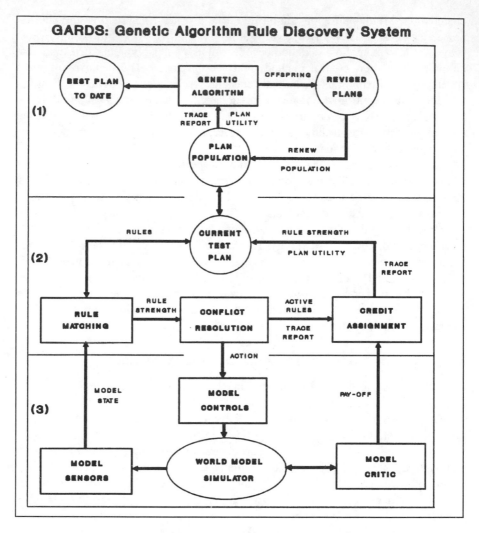

Fig. 1. GARDS' Components: (1) Unsupervised Learner, (2) Plan Manager/Evaluator, (3) Application Domain. Copyright ©1992 by Bowden, Royce O., Jr. Used by permission.

2.1 Application Domain Component

The application domain component provides four elements: (1) simulation model of the task being studied, (2) sensors to reflect the state of the simulation model, (3) controls for the decision-maker(s) to adjust, and (4) a critic to judge the decision maker's performance.

GARDS has been applied to several different simulated manufacturing systems. Here, a realistic cellular manufacturing system (CMS) consisting of four machining cells, connected by a material handling system is presented (Figure 2). Each machine in a cell has a local in-process storage area capable of holding two parts in addition to the one being processed. There is a common, or global, storage space that provides storage for work-in-process and for new job arrivals.

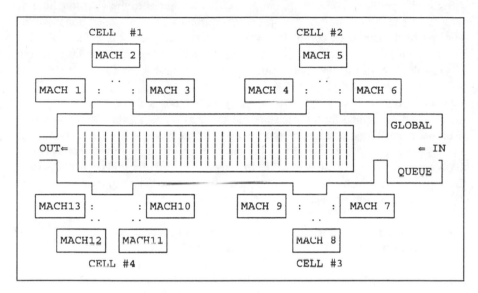

Fig. 2. Hypothetical cellular manufacturing system. Copyright ©1992 by Bowden, Royce O., Jr. Used by permission.

The CMS produces three different part types. Multiple manufacturing process plans (MPP), which allow the part types to be routed to different cells, are available for each part. Part types 1, 2, and 3 can select from three MPPs, four MPPs, and three MPPs, respectively. Each part type has a preferred cell that is specifically designed to produce the part. By selecting the MPP that specifies the preferred cell, one would expect to realize the lowest setup and processing time. However, this time estimate does not include possible queue waiting time and, therefore, does not guarantee the lowest time in the system.

Cells 1, 2, and 3 each consist of three machines and are the preferred cells for part types 1, 2, and 3, respectively. Cell 4 consists of four machines and is the remainder cell (i.c., it can completely produce any of the three part types but is not optimized for any one part type). Parts which are routed to the remainder cell will thus incur increased setup and processing times.

Since the desire to re-route jobs often arises due to a machine breakdown, breakdowns are included in the simulation experiments. Specifically, five of the thirteen machines in the CMS were considered to be less than perfectly reliable, with (identical) normally distributed times between failures and (non-identical) normally distributed times to repair.

The CMS operates as follows. A part surveys the state of the CMS and, based on its learned knowledge, selects an MPP upon arrival. Next, the part enters the global queue, where it waits until the local storage area for the required machine is available. Here, the part waits its turn to be setup on the machine and processed. After each operation is complete, the part either advances to the next machine or returns to the global queue. The process continues until all operations on the selected MPP have been completed, at which time the part exits the CMS. Note that once an MPP is selected, it is followed by the part type through completion. Also, note that within the global queue jobs that have been in the system the longest are given priority.

In addition to capturing the logic of the problem domain, the simulation model must provide a method for the decision-makers (part types) to make and implement their decisions. This is done by providing the part types with information from sensors that reflect the state of the CMS, and also providing them with controls that allow them to select and follow a MPP. In selecting sensors for this application, only those variables that could be easily measured in an industrial setting were considered. The following sensors were chosen:

1-4:   The number of jobs waiting to be processed by a cell. Sensors 1, 2, 3, and 4 correspond to cells 1, 2, 3, and 4, respectively.

5-7:   The ratio of the number of jobs that exit the CMS after their due date to the number of jobs that exit the CMS on or before their due date [(number late) / (number early)]. Sensors 5, 6, and 7 are for job types 1, 2, and 3, respectively.

8-12:   The time since the last failure of a machine. Sensors 8, 9, 10, 11, and 12 are for machines 2, 4, 9, 10, and 11, respectively.

The control adjustments available to the part types are the different MPPs. When a part enters the CMS, it receives information about the state of the CMS through the 12 sensors. Using information from the sensors, a part's task is to develop a set of decision rules for selecting the most appropriate MPP. In short, the parts must learn the mapping between CMS state conditions (sensor readings) and the corresponding correct action. A job's objective is to complete processing on or before its due date.

Learning is unsupervised and is driven by feedback from the critic. Using a formula, pay-off is awarded by the critic at the end of a simulated time period (a trial). For example, the payoff for this CMS takes the following form:

$$\text{pay-off} = 2.0*(\text{no. of non-tardy jobs}) + 0.5*(\text{no. of tardy jobs}).$$

In these experiments, a pay-off bonus of 800 was awarded at the end of the trial if no more than ten percent of the completed jobs were late for each part type. Such a bonus serves to better define what management considers to be an acceptable level of performance. Note that the pay-off formula can take any form as long as it rewards the system for the desired behavior.

2.2   Plan Manager/Evaluator Component

GARDS' interface with the problem domain's simulation model is through the Plan Manager/Evaluator. It is responsible for indexing through the population of plans (control strategies) and having each evaluated in the simulated environment, and performs four main functions: management of the testing of the current plan, rule matching, conflict resolution, and credit assignment.

In most GA applications, a knowledge structure, or individual in the population, is a single rule, usually expressed as a binary string. However, in GARDS' population a collection of rules represents a knowledge structure, or plan. The conditional part of a rule describes a state(s) of the CMS and the action specifies the MPP that a part type is to use when that state(s) is encountered. A rule's IF statement consists of 12 conditions corresponding to the 12 sensors discussed earlier. In addition, each rule has an estimate of its strength (its usefulness for achieving success). Rules are represented as follows:

Rule No: 12   IF   (Part Type = 1) and
Strength: 601.22 $(0 \leq$ Cell 1 Queue $\leq 2)$ and
                                 $(5 \leq$ Cell 2 Queue $\leq 9)$ and
                                 $(1 \leq$ Cell 3 Queue $\leq 3)$ and
                                 $(3 \leq$ Cell 4 Queue $\leq 4)$ and
                                 $(0 \leq$ Type 1 Late/Early $\leq 0.1)$ and
                                 $(0.5 \leq$ Type 2 Late/Early $\leq 1.0)$ and
                                 $(0 \leq$ Type 3 Late/Early $\leq 0.8)$ and
                                 $(80 \leq$ Since Failure of Mach. $2 \leq 95)$ and
                                 $(25 \leq$ Since Mach. 4 Fail $\leq 93)$ and
                                 $(10 \leq$ Since Mach. 9 Fail $\leq 63)$ and
                                 $(90 \leq$ Since Mach. 10 Fail $\leq 970)$ and
                                 $(600 \leq$ Since Mach.11 Fail $\leq 1100)$
                      THEN   use MPP 10.

Each plan in GARDS contains a fixed number of such rules for each part type. Each plan's performance is observed over several simulation runs.

The rule matching algorithm is used to find the rule(s) that most closely matches the current state of the CMS. It is invoked when a decision needs to be made (when a part type arrives to the CMS). For each rule in the rule base, the rule matching algorithm compares the sensor readings with a rule's conditions and counts the number of conditions met. The number of conditions met is referred to as the rule's match score. After the match score has been computed for all rules in the knowledge base, any rule whose match score equals the maximum match score is placed in a firing pool. If the firing pool consists of one rule, then the rule "fires" and specifies the job type's MPP. If multiple rules make it to the firing pool, then conflict resolution must take place. In this event, the rule with the highest strength fires.

Note that even though two rules may have the same match score, this does not mean that they necessarily match the same sensor readings. If this occurs, no attempt is made to rank one rule above the other. Ranking of rules could easily be accomplished by assigning a rank of importance to each sensor. However, this would require that the underlying relationship of the sensors to the problem's solution be known. In many problems, this information may be known and its use might speed the learning process. However, the goal of this research was to construct a learning system that can deal with such uncertainties.

At the end of each simulation trial, the strength of all active rules is adjusted using the Profit Sharing Plan (PSP) [Grefenstette 1988]. There are two ways a rule can become active. When a rule from the firing pool fires and sets a job type's MPP, it becomes active. Additionally, any rule that is a member of the firing pool whose action agrees with the rule that fired, also becomes active. This information is recorded in a trace report as decisions are made in the simulated environment (Fig. 1). A rule's strength is defined as

$$\text{Strength}(\text{Rule}_i) = \mu_i - \sigma_i,$$

where μ_i denotes the estimate of the mean pay-off that will be awarded by the critic if Rule_i is used during a simulated trial, and σ_i denotes the estimate of the standard deviation of the pay-off. In order for a rule to have high strength, it must also have low variance. Therefore, it seems reasonable to resolve rule firing conflicts by selecting the rule with the highest strength, because its use has more consistently demonstrated the most success.

The PSP adjusts a rule's estimated mean and standard deviation of the pay-off by distributing the pay-off received from the critic. It does this by subtracting a fraction of a rule's estimated mean pay-off and adding the same fraction of the pay-off received from the critic back to the rule's estimated mean pay-off. The estimate of the variance is adjusted similarly. Pay-off is distributed as follows:

$$\mu_i = (1 - C)\mu_i + CP, \text{ and}$$
$$\sigma_i^2 = (1 - C)\sigma_i^2 + C(\mu_i - P)^2,$$

where the constant C denotes the fractional adjustment (PSP rate) and P denotes the level of pay-off received from the critic. The result is that if a rule's strength overestimates the pay-off, its strength will be reduced; and if the rule's strength underestimates the pay-off, its strength will be increased. Grefenstette [1988] has shown that the PSP computes a time-weighted estimate of the expected pay-off that will be received at the end of a trial if the rule fires.

2.3 Unsupervised Learner Component

The genetic algorithm is the backbone of the Unsupervised Learner Component used to generate new populations of plans. An outline of the GA designed for GARDS follows:

1. Randomly generate an initial population of m plans, plan, for i = 1, 2, ..., m-1, m.

2. For each plan$_i$, compute and save a measure of its utility (PU$_i$) based on the pay-off awarded by the model critic from the trial runs.

3. Compute the minimum acceptable level of performance (MALP) a plan must achieve.

4. For each plan$_i$, adjust its utility as follows:
   If (PU$_i$ - MALP) < 0 Then PU$_i$ = 0
   Else PU$_i$ = PU$_i$ - MALP.

5. For each plan, compute its selection probability defined by

$$P(Plan_i) = \frac{PU_i}{\sum\limits_{j=1}^{m} PU_j} \,.$$

6. Select plans from the population via the selection probability distribution and apply genetic operators. Replace the existing population with the resulting offspring to form a new population of plausible plans. Return to Step 2.

In Step 1 of the GA, an initial population of plans is created by randomly generating rules for each plan. Initial rules need to be somewhat general in nature because if the rules are too specific (conditional ranges are too narrow), then few conditions will match the sensor values early in the learning phase. If this happens, there would be little correlation between the IF condition of a rule and the resulting success (or failure) gained by its use.

In Step 2 of the GA, a plan's performance is determined through simulation trials. Multiple trials are conducted using each plan to control the selection of MPPs and each plan's utility is computed as the average pay-off received from the critic during the trials. After the measure of utility has been computed for all plans, it is used in Step 3 of the GA to compute the minimum acceptable level of performance (MALP). MALP is computed by taking the mean utility of the population of plans from Step 2 and subtracting one standard deviation. If a plan does not meet the MALP, it is assigned a fitness of zero. Thus, the probability of the plan being selected for reproduction is zero in Step 5.

In Step 6, plans are randomly selected for reproduction via the selection probability distribution determined in Step 5. Therefore, plans with higher utilities are more likely to be selected than those with lower utilities. Plans are selected two at a time and idealized genetic operators crossover and mutation are applied to generate two new offspring plans. This process continues until the population is completely renewed, at which time the algorithm returns to Step 2. Each idealized genetic operator is discussed below.

Since the CMS domain consists of multiple decision-makers (different part types) that must cooperate in order to achieve good performance, a crossover operator had to be designed that would not stifle the cooperative spirit that may develop among the part types. Because, to some extent, part types compete for the same resources, care had to be taken to reduce the greedy behavior of a single part type. First, the critic was designed not to favor any one part type. Second, the crossover operator is restricted so that no rules from one part type mix with rules from another part type. For example, the CMS may be better suited for producing part type 1 than part type 2. If so, then part type 1 strategies may not be appropriate strategies for part type 2. Essentially, the crossover process is performed independently for each part type in a parallel fashion (Figure 3).

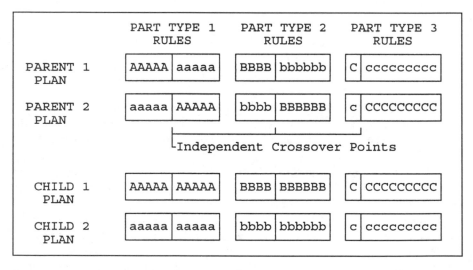

Fig. 3. The parallel crossover operator used in GARDS.

The four step crossover operator is shown in Figure 4. The crossover operator operates at the plan level, swapping rules between two parent plans to create two new plans. First, two parent plans are selected and the most successful trial run for each parent is located. Second, the rules that fired during this trial, as logged in the trace report, are grouped together (clustered) within each parent. The idea is to place rules that work well together in close proximity to one another to increase their chance of staying together as a group during crossover. Third, the positions at which the rules are listed in the parent are randomly adjusted while keeping the clustered rules together. Moving them about reduces any bias that may be created during crossover if they always appeared in the first positions. Fourth, the parallel crossover operator is applied. Although not shown in Figure 4, steps two, three, and four are done for each part type in a parallel fashion.

STEP 1: LOCATE MOST SUCCESSFUL TRIAL

<table>
<tr><td colspan="3" align="center">PARENT 1</td><td colspan="2" align="center">PARENT 2</td></tr>
<tr><td>TRIAL</td><td>TRACE
REPORT</td><td>PAY-OFF</td><td>TRACE
REPORT</td><td>PAY-OFF</td></tr>
<tr><td>1</td><td>R_1 R_2 R_7 R_4</td><td>505</td><td>r_1 r_4 r_3 r_2</td><td>800[*]</td></tr>
<tr><td>2</td><td>R_2 R_1 R_4 R_5</td><td>800</td><td>r_7 r_2 r_6 r_2</td><td>750</td></tr>
<tr><td>3</td><td>R_1 R_2 R_4 R_3</td><td>675</td><td>r_1 r_1 r_1 r_1</td><td>505</td></tr>
<tr><td>4</td><td>R_1 R_2 R_3 R_4</td><td>900[*]</td><td>r_8 r_2 r_2 r_5</td><td>680</td></tr>
</table>

STEP 2: CLUSTER RULES

PARENT 1: R_1 R_2 R_3 R_4 R_5 R_6 R_7 R_8
PARENT 2: r_1 r_4 r_3 r_2 r_5 r_6 r_7 r_8

STEP 3: RANDOMLY ADJUST RULE POSITIONS

PARENT 1: R_7 R_8 R_1 R_2 R_3 R_4 R_5 R_6
PARENT 2: r_5 r_6 r_7 r_8 r_1 r_4 r_3 r_2

STEP 4: PERFORM CROSSOVER

CROSS SITE = 3

CHILD 1: R_7 R_8 R_1 | r_8 r_1 r_4 r_3 r_2
CHILD 2: r_5 r_6 r_7 | R_2 R_3 R_4 R_5 R_6

Fig. 4. The four step crossover operator used in GARDS.

Note that the most successful trial run is not always used in the first step of the crossover operator. Before crossover begins, the trials are ranked from most successful to least successful. When a parent is selected for the first time, GARDS uses the results from the most successful trial. If the same parent is selected a second time (high performing parents can be selected multiple times), the second most successful trial is used, and so on. This technique was adopted because some trial runs may be easier to manage than others. For example, trials with longer time between job arrivals may be easier to manage than those with shorter time between job arrivals. Therefore, if the results of the best trial are always used, GARDS may only learn to deal with the easier case.

As with most GA's reported in the literature, the mutation operator is infrequently applied, leaving the crossover operator with the most responsibility for conducting the search. The probability of applying the mutation operator is the probability that a rule will be mutated. If a rule is marked for mutation, the mutation operator randomly selects one of the rule's conditions or the rule's action to mutate. Therefore, it might change a rule's condition from ($2 \leq$ Cell 1 Queue ≤ 7) to ($9 \leq$ Cell 1 Queue ≤ 12) or an action from (use MPP 10) to (use MPP 12), for example.

The final genetic operator designed for GARDS is called creep, in which the operator makes very small changes to a rule. The operator searches for rule duplication within an offspring after crossover and mutation have been conducted. If duplicate rules are discovered, the creep operator is invoked to make a small change to one of the rules. The first step is to randomly select a rule condition to modify. If the condition is to be generalized, a new condition is created by slightly expanding the range. If the condition is to be specialized, the new range is created by slightly contracting the range.

In summary, the crossover operator operates at the plan level, swapping rules between two parent plans to create two new plans. Mutation and creep function at the rule level, modifying existing rules to create new rules.

3   Results

In this CMS control application, GARDS performs a search for optimal (or near optimal) decision rules. Its search space is defined as all decision rules that can be constructed using the available sensors and actions. Given that sensors 1-4 can take on 31 values each, sensors 5-7 can take on 11 values each, and sensors 8-12 can take on 111 values each, 1.866×10^{17} discrete sensor vectors could be formed as rule conditions. Coupling them with one of the three available actions (MPPs) that part type 1 can select, 5.598×10^{17} part type 1 rules could be formed. Similarly there are 7.464×10^{17} possible part type 2 rules and 5.598×10^{17} part type 3 rules. In fact, the search space is even larger, since GARDS' objective is not only to find a set of useful rules for each part type, but to find a set of useful rules for each part type that cooperates with the other part types in order to maximize total system performance.

Experiments were conducted with GARDS using GATEWAY 2000 4DX2-66V personal computers. The simulation model was developed using SLAMSYSTEM, and Pascal was used to implement the machine learning components. In this experiment, GARDS was allowed to learn for 200 generations. The population consists of 100 plans with each plan containing 90 rules (30 rules for each part type). Each plan is evaluated five times (five trials) during the course of a generation. The results of these five independent trials are averaged and recorded as the plan's utility. In each trial, approximately 125 parts are processed.

Additional GARDS parameter settings were as follows. The probabilities of crossover and mutation are 0.80 and 0.01, respectively. The probability that the creep operator will specialize a rule is 0.40 and the probability that it will generalize a rule is 0.60. The Profit Sharing Plan Rate is 0.01.

GARDS' strategy became apparent early in the learning process. It favored routing part type 1 and part type 3 to their preferred cells (cell 1 and cell 3, respectively), regardless of the state of the CMS. However, by the end of the 200 generations, the top performing plan always routed part type 1 to its preferred cell and for part type 3 it sometimes used the alternate cell (cell 4). For part type 2, GARDS' strategy seemed to be to route jobs to either the preferred cell (cell 2) or to the remainder cell (cell 4). Between these two cells, GARDS seemed to select the one with the fewest number of jobs waiting in its queue. A study of the rules in the best plans suggested the following heuristic:

- Entries to the CMS by part type 1, select MPP 10 (cell 1).
- Entries to the CMS by part type 2:
    IF (cell 2 queue $\leq$ cell 4 queue) THEN select MPP 20 (cell 2)
        Else select MPP 22 (cell 4).
- Entries to the CMS by part type 3, select MPP 30 (cell 3).

Figure 5 shows GARDS' learning curve for this problem. The data for the figure was produced by averaging the results of two replications (the experiment was conducted twice) after every tenth generation. Notice that both the average utility of the population and the population's best performing plan indicate rapid learning during the first 50 generations. Afterwards, the rate of learning slows and begins to cycle. This may indicate that this strategy is near the optimal control strategy for the CMS. Since part type 1 and part type 3 represent the lowest loads, it seems reasonable to route them to their preferred cells and use the extra capacity of the remainder cell for the production of part type 2.

The cycling effect can most likely be attributed to the fact that GARDS is presented with a potentially new set of five independent simulation trials from one generation to the next. In other words, the same five trials are not always used from one generation to the next. Therefore, the utility of a converged population will change from one generation to the next due to the stochastic nature of the manufacturing system (there are variations from one trial to the next in the number of arriving part types, operation processing times, and machine failure and repair times). This creates a good deal of noise for the algorithm but it helps to ensure that only robust plans survive.

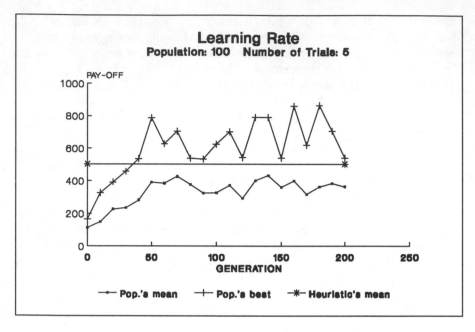

Fig. 5. Part types rate of learning in selecting routes through the system using GARDS.

Figure 5 also illustrates the mean level of performance of the heuristic, noted above, suggested by GARDS. The heuristic was coded and its performance was measured over 200 independent simulation runs. Table 1 further details the performance of the heuristic. On average, the heuristic's performance is very close to the defined management objective of not having more than ten percent of the jobs late for any part type. Also, note that the magnitude of the standard deviation of the pay-off characterizes the dynamic nature of the simulated CMS (which commonly occurs in practice).

The heuristic was compared with the common practice of always routing parts to their preferred cells. For this CMS, fixing a job's route through its preferred cell generated a mean pay-off of 228.6 with a standard deviation of 192.0, based on the same 200 independent simulation runs used above. Using the evolved routing heuristic more than doubled the pay-off.

It is interesting to note that, after about 40 generations, the population's best plan consistently received an average pay-off (based on the five trials) that was above the heuristic's mean level of performance. This is due to GARDS' use of the sensors that report the time since the last machine failure information which is not considered by the heuristic. Using these sensors, GARDS began developing rules that avoided selecting MPPs that used machines that had not failed recently. Additionally, the plan sometimes used the remainder cell for part type 3.

	PART TYPE 1 mean(std.dev.)	PART TYPE 2 mean(std.dev.)	PART TYPE 3 mean(std.dev.)
Completed Early	32.16 (6.69)	47.29 (7.64)	32.66 (6.15)
Completed Late	4.55 (7.98)	5.03 (7.39)	4.42 (7.35)
Late ——— (Early+Late)	0.11 (0.18)	0.09 (0.12)	0.11 (0.17)

Heuristic's mean pay-off was 503.2 with a standard deviation of 388.1.

Table 1. Performance of the Heuristic Based on 200 Observations

4   Summary and Conclusions

The results of applying GARDS to the control of a hypothetical manufacturing system are very encouraging. The control strategies developed by GARDS were straightforward, met the management objective for the manufacturing system, and promoted a high degree of cooperation between the competing part types. In light of developing control policies for manufacturing systems, the simpler the strategy, the easier it is to implement. Given that GARDS has no way of *knowing,* or measuring, whether a strategy is easy or difficult, this speaks well for the approach.

GARDS' ability to deal with the complexity of multiple decision-making agents illustrates that machine learning techniques based on genetic algorithms can be used in domains with multiple competing agents that use high-level rule languages to represent control knowledge. The research is being extended to include additional decision-making agents. The goal is to develop a machine learning technique that allows machines, parts, material handling devices, etc., to collectively evolve behaviors that result in the efficient operation of the complete manufacturing system.

References

Ben-Arieh, D.; Moodie, C. L.; Chi-Chung, C. (1988): Control Methodology for FMS. IEEE Journal of Robotics and Automation 4: 53-59

Bowden, R. O. (1992): Genetic Algorithm Based Machine Learning Applied to the Dynamic Routing of Discrete Parts. Doctor of Philosophy Dissertation, Department of Industrial Engineering, Mississippi State University.

Chandra, J.; Talavage, J. (1991): Intelligent Dispatching for Flexible Manufacturing. International Journal of Production Research 29: 2259-2278

Grefenstette, J. J. (1990): Learning Sequential Decision Rules Using Simulation Models and Competition. Machine Learning 5: 355-381

Grefenstette, J. J. (1988): Credit Assignment in Rule Discovery Systems Based on Genetic Algorithms. Machine Learning 3: 225-245

Lewis, W.; Barash, M. M.; Solberg, J. J. (1987): Computer Integrated Manufacturing System Control: A Data Flow Approach. Journal of Manufacturing Systems 6: 177-191

Maley, J. G. (1988): Managing the Flow of Intelligent Parts. Robotics and Computer-Integrated Manufacturing 4: 525-530

McKay, K. N.; Safayeni, F. R.; Buzacott, J. A. (1988): Job-Shop Scheduling Theory: What Is Relevant? Interfaces 18: 84-90

Shaw, M. J. (1989): A Pattern-Directed Approach to Flexible Manufacturing: A Framework for Intelligent Scheduling, Learning, and Control. The International Journal of Flexible Manufacturing Systems: 121-144

Srihari, K.; Greene, T. J. (1988): Alternate Routings in Capp Implementation in a FMS. Computers in Industrial Engineering 15: 41-50

Determining the Optimal Network Partition and Kanban Allocation in JIT Production Lines

Markus Ettl and Markus Schwehm

IMMD VII, Universität Erlangen-Nürnberg, D-91058 Erlangen, Germany

Abstract. One way to reduce costs in high volume production lines is to smooth and balance the material flow by means of controlled inventories. Kanban systems are now being implemented worldwide due to their ability of reducing inventories and production lead times. This paper addresses two fundamental design issues in kanban systems and presents an efficient heuristic method for designing such systems. An analytical method for modelling kanban systems and a general-purpose genetic algorithm are integrated in a heuristic design methodology which evaluates the performance of kanban systems using alternative network partitions and allocations of kanbans. As we demonstrate, the heuristic method provides a useful procedure to evaluate the impact of design alternatives and can thus serve as a rough-cut decision support tool which assists managers in the planning of large-scale manufacturing systems.

Keywords. Just-in-time, kanban systems, queueing networks, genetic algorithms.

1 Introduction

The manufacturing industries have seen a dramatic change away from high product throughput and high capacity loads towards lower production lead times and work-in-process inventory. Pull-type production control aims at reducing costs through keeping the work-in-process inventory at a minimum level and thus improving the company's ability to adapt to changes, e.g. demand and production fluctuations. Kanban systems are often used to implement the pull-type control in production systems, see for example Schonberger [1982] and Hall [1983]. The success of Toyota's kanban system [Monden 1983] has motivated considerable research of practitioners and analysts in order to gain a better understanding of the operation of pull systems.

In this paper, a pull-type production line is considered which is composed of a sequence of production stages performing various process steps on parts. Each production stage consists of several work stations in tandem. The flow of parts through the overall facility is controlled through a combined push/pull control policy which is implemented by means of kanbans. A push-type policy is used to produce parts within each production stage. Between different production stages, however, the parts are pulled according to the rate at which parts are consumed by the downstream stages. Two well-known kanban systems appear as special cases of the above kanban control policy, i.e., the minimum blocking policy described by Mitra and Mitrani [1990] and the Constant Work-in-Process (CONWIP) system proposed by Spearman et al. [1990].

In order to effectively operate such systems, a design methodology is needed to assist managers in solving the following production plant configuration problems [Tayur 1992]:

Network Partitioning Problem: Given a sequence of work stations, how many production stages should the production line be divided up into? In addition, how many work stations should be assigned to each individual production stage?

Kanban Allocation Problem: Given a partition of the production line, how many kanbans should be assigned to each production stage such that a desired product throughput is achieved while the inventory carrying costs are minimized.

The purpose of this paper is to develop a design methodology which produces reasonably accurate solutions to the above configuration problems. Such a methodology is likely to facilitate the design of kanban systems and should also enhance our understanding of their behavior.

In our methodology, the optimal network partition and kanban allocation is determined from a global optimization model in such a way that the average work-in-process inventory is minimized while a predetermined throughput rate must be guaranteed. In favor of a computationally efficient design process, we use a closed queueing network representation of kanban systems which is evaluated using an approximate analytical method. A general-purpose genetic algorithm package is then used in order to simultaneously determine the optimal network partition and kanban allocation. Applying the genetic algorithm is straightforward, since the output of the modelling process can directly be used as the objective function. We provide numerical tests which demonstrate that the solutions produced by the heuristic method are reasonably accurate and they can be obtained with an acceptable amount of computational effort. The heuristic is well-suited in practice to quickly explore alternative configurations and can thus serve as a rough-cut decision support tool for production planning in large-scale manufacturing systems.

Previous research in this area often uses simulation to study various performance and implementation aspects of pull systems. Chu and Shih [1992] provide a good survey on simulation studies of JIT production systems. Analytical models of kanban systems have been developed only recently, see for example Deleersnyder et al. [1989], Mitra and Mitrani [1990], and Di Mascolo et al. [1992]. The issue of determining the number of kanbans has been addressed by Davis and Stubitz [1987] and Philipoom et al. [1987] by means of simulation. Jothishankar and Wang [1992] developed a stochastic Petri net model to find the optimal kanban allocation in a two-station kanban system. Siha [1994] derived a continuous time Markov model to investigate various kanban allocation patterns for up to five-station kanban systems. In a recent paper, Chang and Yih [1994] described a simulated annealing approach to determining lot sizes and kanban allocations in a generic kanban system.

At this time, little attention has been devoted to the network partitioning problem. Altough the network partitioning problem is related to the assembly line balancing problem [Baybars 1986], the requirement that production stages consist of several work stations, rather than just one, prohibits the use of line balancing results directly. Johri [1992] discussed a shop floor control problem (without kanbans) in semiconductor wafer fabrication and proposed to partition the set of process steps to be performed on the wafer into individual stages called zones. The optimal network partition is determined using a dynamic programming formulation of the problem. Tayur [1992] studied the partitioning problem in serial kanban systems from a theoretical and qualitative point of view. For practical purposes, it is evident that powerful heuristics are necessary in order to solve problems of realistic size. The present paper is a step in this direction.

The remainder of this paper is organized as follows: in Section 2, we describe the operation of kanban systems, discuss the design problem under study, and give an overview of our heuristic optimization approach. The approximation algorithm used to evaluate the performance of kanban systems is reviewed in Section 3. The adaptation of the problem to a genetic algorithm package is described in Section 4. Section 5 provides numerical experiments and Section 6 concludes the paper.

2 Kanban-Controlled Production Lines

The production system studied here is a tandem network of N work stations which are distributed among S production stages as shown in Figure 2.1.

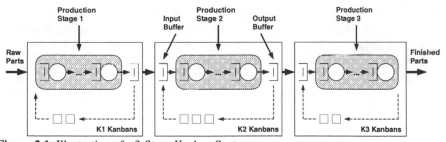

Figure 2.1. Illustration of a 3-Stage Kanban System.

Each production stage is assumed to consist of one or several work stations in tandem, each equipped with an unlimited local buffer to store unfinished parts. In production stage i , there are K_i kanbans and N_i work stations. A part must acquire a free kanban in order to enter production stage i , which is attached to the part as long as it is in that stage. When the processing of a part has been completed in production stage i , the finished part is moved to an output buffer where it waits for admission to the downstream stage (stage $i+1$). The kanban associated with a finished part is detached as soon as the part is withdrawn by the downstream stage.

The unattached kanban is then returned without delay to the input buffer where it serves as a pull signal for the upstream stage (stage $i-1$). Notice that, due to the kanban control policy, the inventory of production stage i can never exceed K_i.

The kanban system produces only one type of parts. Furthermore, it is assumed that an unlimited supply of raw parts is available at the first stage, and an inexhaustible demand for finished parts is present at the output of the final stage. As a consequence, no input buffer is required at the first production stage, and no output buffer is required at the final stage of the production system. The above assumptions are realistic in cases where the demand for finished products is large relative to the plant capacity, that is, the company can sell all it can produce. They are also valid in cases where the plant capacity is limited for strategic purposes below the actual level of demand.

On each work station, a certain amount of time is required to process a part. If the processing times are equal at all work stations, the line is called *homogeneous*; otherwise, the line is called *non-homogeneous*. In real-world production systems, processing times are essentially constant; however, it is often the case that the processing equipment is unreliable. In semiconductor fabrication lines, e.g., machine availablities of 60-75% are quite common [Johri 1993]. Such phenomena in turn result in a highly stochastic production environment. We shall therefore represent processing times as independent and identically distributed random variables in this paper.

2.1 Statement of the Problem

The problem of determining the appropriate network partition and kanban allocation can be stated as an optimization problem where the objective is to minimize the inventory carrying costs and the constraint is the desired throughput rate. Since the inventory carrying costs are directly associated with work-in-process inventory, it is reasonable to choose the average work-in-process as the objective function. The overall design problem can then be stated as a nonlinear integer optimization problem as follows:

$$
\begin{aligned}
\min \quad & w(N_1,\ldots,N_S,K_1,\ldots,K_S) \\
\text{s.t.} \quad & \sum_{i=1}^{S} N_i = N, \quad N_i \geq 1 \text{ and integer} \\
& \sum_{i=1}^{S} K_i \leq K, \quad K_i \geq 1 \text{ and integer} \\
& f(N_1,\ldots,N_S,K_1,\ldots,K_S) \geq f_0
\end{aligned}
\tag{1}
$$

where $w(.)$ denotes the average work-in-process inventory and $f(.)$ denotes the throughput rate of a kanban system with the network partition $N_1,\ldots,N_S$ and the kanban allocation $K_1,\ldots,K_S$. The desired throughput rate f_0 is a strategic decision variable that should be selected by management so as to meet the long-term requirements of the company.

The above formulation of the optimization problem has an additional constraint on the maximum number of kanbans allowed, K, which may be due to costs related to providing buffers or floor space restrictions. Considering the issue of partitioning the production plant, it is assumed that the number of stages, S, is predetermined by the nature of the production process or by other management considerations. Various further constraints on the kanban number, the work station buffer capacities, or the network partition can be included in a straightforward manner.

2.2 Heuristic Design Methodology

The design problem stated in (1) is a combinatorial optimization problem with integer decision variables. Given N work stations, S production stages, and K kanbans, the search space has

$$ST = \binom{N-1}{S-1} \times \sum_{i=S}^{K} \binom{i}{S}$$

different states. It is obvious that a full enumeration is feasible only for production lines of moderate size and small number of kanbans. In addition, notice that design problem (1) is a *structural* optimization problem in which one must first decide the system topology, that is, the size of the various production stages, before determining the allocation of kanbans. Because conventional optimization approaches such as gradient search techniques are in general considered inappropriate for such problems, we advocate the use of a genetic algorithm.

Figure 2.2 is adapted from Biethahn and Nissen [1994] and illustrates our design methodology. In this approach, the performance of kanban systems (the throughput rate and work-in-process inventory) is evaluated using an approximate analytical method while the optimization process is determined through a genetic algorithm.

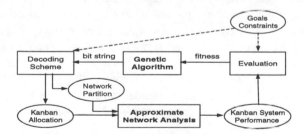

Figure 2.2. Illustration of the Heuristic Design Methodology.

A genetic algorithm is a general-purpose heuristic search and optimization technique which is based on biological evolution, see Goldberg [1989] for an introduction. Genetic algorithms, as well as evolutionary algorithms in general, have been applied recently to combinatorial optimization problems in various domains of management science, see [Nissen 1993] and [Bäck 1992]. They are sufficiently general to cope with arbitrarily constrained search spaces of the decision variables which typically arise in real-world applications.

3   Approximate Analysis of Kanban Systems

A major difficulty is that the performance metrics of kanban systems do not have closed form solutions. As numerical techniques or simulation often become computationally intractable, in particular for problems of realistic size, we have decided to use an approximate procedure to obtain estimates of the performance metrics. We use the approximation algorithm described in [Ettl 1993] to solve the kanban systems under consideration. The algorithm has been shown to provide fairly accurate results in many cases and requires low computation times (less than one second on a Sun Sparc Station 10). Let us briefly describe the procedure.

The approximation algorithm decomposes the original kanban system into a set of subnetworks representing the individual production stages and solves each subnetwork in isolation. The subnetworks are extended by additional queues to account for delays due to blocking and starvation. Blocking occurs if at the instant of completion of a part at production stage i , the input buffer of production stage $i+1$ does not contain any free kanban. Starvation occurs if at the instant of completion of a part at production stage i , the output buffer of production stage $i-1$ does not contain a new part. Since the service time distributions at the additional queues are not known in advance, an iterative algorithm must be used to establish performance metrics of the entire kanban system.

Let us denote the subnetworks by $T(i)$ for $i = 1,...,S$. Each subnetwork $T(i)$, $i = 2,...,S-1$, consists of N_i work stations, an additional *upstream* queue $S_u(i)$ representing the part of the system upstream of stage i , and an additional *downstream* queue $S_d(i)$ representing the part of the system downstream of stage i . The sojourn time at queue $S_u(i)$ models the amount of time that an unattached kanban remains in the input buffer of stage i until a finished part is supplied by stage $i-1$. In a similar way, the sojourn time at queue $S_d(i)$ models the amount of time that a finished part remains in the output buffer of stage i until it is withdrawn by stage $i+1$. As an unlimited supply of raw parts and an unlimited finished-parts demand is assumed, no upstream queue is present in subnetwork $T(1)$ and no downstream queue is present in subnetwork $T(S)$. The decomposition is illustrated in Figure 3.1 for a 3-stage kanban system. Notice that the number of customers in subnetwork $T(i)$ is given by the number of kanbans K_i, respectively.

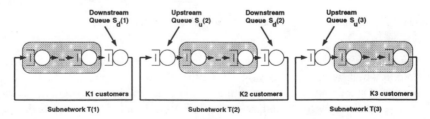

Figure 3.1. Decomposition of the 3-Stage Kanban System.

The approximation is based upon estimating the first two moments of the service time that a job experiences at the additional queues. For that purpose, we condition on the position of customers in subnetwork $T(i)$. To obtain a consistent numbering scheme, we shall use the subscript 0 to denote quantities related to the upstream queues, and the subscript $N_i + 1$ to denote quantities related to the downstream queues as necessary. Let $L_j(i)$ be the number of customers present at work station j in subnetwork $T(i)$ and define

$$\sigma_{n,m}(i) = P\left(L_m(i) > 0, \sum_{p=n}^{m} L_p(i) = K_i \right) \tag{2}$$

for $n, m = 0, 1, \ldots, N_i + 1$ and $n \leq m$. The quantity $\sigma_{n,m}(i)$ denotes the probability that there is at least one customer in service at work station m and all K_i customers are present, that is, either waiting or in service, at work stations n through m.

Denote $b_j(i)$ and $b_j^{(2)}(i)$ the first and second moment of the processing time distribution at work station j in subnetwork $T(i)$ for $i = 1, \ldots, S$ and $j = 1, \ldots, N_i$. Let $b_u(i+1)$ and $b_u^{(2)}(i+1)$ denote the first and second moment of the service time at queue $S_u(i+1)$. Using the probabilities $\sigma_{n,m}(i)$ defined above, we can express the first two moments of the service time at queue $S_u(i+1)$ entirely in terms of quantities related to subnetwork $T(i)$. Conditioning on the position of customers in subnetwork $T(i)$ and applying the law of total probability, we get

$$b_u(i+1) = \sum_{j=0}^{N_i} \sigma_{0,j}(i)\left[\hat{b}_j(i) + \sum_{p=j+1}^{N_i} b_p(i) \right]$$

$$b_u^{(2)}(i+1) = \sum_{j=0}^{N_i} \sigma_{0,j}(i)\left[\hat{b}_j^{(2)}(i) + 2\hat{b}_j(i)\sum_{q=j+1}^{N_i} b_q(i) + \sum_{p=j+1}^{N_i}\left(b_p^{(2)}(i) + 2b_p(i)\sum_{q=p+1}^{N_i} b_q(i) \right) \right]$$

$$\tag{3}$$

where $\hat{b}_j(i)$ and $\hat{b}_j^{(2)}(i)$ denote the first and second moment of the residual service time at queue j in subnetwork $T(i)$. Consider now queue $S_d(i-1)$ and let $b_d(i-1)$ and $b_d^{(2)}(i-1)$ denote the first and second moment of the corresponding service time. Proceeding in a completely analoguous fashion as above, we get

$$b_d(i-1) = \sum_{j=1}^{N_i+1} \sigma_{1,j}(i)\left[\hat{b}_j(i) + \sum_{p=j+1}^{N_i+1} b_p(i) \right]$$

$$b_d^{(2)}(i-1) = \sum_{j=1}^{N_i+1} \sigma_{1,j}(i)\left[\hat{b}_j^{(2)}(i) + 2\hat{b}_j(i)\sum_{q=j+1}^{N_i+1} b_q(i) + \sum_{p=j+1}^{N_i+1}\left(b_p^{(2)}(i) + 2b_p(i)\sum_{q=p+1}^{N_i+1} b_q(i) \right) \right]$$

$$\tag{4}$$

Assuming for a moment that the service time parameters of the additional queues are known, we can solve any subnetwork $T(i)$ using standard approximation techniques for general closed queueing networks.

To compute the performance of the entire kanban system, a two-pass algorithm is developed. The algorithm is initialized by setting the downstream parameters of the subnetworks $T(i)$ to some starting values. The main loop consists of a forward pass moving from stage one to stage $S-1$, and a backward pass moving in turn from stage S to stage two. On the forward pass, it is assumed that the downstream parameters of subnetwork $T(i)$ are known from the previous iteration of the backward pass. The moments of the service time at the upstream queue of subnetwork $T(i+1)$ are revised according to equation (3). On the backward pass, it is assumed that the upstream parameters of subnetwork $T(i)$ are known from the previous iteration of the forward pass. The moments of the service time at the downstream queue of subnetwork $T(i-1)$ are then revised according to equation (4). The probabilities $\sigma_{n,m}(i)$ required in (3) and (4) can be calculated directly from the analysis of subnetwork $T(i)$ once we assume that stages operate independent of each other.

The algorithm iterates between the two passes until an appropriate convergence criterion is met, e.g., if the difference of the throughput rates obtained in the forward and backward pass is less than a given tolerance level $(< 10^{-5})$. The performance metrics of interest of the kanban system can then be derived from the performance metrics of the subnetworks.

4 Genetic Algorithms

The basic idea of genetic algorithms is to maintain a population of candidate solutions which are modified at random, while selective pressure forces the population to increase in quality. Similar to other random search heuristics, the genetic algorithm provides mutation as random modification operator, but here the mutation operates on the binary representation (bit string) of a given solution by inverting randomly chosen bits. A second random modification operator is especially useful in the case of combinatorial optimization: the crossover. Two candidate solutions are chosen from the population to recombine their properties. Again, this operator operates directly on the bit strings of the candidate solutions (parents) by simply concatenating alternate substrings.

Since the genetic algorithm operates blindly on bit strings, a general-purpose genetic algorithm can be applied to the given problem. We used a genetic algorithm package similar to the one described in Schwehm [1993]. The code is written in C++ and runs on Sun workstations and PCs. A distributed implementation of the genetic algorithm to be run on a cluster of workstations is also available [Schwehm 1994]. To apply the genetic algorithm, it remains to define a suitable bit string representation for the candidate solutions.

The genetic algorithm will work with any bit string representation, provided the whole search space can be represented and the modification operators introduce enough variance into the population [Atmar 1994]. Therefore, a working prototype of the design methodology can be implemented rapidly. For an efficient implementation, however, the bit string representation must be chosen carefully, because it significantly influences the speed of convergence of the genetic search. The binary representation is implemented by a decoding scheme, which serves as an interface between genetic algorithm and approximation method as shown in Figure 2.2.

4.1 Standard Coding Scheme

The standard coding scheme for the stated problem maps numbers of kanbans and numbers of work stations to production stages. The bit string is interpreted as gray coded integer vector $(N_1, K_1, ..., N_S, K_S)$. Values N_i, K_i belonging to stage i are placed in pairs on the bit string to reduce the disruptive effect of the crossover operator. The constraints for the N_i and K_i from (1) are introduced by an intelligent decoding scheme similar to voting, which guarantees valid solutions. This decoding scheme uses a bit string of length $S \times \lceil \log_2 N + \log_2 K \rceil$, where $\lceil x \rceil$ denotes the smallest integer larger or equal to x.

Our experience from sample runs using this decoding scheme, however, is that the genetic algorithm ceases to optimize the network partition at an early stage of the optimization run. An explanation for this behavior is that a suboptimal candidate solution decreases in quality if the network partition is changed without a corresponding change of the kanban allocation. Since it is very unlikely that the mutation operator will change the kanban allocation and network partition at the same time, the genetic search almost degenerates to a kanban allocation optimization for the best network partition found in the initial population.

4.2 Alternative Coding Scheme

An alternative coding scheme avoids this problem by first mapping numbers of work stations to production stages, and then *individual* kanbans to work stations. The bit string is divided into two segments: In the first segment, the network partition $(N_1, ..., N_S)$ is coded as in the standard decoding scheme, including a guaranteed fulfilment of the constraints for the N_i from (1). Contrary to the standard coding scheme, in a secon segment each of the K kanbans is assigned to an individual work station or to `nil´, if the kanban is not to be used. The kanban-to-stage allocation is deduced from the kanban-to-station allocation once the network partition from the first segment is known. Obviously, the constraints for the K_i are fulfilled automatically by this decoding scheme. A random change in the network partition segment, e.g. the move of one work station to a neighboring production stage, thus automatically induces a corresponding change in the kanban allocation. This decoding scheme occupies a bit string of length $S \times \lceil \log_2 N \rceil + K \times \lceil \log_2 N \rceil$. Since $K \geq S$, the second decoding scheme in general uses more bits than the standard one.

Using this decoding scheme, the genetic algorithm is able to optimize both network partition and kanban allocation throughout the whole optimization run. We have run many examples with both decoding schemes and have observed that the optimization results were much better with the second decoding scheme, not only with respect to the best solution found but also with respect to convergence speed.

This result – that a longer and thus more redundant bit string representation outperforms a short one – is contradictory to many references in the genetic algorithms literature, where the advice is given to use a representation with as few as possible bits [Goldberg 1989]. For the experiments reported in the following section the second representation scheme was used.

5   Numerical Experiments

We now proceed with numerical experiments in order to study the behavior of the heuristic design method in terms of accuracy and computational efficiency. The genetic algorithm and the analytical method were implemented on a Sun Sparc Station 10. We present here two basic sets of test problems for a 2 work station production line using different processing time distributions and target throughput values. In the first set of experiments (Problems P1-P5), we consider a homogeneous production line in which the processing times at all work stations are exponentially distributed with mean equal to one. In the second set of experiments (Problems P6-P10), we consider a non-homogeneous production line to study the effect of imbalance on our heuristic method. Table 5.1 shows the processing time parameters employed in Problems P6-P10 which are represented in terms of their means b_i and squared coefficients of variation c_i^2. In all experiments, it is assumed that the number of production stages, S, is equal to four, and the maximum number of kanbans allowed, K, is twice the number of work stations, that is, $K = 24$.

Workstation	1	2	3	4	5	6	7	8	9	10	11	12
b_i	0.8	1.0	0.8	0.5	0.6	0.8	1.0	0.6	0.8	0.5	0.8	0.6
c_i^2	0.75	1.0	2.0	0.75	1.0	0.5	2.0	1.0	0.75	1.0	0.75	0.5

Table 5.1. Processing Time Parameters used in Problems P6-P10.

The numerical results presented are based on five independent runs of the genetic algorithm. The five runs differ with respect to the initial population (generation 0) which is selected at random. A population of 64 candidate solutions was used with tournament selection (Size 3) and elitist replacement. A reproduction step consisted of either a mutation with mutation rate 0.01 per bit (with probability 0.9) or a two point crossover (with probability 0.1). The termination condition for the genetic algorithm is fulfilled once a predefined number of 20 generations have been computed, giving a total of 1280 evaluated solutions.

To evaluate the accuracy of the genetic algorithm, an exhaustive search procedure was run for each test problem to find the "optimal" solution (with respect to the approximation method). Table 5.2 compares the solutions found by the genetic algorithm to those obtained from exhaustive search, considering different values of the target throughput f_0. The columns associated with the genetic algorithm represent the average over five runs. The quality of the suboptimal solutions is indicated by the ratio of the work-in-process produced by the genetic algorithm to the optimal one produced by exhaustive search. A total of approximately 1.75×10^6 different evaluations were required for each test problem during the exhaustive search, thereby resulting in computation times of more than 50 hours on a Sun Sparc Station 10.

Problem No.	Target Throughput f_0	Exhaustive Search		Genetic Algorithm		
		Throughput Achieved	WIP Achieved	Throughput Achieved	WIP Achieved	Ratio to Optimal
P1	0.5000	0.5002	10.27	0.5013	10.57	1.029
P2	0.5500	0.5500	12.55	0.5514	12.89	1.027
P3	0.6000	0.6002	15.31	0.6022	15.81	1.032
P4	0.6250	0.6255	17.31	0.6265	17.74	1.024
P5	0.6500	0.6514	19.64	0.6434	19.69	—*
P6	0.6500	0.6502	10.00	0.6520	10.31	1.031
P7	0.7000	0.7001	11.77	0.7009	11.96	1.016
P8	0.7500	0.7501	13.93	0.7551	14.71	1.056
P9	0.7750	0.7759	15.30	0.7776	16.29	1.064
P10	0.8000	0.8040	16.57	0.8055	17.72	1.069

* Target throughput rate not achieved   WIP = work-in-process inventory

Table 5.2. Comparison Between Exhaustive Search and Genetic Algorithm.

It is seen from Table 5.2 that the genetic algorithm performs reasonably well in comparison to exhaustive search. All suboptimal solutions are within 7 percent of optimal for the entire set of problems considered and within 3.8 percent on average. Remarkable is the good quality of the solutions when considering that only 20 generations have been evaluated (less than 0.1% of the entire search space).

We should point out that the termination condition was chosen just to demonstrate that the genetic algorithm converges quickly. There is a potential to obtain better solutions once the number of generations is increased. For the entire set of problems, we performed additional runs in which the number of generations was increased to 80 (roughly 0.3% of the entire search space), resulting in suboptimal solutions within 1.4 percent of optimal on average.

Let us next examine the accuracy of the work-in-process and throughput estimates provided by the approximate analytical method. For that purpose, it is necessary to compute the exact values. Due to lack of any closed-form solution of the performance metrics of kanban systems, a simulation model was implemented using the QNAP2 simulation package [Veran and Poitier 1984]. Table 5.3 reports the differences between the analytical and simulated performance metrics of the "optimal" configurations that were established by exhaustive search. In each case, the simulation model was run with 200,000 jobs, using the independent replication method to obtain simulation point estimates. It can be seen from Table 5.3 that the approximation performs very well in both sets of experiments.

Problem			Throughput Rate			Work-in-Process Inventory		
No.	(N_1,N_2,N_3,N_4)	(K_1,K_2,K_3,K_4)	Approx.	Simul.	Rel. Err.	Approx.	Simul.	Rel. Err.
1a	(5,5,1,1)	(4,6,4,5)	0.5002	0.4818	3.8 %	10.27	10.58	2.9 %
1b	(6,2,1,3)	(6,4,6,6)	0.5500	0.5382	2.2 %	12.55	12.23	2.5 %
1c	(5,2,2,3)	(6,5,7,6)	0.6002	0.5904	1.6 %	15.31	15.17	0.9 %
1d	(3,3,4,2)	(4,6,8,5)	0.6255	0.6175	1.3 %	17.31	16.96	2.1 %
1e	(3,3,2,4)	(5,6,6,7)	0.6514	0.6416	1.5 %	19.64	20.12	2.4 %
2a	(6,4,1,1)	(5,5,5,5)	0.6502	0.6184	5.1 %	10.00	9.56	4.6 %
2b	(6,3,2,1)	(6,5,6,6)	0.7001	0.6656	5.2 %	11.77	11.31	4.1 %
2c	(6,2,1,3)	(7,5,5,7)	0.7501	0.7153	4.8 %	13.93	13.34	4.4 %
2d	(2,4,1,5)	(3,6,5,7)	0.7759	0.7518	3.2 %	15.30	14.94	2.4 %
2e	(2,4,1,5)	(3,7,5,9)	0.8040	0.7705	4.3 %	16.57	15.76	5.1 %

Table 5.3. Comparison Between Simulation and Approximation for Configurations Obtained from Exhaustive Search.

Because of space limitations, we have just presented two sets of examples in this paper. However, the heuristic approach has been tested on numerous other systems of varying degree of complexity. We found that the accuracy of the heuristic is quite satisfactory over a wide range of cases, and the solutions are produced at reasonable computational requirements. The heuristic thus appears to be well-suited to handle complex configuration tasks which may arise in realistic production planning applications.

6   Summary and Conclusions

This paper presented a heuristic design methodology to determine the optimal network partition and kanban allocation in complex production systems. The approach is based on a general-purpose genetic algorithm and an approximate analytical method to evaluate the performance of kanban systems. As the numerical experiments demonstrated, the solutions produced by the heuristic method are reasonably accurate and they can be obtained with an acceptable amount of computational effort. The heuristic is well-suited in practice to quickly explore alternative configurations and kanban settings during the conceptual design phase of the production planning process. One restriction of the proposed methodology is that only suboptimal solutions can be guaranteed. Given the NP-hardness of the underlying nonlinear integer optimization problem, however, a heuristic approach is justified from a practical perspective, in particular if it is intended to solve problems of realistic size. In practice, a rough-cut design is often sufficient, and approximation errors of 10–15% are usually tolerated.

The results of this paper are preliminary and must be confirmed by further study. One way to improve the accuracy of the heuristic method is to employ simulation, rather than an approximation, to evaluate the performance of kanban systems. Combining simulation and optimization, however, usually results in an immense increase of computational requirements which is mainly caused by time consuming simulation runs. To reduce computation times, we are currently integrating simulation into a distributed version of the genetic algorithm package. In any case, it is necessary to find a reasonable trade-off between the desired accuracy of the solutions and additional computational complexity.

Acknowledgements

The authors wish to thank Prof. H. Fromm for valuable suggestions and comments on an early draft of this paper and Thilo Opaterny for implementing the genetic algorithm package.

References

Atmar, W. (1994): Notes on the Simulation of Evolution. IEEE Trans. Neural Networks 5: 130–147

Bäck, T.; Hoffmeister, F.; Schwefel, H.-P. (1992): Applications of Evolutionary Algorithms. Technical Report SYS-2/92, University of Dortmund, Germany

Biethahn, J.; Nissen, V. (1994): Combinations of Simulation and Evolutionary Algorithms in Management Science and Economics. Annals of Operations Research 52: 183–208

Baybars, I. (1986): A Survey of Exact Algorithms for the Simple Assembly Line Balancing Problem. Man. Sci. 32: 909–932

Chang, T.M.; Yih, Y. (1994): Determining the Number of Kanbans and Lotsizes in a Generic Kanban System: a Simulated Annealing Approach. Int. J. Prod. Res. 32: 1991–2004.

Chu, C.H.; Shih, W.L. (1992): Simulation Studies in JIT Production. Int. J. Prod. Res. 30: 2573–22586

Davis, W.J.; Stubitz, S.J. (1987): Configuring a Kanban System Using a Discrete Optimization of Multiple Stochastic Responses. Int. J. Prod. Res. 25: 721–740

Deleersnyder, J.L.; Hodgson, T.J.; Muller, H.; O'Grady, P.J. (1989): Kanban Controlled Pull Systems: An Analytical Approach. Man. Sci. 35: 1079–1091

Di Mascolo, M.; Frein, Y.; Dallery, Y. (1992): Queueing Network Modeling and Analysis of Kanban Systems. 3rd Int. Conf. Computer Integrated Manufacturing. IEEE Computer Society Press

Ettl, M. (1993): An Approximate Method for Evaluating the Performance of Serial Lines with Kanban Control. Technical Report TR 20-93, Universität Erlangen-Nürnberg, Germany

Goldberg, D.E. (1989): Genetic Algorithms in Search, Optimization and Machine Learning. Addison-Wesley

Hall, R.W. (1983): Zero Inventories. Dow-Jones Irvin, Homewood, Illinois.

Johri, P.K. (1992): Optimal Partitions for Shop Floor Control in Semiconductor Wafer Fabrication. Europ. J. Oper. Res. 59: 294–297.

Johri, P.K. (1993): Practical Issues in Scheduling and Dispatching in Semiconductor Fabrication. J. Manufact. Syst. 12: 474–485.

Jothishankar, M.C.; Wang, H.P. (1992): Determination of Optimal Number of Kanbans Using Stochastic Petri Nets. J. Manufact. Syst. 11: 449–461

Monden, Y. (1983): Toyota Production System: Practical Approach to Production Management. Industrial Engineering and Management Press, Norcross, Georgia.

Mitra, D.; Mitrani, I. (1990): Analysis of a Kanban Discipline for Cell Coordination in Production Lines I. Man. Sci. 36: 1548–1566

Nissen, V. (1993): Evolutionary Algorithms in Management Science. European Study Group for Evolutionary Economics (eds.): Papers on Economics & Evolution #9303, Freiburg, Germany

Philipoom, P.R; Rees, L.P.; Taylor III, B.W.; Huang, P.Y. (1987): Dynamically Adjusting the Number of Kanbans in a Just-in-Time Production System Using Estimated Values of Lead Time. IEE Trans.: 199–207

Schonberger, R.J. (1982): Japanese Manufacturing Techniques. The Free Press, New York.

Schwehm, M. (1993):A Massively Parallel Genetic Algorithm on the MasPar MP-1. In: Albrecht, R.F. et al. (eds.): Int. Conf. ANNGA '93. Springer, Wien: 502–507

Schwehm, M.; Opaterny, T. (1994): A Distributed Parallel Genetic Algorithm Package. Working Paper, Universität Erlangen-Nürnberg, Germany

Siha, S. (1994): The Pull Production System: Modelling and Characteristics. Int. J. Prod. Res. 32: 933–949

Spearman, M.L.; Woodruff, D.L.; Hopp, W.J. (1990): CONWIP: A Pull Alternative to Kanban. Int. J. Prod. Res. 28: 879–894

Tayur, S.R. (1992): Properties of Serial Kanban Systems. Queueing Systems 12: 297–318

Veran, M.; Poitier, D. (1984): A Portable Environment for Queueing Systems Modeling. Int. Conf. Modelling Techniques and Tools. North-Holland: 25–63.

On Using Penalty Functions and Multicriteria Optimisation Techniques in Facility Layout

Matthias Krause, Volker Nissen

Abteilung Wirtschaftsinformatik I, Universität Göttingen, Platz der Göttinger Sieben 5, 37073 Göttingen, Germany, vnissen@gwdg.de

Abstract. Constrained optimisation is a research field of great practical relevance. For facility layout problems zoning constraints are typical restrictions. This type of constraint is awkward to deal with using common measures like a tailored solution representation or problem-specific search operators, a repair algorithm or special decoding scheme. Penalty functions are frequently applied in such situations. The general understanding seems to be that well-chosen, graded penalties are better than harsh penalties. We compare different approaches to deal with zoning constraints, and find that laborious finetuning of penalty factors is unnecessary in our application, even when there are only few valid solutions. We also implement two multiobjective optimisation approaches where the minimisation of violated constraints becomes a second objective. One of them employs so called Pareto-selection, the second a best-per-objective selection scheme. The results establish the superiority of the Pareto-selection scheme over the other, when finding an evenly distributed set of efficient (non-dominated) solutions is desired. Both multicriteria techniques are inferior to the other approaches, though, when one is primarily interested in a single valid and good solution.

Keywords. evolution strategy, facility layout, restricted quadratic assignment problem, penalty functions, multicriteria optimisation

1 Introduction

Constrained optimisation problems are frequent in management practice but generally very difficult tasks. Consequently, much research is devoted to coping with various kinds of constraints. Most of the current research in constrained evolutionary optimisation concentrates on Genetic Algorithms. Common measures for incorporating constraints are a tailored solution representation, problem-specific search operators, repair algorithms or special decoding schemes. In contrast, we deal with a combinatorial variant of the Evolution Strategy (ES), and investigate constraints that are awkward to handle using the above measures.

Frequently, in such situations, penalty functions are applied which penalise solutions that fail to respect all constraints.

The general understanding, at least for Genetic Algorithms, seems to be that well-chosen, graded penalties are better than harsh penalties [Richardson et al. 1989]. However, chosing adeqately graded penalty factors may be a laborious task. Moreover, it can lead to penalty factors that depend on the particular problem instance. Graded penalty factors also add complexity to the method - a fact that might affect the acceptance for the entire optimisation concept.

We have experimented with a simple Evolution Strategy on constrained problems of varying complexity in the context of facility layout. Even when only few valid solutions exist, it appears unnecessary in our application to invest much effort in finding nicely graded penalties. We also compare two multicriteria approaches where the number of violated constraints becomes a second objective to be minimised.

The following section illustrates some particular problems in facility layout, our area of application, and describes a set of six testproblems. In section 3 we propose six measures to deal with positive zoning constraints, an important type of restriction in the given context, using an evolutionary approach to facility layout. We build on ideas that were first presented in Nissen and Krause [1994] (see also [Nissen 1994a]). Empirical results, interpretations and conclusions are given in the final section.

2   Modeling Facility Layout

Locating facilities with material flow between them is a difficult layout problem. It is often modelled as a quadratic assignment problem (QAP) [Kusiak and Heragu 1987], one of the toughest combinatorial optimisation problems.

The QAP can be formalised as follows [Burkard 1990]: Given a set $N=\{1,2...n\}$ and real numbers c_{ik}, a_{ik}, b_{ik} for $i,k = 1,2...n$, find a permutation φ of the set N which minimises

$$Z = \sum_{i=1}^{n} c_{i\varphi(i)} + \sum_{i=1}^{n}\sum_{k=1}^{n} a_{ik} b_{\varphi(i),\varphi(k)}$$

where n =   total number of facilities/locations
c_{ij} =   fixed cost of locating facility j at location i
b_{jl} =   flow of material from facility j to facility l
a_{ik} =   cost of transferring a material unit from location i to location k

As a generalisation of the Traveling Salesman Problem, the QAP is NP-hard, and only moderately sized problem instances (approx. $n = 18$) can be solved to optimality with exact algorithms within reasonable time limits. One, therefore, concentrates on developing effective QAP-heuristics.

The QAP is of practical relevance not only in facility layout but also e.g. in machine scheduling and data analysis. But solving the QAP can only be considered a first step to solving real-world problems that frequently involve additional complex and nonlinear constraints. Looking at factory layout as an example, the above QAP-model contains several assumptions, namely:

- The possible locations are specified in advance.
- Machines may be installed at any location.
- They can be independently assigned to locations.
- Accurate material flow and transport cost (distance) data are available.
- Costs vary linearly with distance and material units.
- Single (aggregated) product assumption.
- The location problem can be solved independently of other strategic decisions such as production organisation or choice of transport equipment.

All these assumptions can be questioned in practical applications. For instance, locations may be of unequal size, permitting only a subset of machines to be located at a certain position. The available data on expected material flow might be vague. Fixed costs for material transport can occur. Safety or technical considerations may yield certain assignments invalid. However, few authors have extended the QAP to include such practically relevant constraints so far.

Additionally, one can think of other optimisation criteria than simply minimising some cost-measure. In a multicriteria decision situation aspects like safety or flexibility of a layout as well as environmental objectives might be additional goals.

In this paper, we deal with positive zoning constraints in factory layout problems. These are restrictions on the arrangement of machines. Positive zoning constraints require that certain machines are placed next to each other. This can e.g. be motivated by safety considerations or technical interdependencies between machines. As an example, machines that are operated by the same worker should be placed near each other. Kouvelis et al. [1992] apply Simulated Annealing to a QAP with few zoning constraints and call the resulting model restricted QAP (RQAP). We adopt the term RQAP but develop our own, more demanding set of testproblems.

Our starting point are the well-known QAP instances by Nugent et al. [1968] with $n=15$ (Nug15) and $n=30$ (Nug30) facilities/locations. Without loss of generality, we assume a 6×3 matrix of locations for Nug15 and a 6×5 matrix for Nug30 (figure 1). Machines may be neighbouring each other in vertical or horizontal direction to meet the zoning constraints.

To produce RQAPs of varying complexity, 5 to $n-1$ positive zoning constraints are then added, resulting in six testproblems. The numbers in brackets refer to machines that must be placed next to each other.

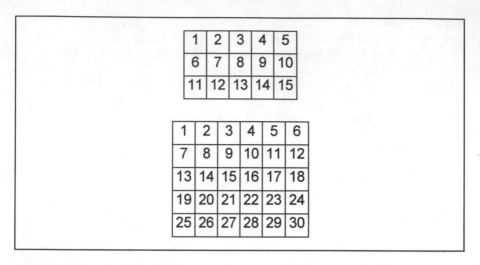

Fig. 1. Assumed matrices of locations for the testproblems with sizes 15 and 30, respectively. Numbered are the locations.

5 constraints (Nug15 and Nug30): (7,11); (8,9); (2,13); (3,13); (5,13). Two pairs ond one cluster of four machines are required.

n-1 constraints (Nug15 and Nug30): (1,2); (2,3); ... ; (n-1, n): Here, all machines make up an ordered sequence (chain). Due to the ground-plans chosen there are still (few) alternative solutions. This constellation is extremely complex for a 'blind' optimisation method, such as our ES.

n-3 (Nug15) and n-5 (Nug30) constraints: These testproblems are essentially the same as those with n-1 constraints, apart from splitting up the sequence in three parts for Nug15 (1–5, 6–10, 11–15) and five parts for Nug30 (1–6, 7–12, 13–18, 19–24, 25–30).

3   An Evolutionary Approach to the RQAP

In our evolutionary approach to the RQAP we employ a modified version of the combinatorial ES by Nissen [1994b] that is quite simple and can be described as follows: The solution representation is a straightforward permutation coding (figure 2). Each position on a solution vector represents a facility and integers are assigned as location numbers.

Our ES uses a simple population concept. Starting from one parent-solution, λ children are generated in each generation by first copying the parent and then mutating the resulting offspring. For the testproblems based on Nug15 $\lambda=15$, while $\lambda=45$ for instances based on the larger Nug30. Mutation is implemented as a single swap of two randomly chosen elements (locations) on the solution vector.

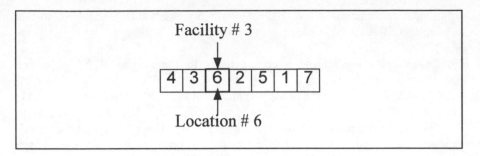

Fig. 2. Solution representation in the combinatorial ES.

The deterministic selection operator then picks the best member (lowest cost value) from the population of children to become the new parent for the next generation. The whole process is repeated for a specified number of generations. The best solution ever discovered is kept in a seperate storage ('golden cage') and updated whenever the heuristic identifies a better individual. This solution is finally output as the ES-result. Our initial solution is randomly generated.

The values for λ were experimentally determined and, when combined with the selection operator, proved large enough to locate good points in the neighbourhood of the current parent. They were also small enough not to get permanently stuck in local optima. Note that the parent is always replaced by the best offspring in each generation to avoid stagnation. This is also denoted (1,λ)-selection.

To account for the presence of zoning constraints we first experimented with the following four approaches:

(1) Transformation of the problem data (DT)
This measure modifies the given flow matrices of the original QAP by artificially raising the material flow between facilities that must be located next to each other. When the objective function value of the final solution is calculated one must, of course, use the original material flow values.

(2) Penalty function ignoring the QAP objective function (PI)
This approach tolerates but penalises illegal solutions. The quality (fitness) of such a solution is not measured with respect to the QAP objective function value. Instead, a harsh penalty factor (10.000 for all testproblems) is multiplied by the number of violated constraints to produce a substitute objective function value for invalid solutions. The penalty factor is chosen so high that feasible solutions are always prefered in the selection process, however bad they may be. By taking the number of violated constraints into account when measuring solution quality, it is presumed that the search process will gradually be lead to a feasible region. When the new parent has to be determined among solutions with an equal number of violated constraints, the selection is done randomly. Note that for infeasible

solutions no calculation of the QAP objective function value is required, so that substantial CPU-time is saved.

(3) Penalty function adding a high penalty to the original QAP objective function value (PH)

In contrast to PI, this time the penalty – calculated as for PI – is added to the QAP objective function value of an invalid solution. Thereby, it is possible to discriminate between solutions of equal infeasibility. The idea is that the search process will not only be guided to a feasible region, but even to a particularly promising part of it. With the high penalty factor of 10.000, valid solutions are still always prefered to invalid ones.

(4) Penalty function adding a moderate penalty to the original QAP objective function value (PM)

The only difference to PH lies in the determination of the penalty factor. This time, it is calculated by taking the product of the maximum distance of any two locations and the highest material flow between any two facilities. For the testproblems based on Nug30 the resulting value is multiplied by two to reflect the more intensive interactions of the machines as compared to Nug15. This procedure is purely heuristic and no claim is made as to its optimality. The moderate penalty allows infeasible solutions that contain good partial assignments and violate only few constraints to successfully compete with rather poor feasible solutions. This should allow the ES to exploit the valuable elements of invalid solutions.

We also investigated two different multiobjective optimisation approaches to the problem. These approaches take the minimisation of violated zoning constraints as a second objective next to cost minimisation. This time, the aim is not to find a single optimal solution but to investigate the tradeoff between both goals (cost minimisation and validity). This requires generating a set of efficient (non-dominated, pareto-optimal) solutions. Solution A is said to dominate solution B, if under all objectives A is as good as B, but there exists at least one objective where A is superior to B.

(5) Pareto-selection (PARETO)

This method shows a certain similarity to an approach put forward for Genetic Algorithms by Louis and Rawlins [1993]. The ES-procedure is modified in the following aspects. The number of children λ equals $3n$, i.e. $\lambda=45$ for the testproblems based on Nug15, and $\lambda=90$ for those based on Nug30.

We use a modified $(\mu+\lambda)$-selection. Thus parents and children are placed in competition, and only the μ best individuals survive to form the next generation. The number of parents μ is variable, however, and embraces all efficient solutions discovered so far (Pareto-set). Should different solutions have identical values w.r.t. both objectives, then one of them is randomly picked for inclusion in the Pareto-set. Note that we have not weighted the constraints.

(6) Best-per-objective selection (BPOS)

This is also an approach to identify efficient (pareto-optimal) solutions, similar in spirit to a proposal by Kursawe [1991]. First, we pick the best individual per objective from the set of children. These two solutions become the new parents for the next generational cycle of the ES. This means a modified $(2,\lambda)$-selection scheme is employed. The value of λ is again $3n$. Additionally, all efficient solutions among the set of children are determined and compared to a seperated set (Pareto-set; kind of 'golden cage') of all efficient solutions discovered so far. The Pareto-set is then updated and is ultimately the final result of the optimisation.

In our experiments with these two multicriteria approaches we were mainly interested in the course of the optimisation, and the distribution of solutions in the Pareto-set that would be generated by the respective methods.

4 Empirical Results and Conclusions

To compare the different approaches we used a software system that was developed by Krause in his diploma thesis [Krause 1994]. It is built around the combinatorial ES-variant described above, allows for comfortable visualisation of results and runs on a PC under Pascal.

Tables 1 and 2 give an overview of our empirical results with DT, PI, PH and PM on all six problem instances, averageing over 10 independent runs on each testproblem. The streams of random numbers are the same for all approaches at identical generation numbers. They are not the same for runs of different length within the same approach to zoning constraints. This allows for a more intensive testing of DT, PI, PH and PM, but very occasionally produces inferior results in a long run as compared to a shorter run of the same method. Results are additionally visualised for two testproblems of different complexity in figures 3 and 4.

The higher the number of constraints the more complex the problems become, which can be easily seen by looking at the percentage of unsuccessful runs. When solution quality (objective function value), reliability (% valid solutions) and CPU-time are simultaneously taken into consideration, then DT is the most successful strategy. However, it has only limited applicability. DT can e.g. not be used to ensure distance constraints, i.e. maximum distances between the locations of two machines.

The approach using moderate penalties (PM) can produce good results when the optimisation problem is of at most medium complexity. It appears less reliable than the other approaches, though, if we look at the percentage of valid solutions. Moreover, when the basic problem involves many machines and zoning constraints, the search process loses orientation.

Method	Gene-ration	5 constraints		12 constraints		14 constraints	
		Mean*	% valid†	Mean*	% valid†	Mean*	% valid†
DT	10	1431.3	30 (1.3)	1492.0	30 (1.0)	1356.0	10 (4.7)
	100	1252.3	80 (1.0)	1465.5	80 (1.0)	1356.0	10 (2.0)
	1000	1217.0	100	1386.8	100	1410.0	60 (1.0)
	10000	1194.2	100	1358.0	100	1383.2	100
PI	10	1525.0	60 (1.0)	1492.0	40 (1.2)	1356.0	10 (2.2)
	100	1282.2	100	1493.7	70 (1.0)	1356.0	20 (1.3)
	1000	1241.8	100	1444.4	100	1413.7	70 (1.0)
	10000	1208.0	100	1373.8	100	1392.8	100
	‡	1204.8	100	1366.4	100	1384.0	100
PH	10	1371.0	20 (1.0)	1492.0	30 (1.1)	1356.0	10 (2.6)
	100	1257.8	100	1461.4	70 (1.0)	1396.0	40 (1.0)
	1000	1232.0	100	1400.4	100	1410.9	70 (1.0)
	10000	1196.0	100	1360.4	100	1364.8	100
PM	10	n.v.s.	0 (1.1)	1492.0	10 (2.2)	1356.0	10 (3.1)
	100	1246.8	80 (1.0)	n.v.s.	0 (1.5)	n.v.s.	0 (2.0)
	1000	1196.4	100	1353.3	30 (1.4)	1364.8	50 (1.2)
	10000	1186.0	100	n.v.s.	0 (1.9)	1356.0	90 (1.0)

n.e. = not executed

n.v.s. = no valid solution found

*   Mean objective function value of valid solutions.

†   Percentage of successful runs (valid solution). The figure in brackets refers to the average number of violated constraints in the final solution of all unsuccessful runs.

‡   Max. number of generations was set to a value that would lead to similar CPU-requirements as 10,000 generations of PH or PM.

Table 1. Empirical results for the RQAPs based on Nug15 (average values of 10 runs on a PC with 66 Mhz). CPU-times are in the range of 7.6 (PI) to 20.5 (PH, PM) seconds for a run of 10,000 generations, depending on the number of constraints and the penalty approach employed.

Method	Gene-ration	5 constraints		25 constraints		29 constraints	
		Mean*	% valid[†]	Mean*	% valid[†]	Mean*	% valid[†]
DT	10	7254.7	30 (1.3)	n.v.s.	0 (1.0)	n.v.s.	0 (8.5)
	100	6520.6	100	8060.0	70 (1.0)	n.v.s.	0 (6.2)
	1000	6365.0	100	7786.0	80 (1.0)	8004.0	10 (3.6)
	10000	6311.4	100	7407.8	100	7848.0	10 (1.8)
	100000	n.e.	n.e.	n.e.	n.e.	7604.9	90 (1.0)
PI	10	7540.0	20 (1.3)	8060.0	10 (1.0)	n.v.s.	0 (4.8)
	100	6513.8	80 (1.0)	8060.0	50 (1.0)	n.v.s.	0 (3.3)
	1000	6405.6	100	7955.0	100	n.v.s.	0 (1.9)
	10000	6308.6	100	7671.6	100	7954.7	60 (1.0)
	100000	n.e.	n.e.	n.e.	n.e.	7936.4	100
	‡	6301.4	100	7565.2	100	8034.7	60 (1.0)
PH	10	7298,8	50 (1.0)	n.v.s.	0 (1.0)	n.v.s.	0 (4.9)
	100	6520.2	90 (1.0)	7959.3	60 (1.0)	8004.0	10 (4.1)
	1000	6363.8	100	8015.0	60 (1.0)	n.v.s.	0 (1.9)
	10000	6307.0	100	7407.0	100	n.v.s.	0 (1.1)
	100000	n.e.	n.e.	n.e.	n.e.	7732.0	40 (5.0)
PM	10	n.v.s.	0 (1.2)	n.v.s.	0 (1.7)	n.v.s.	0 (5.8)
	100	6537.6	90 (1.0)	7758.0	40 (2.8)	n.v.s.	0 (3.9)
	1000	6382.4	100	7472.0	10 (2.3)	n.v.s.	0 (2.6)
	10000	6315.0	100	7264.0	20 (1.4)	n.v.s.	0 (2.5)
	100000	n.e.	n.e.	n.e.	n.e.	n.v.s.	0 (1.6)

n.e. = not executed

n.v.s. = no valid solution found

*   Mean objective function value of valid solutions.

†   Percentage of successful runs (valid solution). The figure in brackets refers to the average number of violated constraints in the final solution of all unsuccessful runs.

‡   Max. number of generations was set to a value that would lead to similar CPU-requirements as 10,000 generations of PH or PM.

Table 2. Empirical results for the RQAPs based on Nug30 (average values of 10 runs on a PC with 66 MHz). CPU-times are in the range of 38 (PI) to 118 (PH, PM) seconds for a run of 10,000 generations, depending on the number of constraints and the penalty approach employed.

162

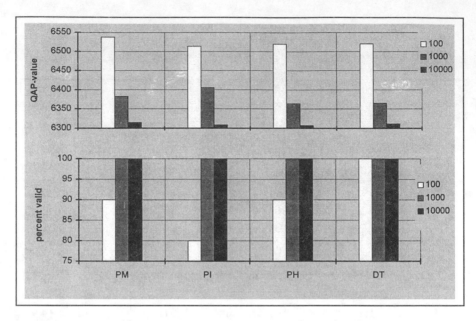

Fig. 3. Empirical results for the first four approaches on the testproblem with 30 machines, 30 locations, and 5 positive zoning constraints (run length indicated in generations).

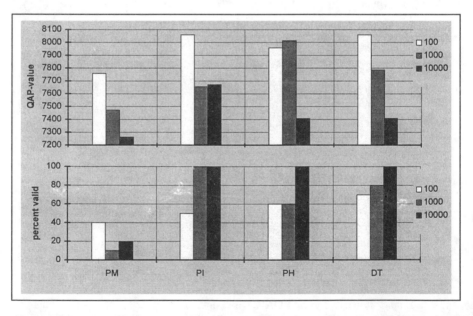

Fig. 4. Empirical results for the first four approaches on the testproblem with 30 machines, 30 locations, and 25 positive zoning constraints. Note the different scaling on the ordinates as compared to fig. 3.

One could argue this result is due to missing tuning of the penalty factors. However, a heuristic that requires problem-specific adaptations of strategy parameters must be considered rather uncomfortable. Moreover, the good results with PH and PI demonstrate that the considerable effort for finetuning graded penalty-factors is unnecessary, at least in the case of the RQAP.

Comparing the penalty approach that ignores the cost-value (PI) to the one that adds a high penalty (PH), both perform well even in the presence of many zoning constraints. While the first method is quicker, avoiding the time-consuming QAP-evaluations, the second approach tends to produce slightly better solutions by using the cost information. Interestingly, in the extremely complex case of 29 constraints (very few valid solutions exist at all) on the modified Nug30 problem, using the cost-value can lead to a deception of the search.

11	10	1	26	27	16
12	9	2	25	28	17
13	8	3	24	29	18
14	7	4	23	30	19
15	6	5	22	21	20

Fig. 5. Example of an invalid assignment for Nug30 with 29 constraints where only one restriction (machines 15 and 16 next to each other; numbered are the machines) is violated, but with the given swap-operator a feasible solution is very hard to reach.

Here, PH rather often ends up with a locally optimal assignment that looks something like the example in figure 5. Very few constraints are violated while a massive restructuring of the solution would be necessary to reach a feasible layout. A different mutation operator that changes each solution more strongly (destabilisation) would be helpful here. Alternatively, not using the QAP objective function information (as done by PI) is a useful measure to cope with the problem. However, this particular testproblem seems too extreme to reflect real-world requirements.

Let us now look at the results of the two multicriteria approaches PARETO and BPOS. In short, they are not competitive with the other approaches when the primary goal is generating feasible solutions with a low cost value. Nevertheless, they are very useful in visualising the tradeoff between both objectives by identifiying a Pareto-set of efficient (non-dominated) solutions. The efficiency of both approaches is quite different, though, as can be seen from figure 6.

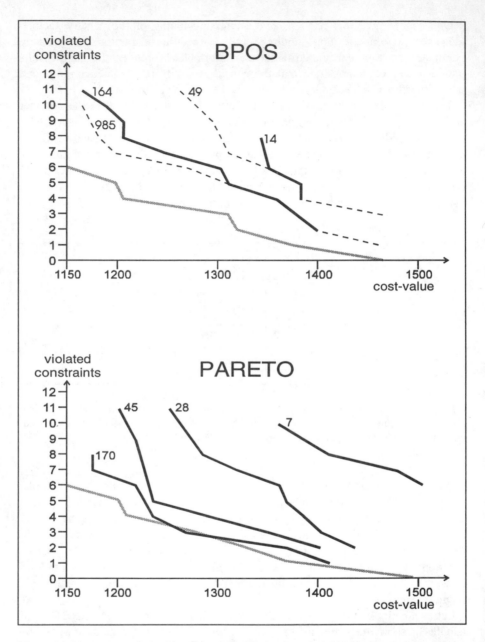

Fig. 6. Multicriteria optimisation where the minimisation of violated constraints becomes a second objective next to cost minimisation. This testproblem involves 15 machines, 15 locations, and 14 positive zoning constraints. Course of optimisation (generation numbers indicated) for best-per-objective selection (upper chart) and Pareto-selection (lower chart). Grey line indicates a long-term Pareto-set achieved with the respective approach.

Depicted are typical courses of optimisation for PARETO and BPOS respectively for the testproblem with 15 machines and 14 zoning constraints. Charts for the other testproblems look very alike. Note that solutions with 12 or more violated constraints do not appear in the graphs since the same cost-values are achieved with fewer violations (dominance).

The software system we used allows for continuos monitoring of the optimisation process, leading to the following observations:

- Pareto-selection quite quickly and more reliably than best-per-objective selection produces an approximation of the long-term Pareto-set achievable.
- Best-per-objective selection tends to focus on the margins of the Pareto-set where one objective is particularly well satisfied.
- The course of optimsation is smooth with Pareto-selection, and rather discontinuous with best-per-objective selection.
- Fully valid solutions are rarely discovered in both approaches.

Therefore, when identifying an evenly distributed set of efficient solutions is desired, Pareto-selection produces better results than best-per-objective selection. PARETO can be particularly time-consuming, though, when many different objectives have to be taken into account (not the case here).

On a more general level, the empirical results show that complex zoning constraints which are awkward to deal with by chosing a tailored solution representation, problem-specific operators, repair algorithms or a special decoding scheme, can effectively be dealt with by a simple combinatorial variant of the Evolution Strategy, completed by a transformation of the problem data or an almost trivial penalty function approach that works with harsh untuned penalties. The common understanding seems to be that nicely graded penalties are better than harsh penalties. We find that the required effort to develop graded penalty factors is unnecessary in our case, and would add undesired complexity to the approach. This might well extend to other applications. Pareto-selection is the method of choice when generating a set of efficient solutions is desired that shows the tradeoff between (few) different objectives.

We currently work on an extension of the employed software to account for more types of layout constraints. Other avenues for further research include changes in the concept of the underlying Evolutionary Algorithm, as well as the investigation of further testproblems with different structure, or from other application domains.

References

Burkard, R.E. (1990): Locations with Spatial Interactions: The Quadratic Assignment Problem. In: Mirchandani, P.B.; Francis, R.L. (eds.): Discrete Location Theory. Wiley, New York: 387–437

Kouvelis, P.; Chiang, W.-C.; Fitzsimmons, J. (1992): Simulated Annealing for Machine Layout Problems in the Presence of Zoning Constraints. EJOR 57: 203–223

Krause, M. (1994): Praxisnahe Fertigungs-Layoutplanung mit evolutionären Lösungsverfahren, Diploma Thesis, University of Göttingen, Department of Economics, Göttingen

Kursawe, F. (1991): A Variant of Evolution Strategies for Vector Optimization. In: Schwefel, H.-P.; Männer, R. (eds.): Parallel Problem Solving from Nature. Springer, Berlin: 193-197

Kusiak, A; Heragu, S.S. (1987): The Facility Layout Problem. EJOR 29: 229–251

Louis, S.J.; Rawlins, G.J.E. (1993): Pareto Optimality, GA-easiness and Deception. In: Forrest, S. (ed.): Proceedings of the Fifth International Conference on Genetic Algorithms. Morgan Kaufmann, San Mateo/CA: 118-123

Nissen, V. (1994a): Evolutionäre Algorithmen. Darstellung, Beispiele, betriebswirtschaftliche Anwendungsmöglichkeiten. DUV, Wiesbaden

Nissen, V. (1994b): Solving the Quadratic Assignment Problem with Clues from Nature. IEEE Transactions on Neural Networks 5 (Special Issue on Evolutionary Programming): 66–72

Nissen, V.; Krause, M. (1994): Constrained Combinatorial Optimization with an Evolution Strategy. In: Reusch, B. (ed.): Fuzzy Logik. Theorie und Praxis. Springer, Berlin: 33-40

Nugent, E.N.; Vollmann, T.E.; Ruml, J. (1968): An Experimental Comparison of Techniques for the Assignment of Facilities to Locations. Operations Research 16: 150–173

Richardson, J.T.; Palmer, M.R.; Liepins, G.; Hilliard, M. (1989): Some Guidelines for Genetic Algorithms with Penalty Functions. In: Schaffer, J.D. (ed.): Proceedings of the Third International Conference on Genetic Algorithms. Morgan Kaufmann, San Mateo/CA: 191-195

Tapping the Full Power of Genetic Algorithm through Suitable Representation and Local Optimization: Application to Bin Packing

Emanuel Falkenauer

CRIF - Research Centre of the Belgian Metalworking Industry
Department of Industrial Management and Automation
CP 106 - P4, 50 av. F.D.Roosevelt, B-1050 Brussels, Belgium

Abstract. The Genetic Algorithm (GA) is a powerful technique that has been applied with fair success to various optimization problems. In this chapter, we discuss two ways of significantly improving the power of the GA: choosing a representation of solutions that reflects the structure of the problem being optimized, and using a powerful local optimization. The impact of these improvements is illustrated on a combinatorial problem of considerable industrial importance, the Bin Packing Problem (BPP).

Keywords. Grouping, partitioning, bin packing, genetic algorithm, solution representation, dominance, reduction

1 Introduction

1.1 The Bin Packing Problem

1.1.1 Definition

The Bin Packing Problem (BPP) is defined as follows [Garey and Johnson 1979]: given a finite set O of numbers (the item sizes) and two constants C (the bin capacity) and N (the number of bins), is it possible to 'pack' all the items into N bins, i.e. does there exist a partition of O into N or less subsets, such that the sum of elements in any of the subsets doesn't exceed C?

This NP-complete decision problem naturally gives rise to the associated NP-hard optimization problem, the subject of this chapter: what is the *best* packing, i.e. what is the *minimum* number of subsets in the above mentioned partition?

Being NP-hard, there is no known optimal algorithm for BPP running in polynomial time. However, Garey and Johnson cite simple heuristics which can be shown to be no worse (but also no better) than a rather small multiplying factor above the optimal number of bins. The idea is straightforward: starting with one empty bin, take the items one by one and for each of them first search the bins so far used for a space large enough to accommodate it. If such a bin can be found, put the item there, if not, request a new bin. Putting the item into the first available bin found yields the First Fit (FF) heuristic. Searching for the most filled bin still having enough space for the item yields the Best Fit, a seemingly better heuristic, which can, however, be shown to perform as well (as bad) as the FF, while being slower. In the realm of Operations Research methods, Martello and Toth [1990a] have recently introduced a more powerful approximation algorithm for BPP, discussed below.

1.1.2   Applications

The Bin Packing Problem underlies many optimization problems of practical importance. Indeed, economies can be made whenever 'objects' of various dimensions have to be packed into 'boxes' or cut from 'sheets' or 'plates'.

In construction, tubes and rods must often be cut from a stock of constant lengths. Wires for electric wiring come in coils of constant length. Wallpaper sheets must be cut from packs of a given length. Stones of various lengths (but constant width) have to be transported on pallets to the construction site.

In metalworking industry, steel sheets must be cut from master sheets.

However, the dimension of the 'objects' does not have to be geometrical. For instance, in electronics industry, microcode routines of various sizes (in bytes) have to be stored in microprocessor memory divided into banks of a given size.

In transportation industry, it is often the case that only the weight of the various loads counts in distributing them over trucks of a given maximum load.

In entertainment industry, song collections are released on media (CDs, cassettes) of a given maximum capacity.

In operations management, tasks of various durations must be allocated to workers under the constraint of a given time for completing all the tasks[1] . The important problem of Line Balancing (allocation of tasks to workstations along a production line) is a BPP with additional precedence constraints, and Falkenauer [1992] shows how an algorithm for the latter can be used to solve the former.

1.2   The Grouping Problems

The Bin Packing Problem is member of a large family of problems which consist in *partitioning* a set U of items into a collection of mutually disjoint subsets U_i of U, i.e. such that

$\cup \, U_i = U$ over all i, and

$U_i \cap U_j = \varnothing$, i≠j.

One can also see these problems as ones where the aim is to *group* the members of the set U into one or more (at most **card(U)**) *groups* of items, with each item in exactly one group, i.e. to find a *grouping* of those items.

---

[1] The author was recently confronted with the following Bin Packing Problem: how many computers are required for running a battery of tests of various durations, in order to meet the deadline for the paper reporting the results of those tests?

In most of these problems, not *all* possible groupings are allowed: a solution of the problem must comply with various *hard constraints*, otherwise the solution is invalid. That is, usually an item cannot be grouped with all possible subsets of the remaining items.

The objective of the grouping is to optimize a *cost function* defined over the set of all valid *groupings*. Thus the grouping problems are characterized by cost functions which depend on the *composition of the groups*[2], that is, where one *item* taken isolately has little or no meaning.

Many grouping problems are NP-hard [Garey and Johnson 1979], which implies that any known *exact* algorithm will run in time *exponential* in the size of the problem instance. Such an algorithm is thus in most cases unusable for real-world size problems. The encouraging record of GAs on NP-hard problems makes them a candidate for solving the grouping problems.

In this chapter, we discuss two ways of enhancing significantly the power of a GA, which we illustrate on the grouping problems in general and the Bin Packing Problem in particular.

The first GA enhancement consists in choosing a chromosomal *representation* of solutions and genetic *operators* which closely reflect the structure of the problem on hand, rather than using standard operators and a decoder/encoder which would translate each solution to and from a standard chromosome. This approach is illustrated by the Grouping Genetic Algorithm (GGA), i.e. a GA adapted to suit the structure of grouping problems.

Given the representation and the genetic operators, the second enhancement consists in applying a *local optimization* technique which produces high-quality building blocks that are then usefully processed by the GA. This is illustrated on a hybridisation of the GGA with a recent OR technique for Bin Packing, the Dominance Criterion of Martello and Toth [1990a].

A successful application of the two enhancements can lead to a very efficient optimization technique, which is illustrated by an experimental comparison of the hybrid GGA with a very powerful enumerative technique, the MTP procedure of Martello and Toth [1990b].

The rest of the chapter is organized as follows. In sections 2 and 3 we point out the main weaknesses of standard and ordering GAs when applied to grouping problems. In section 4, we present the Grouping GA (GGA) which addresses those drawbacks. The ideas behind the Dominance Criterion of Martello and Toth are presented in section 5. Section 6 introduces the Hybrid GGA (HGGA) for BPP resulting from a 'marriage' of the two techniques. An experimental comparison of the HGGA with the MTP procedure is carried out in section 7. Conclusions are drawn in section 8.

---

[2] This is why we talk about *grouping* problems, rather than *partitioning* - we thus emphasize the importance of the groups, rather than the 'cuts'.

2 Standard GA and Grouping Problems

The most straightforward application of the GA technique to a grouping problem encodes the *membership* of items in the groups in the solution. For instance, the chromosome ADBCEB would encode the solution where the first item is in the group A, the second in the group D, third in B, fourth in C, fifth in E and sixth in the group B.

This approach has the advantage that the chromosomes are of constant length (equal to the number of items), which allows for application of standard genetic operators. However, as Falkenauer [1994a] points out, this encoding suffers several drawbacks, two of which are discussed below.

2.1 Redundancy of Encoding

The straightforward encoding above is highly redundant. Indeed, the cost function of a grouping problem depends only on the grouping of the items, rather than the numbering of the group. For instance, in the Graph Coloring Problem, only the distribution of colors over the nodes counts[3], whatever the actual colors (their *names*) used. Thus with A standing for Amber, B for Blue, C for Crimson and D for DarkRed, ABCADD and CADCBB both encode the same solution of the problem, namely the one where the first and fourth nodes of the graph are assigned one color, the fifth and sixth nodes a second color, and the second and third nodes a third and fourth color respectively.

The degree of redundancy (i.e. the number of distinct chromosomes encoding the same solution of the original problem) of this scheme grows *exponentially* with the number of groups, that is, indirectly, with the size of the problem. Thus the size of the space the GA has to search is *much* larger than the original space of solutions. Consequently, the power of the GA is *seriously* impaired.

2.2 Context Insensitivity of Crossover

The straightforward encoding leads to the highly undesirable effect of casting context-dependent information *out of context* under the standard crossover. Indeed, in the first chromosome above (ABCADD), the C affected to the third gene only has sense in the context of that particular chromosome, where it means that the third node is not grouped with any other node. Taking that C out of the context during crossover has disastrous consequences. To see this, let us apply the standard two-point crossover to the two chromosomes above:

A | BC | ADD   crossed with
C | AD | CBB   would yield
   CBCCBB   as one of the two children.

---

[3] The resulting *number* of colors, i.e. the value of the cost function, results from a given distribution of colors over the nodes of the graph.

In absence of mutation, a recombination of two *identical* individuals must produce progeny which is again identical to the parents. The two parents above *are* identical with respect to the problem being solved by the GA, because they both encode the same solution of the problem. Hence a correct recombination operator should produce an individual which again encodes the same solution. However, the resulting child above encodes a 'solution' which has *nothing* in common with the solution its parents encode, since there are two groups instead of four.

In other words, while the schemata are well transmitted with respect to the *chromosomes* under the standard encoding/crossover, their meaning with respect to the *problem* to solve (i.e. the cost function to optimize) is lost in the process of recombination.

3 Ordering GA and Grouping Problems

Another way of tackling the grouping problems has been to use chromosomes which encode *permutations* of the items, and apply a decoder to retrieve the corresponding solutions (the distributions of items among groups).

As for the representation encoding group memberships described in the previous section, the resulting chromosomes allow for application of classic ordering operators. However, this approach also suffers of various drawbacks, two of which are described below.

3.1 Redundancy of Encoding

For the sake of clarity, let's consider the Bin Packing Problem. Suppose there are ten items to pack, numbered 0 through 9. A valid chromosome is one where each item appears exactly once, for example 0123456789. This encoding is highly redundant. Indeed, suppose that the items in the above chromosome are partitioned as follows: 0123 | 45678 | 9, i.e. there are three bins, one containing the items 0 through 3, the second containing the items 4 through 8, and the third containing the item 9. Now any permutation of the items having the same bin contents, such as 3210 | 45678 | 9 or 87645 | 1032 | 9, encodes *the same* solution of the original Bin Packing Problem. As for the straightforward encoding in section 2, the degree of redundancy of this encoding grows *exponentially* with the size of the instance. Again, the power of the GA is seriously diminished.

3.2 Context Insensitivity of Crossover

Given the fact that the decoder retrieves the groups corresponding to a given permutation by considering the items from left to right, the meaning of the position of a given item strongly depends on the 'head' of the chromosome, i.e. on all the items on its left. Nevertheless, it is precisely the positions of the items on the chromosome, i.e. the *o-schemata* of Goldberg [1989], that are transmitted by an ordering crossover. Consequently, when the 'head' of an o-schema changes after inheritance from another chromosome, the meaning of the schema is lost.

To see this, consider the instance of the Bin Packing Problem where items of sizes 1, 2, 3, 4, 6, 7, ..., have to be packed inside bins of size 10, and the o-schema ??**32**??...[4]. The following is a sample of the chromosomes belonging to the schema:

Chromosome/solution	First two bins	Rest to pack	Composition of bin(s) containing the items in the schema
1**43**2|6|7...	10,6	7	1234
17|**32**|64|...	8,5	10	23
16**3**|**2**7|4...	10,9	4	136 and 27 (schema broken)
4|7**3**|**2**16...	4,10	9	37 and 126... (schema broken)

The diversity of the sample is remarkable, even though all those solutions belong to the above o-schema. Clearly, there is little insight concerning the grouping problem that can be gained by sampling o-schemata. This is because they do not convey information *relevant* to a grouping problem. Consequently, they are *not* the building blocks to work with.

Needless to say, the corresponding o-schema which would express the *relative* positions of the genes[5] would lead to an even greater diversity of a corresponding sample, which means that crossovers transmitting well the relative positions are not a cure either.

4 The Grouping GA

The Grouping Genetic Algorithm (GGA) differs from the classic GA in two important aspects. First, a special encoding scheme is used in order to make the relevant structures of grouping problems become genes in chromosomes, i.e. the building blocks the GA works with[6]. Second, given the encoding, special genetic operators are used.

4.1 The Encoding

As we have seen, neither the standard nor the ordering GAs are suitable for grouping problems. The reason is that the simple chromosomes (which the above GAs work with) are *item* oriented, instead of being *group* oriented. In short, the above encodings are not adapted to the cost function to optimize, because the cost function of a

---

[4] Writing the *sizes* rather than the *numbers* of the items, this o-schema is the set of all chromosomes having the item of size 3 in the third position, and the item of size 2 in the fourth.

[5] The so-called *type r* o-schema.

[6] The smallest building blocks are single genes, i.e. schemata of length 1. Larger building blocks are aggregates of smaller ones, i.e. the building blocks as a whole are aggregates of genes.

grouping problem depends on the *groups* (i.e. their composition), but there is no structural counterpart for them in those chromosomes.

Note that these remarks are nothing more than a call for compliance with the *Thesis of Good Building Blocks*, central to the GA paradigm. The GA proceeds in the exploration of the search space by increasing the search effort in regions surrounding the promising solutions so far visited, acording to the optimal strategy of trial allocation worked out by Holland [1975]. The mechanism that implements that strategy is the inheritance of genes, and the Thesis expresses the idea that the the genes are indeed the building blocks that should be manipulated.

Since the GA processes (through inheritance) genes in chromosomes, and since it is the groups (rather than the items) that are meaningful to a grouping problem, it follows that a suitable representation of solutions of a grouping problem must cast *groups as genes* in the chromosomes. This conclusion has led us to the introduction of the Grouping GA (GGA), first in [Falkenauer 1991].

To follow the above remarks, we have chosen the following encoding scheme in the GGA: the standard chromosome from section 2 is augmented with a *group part* encoding the groups on a *one gene for one group* basis. More concretely, let us consider the first chromosome in section 2 and the Bin Packing Problem. Numbering the items from 0 through 5, the *item* part of the chromosome can be explicitly written

```
012345
ADBCEB:...,
```

meaning that the item 0 is in the bin *labeled* (named) A, 1 in the bin D, 2 and 5 in B, 3 in C, and 4 in E. This is the straightforward chromosome from section 2. The *group* part of the chromosome represents *only the groups* (bins in BPP). Thus

```
...:BECDA
```

expresses the fact that there are five bins in the solution. Of course, what *names* are used for each of the bins is irrelevant in the BPP: only the *contents* of each bin counts in this problem. We thus come to the *raison d'être* of the item part. Indeed, by a lookup there, we can establish what the names stand for, namely A={0}, B={2,5}, C={3}, D={1} and E={4}. In fact, the chromosome could also be written

```
{0}{2,5}{3}{1}{4}.
```

The important point is that the genetic operators will **work with the group part** of the chromosomes, the standard item part merely serving to identify which items actually form which group. Note in particular that this implies that the operators will have to handle chromosomes of *variable length*.

4.2   Crossover

As pointed out in the previous section, a GGA crossover will work with variable length chromosomes with genes representing the groups[7].

Given the fact that the hard constraints and the cost function vary among different grouping problems, the ways groups can be combined without producing invalid or too

---

[7] In other words, the GGA works with the group part of the chromosomes. Naturally, the item part of the chromosome is adjusted accordingly.

bad individuals are not the same for all those problems. Thus the crossover used will *not* be the same for all of them. However, it will fit the following pattern, illustrated in Figure 4.1[8].

1. Select at random two crossing sites, delimiting the *crossing section*, in each of the two parents.
2. *Inject* the contents of the crossing section of the first parent at the first crossing site of the second parent. Recall that the crossover works with the group part of the chromosome, so this means injecting some of the *groups* from the first parent into the second.
3. Eliminate all *items* now occurring twice from the groups they were members of in the second parent, so that the 'old' membership of these items gives way to the membership specified by the 'new' injected groups. Consequently, *some* of the 'old' groups coming from the second parent are altered: they do not contain all the same items anymore, since some of those items had to be eliminated.
4. If necessary, *adapt* the resulting groups, according to the hard constraints and the cost function to optimize. At this stage, local problem-dependent heuristics can be applied.
5. Apply the points 2. through 4. to the two parents with their roles permuted to generate the second child.

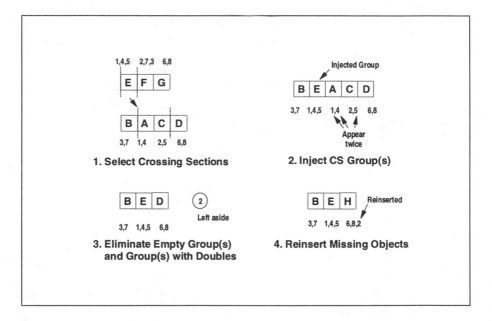

Fig. 4.1 The GGA Crossover

---

[8] The stage 4 of the crossover depicted in the figure first empties all groups modified by the injection and then reinserts the resulting unassigned items (item 2 in this case).

4.3   Mutation

A mutation operator for grouping problems must work with groups rather than items. As for the crossover, the implementation details of the operator depend on the particular grouping problem on hand. Nevertheless, two general strategies can be outlined: either *create* a new group or *eliminate* an existing one.

5   Dominance in Bin Packing

Martello and Toth [1990a] have recently introduced an approximation algorithm for the Bin Packing Problem based on a simple yet powerful observation illustrated in the following figure. Given the contents of two bins B_1 and B_2, if there exists a subset $\{i_1, \dots i_n\}$ of items in B_2 and a partition $\{P_1, \dots P_n\}$ of items in B_1 such that for each item i_i there is a corresponding P_i not larger than i_i[9], then B_2 is said to *dominate* B_1, because a solution obtained with B_2 as one of the bins requires no more bins than one with B_1.

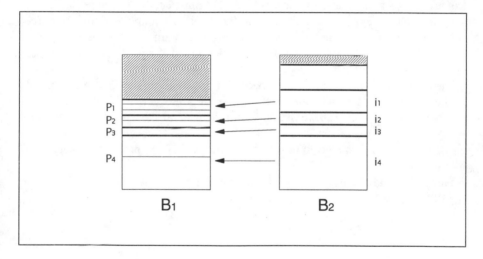

Fig. 5.1 The Dominance Criterion: B_2 dominates B_1.

A Bin Packing algorithm would repeatedly find a bin dominating *all* others, add that bin to the solution and *reduce* the problem by removing the items just assigned. However, that procedure would run in exponential time. In order to obtain a procedure of a reasonable complexity, Martello and Toth propose to consider only sets of size three or less.

---

[9] That is, the total size of items in P_i is less than or equal to the size of i_i.

An effective approximation algorithm can be obtained from the above procedure as follows. When no set dominating all others can be found anymore, the problem is *relaxed* by removing the smallest item among those which are not yet assigned to any bin, and the procedure is repeated. Martello and Toth use this algorithm to compute lower bounds on the number of necessary bins for BPP instances.

We use the concept of dominance in conjunction with the Grouping GA described above. It serves as a *local optimization* producing high-quality bins which are then efficiently processed by the GGA.

6   The Hybrid GGA for Bin Packing

In this section, we first define a suitable cost function for the Bin Packing Problem, and then show how the Grouping Genetic Algorithm can be combined with the concept of dominance in a hybrid GGA (HGGA).

6.1   The Cost Function

Let us define a suitable cost function for the Bin Packing Problem defined in section 1.1.1. The objective being to find the minimum number of bins required, the first cost function which comes to mind is simply the number of bins used to 'pack' all the items. This is correct from a strictly mathematical point of view, but is unusable in practice. Indeed, such a cost function leads to an extremely 'unfriendly' landscape of the search space: a very small number of optimal points in the space are lost in an exponential number of points where this purported cost function is just one unit above the optimum. Worse, all those slightly suboptimal points yield the *same* cost. The trouble is that such a cost function lacks any capacity of *guiding* an algorithm in the search, making the problem a 'Needle-in-a-haystack'.

Falkenauer and Delchambre [1992] thus settled for the following cost function for the BPP: maximize

$$f_{BPP} = \frac{\sum_{i=1..N}(F_i / C)^k}{N}$$

with   N being the number of bins used in the solution,
F_i the sum of sizes of the items in the bin i (the fill of the bin),
C the bin capacity and
k a constant, k>1.

The constant k expresses our concentration on the 'elite' bins in comparison to the less filled ones. The larger k is, the more we prefer a few well-filled bins as opposed to a collection of about equally filled bins. We have experimented with several values of k and found out that k=2 gives good results. Larger values of k seem to lead to premature convergence of the algorithm, as local optima due to a few well-filled bins become too hard to escape.

6.2 BPRX - the Bin Packing Crossover with Replacement

The most important operator of a Genetic Algorithm is crossover. The algorithm described here being a GGA, its crossover follows the pattern given in section 4.2 above. We describe here the application of that operator to the particular problem of Bin Packing, including the involvement of the Dominance Criterion.

6.2.1 The Mechanism

In the phase 4 of the GGA crossover, we eliminate all the bins which have been modified by the elimination of doubles performed in phase 3. This leaves us with a partial solution to the BPP consisting of the bins injected from the first parent and those from the second parent that have not been modified by the elimination, and a set of isolated items that have to be reinserted into the solution.

To fix this last problem, in our previous work we used the First Fit Descending (FFD) heuristic to reinsert again the missing objects [Falkenauer and Delchambre 1992]. That is, they were sorted in descending order of their sizes and then put one by one into the solution, each time into the first sufficiently empty bin.

In the hybrid algorithm, we first perform a *local optimization* inspired by the ideas of Martello and Toth [1990a] in the following way. Taking one by one the bins so far in the solution, we check whether it is possible to **replace** up to three items in the bin by one or two items from those currently missing in the bins, in such a way that the total size of the items in the bin increases without overflowing the bin. If so, we perform the replacement, which means that some of the previously unassigned items are assigned to the bin, while some of the items previously assigned to the bin become 'unassigned'.

Note that the replacement has two important consequences. First, it *fills better* the target bin than it was before. Since a good packing has well-filled bins, this improves the quality of the solution on the one hand. On the other hand, since the total size of the items is a constant, it also leaves more space in the other bins (indirectly), which makes them more amenable to accommodate additional items, and that eventually leads to the desired reduction of the number of necessary bins. Second, the exchange makes available (i.e. 'unassigns') *smaller items* than before the exchange, which makes easier the task of adding those items to bins already in the solution.

This process is repeated as long as such exchanges are possible. When none is possible anymore and there are still items to be reinserted, the usual FFD heuristic is applied to complete the solution (i.e. assign all items to bins).

6.2.2 The Rationale

The method of Martello and Toth aims at identifying bins which *dominate* the others, so that they can be fixed, thus reducing the effective size of the problem. However, because of the size of the search space, it is impossible to verify in a reasonable time that a given bin dominates *all* the others. The approximation described in section 5 above solves the problem of complexity of the algorithm, but introduces a new one: it happens that the simplified method does *not* find a bin which dominates the others. In order to continue towards *some* solution, rather than stopping the algorithm with a "do not know" answer, the problem is *relaxed* in some way[10] and the reduction procedure is reapplied.

However necessary to keep the algorithm practically useful, the relaxation step introduces an extraneous element into the procedure: there is little guarantee that the relaxation applied will preserve the global optimality of the solution under construction. Since there is no backtracking allowed (for efficiency reasons), once a wrong relaxation is performed, the global optimum is out of reach and the method will settle to a local one.

The replacement stage in the BPRX was inspired by the method of Martello and Toth. Indeed, what is done during that stage is nothing else than a local search for dominant bins, using an approximative criterion very similar to the one used by Martello and Toth. However, the Grouping GA does not suffer the drawback of convergence to a local optimum. Since *whole bins* are transmitted during a crossover, each improvement is usefully propagated throughout the population, by means of transmission from parents to offspring. That makes it possible to 'test' the quality of each bin in numerous contexts, which is analogous to testing the dominance of each bin under many different relaxations.

Indeed, consider a bin in one individual in the population and recall that in the Grouping GA, the bins correspond to genes in the chromosomes. If the gene is transmitted without modification over the succesive generations of the GGA, then it probably dominates most of the other bins that could be made with the items it contains. On the other hand, if it *is* modified, then it is because there is a bin which dominates it.

Finally, the recombining power of the BPRX crossover takes still further advantage of an approximated dominance criterion. Consider two bins having no item in common and suppose each is part of one individual in the population. Since both individuals have survived the evolutionary competition, the bins they are made of dominate, under the approximated criterion, all other bins which could be formed with the items the bins contain[11]. Now since the BPRX crossover combines whole bins and the bins have no item in common, they can be *both* inherited in a child, without a need of new verification of their dominance. In short, the crossover constructs solutions that *automatically* contain bins dominating the others.

6.3   Mutation

The second important GA operator is mutation. The HGGA mutation operator is simple. Given a chromosome, we select at random a few bins (i.e. *genes*) and eliminate them. The items which composed those bins are thus missing from the

---

[10] Martello and Toth [1990a] propose three sensible ways of relaxing a problem, but there are numerous other ways of relaxing a given instance.

[11] This does not mean that they dominate *all* the others though, because a more thorough (less approximated) criterion could reveal that they are themselves dominated.

solution and must be inserted back. To do so, we again use the ideas applied for the crossover. Namely, the eliminated items first serve as the basis for eventual improvement of the bins left unchanged, during a stage of replacement. When no replacement is possible anymore, the FFD heuristic is used to complete the solution.

7   Experimental Results

The HGGA issued from the above considerations has been thoroughly experimentally tested through a comparison with the MTP procedure of Martello and Toth [1990b], i.e. a sophisticated branch-and-bound procedure that has the Dominance Criterion embedded. We chose the MTP as the benchmark because it is considered by many to be one of the best methods for the BPP to date.

Two sets of experiments were performed. One was designed to see how the HGGA fares on the MTP's "turf", i.e. we generated instances of the kind considered by Martello and Toth. The second set of experiments was designed to assess the practical limits of the two algorithms. To do so, we generated what seems to be the *hardest* BPP instances.

Each instance was submitted both to the MTP procedure and to the Hybrid GGA, which means that the performances of the two algorithms were compared on the *same* instances. Note however that the enumerative nature of the MTP procedure makes it take an excessive time when confronted with difficult instances, and an artificial shutoff is required in order to obtain *some* result. We thus allowed the MTP to perform at most 1500000 (one and a half million) backtracks on any of the instances. In some cases though, this shutoff aborted the MTP sooner than after the amount of time (in CPU seconds) we gave to the HGGA, which could be perceived as an unfair comparison. Consequently, whenever this was the case, we increased the backtrack limit accordingly and rerun the MTP.

The detailed results of the statistics over 160 BPP instances can be found in [Falkenauer 1994b] and we will not repeat them here for space reasons. The following is a summary of those results.

7.1   Uniform Item Size Distribution

In the first set of tests, we generated instances with items of sizes uniformly distributed between 20 and 100 to be packed into bins of capacity 150, with 120, 250, 500 and 1000 items respectively. We generated 20 instances of each.

Among the instances of 120 items, in two out of the twenty cases, neither algorithm came up with a solution having the theoretical number of bins, so we conjecture that there is no such solution. However, the MTP had to be aborted prematurely, so we have no proof. Apart from those two instances, the 120-item data proved to be easy for the MTP, which was faster than the HGGA. Nevertheless, the difference was only marginal.

From 250 items up, the 'explosive' nature of MTP started to show, and the results show a superiority of the HGGA in two respects: the HGGA supplies *better* solutions, and it does so *faster* than the MTP procedure.

For seventeen out of the twenty instances of 250 items, the HGGA has discovered a solution in the theoretical number of bins, i.e. a global optimum. For the remaining three, the HGGA's solution had the same number of bins as the MTP's, so we again conjecture that these were globally optimal as well, although we again have no proof, as the MTP had to be aborted in all three cases.

The MTP procedure was less successful in finding the global optima for these instances: in nine out of the twenty cases, it was unable to find a solution as good as the HGGA's, the difference being two bins in one case.

The results on instances of 500 and 1000 items confirmed the superiority of the HGGA: in all cases, the HGGA found a globally optimal solution, while the MTP never did. In addition, the meaning of the time taken by the MTP became especially clear: for all but four of the 500 item instances, and for all with 1000 items, the difference between the solutions of the two algorithms was two bins or more. This means that even if we increased the backtrack limit for the MTP so that it could improve the solution by one bin, which would undoubtedly lead to extremely long execution times, the MTP would still end up with a solution worse than the HGGA. Consequently, the HGGA fared better in both *quality* of the solution and the *speed* of their delivery.

7.2   Triplets

With the second class of tests, we tried to establish the practical limits of the HGGA. Following van Vliet [1993], we considered problems with item sizes between the quarter and the half of the bin capacity. In these problems, a well-filled bin must contain one 'big' item (larger than the third of the bin capacity) and two 'small' ones, which is why we term them 'triplets'. What makes these problems difficult is the fact that putting two 'big' or three 'small' items into a bin *is* possible, but inevitably leads to a waste of space (the bin cannot be completely filled by an additional item), implying a suboptimal solution.

In order to preserve the difficulty of the problem, we generated instances of *known optima*[12] as follows. First, an object was generated with a size drawn uniformly from the range [380,490]. That left a space S of between 510 and 620 in the bin of 1000. The second object was drawn uniformly from [250,S/2). The third object in the bin completed the size of the bin. We generated 'triplets' with 60, 120, 249 and 501 items, 20 instances of each.

The performance of the MTP procedure showed that 'triplets' are indeed very hard problems. The MTP was able to finish only on six of the twenty instances of 60 items, and it never finished on any of the bigger ones.

---

[12] As the MTP's performance revealed, it was impossible to generate triplets at random and then *compute* the global optima by an exact method.

In two runs of 60 items, the HGGA failed to find the optimal solution. Obviously, the limit we imposed (maximum 67000 cost function evaluations) was too tight. However, on both these instances, the MTP fared one bin worse yet.

Among the six 60 item runs which the MTP was able to optimize completely, in only two cases was the MTP faster than the HGGA. Except for these, the MTP took longer than the HGGA to find an equally good solution. In sixteen out of twenty cases, it took longer to find a *worse* solution.

From 120 items up, the HGGA fared better than the MTP procedure in all respects. It always found a globally optimal solution, while the MTP never did. The HGGA was also much faster.

8   Conclusions

The GGA's distinctive features allow it to *exploit* the very structure of the grouping problems that makes the standard and the ordering GAs fail. This is achieved by using a represenation of solutions that allows the GGA to manipulate building blocks *relevant* to the grouping problems. Joining this ability with an efficient OR technique for *generating* those blocks leads to a hybrid GGA performing better than either of its components separately.

The superiority of the hybrid GGA over the MTP procedure of Martello and Toth on difficult instances, in both the quality of the solutions supplied and the speed of their delivery, was confirmed by an extensive experimental comparison.

The respective performances of the two algorithms inspire an important conclusion. Both methods use the same *local* techniques (both FFD and the Dominance Criterion are embedded in MTP), but they use different *global* mechanisms for generating candidate solutions (like all GAs, the HGGA uses crossover, while the MTP follows a branch-and-bound search tree). Given the superiority of the HGGA demonstrated above, we hope that the search mechanism of the GA[13] will be recognized as a *very* viable instrument in searching the vast search spaces of difficult problems. In particular, we hope that the results presented in this chapter will contribute to a wider acceptance of the GA paradigm by the Operations Research community.

Besides the Bin Packing Problem, the GGA holds a promise for many other grouping problems [Falkenauer 1994a]. If the concept of dominance of Martello and Toth can be shown to carry over to other grouping problems, then the marriage of the two paradigms should prove useful there as well.

Acknowledgment. The research reported in this chapter has been supported in part by the ESPRIT III Project n. 6562 SCOPES.

---

[13] Note that, as we have shown above, the use of an *adequate encoding and operators* is **fundamental** in a GA.

References

Falkenauer, E. (1991): A Genetic Algorithm for Grouping. R.Gutiérrez and M.J.Valderrama (Eds), Proceedings of the Fifth International Symposium on Applied Stochastic Models and Data Analysis, April 23-26, 1991, Granada, Spain. World Scientific Publishing Co. Pte. Ltd. Singapore: 198-206

Falkenauer, E.; Delchambre, A. (1992): A Genetic Algorithm for Bin Packing and Line Balancing. Proceedings of the IEEE 1992 Int. Conference on Robotics and Automation (RA92), May 10-15, 1992, Nice, France. IEEE Computer Society Press: 1186-1192

Falkenauer, E. (1994a): New Representation and Operators for GAs Applied to Grouping Problems. Evolutionary Computation, Vol.2, N.2

Falkenauer, E. (1994b): A Hybrid Grouping Genetic Algorithm for Bin Packing. CRIF Industrial Management and Automation, Brussels, Belgium

Garey, M. R.; Johnson, D. S. (1979): Computers and Intractability - A Guide to the Theory of NP-completeness. W.H.Freeman Co., San Francisco

Goldberg, D. E. (1989): Genetic Algorithms in Search, Optimization and Machine Learning. Addison-Wesley

Holland, J. H. (1975): Adaptation in Natural and Artificial Systems. University of Michigan Press, Ann Arbor

Martello, S.; Toth, P. (1990a): Lower Bounds and Reduction Procedures for the Bin Packing Problem. Discrete Applied Mathematics 22: 59-70

Martello, S.; Toth, P. (1990b): Bin-packing problem. Knapsack Problems, Algorithms and Computer Implementations. John Wiley & Sons, England: 221-245

Radcliffe, N. J. (1991): Forma Analysis and Random Respectful Recombination. Proceedings of the Fourth International Conference on Genetic Algorithms, University of California, San Diego, July 13-16, 1991. Morgan Kaufmann Publishers, San Mateo/Cal: 222-229

van Vliet, A. (1993): Private communication. Econometric Institute, Erasmus University Rotterdam, The Netherlands

A Hybrid Genetic Algorithm for the Two - Dimensional Guillotine Cutting Problem

Víctor Parada Daza[1] , Ricardo Muñoz[1] and Arlindo Gómes de Alvarenga[2]

[1] Depto. Ingeniería Informática - Universidad de Santiago de Chile Av.
Ecuador 3659, Santiago - Chile
[2] Departamento de Informática, Universidade Federal do Espírito Santo
Vitoria-ES-Brasil, 29060-900

Abstract. In this article an algorithm to solve the two-dimensional guillotine cutting problem is proposed. This problem considers the cut of a number of rectangular pieces from a single large rectangular plate. Two restrictions are considered: all cuts must be of guillotine type and, the number of time a piece can be cut from the plate has an upper bound. The aim is to generate a cutting pattern with minimum trim loss. The algorithm is based on the enumeration of parts of the problem domain by using ideas from the genetic algorithms. A cutting pattern is represented by means of a string which is obtained from a syntactic binary tree associated with the pattern. Reproduction and crossover operators are adequately defined in order to guarantee that all newly generated strings correspond to feasible solutions. The successive generation of string populations permit to obtain better strings that correspond to cutting pattern with smaller trim losses. The encoding used not only optimizes the memory required to solve the problem but simplifies the process of pattern generation. In order to evaluate the performance of this method a set of numerical experiments is performed. It is shown that this method can manage instances greater than those the algorithm of Oliveira and Ferreira can handle, considering the same computational resources. Furthermore, even considering the problem with pieces rotation, the quality of the obtained solutions is improved in terms of trim loss, when compared to the modified Wang's algorithm.

Keywords. Cutting problem, trim loss problem, genetic algorithms

1   Introduction

The constrained two-dimensional guillotine cutting problem considers a large rectangular plate of length L and width W from which a set of p types of smaller pieces must be cut. Each ith type of piece has dimensions (l_i, w_i) and a demand constraint value b_i. All cuts must be of guillotine type, i.e. orthogonal to some of the plate's sides. A cutting pattern must be generated specifying the locations in

184

which each cut should be executed over the plate, in order to get a minimum trim loss and avoiding overlapping between pieces. Figure 1 shows a feasible solution for this problem. Black rectangles represent the trim loss. It must be noted that all pieces can be separated by means of guillotine cuts.

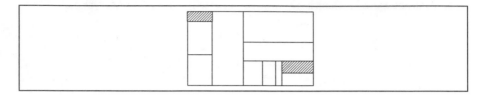

Figure 1 Example of a feasible solution for the problem.

This problem is a special case of the cutting stock problem class. Reviews about this problem class can be found in the studies of Hinxman [1980] and Dyckhoff [1990]. Related to the problem considered here, several studies have been appeared lately. Christofides and Whitlock [1977] proposed an exact tree-search procedure by using the previously proposed algorithm of Gilmore and Gomory [1967], which solves the same problem ignoring the demand constraint. Wang [1983] proposed an incremental development algorithm to generate a cutting pattern. Numerical improvements of this algorithm were proposed by Vasko[1989] and Oliveira and Ferreira [1990]. Hinxman [1976] and Morabito et. al. [1992] presented studies that consider a problem reduction methodology of artificial intelligence [Pearl, 1984] to solve the problem. An And/Or graph is used to represent a constructive solution process. Following this ideas Viswanathan et al. [1993] and Parada et al. [1995] have proposed best-first search approaches to find an optimum solution.

In this study we propose to use some ideas from genetic algorithms [Goldberg 1989; Michalewicz 1992] to scan the problem domain. A feasible solution to this problem is represented by means of a string. From an initial set of strings, successive populations are generated, all of them corresponding to new feasible solutions. After a finite number of generations a good solution for this problem is found.

In the second section, both the formulation of the problem and the method here proposed are presented. In the third section an analysis of numerical results is given and finally, in the fourth section the main conclusions are drawn.

2 Formulation of the Problem

2.1 Definition of Individual and String

Any guillotine cutting pattern of n pieces ($n > 1$) has at least one horizontal or vertical cut that divides it in two new also guillotine cutting patterns. Each part contains *k* and *n-k* pieces ($1 < k < n$) respectively. By decomposing the pattern in that way, in the last level the original pieces are found. This decomposition process can be represented as a binary tree as shown in figure 2, where intermediate nodes correspond to partial cutting patterns.

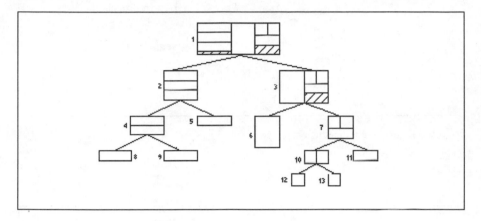

Figure 2 A binary tree associated with a cutting pattern.

Wang's algorithm build a cutting pattern combining pairs of rectangles. We represent this incremental combination as a binary tree. So, two child nodes are combined to give rise to a father node by means of a vertical or a horizontal cut. Then in each new node composed in that way an internal trim loss is generated, see for instance nodes 1 and 3 in figure 2. It should be noted that while node 2 is generated by an horizontal composition, the node 3 is composed by joining vertically nodes 6 and 7. To see whether a cut is horizontal or vertical an equivalent trec can be used, such as it is shown in figure 3. We define operators representing vertical and horizontal cuts and denote them by the characters 'V' and 'H' respectively. Similarly we denote pieces as lowercase letters beginning with letter 'a', such that: $p1='a'$, $p2='b'$, $p3='c'$, etc. Using this notation the tree in figure 3 can be stated as in figure 4 where each node represents an operator and its children the operands. It should be noted that it is a binary syntactic tree.

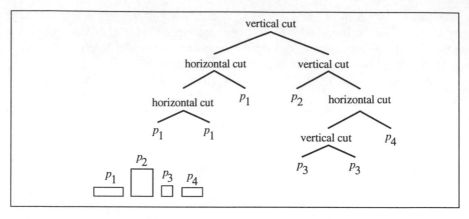

Figure 3 Binary tree indicating each type of cut.

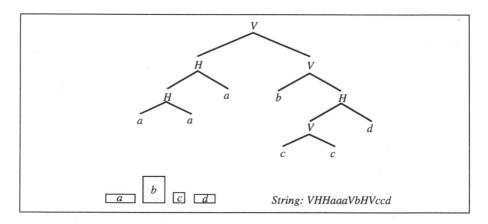

Figure 4. Syntactic binary tree.

It is not difficult to see that by performing a depth-first search on the syntactic binary tree a string can be retrieved. For example, in figure 4 we have represented the string *VHHaaaVbHVccd* corresponding to the cutting pattern defined in figure 2 and composed by pieces *a*, *b*, *c* and *d*. Obviously, associated with each string we need other information in order to completely describe the specific, pattern such as the size of the rectangle (length and width) and the area effectively occupied by the pieces. We identify an *individual* as the string and the complementary information associated with it.

A string as defined above, can be described hierarchically, according to its syntax [Aho, 1986], with the following production rules:

$$string \rightarrow V\ string\ string$$
$$string \rightarrow H\ string\ string$$
$$string \rightarrow p_i \forall p_i \in P = \{\,'a','b','c','d',..\}$$

Where the arrow is read as 'has the form'. $'V'$ and $'H'$ represent the operators and constitute the non terminal symbols. The p_i 's are characters representing pieces of the set of demand pieces P and correspond to the terminal items in the tree.

From the explanation above we know how to build an individual from a cutting pattern. But now, given an individual it is necessary to translate its information content in order to determine the location of each piece within the layout. We use a recursive decoding process: $decode(x, y, W, L)$, that starts from the piece information and gradually obtains all needed data. In this way, considering a string to decode:

$$s = s_1 s_2 \ldots s_m$$

and an initial call to the procedure with the input data $x=y=0$ and $i=1$, the location of the left superior vertex from each piece allocated on the plate is obtained as the output. Such steps are indicated in algorithm 1.

Algorithm 1
Decode (input: x,y; output: W, L);
Begin

> $c \leftarrow s_i;$
> IF $c = "V"$ THEN
> > $Decode(x, y, W1, L1);$
> > $Decode(x, y + L1, W2, L2);$
> > $W \leftarrow maximum\{ W1, W2 \};$
> > $L = L1 + L2;$
>
> IF $c = "H"$ THEN
> > $Decode(x, y, W1, L1);$
> > $Decode(x + W1, y, W2, L2);$
> > $W \leftarrow W1 + W2;$
> > $L = maximum\{ L1, L2\};$
>
> IF $c = "p_i"$ THEN
> > $W \leftarrow w_i;$
> > $L = l_i;$
> > $print(Piece\ p_i\ on\ position\ x + W,\ y + L);$
> > $Return;$

End.

By using the procedure above with a set of pieces $P = \{a, b, c, d\}$ and the string $s = "VHHaaaVbHVccd"$, figure 5 shows the location of each piece on the plate. If we consider in this figure the origin of the coordinates on the left superior corner of the plate then, (L, W, x, y) indicates the left superior corner of the rectangle (x, y), and its dimensions (L, W).

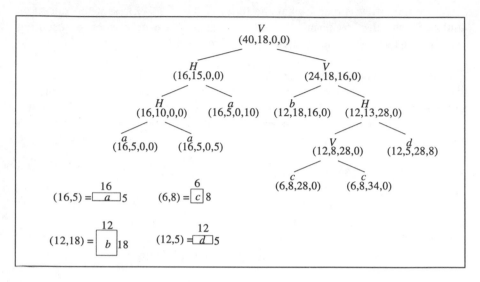

Figure 5 Tree of pieces location on the plate.

The data of terminal nodes i.e., position within the plate (x, y) and dimensions (l_i, w_i) give rise to table 1 that describes completely the retrieved cutting pattern.

Table 1. Sizes and coordinates of each piece on the plate

Piece	Width	Length	X axis	Y axis
a	16	5	0	0
a	16	5	0	5
a	16	5	0	10
b	12	18	16	0
c	6	8	28	0
c	6	8	34	0
d	12	5	28	8

It can be appreciated that, as opposed to the traditional genetic algorithms, the string here defined has variable length and even more, it increases gradually as the generation process proceeds. However the string growth is limited. A crossover is feasible, if the newly generated individual can be cut from the plate and the number of times a piece is cut does not exceed its upper limit.

Consider now that pieces can be rotated in 90°. In this way, the problem domain is extended and the final trim loss can be improved considerably. To include this issue in the model it is necessary to incorporate a new sort of operator between rectangles. We define thus, the rotated vertical operator that is denoted by *'W'*, and the rotated horizontal operator *'I'*. So, the strings now could have four characters: *'H'*, *'V'*, *'W'*, and *'I'*. Figure 6 illustrates the two new operators.

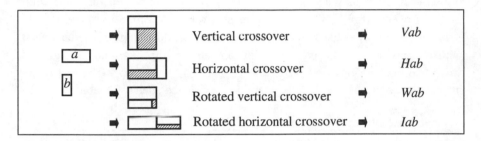

Figure 6. Operators with pieces rotation.

These two new sort of operators, that are added to the already described, represent rotation in 90° of the second individual of a combination. As an example consider the string *s=IWIdcWHaaVbbIVcca* that represents a cutting pattern from the set of pieces *a,b,c,d*. The associated binary tree is shown in figure 7.

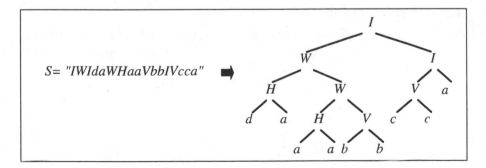

Figure 7 Syntactic tree of a cutting pattern considering piece rotation.

The decoding procedure presented in the algorithm 1 can be easily extended to handle the rotation of pieces. Although the computational effort is greater using such rotation it is rewarded in terms of solution quality.

We denote an individual as:

$$\gamma_i = (\sigma, \alpha, \lambda, \varepsilon).$$

where σ corresponds to the string, α and λ are the rectangle width and length respectively, and ε is the affective area occupied by pieces.

2.2 Crossover Operator

From two individuals γ_i and γ_j other four $(\gamma_l, \gamma_o, \gamma_p, \gamma_m)$ can be generated according to use of operators 'V', 'W', 'H' and 'I' respectively. Considering σ_i and σ_j , the strings of the individuals γ_i and γ_j, we can obtain child strings concatenating σ_i with σ_j and putting the corresponding operator at the beginning of the new string. So, new strings are: 'V$\sigma_i\sigma_j$', 'W$\sigma_i\sigma_j$', 'H$\sigma_i\sigma_j$' and 'I$\sigma_i\sigma_j$'. The rest of the information associated with individuals can be updated such as in table 2.

Table 2. Results of the crossover

Vertical crossover	Rotated vertical crossover	Horizontal crossover	Rotated horizontal crossover
$\gamma_l = (\sigma_l, \alpha_l, \lambda_l, \varepsilon_l)$	$\gamma_o = (\sigma_o, \alpha_o, \lambda_o, \varepsilon_o)$	$\gamma_m = (\sigma_m, \alpha_m, \lambda_m, \varepsilon_m)$	$\gamma_p = (\sigma_p, \alpha_p, \lambda_p, \varepsilon_p)$
$\sigma_l = V\sigma_i\sigma_j$	$\sigma_o = W\sigma_i\sigma_j$	$\sigma_m = H\sigma_i\,\sigma_j$	$\sigma_p = I\sigma_i\,\sigma_j$
$\alpha_l = \alpha_i + \alpha_j$	$\alpha_o = \alpha_i + \lambda_j$	$\alpha_m = \max(\alpha_i, a_j)$	$\alpha_p = \max(\alpha_i, \lambda_j)$
$\lambda_l = \max(\lambda_i, \lambda_j)$	$\lambda_o = \max(\lambda_i, \alpha_j)$	$\lambda_m = l_i + l_j$	$\lambda_p = \lambda_i + \alpha_j$
$\varepsilon_l = \varepsilon_i + \varepsilon_j$	$\varepsilon_o = \varepsilon_i + \varepsilon_j$	$\varepsilon_m = \varepsilon_i + \varepsilon_j$	$\varepsilon_p = \varepsilon_i + \varepsilon_j$

2.3 Updating the Trim Loss

Given a plate of length L and width W, and an individual to be cut from it, the total trim loss p_T corresponds to the area of the plate not used by any piece. This includes the internal trim loss p_I that according to the individual definition, is determined as the total area of the rectangle less the area occupied by pieces. So, we have:

$$p_T = LW - \varepsilon \tag{1}$$
$$p_I = \alpha\lambda - \varepsilon \tag{2}$$

Note that $p_I \le p_T$ and if the rectangle cover completely the plate, then $p_I = p_T$.

2.4 Evaluation Function

A cutting pattern is better than an other one if it has a lower trim loss. In this sense, we define the evaluation function to be maximized as the ratio between the area occupied by pieces and the plate area, it means:

$$f(\gamma) = \varepsilon / WL \tag{3}$$

2.5 Algorithm

The operations to incrementally generate cutting patterns, such as was explained above, can be represented through an And /Or graph [Parada et al. 1995]. Considering this representation we denote the proposed algorithm as *GAO* (Genetic - And /Or algorithm).

The proposed algorithm consists of an iteration cycle in which, from a given population of individuals a new population is obtained applying the operators above defined. The initial population consists of a set of minimal individuals, one for each piece. From these, other individuals representing more complex patterns and containing a greater number of pieces are obtained. The process continues until a total trim loss equal to zero is found or till, no new individual can be generated or finally when the number of iterations exceeds a termination value. The algorithm works with three sets of individuals $A(t)$, $B(t)$ and C, described below:

$A(t)$: Set of the best generated individuals during the process at iteration t. This set is modified in each iteration, by replacing individuals by superior solutions. Initially this set is empty. This set has a limited size.

$B(t)$: Set containing the population of individuals in each iteration t. The elements of $B(t)$ are obtained selecting the better individuals after the crossover among elements from $A(t)$ and $B(t)$ plus all those elements resulting from the crossovers among elements of $B(t)$. Initially $B(t)$ contains those elements corresponding to the pieces.

C: This auxiliary set is used to update $B(t)$ in each cycle.

Algorithm GAO

Begin

    $B(0) \leftarrow$ *Set of initial individuals;*

    $A(0) \leftarrow \varnothing$ *;* $t = 0$*;*

    Repeat

        $t = t + 1$*;*

        $C \leftarrow \varnothing$ *;*

        $C \leftarrow$ *Selection of better individuals of feasible crossovers from*

                $A(t-1) \times B(t-1)$ *and* $B(t-1) \times B(t-1)$*;*

        $B(t) \leftarrow C$ *;*

        Update $A(t)$*;*

    Until an optimum criterion is satisfied;

end.

It must be noted that this algorithm does not employ the mutation operator because the, crossover operator alone can produce any conceivable solution. On the other hand, an additional issue is incorporated in the algorithm by means of the use of $A(t)$ that, implements a sort of memory throughout successive generations.

3   Numerical Results

In order to estimate the performance of the proposed algorithm, in terms of required memory and CPU time, it was tested a set of instances of cutting problems. In particular, a set of comparative numerical results was obtained implementing the Oliveira and Ferreira's method MWA, which is clearly superior over Wang's method [1983]. Results are presented for the problem with and without piece rotation.

A set of ten instances of the cutting problem with several plate and piece sizes. Some of them have been extracted from Christofides and Whitlock's paper [1977] since they have been used as tests in some subsequent studies. Others instances were defined by Oliveira and Ferreira[1990], and the rest was extracted from study of Parada et al. [1995].

It is important to note that the proposed algorithm is designed for any plate size, and for integer or real values. The algorithm MWA does not present good results for large plates, i.e. over 200 units of length and width. MWA is also satisfactory when dimensions of pieces or plates are measured as real values, because its performance depends on Gilmore and Gomory's method to solve the unconstrained problem. This method generates a large matrix that must be stored in memory during the execution of MWA.

Numerical results have been obtained from a C language implementation on a SUN-Sparc Station. All given results correspond to the required effort to find the optimum solution to each problem. Parameters of GAO were fine-tuned using a set of representative instances. So, the size of the population was varied, while for MWA parameter corresponding to the percentage of acceptable trim loss were adjusted for each individual problem instance. Results obtained in numerical tests for problem with and without rotation of pieces are summarized in figures 8 to 11.

In order to appreciate the relationship among the required resources in terms of memory and time, it is necessary to trace the results proportionally. In this sense, a ratio of the resources used by each implementation and the sum of resources used by both methods is used. Bar charts, show such percentages in terms of both time and memory required by each method in order to reach the optimum solution. Additionally, pie charts show the total amount of resources for both methods.

As a rule, for problems without pieces rotation one can not establish the superiority of one or the other method concerning CPU time, since the obtained results are quite similar. This can be appreciated from the pie chart in figure 8, where the percentages of CPU time are 47.2% and 52.8% for GAO and MWA respectively. However, as can be seen in the same figure, some problems are solved with more efficiency by MWA.

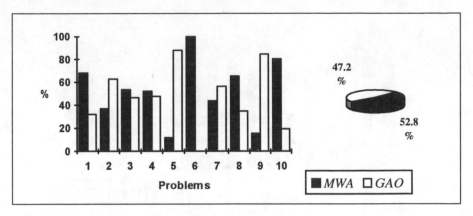

Figure 8 CPU time for problems without rotation of pieces.

In terms of the required memory one can note a categorical superiority of *GAO* related to *MWA*. In fact, looking at the pie chart in figure 9 we can see that *GAO* uses only 11.5% of total required memory by both methods to find the optimum solution. The corresponding bar chart shows that memory is used more efficiently by *GAO* for all cases.

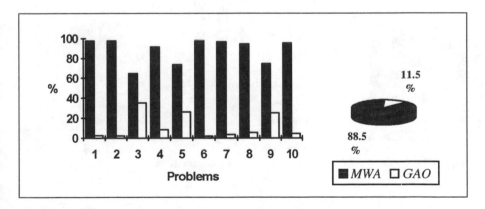

Figure 9 Required memory for problems without rotation of pieces.

For problems with pieces rotation a marked superiority of *GAO* over *MWA* can be demonstrated. As is shown in figure 10, *GAO* uses only 27.8% of the total time used by both algorithms. In terms of required memory the discrepancy is stressed even more. In fact, to reach the optimum solution in all cases using *GAO* requires 2.5% of the total resources used by both algorithms. So we can establish that in terms of memory *GAO* acts with more efficiency than *MWA*.

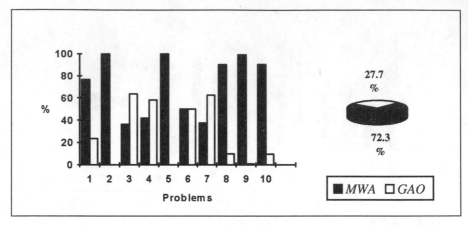

Figure 10 CPU time for problems with pieces rotation.

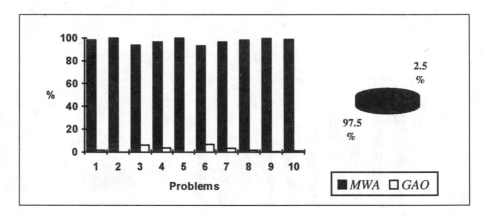

Figure 11 Required memory for problems with pieces rotation.

It is important to note that for problems 2 and 5 considering pieces rotation, *MWA* is not able to produce the optimum solution since available computer memory is exceeded. When comparing results in problems without rotation against those with pieces rotation, *GAO* obtains better results in the latter case. So, *GAO* has better performance than *MWA* as solution space increase.

Figure 12 is a convergence chart for both solution methods on problem 1 without pieces rotation. This chart, that is a representative example of the studied problems shows that *GAO* initially presents a fluctuating behavior, but reaches trim losses significantly less than *MWA* within a short time.

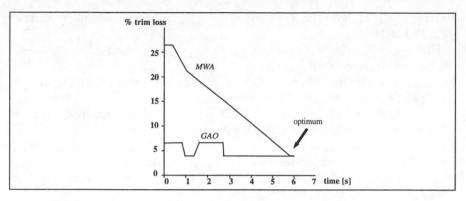

Figure 12 Best solution vs. CPU time for both algorithms.

4 Conclusions

In this article we propose an algorithm to solve the two-dimensional, constrained guillotine cutting problem. The algorithm is based on the enumeration of part of the feasible solution space by using ideas from genetic algorithms. A string represent a cutting pattern and successive populations generate strings corresponding to other feasible solutions with smaller trim losses. The used coding not only optimizes the memory requirements but, furthermore, simplifies the process of storage and manage cutting pattern in a computer. According to this other methods such as *MWA* could also use this representation in order to enhance their performance. Numerical results establish that the proposed method can handle problem instances greater than those the Oliveira and Ferreira's algorithm can handle.

References

Aho , A.; Sethi, R. and Ullman, J. (1986): Compilers: Principles, Techniques and Tools. Addison Wesley Publishing Company. Reading MA.

Christofides, N. and Whitlock, C. (1977): An Algorithm for Two-Dimensional Trim-Loss Problems. AI and Simulation, Summer Conference, Univ. of Edinburgh, 158-165.

Dyckhoff, H. (1990): A Typology of Cutting and Packing Problems, *EJOR* 44, 145-159.

Gilmore, P.C. and Gomory, R.E. (1967): The Theory and Computation of Knapsack Functions. *Operations Research* 15, 1045-1075.

Goldberg, D. (1989): Genetic Algorithms in Search, Optimization and Machine Learning. Addison Wesley,. Reading/ Mass.

Hinxman, A.I. (1976): Problem Reduction and the Two-dimensional Trim-loss Problem. A. I. and Simulation. Summer Conference, Univ. of Edinburgh, 158-165.

Hinxman, A.I. (1980): The Trim - Loss and Assortment Problems :A Survey. *EJOR* 5, 8-18.

Michalewicz, Z. (1992): Genetic Algorithms + Data Structure = Evolution Programs. Springer Verlag, Berlin.

Morabito, R. ; Arenales, M. and Arcaro, V. (1992): An And-Or-Graph Approach for Two Dimensional Cutting Problems. *EJOR* 58, 263-271.

Oliveira, J. F. and Ferreira, J. S. (1990): An Improved Version of Wang's Algorithm for two-dimensional Cutting Problems. *EJOR* 44, 256-266.

Parada, V.; Gómes, A. and De Diego, J. (1995): Exact Solutions for Constrained Two-Dimensional Cutting Problems. To appear in *EJOR*.

Pearl, J. (1984): Heuristics: Intelligent Search Strategies for Computer problem Solving. Addison-Wesley, Reading/Mass.

Vasko, F.J. (1989): A Computational Improvement to Wang's Two-Dimensional Cutting Stock Algorithm. *Computers and Industrial Engineering* 16, 109-115.

Viswanathan, K. and Bagchi, A. (1993): Best-First Search Methods for Constrained Two-Dimensional Cutting Stock Problems. *Operations Research*, 41, 768-776.

Wang, P. Y. (1983): Two Algorithms for Constrained Two-Dimensional Cutting Stock Problems. *Operations Research* 31, 573-586.

Part Three
Applications in Trade

Facility Management of Distribution Centres for Vegetables and Fruits

Rob A.C.M. Broekmeulen

ATO-DLO, P.O. Box 17, 6700 AA Wageningen, The Netherlands

Abstract. We present a hierarchical algorithm to solve the facility management problem in a distribution centre for vegetables and fruits. The facility management problem is formulated as a multi criteria decision model. The hierarchical algorithm consists of two stages: determination of cluster properties and product group assignment to clusters. Cluster properties such as capacity and temperature of the cold store are determined with a genetic algorithm. For the assignment of clusters to product groups we linearized the multi criteria decision problem. The resulting linear assignment problem was solved with the simplex method. This solution strategy was applied to a distribution centre in the Netherlands to demonstrate that the suggested approach works for real life problems.

Keywords. decision support system, genetic algorithm, distribution centres, vegetables and fruits

1   Introduction

1.1   Physical Distribution of Vegetables and Fruits

Vegetables and fruits are products that are susceptible to quality loss such as aging and breakdown. Physical distribution includes all activities associated with the shipment of products from the manufacturer to the consumer. The distribution of vegetables and fruits usually starts after the harvest and includes activities such as transportation, handling in and out of storage and conditioning. A lot of these activities are carried out in a *distribution centre*.

The share of distribution cost in the consumer price of vegetables and fruits is nearly twice as high as the distribution cost of non-perishables [Hoogerwerf *et al* 1990]. This difference is due to two complicating factors: fast handling and special storage conditions. Vegetables and fruits are distributed in a relatively short time to minimize the quality loss [Chung and Norback 1991]. Adequate storage conditions such as relative humidity and temperature, minimal handling and avoidance of product interactions such as odour and hormone transmission can also reduce quality loss [Petropakis 1989]. The management of a distribution centre for vegetables and fruits aims at minimizing quality loss and the amount of handling. This must be realized with minimal investments and low operational cost.

1.2 Distribution Centre

The *assortment* of a distribution centre is a list of *articles*. An article is defined by attributes such as country of origin, quality class, sorting and packaging. A *product group* consists of articles with the same *quality change characteristics*. These characteristics include optimal storage temperature and relative humidity, production of and sensitivity to odours and hormones [Kopec 1983].

The efficiency of a distribution centre plays a crucial role in the distribution process. The *layout* and *storage methods* influence the amount of quality loss. A distribution centre for vegetables and fruits consists of an air-conditioned storage accommodation and several cold stores. A *cluster* is a storage space with specific conditions and a maximum storage capacity. Each cold store should be matched with at least one cluster. An example of a *physical layout* is shown in **Fig. 1.1**. All articles have a fixed *location* or position in the storage area due to the absence of a uniform article coding.

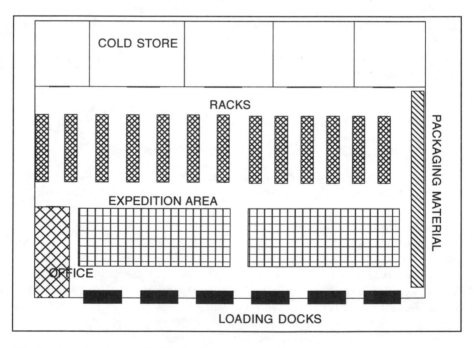

Fig. 1.1 A typical layout of a distribution centre for vegetables.

The supply and sometimes the quality of many vegetables and fruits depend on the seasons. Lack of harmonization in the post-harvest chains limits the availability of vegetables and fruits further. The mismatch between the long, seasonal production pattern and the short, day-to-day fluctuating consumption pattern makes the stock levels in a distribution centre unpredictable. The numerous changes in the assortment during the year make the activities in a distribution centre non-repetitive. Concepts such as Material Resource Planning, Distribution Resource Planning and Just In Time Planning do not seem to be applicable for the distribution of vegetables and fruits because of the unpredictable and non-repetitive nature of the activities involved [Browne *et al* 1988].

To minimize the quality loss and the amount of handling in a distribution centre for vegetables and fruits the management has to make decisions about the conditioning and the assignment of the articles. There is a need for a procedure that deals with these decisions in a structural and integral way. The procedure developed for warehouses by Gray *et al* [1992] does not take into account the influence of the conditions on the quality loss of vegetables and fruits.

1.3   Problem Definition

The management of a distribution centre has to deal with questions concerning storage and handling of the articles such as the ones below.
- How much capacity is needed?
- What kind of conditions do we need in each cold store?
- Where must the articles be placed in the distribution centre?

When the management tries to answer these questions their main objective is to minimize quality loss and the amount of handling. This means that the management searches for a tradeoff between quality loss, investment and handling costs.

1.4   Overview of the Article

- In our research we concentrate on the problem of the facility management of distribution centres for vegetables and fruits. The quality change properties of vegetables and fruits are described in Section 2. We state the developed decision model in Subsection Multi Criteria Decision Model. The applied solution strategy is explained in Subsection 3.2 followed by the implementation issues in Subsection 3.3. In Section 4 we discuss the application of the proposed strategy to the facility management of a distribution centre in the Netherlands.

2   Quality Change Models for Vegetables and Fruits

Vegetables and fruits require product specific conditions for a better keeping quality.
- **Temperature**: Each product has its own optimal temperature. A lot of products that now or in the past originated from tropical or subtropical

climates are susceptible to low temperature breakdown. Each cluster has a specific temperature that will always be a compromise between the optimal temperatures of the product groups that are present in that cluster.

- **Utilization**: Handling has a negative effect on keeping quality. The storage types available at a cluster determine the accessibility of that cluster for handling. High levels of utilization increase the amount of handling.
- **Interactions**: Interactions between products caused by the hormone ethylene and odours have to be avoided by spatially separating the product groups or by ventilation of the cluster. The production of ethylene and odours as well as the influence of these product interactions on the keeping quality are dependent on the temperature.

QUALITY CHANGE MODEL

Declaration of the symbols

•Dimension

$P \in \mathbf{N}$ = total number of product groups

•Variables

$x_{pk} \in \{0,1\}$ = assignment of cluster k to product group p

•Coefficients

$A_k \in [0,1] \subset \mathbf{R}$ = accessibility for handling of cluster k

$B_p \in \mathbf{R}^+$ = average storage time of product group p [days]

$C_k \in \mathbf{R}^+$ = storage capacity of cluster k [m^3]

$E_k \in \mathbf{R}^+$ = ethylene concentration in cluster k [mol / m^3]

$K_p \in \mathbf{R}^+$ = initial keeping quality of product group p [days]

$L_{pk} \in \mathbf{R}^+$ = loss of keeping quality of product group p in cluster k [days / days]

$Q^E_{pk} \in [0,1] \subset \mathbf{R}$ = ethylene effect of cluster k on the keeping quality of product group p

$Q^H_{pk} \in [0,1] \subset \mathbf{R}$ = handling effect of cluster k on the keeping quality of product group p

$Q^T_{pk} \in [0,1] \subset \mathbf{R}$ = temperature effect of cluster k on the keeping quality of product group p

$S_p \in \mathbf{R}^+$ = stock level of product group p [m^3]

$T_k \in \mathbf{R}^+$ = temperature of cluster k [$^\circ C$]

$U_k \in \mathbf{R}^+$ = utilization of cluster k

$V_k \in [0,1] \subset \mathbf{R}$ = volume of cluster k [m^3]

$W_k \in \mathbf{R}^+$ = ventilation rate in cluster k [m^3 / m^3]

$$L_{pk} = \frac{B_p}{Q_{pk}^E Q_{pk}^H Q_{pk}^T K_p} \tag{1}$$

$$Q_{pk}^E = \text{ETHS}_p(E_k, T_k) \tag{2}$$

$$Q_{pk}^H = \text{HAND}_p(A_k, U_k) \tag{3}$$

The quality change model equations:
$$Q_{pk}^T = \text{TEMP}_p(T_k) \tag{4}$$

$$E_k = \frac{\sum_{p=1}^P \text{ETHP}_p(T_k) S_p x_{pk}}{W_k \left(V_k - \sum_{p=1}^P S_p x_{pk}\right)} \tag{5}$$

$$U_k = \frac{1}{C_k} \sum_{p=1}^P S_p x_{pk} \tag{6}$$

The generalized quality change model describes for each product group the loss in keeping quality dependent on the average time in storage, the cluster conditions and the interactions between the product groups. At the moment the ethylene effect is the only interaction considered between product groups. In Equation 1 quality loss is expressed as the fraction of the initial keeping quality that is lost. Equation 5 calculates the ethylene concentration in the clusters and Equation 6 calculates the utilization. The effects of ethylene, handling and temperature on the quality loss are described by the product group specific functions mentioned in Equations 2, 3 and 4. The functions for the ethylene effect are generalized from Woltering et al [1987]. The function TEMP_p is based on Tijskens et al [1995].

3   Facility Management Problem

3.1   Multi Criteria Decision Model

A storage location or cluster must be assigned to every article. The main goal is to reduce the quality loss due to inadequate storage conditions. It is impractical to give each product group its own storage room. The system tries to balance quality loss against utilization of storage capacity.

MULTI CRITERIA DECISION MODEL

Declaration of the symbols
* Dimensions
  $P \in \mathbf{N}$ = number of product groups
  $K \in \mathbf{N}$ = number of clusters
  $T \in \mathbf{N}$ = number of periods

- Variables

$x_{kp} \in \{0,1\}$ = assignment of cluster k to product group p

$o_{kt} \in \mathbf{R}^+$ = capacity overflow of cluster k in period t

$e \in \mathbf{R}^+$ = maximum capacity overflow as fraction of the available capacity

- Coefficients

$w^L \in \mathbf{R}^+$ = weightfactor of loss of keeping quality

$w^C \in \mathbf{R}^+$ = weightfactor of the capacity overflow

$L_{pk} \in \mathbf{R}^+$ = loss of keeping quality of product group p in cluster k

$C_k \in \mathbf{R}^+$ = capacity of cluster k

$S_{pt} \in \mathbf{R}^+$ = peak stock level of product group p in period t

Given a set of values of the coefficients and values of the dimensions, find values of x_{pk} such that

$$w^L \sum_{p=1}^{P} \sum_{k=1}^{K} L_{pk} x_{pk} + w^C \left(e + \sum_{k=1}^{K} \sum_{t=1}^{T} o_{kt}\Big/ C_k \right) \quad (7)$$

is minimal, subject to

$$\sum_{k=1}^{K} x_{pk} = 1 \qquad \text{for all } p = 1,\ldots,P, \qquad (8)$$

$$\sum_{p=1}^{P} S_{pt} x_{pk} \leq C_k + o_{kt} \quad \text{for all } k = 1,\ldots,K \text{ and } t = 1,\ldots,T, \quad (9)$$

$$o_{kt}\Big/ C_k \leq e \qquad \text{for all } k = 1,\ldots,K \text{ and } t = 1,\ldots,T. \quad (10)$$

The first step in the proposed decision model is the definition of a fixed amount of clusters of storage space. The layout of the distribution centre restricts the number of the clusters. Each cold store should be matched with at least one cluster.

The first part of Objective function 7 considers the loss in keeping quality due to location dependent properties, product group interactions and amount of handling, the second part deals with the capacity overflow. Quality loss is calculated with functions described in Section 2. Constraint 8 ensures that a cluster is assigned to every product group. Constraint 9 calculates the capacity utilization of each cluster in all periods. Constraint 10 calculates the maximum overflow.

The sum of the peak stock levels in a cluster normally exceeds the available capacity of a cluster. In practice these peaks do not occur at the same time during a given period. The resulting hypothetical capacity overflow is equally divided over the clusters and the periods by minimizing the maximum overflow.

The product group interactions make the model non-linear because the loss in keeping quality in a cluster depends on the presence of other product groups in that cluster. A typical distribution centre has two hundred product groups and about ten clusters. These problem instance dimensions make a traditional solution approach impractical.

3.2   Hierarchical Solution Strategy

Solving the non-linear decision model in one stage is intractable for real world instances. Instead, we developed a hierarchical solution approach for the different, functionally related decisions in the problem. The approach divides the decision variables into separate nested or hierarchical levels. We have chosen a hierarchical decomposition into two decision levels as shown in **Fig. 3.1**. The main advantage of this solution approach is a reduction of the decision space at the expense of optimality.

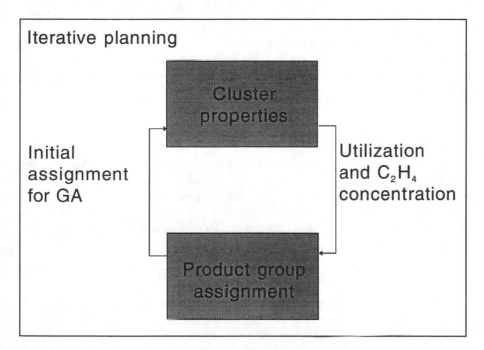

Fig. 3.1 Decomposition of the facility management problem of a distribution centre for vegetables and fruits.

Cluster properties. In the first level we allocate capacity to the clusters and determine the conditions such as temperature in the different clusters. The initial product group assignment together with the cluster properties determine dependent conditions such as the ethylene concentration. We use at this level a *genetic algorithm* that is explained further in Subsection 3.3.

Product group assignment. A cluster is assigned to every product group with respect to quality loss and capacity utilization. The original multi criteria decision model is linearized by fixing the capacity (C_k^F), the utilization (U_k^F) and the ethylene concentration (E_k^F) of each cluster in the calculation of the loss of keeping quality and the capacity overflow. For this purpose the maximum values during the total planning period are used. The following two sets of constraints replace the corresponding equations in the quality change model to keep the deviation from the exact loss of keeping quality within bounds.

$$\frac{\sum_{p=1}^{P} \text{ETHP}_p(T_k)S_{pt}x_{kp}}{W_k(V_k - C_k^F U_k^F)} \leq E_k^F \quad \text{for all } k = 1,...,K \text{ and } t = 1,...,T \quad (11)$$

$$\sum_{p=1}^{P} S_{pt}x_{pt} \leq C_k^F(1+\varepsilon)U_k^F \quad \text{for all } k = 1,...,K \text{ and } t = 1,...,T \quad (12)$$

The resulting product group assignment problem can be solved with an algorithm that is based on the simplex method.

During the solution process the user has to iterate between the decision levels to improve the solution quality. The output of the first level can be used as input for the second level and vice versa. The procedure will typically converge after a few iterations to a solution with minimal quality loss and minimal capacity overflow.

3.3   Implementation

The solution strategy is implemented in a decision support system. The manager can interact with the solution process by identifying interesting alternatives and steering towards superior and practical facility plans. The user-friendly implementation makes revisions of the facility plan an easy and straightforward job. The solution can be fine-tuned with detailed simulation experiments to examine effects that have been overlooked or discarded in the models.

3.3.1   Genetic Algorithm

A genetic algorithm is a random search technique that is based on the concept of natural selection in the evolution of species [Goldberg 1989]. The genetic algorithm for the studied problem was implemented with the Heuristic Optimization Shell (HOS), developed at ATO-DLO. The user must supply the HOS with a description of the type and position of the decision variables on the strings or chromosomes and the corresponding fitness function of the problem. The alphabet-size of the coding can vary between 2 and 255. Each chromosome is an instance of the problem. The number of chromosomes in the population is fixed. We used a population of 100 chromosomes with a binary coding (alphabet-size = 2).

The neighbourhood space is searched with the following two operators:
- **Mutation**: One byte at a single position of a randomly selected chromosome is replaced with a random number in the range of the chosen alphabet.
- **Crossover**: Two parents are selected at random from the whole population without regard to fitness. The chromosomes exchange parts of the string with a two-point crossover. Only the resulting children return to the population.

The mutation rate and the crossover rate are dynamically adjusted during the search process and depend on the variation in the population. Crossover has less effect in a population with low variation. A high mutation frequency can introduce higher variation on all positions. High variation restores a low mutation frequency and a high crossover frequency.

The selection operator is not linked with the mutation and crossover operators. Every selection operation starts with taking a sample of the population. We used a sample size of 10 chromosomes. The chromosomes in the samples are ranked according to the fitness value. The chromosome with the best fitness value in the sample is duplicated at expense of the worst chromosome in the sample that most closely resembles the best chromosome. This selection process based on the crowding model ensures high diversity in the population. An elitist strategy protects the best chromosome of the population against being destroyed by crossover or mutation.

The search process is stopped after a fixed amount of operations instead of generations because the described genetic algorithm has no clearly defined generations.

Each chromosome codes for a different set of cluster properties for the distribution centre as shown in part A of **Fig. 3.2**. The fitness function is based on the multi criteria decision model. An initial assignment is needed to calculate the fitness of the chromosome. We have chosen a genetic algorithm for the determination of the cluster properties because these algorithms typically perform rather well on non-linear problems with 'soft' constraints. Obtaining a good product group assignment by extending the coding on the chromosome, as shown in part B of **Fig. 3.2** is on the other hand difficult because the algorithm is 'blind' for combinatorial problems. Crossover does not speed up the search for better assignments because of the GA-deceptive nature of these problems. The performance of a genetic algorithm is based on the propagation of short, low-order schemata or building blocks in the population. Product groups with adjacent positions on the chromosome have not necessarily a direct relation but in this combinatorial problem do have a epistatic effect. Such a GA-deceptive problem can combine low-order building blocks to suboptimal longer, higher order building blocks that destroys the positive effect of crossover. A GA-deceptive problem does not have to be GA-hard which means that it diverges from the global optimum.

A. Cluster properties

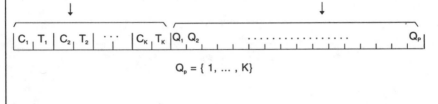

B. Cluster properties plus product group assignment

Fig. 3.2 Possible chromosome codings for the facility management problem of a distribution centre for vegetables and fruits

The effect of crossover was investigated with two experiments on the extended coding. In the first experiment we replaced the crossover operator with an operator that exchanges on both chromosomes the string between the crossover points with a string of random bytes. Crossover is now reduced to an intensive mutation. In the second experiment we reordered the position of the product groups on the chromosome. In both experiments the quality of the results of the genetic algorithm did not improve and the required CPU-time stayed roughly the same as the genetic algorithm with 'real' crossover and standard product group ordering. We could not find a speed-up of the search process by a crossover operator that uses information from the population. We do not know if the use of Gray-codes overcomes the deceptive nature of the studied problem.

3.3.2 Simplex Method

The assignment problem is relaxed by allowing all assignment variables to be continuous between zero and one. The resulting continuous problem can be solved with the simplex method. A branch and bound procedure with a limited search time can find better integer solutions than the genetic algorithm. If no integer solutions are found after a preset amount of time with the branch and bound procedure, the algorithm proceeds with a rounding procedure. If more than one cluster is assigned to a product group, then the cluster with the highest value of the assignment variable is assigned to the product group. This heuristic approach was necessary because of the large number of product groups.

4 Case Study and Discussion

To test our solution strategy we studied the logistic operations of a major distribution centre for vegetables and fruits in the Netherlands. The distribution centre is a 40000 m^3 facility with four cold stores of 1500 m^3 each. The complete assortment lists more than 5000 articles divided into 250 product groups. On a single day not more than 750 different articles are in stock because of seasonal variations in the assortment. The turnover is about 400 pallets per day. Six days a week the distribution centre buys vegetables and fruits on order at auctions and directly from growers for about 20 customers. These customers are large supermarket chains.

During the implementation of our procedure we had a problem with obtaining a complete and accurate set of data. The installed administrative system cannot keep up with the pace of the physical transactions in the distribution centre. The management is improving the current system to let it log the activities real-time. We expect better input data for our solution strategy in the near future.

The use of the prototype of the decision support system gave the management already better insight in the current problems with quality loss. The effect of ethylene and high storage temperatures had been underestimated. The distribution centre has added three new cold stores with facilities for ventilation. The solutions presented by the system did not result in less capacity overflow of the storages compared to the current situation. This can be attributed partly to the inaccurate historical data that exaggerated the utilization in the past years.

5 Conclusions

The hierarchical solution strategy seems to work for the facility management problem of a distribution centre for vegetables and fruits. The expert knowledge contained in the quality change models plays an important role in the acceptance of the presented solutions. The potential of the solution strategy to reduce the amount of handling has still to be proven.

Acknowledgments

I thank Emile Aarts for the valuable discussions and support during this work. Mark Sloof assisted with the layout of the final version of this text.

References

Browne, J.; Harhen, J.; Shivnan, J. (1988): Production Management Systems. Addison-Wesley Publishing Company, 259-265

Chung, H.K.; Norback, J.P. (1991): A clustering and insertion heuristic applied to a large routing problem in food distribution. Journal of the Operations Research Society 42(7):555-564

Goldberg, D.E. (1989): Genetic Algorithms in Search, Optimization and Machine Learning}. Addison-Wesley, Reading MA

Gray, A.E.; Karmarkar, U.S.; Seidmann, A. (1992): Design and operation of an order-consolidation warehouse: Models and application. European Journal of Operations Research 58:14-36

Hoogerwerf, A.; Reinders, M.P.; Oosterloo, S.K., Kanis, J. (1990): Eindrapport van de programmeringsstudie agrologistiek. ATO/NEHEM, Technical report, Wageningen, (in Dutch)

Kopec, K..(1983): Effect of storage condition on harvested vegetables and their mathematical simulation. Acta Horticulturae 138:343-354

Petropakis, H.J. (1989): Transport of chilled agricultural products. In: Zeuthen, P.; Cheftel, J.C.; Eriksson, C.; Gormley, T.R.; Linko, P.; Paulus, K. (eds.): Chilled Foods: the revolution in freshness}, COST 91, London, Elsevier Applied Science, 234-243

Tijskens, L.M.M.; Polderdijk, J.J. (1995): Keeping quality of vegetable produce during storage and distribution. Agricultural Systems, (submitted)

Woltering, E.J.; Harkema, H. (1987): Effect of exposure time and temperature on response of carnation cut flowers to ethylene. Acta Horticulturae 216:255-262

Integrating Machine Learning and Simulated Breeding Techniques to Analyze the Characteristics of Consumer Goods

Takao Terano, Yoko Ishino, Kazuyuki Yoshinaga

Graduate School of Systems Management, The University of
Tsukuba 3-29-1, Otsuka, Bunkyo-ku, Tokyo 112, Japan

Abstract. This paper describes a novel method to analyze the data on consumer goods gathered via questionnaires. In the task domain, although we can only gather noisy sample data, it is critical to get simple but clear classification rules to explain the characteristics of the data in order to make decisions for promotion. In this paper, we integrate machine learning to acquire simple decision rules from data and simulated breeding to get the effective features. Simulated breeding is one of the GA-based techniques to subjectively or interactively determine the objective function values of offspring generated by genetic operations. The proposed method has been validated in a case study of oral care products (toothpaste) analysis data with 16 concepts, 16 features, and 2,300 cases. The results suggest that the prerequisites of the method are so simple that it can be used for various problems.

Keywords. Machine Learning, C4.5, Genetic Algorithms, Simulated Breeding, Marketing Data Analysis, Feature Selection Problem

1   Introduction

This paper describes a novel method to analyze the data of consumer goods gathered via questionnaires. We apply machine learning and genetic algorithm (GA)- based techniques for this purpose.

In a saturated market domain such as oral care products, marketing decision analysts must determine the promotion strategies of new products according to the abstract image of the products to be produced. In the task domain, although we can only gather noisy sample data from complicated information sources including questionnaires from candidate users, it is critical to get simple but clear classification rules to explain the characteristics of the products in order to make decisions for promotion (please refer to Aaker, et al. [1980]). Furthermore, the actual features of the product to realize the product image are often left to the discretion or intuition of marketing analysts and are determined in a very unclear manner. It is necessary to organize the information in a simple and useful format in order to understand the relationship between product images and features from the results of a questionnaire, and in order to use this understanding in the decision making processes.

Conventional statistical methods are too weak because they usually assume linearity of the models and the form of distributions of the data. For example, multivariate analysis [Kendall 1980] has been the main statistical tool used for analysis of questionnaire data. During the analysis, emphasis has been placed on understanding trends after identifying target data. Furthermore, marketing requires use of quantitative as well as qualitative analysis. Unfortunately, there are no statistical tools which facilitate to satisfy both requirements simultaneously.

AI-based techniques for concept learning do not assume such conditions, however, they may involve combinatorial feature selection problems. Feature selection in machine learning and statistical research is the problem to choose a small subset of features that is necessary and sufficient to describe the target concept. If we were able to have well-defined objective functions to be optimized, we could apply well- known GA techniques to choose appropriate features. In the task domain, this is not the case. We must interactively evaluate the resulting decision rules.

In this paper, we propose a method which integrates (1) machine learning to acquire simple decision rules from questionnaire data for clarification of the relationships between product image and features and (2) simulated breeding to get the effective features. Simulated breeding is one of the GA-based techniques to evolve offspring [Unemi 1994].

This paper is organized as follows: In Section 2, discussions on related work are given. In Section 3, the research problem is defined. Section 4 explains and summarizes the procedure of the proposed method, while Section 5 explains the results of some experiments conducted to validate the effectiveness of the method, using the data obtained from a questionnaire survey on oral care products (toothpaste). Section 6 contains some concluding remarks.

2 Related Work

In this section, we outline previous research and clarify the principles of the proposed new method with respect to its relationship with research in the literature.

The method most representative of inductive machine learning is ID3 [Quilan 1986] which produces a decision tree or a set of decision rules as the result of a classification analysis on features and attribute-value pairs. Our research adopts C4.5 [Quilan 1993], a successor of ID3 for inductive learning.

As stated in Weiss et al. [1991], inductive learning or concept learning techniques in Artificial Intelligence, and classification of data via statistical methods (for example, the linear discrimination method) will give similar classification results, if we are able to assume the linear distribution of sample data. The performance of the results are compatible. However, we believe that the explainability of the results for domain experts from machine learning is better than the one from statistical methods.

On the other hand, machine learning which attempts to incorporate all features in a decision tree is too complex [Mingers 1989]. Hence, selection of appropriate features becomes necessary. When defined broadly, feature selection involves inductive learning. Feature selection intrinsically has combinatorial characteristics. Thus, methods to search for appropriate features must be used. Various studies have been conducted to deal with the problem of interactions between features. Recently, Kira, et al. [1992] have proposed new algorithms.

Research to integrate inductive learning and genetic algorithms is not quite novel in the multistrategy learning literature. For example, Vafaie, et al. [1994] have investigated automated feature selection for the inductive learning program AQ with GA-based techniques. Bala, et al. [1994] have proposed another multistrategy approach to integrate AQ and GA in order to reduce computation time. The domain of these investigations is image understanding and classification. They differ from our problem in the aspect that an objective function is not explicitly given in our case.

The basic idea of *simulated breeding* [Unemi 1994] is similar to the ones of *simulated evolution* or *interactive evolution* in computer graphics arts [Sims 1992]. Conventional GA procedures (e.g., [Davis 1991]) consist of (1) selection of individuals based on a given evaluation function for phenotypes, (2) generation of offspring from selected individuals via crossover and mutation operators applied to genotypes, and (3) deletion of inferior individuals. When using standard genetic algorithms, it is necessary to define the evaluation function to execute step (1). However, for problems where human subjective judgments play an important role, the definition of an evaluation function is not an easy task. In contrast, for simulated breeding, step (1) consists of interactive selections by humans of good individuals exhibiting preferred characteristics without an explicit evaluation function. The other steps in simulated breeding are similar to the ones in GAs. Using simulated breeding, we can improve offspring by selecting the parent for the next generation based on human preference.

For example, in Unemi [1994], he has generated beautiful graphic images based on the user's preferences of colors, figures, and texture of the individual images, which represent the implicit evaluation criteria. Another example of an earlier system related to simulated breeding was developed by R. Dawkins in the Blind Watchmaker [Dawkins 1986]. In this system, a genetic algorithm with coded parameters of an *L-system* [Lindenmayer 1968] to produce shapes that resemble living objects is used. After breeding of individuals with only random mutation, offspring can be selected from the phenotypes based on human preference.

Hence, this method allows for the development of objects reflecting human preference. We do not adopt the selection procedure from standard GAs for the following reasons: (1) It is necessary to support the creativity of the marketing staff who try to develop appropriate explanations, and (2) the domain of our problem involves human subjective judgments which make the definition of evaluation functions and the formalization of optimization problems difficult.

Therefore, in a general sense, we propose in this paper a method to solve the feature selection problem in machine learning by the simulated breeding method. As a result, it is possible to develop a decision tree based on a smaller number of features, and which incorporates human subjective evaluations.

3 Problem Description

The focuses of this research are (1) to classify data with multiple features, (2) to select necessary and sufficient features to explain the characteristics of the data, and (3) to generate effective interpretations provided by decision trees or a set of decision rules.

The difficult points are that (1) the data involves noise, (2) the distribution of data cannot be previously determined, (3) selection of appropriate features of the data is inevitable, and (4) it is difficult to determine well-defined objective functions for decision making.

The method proposed in this paper has the following novel characteristics:

(1) inductive learning in Artificial Intelligence is used to classify the data,
(2) genetic operations are used to enhance the flexibility for feature selection,
(3) appropriate decision trees are selected based on the judgments of human experts, and
(4) decision trees which necessarily and sufficiently explain the model can be developed using a small number of features.

This is the first application of such an integration for the real world management analysis of marketing data. Specifically, this paper addresses the problem of clarifying the relationship between product images and product features through the usage of questionnaire data.

4 Outline of the Proposed Method

The procedure of the proposed method is shown in Figure 1. Descriptions of the steps involved in Figure 1 are presented below.

(1) Initialization

We define a set of target concepts to be explained by decision trees. In the problem, we select n number of image words to explain the characteristics of the product. If we are able to use only one word to represent the target concept, it is relatively easy to make clear the characteristics of the product. However, this case is not a frequent one. Therefore, by defining and explaining multiple image words simultaneously, we try to solve multi-objective optimization problems.

We generate the initial population, that is, we select m sets of individuals with less than or equal to l features. The m and l respectively represent the number of individuals and the length of their chromosomes. In principle, the more individuals we have, the more we obtain *good* evaluation results. However, the number m in simulated breeding is set to a very small value compared with standard GA-based applications, because the evaluation process in step 2 requires much more effort of a human expert than the automated evaluation of standard GAs. In our implementation, m and l are respectively set to 5 and 16. The chromosomes to represent the features are coded in binary strings, in which a 1 (respectively 0) means that a feature is (not) selected for inclusion in the inductive learning process in step 2.

```
Step 1: Initialization
    Select plural number of image words to be explained by decision
    rules.
    Randomly select m individuals with the features up to l.

Repeat Step 2-4 until
    an appropriate decision tree or a set of decision rules are
    obtained.

Step 2: Inductive Learning
    Apply inductive learning programs to the m individuals.
    Obtain corresponding decision trees or sets of decision rules.

Step 3: Interactive Evaluation of Individuals
    From among the obtained decision trees or decision rules, two are
    selected by a user based on their simplicity, correctness,
    reliability, and the understandability of the decision tree.

Step 4: Application of Genetic Algorithms
    Select two best offspring as parents.
    Apply uniform crossover operations to them in order to obtain new
    sets of features. Then, generate corresponding offspring.
```

Fig. 1. Algorithm for the Proposed Method

(2) Application of Inductive Learning

Inductive learning is applied to each of the m individuals with the selected features suggested as 1 in the chromosome. The data acquired from the questionnaire is aggregated, each of which has the corresponding features in it. Then the m sets of the data are processed by inductive learning programs. As stated earlier, we use C4.5 programs without modifications. As a result, m sets of decision trees with selected features or the corresponding set of decision rules are generated.

(3) Selection by Interactive Evaluation

In this step, a user, or a domain expert must interact with the system. This is a highly knowledge-intensive task.

Observing the forms of the decision trees, sets of decision rules, and combinations of selected features, the domain expert subjectively and interactively evaluates the intermediate results to explain the characteristics of the predetermined n image words. The domain expert judges them based on simplicity, understandability, accuracy, reliability, plausibility, and applicability of the represented knowledge. The implicit integration of these criteria plays the role of the evaluation function in standard GAs. This is a unique point of simulated breeding techniques.

From among the obtained decision trees or decision rules, two are selected as parents based on the judgment of the domain expert.

(4) Application of Genetic Algorithms

The trees selected in Step 3 are set as parents, and new product characteristics are determined by genetic operations. The GA techniques we have adopted are based on the Simple GA found in Goldberg [1989].

The corresponding chromosomes of the selected decision trees become parents for genetic operations. We apply uniform-crossover operations [Syswerda 1989] to them in order to get new sets of features to broaden the variety of offspring. Prior experiments with this problem have revealed that the standard one-point crossover operation is not adequate, because it usually results in locally optimal solutions within a few steps. No mutation operators are applied in our implementation in order to preserve the features the user has specified, however, the effects of mutation operations have not been investigated in detail in the experiments.

The selected two parents are preserved for the next generation. The rest $m-2$ offspring are replaced by the corresponding new $m-2$ offspring.

(5) Repeat the Steps

Steps 2 to 4 are repeated until an appropriate decision tree or set of decision rules is obtained. As are illustrated in Dowkins [1986] and Unemi [1994], only a few iterations are required to obtain appropriate results. In our experiments, it usually takes only less than 10 steps.

5 Experimental Results

5.1 Outline of the Experiments

Data obtained from a toothpaste questionnaire was used as an example for the analysis of product features. The outline of the experiments is summarized as follows.

(a) Questionnaire survey conducted with 2,300 respondents by a manufacturing company in 1993.

(b) 16 image words were selected to define product image. Respondents evaluated how well each of the 16 image words fit the toothpaste brand they mainly use ("*Fit*", „*Neither Fits nor Does not Fit*", and „*Does not Fit*"; these words are respectively represented by the marks *O*, *M*, and *X* in Figures 3 and 5 in the following subsections).

(c) 16 features were established. Respondents evaluated whether they were „*satisfied*" or „*not satisfied*" with their toothpaste brand with regard to each of the 16 features. The words „*satisfied*" and „*not satisfied*" respectively correspond to: *YES* and *NO* in the answers on the questionnaire. Because we have 16 features, the size of the search space for GA operations is 2**16. This space seems small compared to standard GA applications. However, the size is comparable to other publications on solving feature selection problems using GA techniques [Bala et al. 1994, Vafaie et al. 1994]. This means that the selection of appropriate features from only 16 candidates requires various kinds of efforts.

(d) Evaluation of the decision trees was conducted by the second author who is practicing marketing analysis. The user is required to have the expertise in marketing decision making, the knowledge of the principles of inductive learning techniques, and the ability to understand the output forms of decision trees or sets of decision rules.

The experimental system is implemented on a Sun Sparc Station. The GA programs are written in Common LISP language based on the Simple GA programs [Goldberg 1989], and C4.5 programs are used as an inductive learning tool. Figure 2 shows a sample of the display images we have implemented. At each step of the iteration, observing the forms of decision trees, set of decision rules, and combinations of selected features shown in the display, market analysts interactively judge the effectiveness of the intermediate results, then select two of the decision trees as parents for the next generation.

5.2   Results and Discussion

This section presents the results of experiments for two selected images: *innovative* and *effective*. In the experiments, we have tried to acquire the knowledge to represent both of the two image words simultaneously. We have conducted two experiments using the same data but different initial populations. Prior to the experiments, as an initial investigation, we applied C4.5 to the data with all 16 features . The result was terrible; C4.5 programs generated a huge *pruned* decision tree with 112 nodes, which was impossible for even experienced analysts to correctly interpret.

218

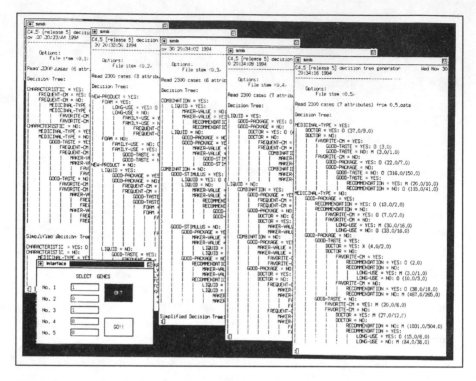

Fig. 2. Sample Display of the Experimental System

Figure 3 shows the results of the first experiment. The figure shows the changes in the selected product characteristics in chromosomes represented by bit strings. The *1* or *0* respectively mean selected or unselected features in each offspring. Black dots and a star mark respectively mean selected parents and the final offspring considered to be adequate. It took seven generations to obtain the results, which the user judged adequate. The final decision tree is shown in Figure 4. The decision tree is represented in the form of standard outputs of C4.5 programs. The top left node means the top decision node. The lower decision nodes follow to down and right directions. Roughly speaking, the numbers in parentheses of the nodes (for example, 293.0/117.3 of the top node in Figure 4) indicate the estimated number of sample cases associated with each node and the number of them misclassified by the node (for example, among 293.0 data, 117.3 data are estimated to be misclassified). Please refer to Quinlan [1994] for detailed explanations.

Figure 5 also shows the results of the second experiment with the same data but different initial populations. For this case, it took only three generations to obtain the results. The final decision tree is shown in Figure 6.

Since one of the objectives of this research is to support the creativity of marketing analysts for determining the promotion strategies of new products, there is more than one right answer to the interpretation problem of decision trees we are investigating, and there are several potential answers left uncovered by the GA-results. With this in mind, the interpretations of the simulation results are described below.

Generations	Good for Combination	Have Unique Chrctrstcs.	Medical Type	Liquid Type	Bubbly Paste	Frequent Commercials	Favorite Commercials	Reliable Manufacturer	Innovative & Effective	Good Taste and Flavor	Familiar Goods	Stimulating Taste	Recommended by Dentists	Recommended by Friends	Good for Family Use	Good Packaged	Selected or Best Children
Gen 0	0	1	0	0	0	1	1	1	1	1	0	0	0	1	0	0	
	0	1	0	1	0	0	0	1	1	0	1	0	0	0	1	1	
	1	0	0	0	1	1	0	1	1	1	0	0	1	1	1	0	
	0	1	0	0	0	0	1	1	1	0	1	0	0	1	1	1	●
	1	1	0	1	1	1	0	1	0	0	0	0	1	0	0	0	●
Gen 1	0	1	0	0	0	0	1	1	1	0	1	0	0	1	1	1	
	1	1	0	1	1	1	0	1	0	0	0	0	1	0	0	0	
	0	1	0	1	0	0	1	1	1	0	0	0	0	1	1	0	●
	1	1	0	0	1	1	0	1	0	0	0	0	0	1	1	0	●
	0	1	0	1	0	1	0	1	0	0	1	0	0	0	0	1	
Gen 2	0	1	0	1	0	0	1	1	1	0	0	0	0	1	1	0	●
	1	1	0	0	1	1	0	1	0	0	0	0	0	1	1	0	●
	1	1	0	0	1	1	1	1	0	0	0	0	0	1	1	0	
	0	1	0	1	1	0	1	1	0	0	0	0	0	1	1	0	
	1	1	0	0	0	0	0	1	1	0	0	0	0	1	1	0	
...					...						...						...
Gen 6	1	1	0	0	1	1	0	1	0	0	0	0	0	1	1	0	●
	1	1	0	1	0	1	0	1	1	0	0	0	0	1	1	0	●
	1	1	0	0	1	1	0	1	0	0	0	0	0	1	1	0	
	1	1	0	0	1	1	0	1	1	0	0	0	0	1	1	0	
	1	1	0	0	0	1	0	1	1	0	0	0	0	1	1	0	
Gen 7	1	1	0	0	1	1	0	1	0	0	0	0	0	1	1	0	
	1	1	0	1	0	1	0	1	1	0	0	0	0	1	1	0	
	1	1	0	0	0	1	0	1	1	0	0	0	0	1	1	0	
	1	1	0	1	0	1	0	1	0	0	0	0	0	1	1	0	○
	1	1	0	1	1	1	0	1	1	0	0	0	0	1	1	0	

SELECTED FEATURES

Fig. 3. Generation Changes from Experiment (1)

```
CHARACTERISTIC = YES: O (293.0/117.3)
CHARACTERISTIC = NO:
|  LIQUID = YES: O (48.0/21.9)
|  LIQUID = NO:
|  |  COMBINATION = YES: O (120.0/59.3)
|  |  COMBINATION = NO:
|  |  |  FREQUENT-CM = YES: O (198.0/115.3)
|  |  |  FREQUENT-CM = NO:
|  |  |  |  MAKER-VALUE = NO: M (1191.0/595.4)
|  |  |  |  MAKER-VALUE = YES:
|  |  |  |  |  RECOMMENDATION = YES: O (33.0/14.5)
|  |  |  |  |  RECOMMENDATION = NO: M (417.0/236.5)
```

Fig. 4. Resulting Decision Tree from Experiment (1)

Generations	Good for Combination	Have Unique Chrcrstcs.	Medical Type	Liquid Type	Bubbly Paste	Frequent Commercials	Favorite Commercials	Reliable Manufacturer	Innovative & Effective	Good Taste and Flavor	Familiar Goods	Stimulating Taste	Recommended by Dentists	Recommended by Friends	Good for Family Use	Good Packaged	Selected or Best Children
Gen 0	0	1	1	0	0	1	1	1	0	1	0	0	0	0	0	0	●
	0	0	0	1	1	1	0	0	1	1	1	0	0	0	1	1	
	1	0	0	1	0	0	0	1	0	0	0	1	0	1	0	1	●
	1	0	0	1	0	1	1	1	0	0	0	0	1	0	0	1	
	0	0	1	0	0	0	1	0	0	1	1	0	1	1	0	1	
Gen 1	0	1	1	0	0	1	1	1	0	1	0	0	0	0	0	0	
	1	0	0	1	0	0	0	1	0	0	0	1	0	1	0	1	●
	0	1	0	1	0	1	1	1	0	0	0	0	1	0	0	1	●
	1	1	1	0	0	0	0	1	0	1	0	0	0	0	0	1	
	0	1	0	1	0	0	0	1	0	1	0	0	0	1	0	0	
Gen 2	1	0	0	1	0	0	0	1	0	0	0	1	0	1	0	1	●
	0	1	0	1	0	1	1	1	0	0	0	1	0	0	0	1	●
	0	0	0	1	0	1	0	1	0	0	0	1	0	1	0	1	
	1	0	0	1	0	0	0	1	0	0	0	1	0	0	0	1	
	0	1	0	1	0	0	1	1	0	0	0	1	0	0	0	1	
Gen 3	1	0	0	1	0	0	0	1	0	0	0	1	0	1	0	1	
	0	1	0	1	0	1	1	1	0	0	0	1	0	0	0	1	
	1	0	0	1	0	0	1	1	0	0	0	1	0	0	0	1	
	1	1	0	1	0	1	0	1	0	0	0	1	0	1	0	1	○
	1	0	0	1	0	0	0	1	0	0	0	1	0	1	0	1	

Fig. 5. Generation Changes from Experiment (2)

```
CHARACTERISTIC = YES: O (293.0/117.3)
CHARACTERISTIC = NO:
| LIQUID = YES: O (48.0/21.9)
| LIQUID = NO:
| | COMBINATION = YES:
| | | GOOD-PACKAGE = NO: O (110.0/53.1)
| | | GOOD-PACKAGE = YES:
| | | | FREQUENT-CM = YES: M (3.0/1.1)
| | | | FREQUENT-CM = NO:
| | | | | MAKER-VALUE = YES: O (2.0/1.0) 1)
| | | | | GOOD-STIMULUS = NO: M (2.0/1.0)
| | COMBINATION = NO:
| | | | MAKER-VALUE = NO:
| | | | | GOOD-STIMULUS = YES: O (3.0/2.0)
| | | GOOD-STIMULUS = YES:
| | | | RECOMMENDATION = YES: M (21.0/13.0)
| | | | RECOMMENDATION = NO: O (274.0/145.2)
| | | GOOD-STIMULUS = NO:
| | | | RECOMMENDATION = NO: M (1409.0/736.5)
| | | | RECOMMENDATION = YES:
| | | | | MAKER-VALUE = YES: O (29.0/12.3)
| | | | | MAKER-VALUE = NO: M (106.0/48.0)
```

Fig. 6. Resulting Decision Tree from Experiment (2)

As depicted in the decision trees obtained, toothpaste with the images of *innovative* and *effective*, was explained by seven features in the first experiment and eight features in the second experiment. The sets of rules which explain that both image characteristics *innovative* and *effective* fit the data are described below.

5.2.1   Interpretation of Decision Tree and Rules (1)

C4.5 programs have functions to make a simplified or *pruned* decision tree from an original decision tree generated from data. The *pruning* strategies are based on heuristics. The following decision rules have been automatically generated by C4.5 programs from the corresponding *pruned* decision tree. The rule numbers (for example, Rule 9) and the estimated correctness (for example, 74.7%) have also been automatically calculated from the pruned decision tree by C4.5 programs. Rules obtained from the first experiment, which are translated into natural language sentences, are as follows:

Rule 9:   If [liquid type] and [frequently seen on commercials], then [innovative and effective toothpaste]. (74.7%)

Rule 27: If not [frequently seen on commercials], but [manufacturer is reliable] and [recommended by family, friend, acquaintances], then [innovative and effective toothpaste]. (70.3%)

Rule 4: If [have unique characteristics other brands do not have], then [innovative and effective toothpaste]. (60.0%)

Rule 16: If [combination of tooth brush and mouth wash which is easy to use], then [innovative and effective toothpaste]. (56.1%)

From the above rules, for example, by combining Rules 9, 4, and 16, we can derive the strategy: „*Develop a line-up of toothpaste with technical characteristics other brands do not have, a liquid toothpaste, and a combination toothbrush/toothpaste brand.*" This strategy is similar to the marketing strategy of an actual producer of oral care products for its brand, however, the brand was not in the market at the time the questionnaire survey was conducted. Furthermore, this brand aimed at establishing the image of being innovative and effective.

Also, by combining Rules 27 and 4, the following strategy is conceivable: „*Develop a toothpaste brand with technical characteristics other brands do not have, advertise on certain magazines rather than on television, and develop word of mouth communication.*" This strategy is considered to be valid for a product with focused target users.

5.2.2 Interpretation of Decision Tree and Rules (2)

The rules developed in the second experiment which explain that both image characteristics *innovative* and *effective* fit the data are as follows.

Rule 8: If [liquid type] and [good packaged], then [innovative and effective toothpaste]. (78.4%)

Rule 9: If [liquid type] and [frequently seen on commercials], then [innovative and effective toothpaste]. (74.7%)

Rule 27: If [manufacturer is reliable], and [recommended by family, friend, acquaintance] then [innovative and effective toothpaste]. (68.4%)

Rule 7: If [have unique characteristics other brands do not have], then [innovative and effective toothpaste]. (60.0%)

Rule 18: If [combination of tooth brush and mouth wash which is easy to use], then [innovative and effective toothpaste]. (56.1%)

Rule 25: If [stimulating taste] and not [recommended by family, friend, acquaintance] and not [good packaged] then [innovative and effective toothpaste]. (50.9%)

Many of the rules as well as their interpretations are the same as those in the first experiment. It can be seen from the comparison of experiments 1 and 2 that if decision trees are constructed with the same set of image characteristics such as *innovative* and *effective*, then the resulting trees and set of rules are similar, although the processes to obtain the results and the features selected by the method are different. For example, the initial populations, features selected by the interactive evaluation, and the intermediate decision trees are quite different. This shows that, if an experienced human expert uses the proposed method, the methodology is repeatable and that the evaluation function assumed by the expert (not explicitly expressible) is effective for the optimization of decision trees and is a useful aid in decision making.

6 Conclusion

In this paper, we have investigated the relationship between product characteristics represented by a set of image words and product features through the application of simulated breeding, a genetic algorithm-based method, on decision trees and rules obtained by inductive inferences from questionnaire data. As a result, we have succeeded in obtaining a decision tree or set of rules with a comparatively small number of features in the questionnaire, which incorporates human subjective evaluations.

In the experiments, the user or marketing analyst is able to understand the meaning of the generated decision trees, and the basic principles of genetic algorithms and inductive learning programs. If this were not the case, the naive user interface shown in Figure 2 would not work well and a more sophisticated interface should be developed. This suggests further improvement of the proposed method. We are currently exploring methods to explicitly define the evaluation function which we have already implicitly defined in a subjective and interactive manner. If our investigation is successful, it will become possible to automate the analysis of the system.

The prerequisites of the proposed method are quite simple and the algorithm is easy to implement. Therefore, we conclude that the proposed method is applicable to other domain problems including some subset selection tasks.

Acknowledgments

The authors wish to express their thanks to the editors for giving detailed comments and constructive suggestions on the earlier version of the paper. This research is supported in part by Grant-in-Aid for Scientific Research (A-06402060) of the Ministry of Education and Culture of Japan.

References

Aaker, D. A.; Day, G. S. (1980): Marketing Research: Private and Public Sector Decisions. John-Wiley, New York/NY

Bala, J. W.; De Jong, K.; Pachowicz, P. W. (1994): Multistrategy Learning from Engineering Data by Integrating Inductive Generalization and Genetic Algorithms. in Michalski, R.; Tecuci, G. (eds.) (1994): Machine Learning IV: A Multistrategy Approach. Morgan-Kaufmann, San Francisco/CA: 471-488

Davis, L. (ed.) (1991): Handbook of Genetic Algorithms. Van Nostrand Reinhold, New York/ NY

Dawkins, R. (1986): The Blind Watchmaker. W. W. Norton, New York/NY

Goldberg, D.E.(1989): Genetic Algorithms in Search, Optimization and Machine Learning. Addison-Wesley, Reading/Mass.

Kendall, M. (1980) : Multivariate Analysis, 2nd Edition. Charles Griffin, High Wycombe/England

Kira, K.; Rendell, L. A. (1992): The Feature Selection Problem: Traditional Methods and a New Algorithm. Proc. AAAI-92, MIT Press, Cambridge/Mass., 129-134

Lindenmayer, A. (1968): Mathematical Models for Cellular Interaction in Development, Parts I and II. Journal of Theoretical Biology 18: 280-315

Mingers, J. (1989): An Empirical Comparison of Selection Measures for Decision-Tree Induction. Machine Learning 3: 319-342

Quinlan, J. R. (1986): Induction for Decision Trees. Machine Learning 1-1: 81-106

Quinlan, J. R. (1993): C4.5: Programs for Machine Learning. Morgan-Kaufmann, San Francisco/CA

Sims, K. (1992): Interactive Evolution of Dynamical Systems. Varela, F. J., Bourgine, P. (eds.) : Toward a Practice of Autonomous Systems - Proc. 1st European Conf. Artificial Life, MIT Press/Mass.: 171-178

Syswerda, G. (1989): Uniform crossover genetic algorithms. J. David Schaffer(ed.), Proceedings of the Third international Conference on Genetic Algorithms. Morgan Kaufmann, San Mateo/CA

Unemi, T.: Genetic Algorithms and Computer Graphics Arts (in Japanese). Journal of Japanese Society for Artificial Intelligence 9-4: 42-47

Vafaie, H.; De Jong, K. A. (1994): Improving a Rule Induction System Using Genetic Algorithms. in Michalski, R., Tecuci, G. (eds.): Machine Learning IV: A Multistrategy Approach. Morgan-Kaufmann, San Francisco/CA: 453-470

Weiss, S. M.; Kulikowski, C. A. (1991): Computer Systems that Learn: Classification and Prediction Methods from Statistics, Neural Nets, Machine Learning and Expert Systems. Morgan-Kaufmann, San Francisco/CA

Adaptive Behaviour in an Oligopoly

Robert E. Marks[1], David F. Midgley[1], and Lee G. Cooper[2]

[1] Australian Graduate School of Management, The University of New
  South Wales, Sydney, NSW 2052, AUSTRALIA
[2] Anderson Graduate School of Management, University of California,
  Los Angeles, CA 90024-1481, USA

Abstract. Advances in game theory have provided an impetus for renewed
investigation of the strategic behaviour of oligopolists as players in repeated
games. Marketing databases provide a rich source of historical evidence of such
behaviour. This paper uses such data to examine how players in iterated
oligopolies respond to their rivals' behaviour, and uses machine learning to derive
improved contingent strategies for such markets, in order to provide insights into
the evolution of such markets and the patterns of behaviour observed. The paper is
an application of repeated games and machine learning to adaptive behaviour over
time in the retail market for ground coffee. Using empirical data on the weekly
prices and promotional instruments of the four largest and several smaller coffee
sellers in a regional U.S. retail market, and using a market model to predict sellers'
market shares and profits in response to others' actions in any week, we examine
the adaptive strategic behaviour of the three largest sellers. We model the sellers'
strategic behaviours as finite automata with memory of previous weeks' actions,
and use the Axelrod/Forrest representation of the action function, mapping state to
action. We use a genetic algorithm (GA) to derive automata which are fit, given
their environment, as described by their rivals' actions in the past and the implicit
demand for coffee.

Keywords. iterated synchronised oligopoly, asymmetrical competition, pricing,
marketing strategies, stimulus-response behaviour

1   The Issues

We are interested in the strategic implications of asymmetric competition.
Previous work [Carpenter, Cooper, Hanssens & Midgley 1988] (CCHM) has
estimated the Nash-equilibrium prices and advertising expenditures for asymmetric
market-share models in the extreme cases of *no competitive reaction* and *optimal
competitive reaction*. There are, however, three important limitations to building
marketing plans on either of these competitive scenarios.

First, such *static*, single-period strategies do not provide insight into the actions
undertaken over time by major manufacturers and retailers. As was called for in
the CCHM study, it is time to investigate dynamic, multiperiod strategies.

Second, major sources of asymmetries are missing from the CCHM equilibrium analysis. There are two main sources of asymmetries. They can arise from stable, cross-competitive effects, but can also arise from temporary differences in marketing offerings. One brand on sale by itself might gain much more than if it were promoted along with four other brands in the category. While the CCHM study incorporated measures of distinctiveness into their development of methods for reflecting asymmetric competition, the equilibrium analysis used a simpler model that did not account for this source of asymmetries.

Third, the CCHM effort studied market share, while we here investigate multi-period strategies, when the market response is fundamentally asymmetric in both sales volume and market share.

There are major barriers to traditional avenues of investigation. Mathematical exploration is hampered because sources of asymmetry explicitly violate the global-convexity requirements of most economic models. One major alternative to mathematical exploration is multi-period simulations, such as Axelrod's first tournament [Axelrod 1984] or the Fader/Hauser tournament [Fader & Hauser 1988]. While these have the advantage of allowing strategies to be played out over time, they have previously only been undertaken with symmetric and hypothetical market-response functions. We want to use asymmetric market-response functions that characterize brand behaviour in actual markets to study the evolution of robust strategies.

Data from an asymmetric model of a regional U.S. coffee market are used to breed simple artificial agents. *We shall demonstrate that, in the limited tests we can feasibly conduct, these agents outperform the historical actions of brand managers in this regional market.*

2 Modelling the Managers

Competitive marketing strategies can be represented as sets of rules that map states of the market to actions undertaken by brands, brand managers or retailers. These *sets of rules*, in turn, can be represented as chromosome-like *strings*. The *fitness* of each string can be judged by the profits it produces over a period of many interactions, following Axelrod [1987].

A player choosing a strategy can be thought of as choosing a *machine* (a *finite automaton*) or *artificial agent* that will play instead of the player [Marks 1992a]. Such a machine is designed to have a unique action in response to each possible state.[1] The *state* is defined by the history of actions taken by the player and the historic actions and reactions of other players. This line of reasoning builds on developments by Axelrod and Forrest [Axelrod 1987]. They view *players* (e.g., managers) as being characterized by *bounded rationality* [Simon 1972], in which *memory, computing ability,* or *competence at pattern recognition* is limited. The *states of the market* are the number of past actions of all players in *limited*

---

[1] This is a pure-strategy machine (i.e., a strategy chosen with probability 1.0); no mixed strategies are allowed.

memory. If there are p players, a possible actions per round, and m rounds of memory, then the number of states is a^{mp} .

The Axelrod and Forrest study demonstrated that genetic algorithms (GAs) could take the place of the human programmers used in the original Axelrod tournament [Axelrod 1984] or the Fader & Hauser [1988] tournaments. Axelrod reports that the GA evolved strategy populations whose median member resembled *Tit for Tat* and was just as successful. In some cases the GA, which does not require well-behaved, differentiable, globally-convex objective function, was able to generate highly specialized adaptations to a specific population of strategies for particular situations that performed substantially better than *Tit for Tat*.

After Axelrod's pioneering study, other applications of GAs to economics have appeared [Miller 1989; Eaton & Slade 1989; Marks 1992a, 1992b; Marimon, McGrattan & Sargent 1990; Arthur 1990; and Arifovic 1994], with one application in marketing [Hurley, Moutinho, & Stephens 1994].

Our challenges are (i) to develop strings that represent real strategies in asymmetric markets, and (ii) to calibrate asymmetric market-response functions that translate the market states into fitness measures for each brand.

We can coevolve artificial agents, using the asymmetrical profit functions, and then take each of the coevolved agents in the final generation and separately play it against the actual history of the other $n-1$ brands, and assess its performance against that actually achieved by human brand managers. That is, we can ask if our procedure of encoding, breeding and testing has evolved a strategy for Folgers (say) which would have been more profitable than Folgers was historically at competing in the retail coffee market.

3 Asymmetric Competition in a Regional U.S. Coffee Market

3.1 Choice of Market Example

We want to work with an example of competition that exhibits four aspects of real-world markets:

(I) *Differential effectiveness of marketing-mix instruments across brands*. Each brand may have its own unique sensitivity to consumer response to its marketing actions.

(II) *Stable cross-competitive effects*. Some brands gain much more from the losses of certain rivals than would be dictated by market share alone, while other brands are far more insulated by competitive boundaries than the symmetric-market hypothesis would allow.

(III) *Asymmetries due to the temporal distinctiveness of marketing actions*. That is, representing the role of choice context on what brands are chosen: marketing actions must be distinctive to be effective.

(IV). *The dramatic swings in volume that characterize promotion response.* Scanner data reveal that, when viewed at the store or chain level, market response to tactical market-mix decisions is abrupt and dramatic.

The retail coffee market analyzed in Cooper & Nakanishi [1988] satisfies all four criteria. There are eight brands: Folgers, Maxwell House Regular, MH Master Blend, Hills Bros., Chock Full O'Nuts, Chase & Sanborne, Yuban, and an aggregate of premium brands called All Other Branded (AOB). The data track the sales impact of price per pound (net of coupons redeemed), major newspaper ads, in-store displays, and store (not manufacturer) coupons, for 80 weeks in three grocery chains operating in this two-city market. For the sake of simplicity, however, we focus on the 52 weeks of data for Chain One.

The asymmetric market-share model and the category volume model have been combined into a single-shot market simulator called *Casper* (Competitive analysis system for promotional effectiveness research) [Cooper & Nakanishi 1988, pp. 219-257]. In order to use this simulator as an instructional device, manufacturers' unit costs and promotional costs have been estimated for each brand. This allows us to estimate total profits for each brand for any market scenario. These estimates are thought to be roughly accurate.[2]

Typical behaviour of some brands is to cut their price and engage in newspaper advertising, in-store displays, and coupon distribution after a period of higher prices and no other activity. The effect, not unexpectedly, is usually to increase sales and market share, and perhaps total profits in the market, depending on the costs of the promotions and the activities of other brands in the market—this is a strategic interaction. The overall patterns of prices and sales for the three major brands available in Chain One (Folgers (F), Maxwell House Regular (M), and Chock Full O'Nuts (C)) are depicted in Figure 1 and the average prices and annual market shares for all brands are shown in Table 1.

There are at least three main ways we might breed artificial agents.

(I). Breed populations of each of the eight brands against the history of the other seven for *each* of the 52 weeks. The procedure would be repeated for each of the eight brands. While this procedure will quickly breed agents to maximize profits against the fixed moves of the other seven in any week, it is essentially static and ignores the multi-period nature of strategic interactions.

(II). Breed populations of each of the eight brands against the history of the other seven over the time frame, with g agents each playing against the entire 52-week period, until convergence. This approach is better, since each brand's g agents are exposed to 52 weeks of the other brands' actions. But the 52-week pattern is still static in that the focal brand's competitors do not react to the actions of its artificial agent, they simply repeat history.

---

[2] Profit margins and hence unit costs were estimated from publicly available corporate and SBU-level accounting information rather than provided by the companies concerned. To the extent these estimates are inaccurate, the validity of our results for the coffee market may be reduced.

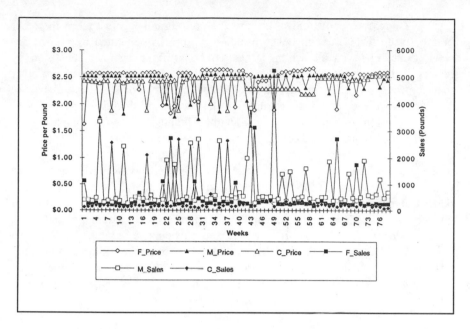

Figure 1. Prices and sales of the three strategic brands

Table 1. Average prices and annual market shares

Brand	Price per pound	Market share
Maxwell House Regular	$2.40	37%
Folgers	$2.45	24%
Chock Full O'Nuts	$2.36	16%
MH Master Blend	$2.78	13%
Chase & Sanborne	$2.36	2%
Hills Bros.	$1.91	2%
Yuban	$3.13	<1%
All Other Branded	$2.56	6%

Furthermore, there is no way around the static nature of the data, since they do not reveal what the contingent strategies of the competing brands might have been. As these contingent strategies are what we are trying to evolve, we believe breeding our agents against historical actions is not adequate.

(III). Coevolve populations of each of the eight brands against all of the other brands, using the *Casper* model to estimate the profits generated from each 52-week game, but with all actions generated by artificial agents rather than by history. This is analogous to breeding the agents in a laboratory experiment rather than the field, as in (I) and (II) above. We would then trial the best artificially bred agents for each brand against the historical actions of the other seven over 52 weeks. This approach reveals the best-adapted brand strategy by comparing the brands' scores against actual profits over the historical periods.

Two tests of the artificial agents are explicit in the third approach. One is their profit performance against other artificial agents in the laboratory, the other is the field test of each against the historical actions of the others. Neither of these is perfect, the laboratory test because it is entirely artificial and moreover because convergence of behaviour and genetic drift result in a smaller number of states and so a smaller number of positions on each string being tested for, the field test because it suffers from the lack of learning noted in (II) above. But the only better tests we can currently envisage are to play an artificial agent against the future actions of coffee brand managers either in a brand management game or in the real market. We have not yet conducted such tests.

There are significant problems of complexity with an eight-brand example, especially if a wide range of possible actions are allowed, and hence a large number of possible states of the game need to be encoded for in an agent's bit string. With only 52 weeks of data, we might not have an adequately rich environment in which to test a complex agent. By this we mean that some contingent strategies might not be invoked by the environment (with a maximum of 51 distinct states) and therefore their fitness never tested. For these reasons we sought to simplify the problem.

3.2 Modelling the Coffee Players

We want to reduce the number of possible states for computational reasons, and, more importantly, for data reasons. We can do this by reducing the number of rounds of memory, which is probably not realistic, by reducing the number of actions of the players (again, not realistic), and by reducing the number of strategic players (again, not realistic). This implies that any economy will occur only with a cost to realism. So the question becomes, what can we do with the smallest sacrifice of realism?

First, we assume that the decision to use coupons is simply a decision to lower price (which is net of coupons). Rather than considering price to be a continuous variable, with a consequently very high number of states, we represent four price levels. Figure 2 shows that the smoothed frequency polygon for Folgers' prices has four rough peaks. The right-hand or most common peak relates to the shelf price of Folgers, while the others denote promotional prices. The frequency polygons for other major brands have similar quadrimodal characteristics.

Given that each brand has a choice of four prices and also whether to *display* or not, and to *feature* or not, there are 16 possible actions per week per state. In the historical data, features and displays only occur with low prices, and therefore we might reduce the number of actions per brand per week to four, where each price level had an associated feature and display value. Four actions can be coded in two bits, considerably reducing the complexity of the problem.

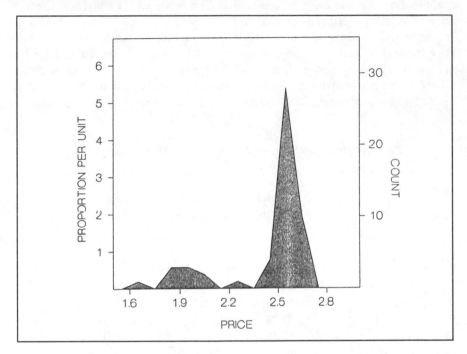

Figure 2. Folgers' price distribution

We model the market as having three strategic players (Folgers, Regular Maxwell House, and Chock Full O'Nuts), with the other brands as fringe players, who act as non-strategic price takers. This means there are only 64 possible states (three players, each with four possible actions) which results in strings of 128 bits. A one-round memory game with three strategic players also requires six bits of phantom memory, resulting in 134 bit strings for strategies. Strings of 134 bits are not only easy to estimate, but the 52-week environment is adequate to evolve effective agents of this length. The three strategic brands emphasized in this simplification are by far the major players in this market.

We used a version of the GA[3] to simulate the actual behaviour of the brands in a realistic manner. To reduce complexity we set up the algorithm using a single

---

[3] We adapted GAucsd, the U.C. San Diego version of GENESIS, originally written by John Grefenstette at the U.S. Naval Research Laboratory.

population of strings for the three brands rather than three separate populations. With coevolution, we did not use the historical pattern of actions, but only the payoffs (profits) as estimated by the *Casper* model, which were used to derive a 4∞4∞4 payoff matrix for each of the three major brands. The four possible actions that define each face of this payoff cube were a *High* price to approximate the co-operative or collusive price, a *high* price to approximate the two-person coalition price, a *low* price to approximate the non-cooperative, Nash-Cournot price, and a *Low* price to approximate the envious price. We had also to determine the amounts of feature and display promotions associated with each price level. (See Midgley Marks & Lee [1994] for details). See Table 2 for the marketing mix associated with each action for each brand. The non-strategic sellers' prices per pound are: MH Master Blend $2.90, Hills Bros. $2.49, Yuban $3.39, Chase & Sanborne $2.39, and All other brands $3.68.

Table 2. Possible actions for each strategic brand

Action	Price ($/lb)	Feature (% stores)	Display (% stores)
Folgers			
Low	$1.87	79	68
low	$2.07	82	53
high	$2.38	0	0
High	$2.59	0	0
Maxwell House Regular			
Low	$1.96	95	68
low	$2.33	84	0
high	$2.46	0	0
High	$2.53	0	0
Chock Full O'Nuts			
Low	$1.89	100	77
low	$2.02	99	64
high	$2.29	0	0
High	$2.45	0	0

Each brand participates in 50-round games, with all possible combinations of the other two brands. Although the number of rounds is fixed, the one-round memory eliminates end-game strategies. With a population of size 25, testing each generation of strings requires 8,125 50-round games (325 games per string per generation). Each brand has complete information on all previous actions, but not on other brands' profits (payoffs).

4 Results

4.1 First Experiments—Unconstrained

The first computer experiments found convergence, with all brands pricing at their *Low* price with promotions—not a collusive high price. This finding is the result of including a model for category volume as well as market shares. If only shares were modeled, strategies would probably have converged on the collusive price. But historically most of the sales and profits in this market have occurred at *Low* prices with promotions, because of stockpiling, forward buying, and brand switching (if not all brands are at *Low* prices), rather than through increased consumption. At least for the period we have data for, we can consider coffee as a mature category with stable long-term consumption rates.

4.2 Second Experiments—Institutional Constraints

To increase realism, we added some institutional constraints. Chain 1 does an excellent job, long run, of maximising profits while not exhausting demand. Its policy is to promote (*Low*) only one major brand at a time for the duration of one week. We mimicked this policy by saying no player could follow one week's *Low* with another *Low*, and only one player per week at *Low*. Ties of two or more strings (brands) that, given the state of the oligopoly as a result of past actions, would simultaneously price at *Low* are broken by random choice; the loser(s) arbitrarily price at *high*.

These constraints resulted in an interesting pattern of behaviour in which brands roughly alternated in pricing *Low*, with the other two brands pricing *low*, *high*, or *High*. But too frequent pricing of *Low* and *low* results in saturation of demand.

4.3 Third Experiments—Demand Saturation

To make the experiments even more realistic, we introduce time into the demand side by adding demand saturation. *Casper* is a one-shot, brand planning simulator that does an excellent job of forecasting single-period demand. But while this market is very volatile in the short run, it is very stable in the long run. For details of the demand-saturation implementation, see [Midgley Marks & Lee 1994]. Two things follow if the degree of saturation is greater than 100%: the total sales volume for the latest week is reduced by the degree of saturation, and the profits of the brands are reduced for each of the three competing brands.

With institutional and demand constraints in place, two patterns of competition evolved. In some cases we got convergence to all *low* pricing. In other cases we got patterns of behaviour similar to that observed historically in Chain 1. Figure 3 shows the simulated behaviour of the three strategic brands with the institutional and demand constraints.

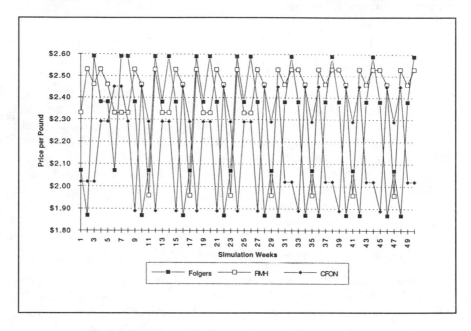

Figure 3. Price paths for the three artificial competitors

It is important to note that the results shown in Figure 3 are for three optimized (coevolved) agents competing against each other over fifty weeks. As such, the frequency of price competition is higher than we observe in the actual market, because the optimized agents invariably respond to the previous week's actions of their competitors. For example, the artificial agent for Folgers reduces its price thirty-seven weeks out of fifty, whereas the brand managers for Folgers only promoted fourteen weeks out of fifty. Similar statistics for Maxwell House are thirty weeks out of fifty for the artificial agent, versus eleven weeks in the data. For Chock Full O'Nuts the artificial agent promotes thirty-seven weeks out of fifty, versus seventeen weeks in the data. Over the three brands the artificial agents reduce their prices approximately 2.5 times as often as we observe in the market. If we focus on deep price reductions, the artificial agents employ these 1.9 times as often as we observe in the market. In itself this 'over-competition' is not unexpected, as our artificial agents do not face the practical barriers encountered by brand managers. In the artificial laboratory, information on competitors' actions is received instantaneously, and promotional responses can be implemented within one or two weeks.

In the course of the 'laboratory' simultations the best performing string improved over the 325 50-round games per string per generation by 1.4 times. The best string emerged in the 63rd generation, and remained unbeaten (in terms of its average profit) for the next 37 generations.

4.4   Fourth Experiments—Tests Against Historical Actions

The final series of experiments is not concerned with breeding better agents as such; rather, we took the best agents from the third series of experiments and tested each in turn against the historical actions of their two major competitors[4]. We did this by taking an artificial agent, assigning it to one of the three brands, and allowing it to respond to the historical actions of all other brands over a 52-week period[5]. In fact, as the GA was set to evolve a population of 25, we had 25 'best' agents, and so the test could be repeated 25 times. How well do these strings perform in comparison to human brand managers?

Figure 4 shows that when the final generation of agents is assigned to the Folgers brand most of them do markedly better than human brand managers (as measured by Folger's historical average profit over the 52 weeks). Indeed we have also placed a control line of 25% better than history on the figure and it can be seen that 14 of the 25 agents exceed this. Even the two worst agents generate average profits of 96% and 93% of the historical figure, whereas the best agent does over 240% better than the human brand managers. Although not detailed here, similar results can be generated for Chock Full O'Nuts and Maxwell House, whose best agents do 233% and 120% better than human brand managers do.

While the historical test is limited, in that the competitors do not learn from the changed actions of the brand managed by the artificial agent, these results are impressive. They demonstrate that the 'laboratory' results can be translated to the field. Moreover, given the simplicity of the agents (one-round memory, limited to 4 actions) it is remarkable that they can out-perform human managers. Before we discuss the reasons for this performance, we should ask what the patterns of agent behaviour are that lead to improved profits. This is not an easy question to answer because of the difficulties of presenting all the data in an understandable form. But Figures 5 and 6 shed some light on the issue. Figure 5 shows the historical price actions of Folgers compared with the price actions of the best agent (string 24). Figure 6 shows the same historical actions compared with the worst agent (string 20 of the final generation).

---

[4] With the historical actions of the other five brands input to the profit calculations but not 'recognised' by the agent: the perceived market state is invariant to the other five's actions.

[5] In performing this test it is necessary to classify the historical actions of the other major brands into *Low, low, high* and *High*. We did this by inspection, partitioning the price distribution into four roughly equal levels, using Figure 2 for Folgers, etc.

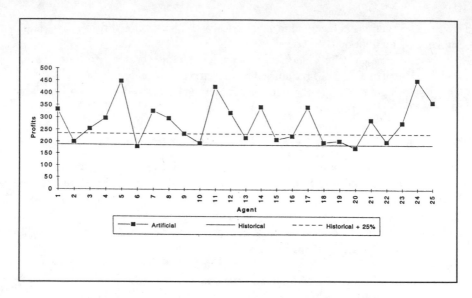

Figure 4. Profits for Folgers: artificial agents versus history

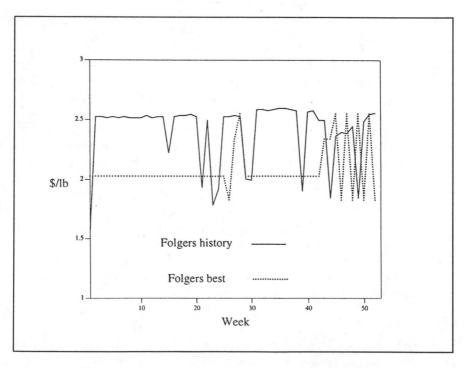

Figure 5. Folgers' price paths—best agent versus history

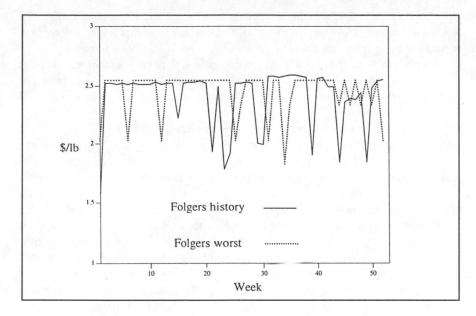

Figure 6. Folgers' price paths—worst agent versus history

The comparison between these two figures suggests that while the "worst" agent behaves quite similarly to the human manager, the "best" agent is prepared to keep the price low and promote more frequently. Although we do not present the figures here, similar conclusions can be drawn for Chock Full O'Nuts and Maxwell House.

5 Conclusion

The general conclusion is that the artificial agents price promote more frequently than human managers. We observe the highest level of promotion when the three optimized agents are competing with each other in our 'laboratory'—an environment which perhaps represents the most competitive scenario we can achieve. Indeed, we might define these results as the maximum competitive intensity possible in this market (given our sales model and institutional constraints). All actual markets would be likely to show less intense competitive activity. Hence, it is not surprising that when we place one of these optimized agents back into the historical market we observe a lower frequency of promotion. This is the case for many of the final strings—whose behaviour more resembles human managers. But it is still true that the best of our agents promote more frequently than do their human counterpoints and we can speculate on the reasons why this might be so.

One reason may be that human brand managers are not in a position to respond to competition on a week-by-week basis. More likely, they negotiate with the chains for a series of promotions to occur across a defined promotional period (often of thirteen weeks duration). Major responses to competitive actions then occur in the next promotional period, rather than by immediate adjustments to the current promotional plan. This suggests that competitive response in real markets may be more measured and less immediately reactive than that generated by our optimized artificial agents. *Institutional constraints may therefore serve to dampen competition.*

But there may be reasons for the greater level of promotion which have more to do with our agents than with the institutional constraints and brand managers: the choice of one-round memory and the selection of the four reference prices. One-round memory restricts the agent to only being directly 'aware' of the most recent actions of its competitors. Two or more rounds of memory would allow the agent to take a more balanced approach to competitive reaction, since the agent might then 'assess' how aggressive a competitor's strategy was across a greater number of instances of market-place behaviour. For example, observing that a competitor has promoted for two consecutive periods implies greater aggression than if that competitor has only promoted for one period out of two.

What then are the managerial implications of this approach? We believe these are threefold. First, the artificial agents allow the managers of any brand to check future promotional plans against the likely response of their competitors. Promotional plans can be input for their own brand, and the competitive responses to these plans generated from the agents of the other brands. Second, the agents also enable managers to test 'what-if' scenarios, both for their own brands and for the brands of their competitors. Both these may help alleviate the resistance to market modelling which is observed in many consumer product companies. In our opinion some part of this resistance stems from the static or competitively myopic nature of current modelling approaches. Managers expect models to be able to simulate the consequences of a planning period (often four promotional periods or a year) and to factor in likely competitive responses. Third, the agents may be useful in training junior brand managers: the agents could form the basis of a game whereby junior managers make decisions for one brand and the agents for other brands provide the competitive test of these decisions. With appropriate agents this would inject an element of realism into training by simulation games. This element is missing from many games at present because they use other teams of junior managers to make the competitors' decisions and also often have unrealistic algorithms for market response.

Acknowledgements

The authors wish to thank Information Resources, Inc. for providing the data used in this study and Joel Steckel for his assistance in estimating the profit margins for the brands. This research is supported, in part, by the Anderson Graduate School of Management, UCLA, the Australian Graduate School of Management, UNSW, the Australian Research Council, the Graduate School of Business at Stanford

University, and the Santa Fe Institute. Earlier versions of this paper were presented at the Santa Fe Institute, the TIMS Marketing Science Conference in St. Louis, Missouri, the Society of Economic Dynamics and Control Conference in Nafplion, Greece, and the Australasian meeting of the Econometrics Society in Armidale, N.S.W.

References

Arifovic, J. (1994): Genetic algorithm learning and the cobweb model, *Journal of Economic Dynamics and Control*, 18: 3–28.

Arthur W.B. (1990): A learning algorithm that mimics human learning, Working Paper 90-026, SFI Economics Research Program, Santa Fe Institute.

Axelrod R. (1984): *The Evolution of Cooperation*, Basic Books, New York.

Axelrod R. (1987): The evolution of strategies in the iterated Prisoner's Dilemma, *Genetic Algorithms & Simulated Annealing*, L. Davis (ed.), Pittman, London.

Carpenter G.S., Cooper L.G., Hanssens D.M., and Midgley D.F. (1988): Modeling asymmetric competition, *Marketing Science*, 7(4): 393–412.

Cooper L.G. and Nakamishi M. (1988): *Market-Share Analysis: Evaluating Competitive Marketing Effectiveness*, Kluwer, Boston.

Eaton B.C. and Slade M.E. (1989): Evolutionary equilibrium in market supergames, mimeo., November.

Fader P.S.and Hauser J.R. (1988): Implicit coalitions in a generalised Prisoner's Dilemma, *Journal of Conflict Resolution*, 32: 553–582.

Hurley S. Moutinho L., and Stephens N.M. (1994): Applying genetic algorithms to problems in marketing, *Proceedings of the 23rd EMAC Conference, Marketing: Its Dynamics and Challenges*, ed. by J. Bloemer, J. Lemmink, H. Kasper, European Marketing Academy, Maastricht.

Marimon R., McGrattan E, and Sargent T.J. (1990): Money as a medium of exchange in an economy with artificially intelligent agents, *Journal of Economic Dynamics and Control*, 14: 329–373.

Marks R.E. (1992*a*): Repeated games and finite automata, *Recent Advances in Game Theory*, ed. by John Creedy, J. Eichberger, and J. Borland, Edward Arnold, London, pp.43–64.

Marks R.E. (1992*b*): Breeding optimal strategies: optimal behaviour for oligopolists, *Journal of Evolutionary Economics*, 2: 17–38.

Midgley D.F, Marks R.E, and Lee L.G. (1994): Breeding competitive strategies, UCLA Anderson Graduate School of Management Working Paper No. 242.

Miller J.H. (1989): The coevolution of automata in the repeated Prisoner's Dilemma, Working Paper 89–003, SFI Economics Research Program, Santa Fe Institute, July.

Simon H. A. (1972): Theories of bounded rationality, from: *Decision and Organisation: A Volume in Honor of Jacob Marschak*, C. B. McGuire & R. Radner (eds.), Chapters 8 & 9, North-Holland, Amsterdam, pp.161–188.

Determining a Good Inventory Policy with a Genetic Algorithm

Volker Nissen, Jörg Biethahn

Abteilung Wirtschaftsinformatik I, Universität Göttingen, Platz der Göttinger Sieben 5, 37073 Göttingen, Germany, {vnissen, jbietha}@gwdg.de

Abstract. A fruitful approach for the optimisation of complex systems is to model the real system in a simulation and use a powerful optimisation technique to determine good decision parameter settings for the simulation model. The simulation serves as an evaluation component, measuring the quality of individual solutions (parameter settings). In this paper, we have modeled a stochastic inventory problem as an event-driven simulation. We compare results achieved with a GA and two more conventional optimisation methods, a simplified gradient search and an alternating variable search. The GA, though having higher computational requirements, produces better solutions with greater reliability when optimising the decision variables of the stochastic inventory simulation. Moreover, we find indications that the GA is also more robust when only few simulations of each trial solution are performed. This characteristic may be used to reduce the generally higher CPU-requirements of population-based search methods like GA as opposed to point-based traditional optimisation techniques in stochastic problems. Though being in good agreement with earlier empirical results on sampling based evaluation, this indication requires further study.

Keywords. simulation, stochastic optimisation, genetic algorithm, inventory management

1 Introduction

Simulation can be regarded as a well established method to analyse complex systems. It is generally viewed as one of the most versatile methods in operations research, applicable in domains where adequate analytical models cannot be developed or solved. However, in the majority of management applications simulation seems to be used in a rather intuitive way, aiming at studying the behaviour of a system through some form of what-if analysis.

The explicit attempt to optimise complex real systems using simulation, on the other hand, is frequently a very difficult task. It is complicated by factors such as a large number of possible system configurations, and complex constraints that lead to a high dimensional and complex solution space. Therefore, one is generally happy, if simulation helps to avoid implementing particularly bad system configurations.

In this paper, we deal with a stochastic inventory problem. It is modeled as an event-driven simulation, and three optimisation techniques are compared to determine a good inventory policy for the given problem. The implemented optimisers are a simplified gradient search, an alternating variable search, and a genetic algorithm. The first two methods were chosen since Biethahn [1978] rates them high in an earlier investigation on this same problem. The following section further elaborates the combination of simulation and optimisation. Section three presents the investigated inventory problem. Section four describes the implemented methods. In section five we present and interpret empirical results on the given inventory problem and give suggestions for further research.

2 Tuning Decision Variables of a Simulation Model

The general approach for combining simulation and optimisation is shown in figure 1. As far as the combination of simulation and Evolutionary Algorithms (EA) is concerned, this is only one of at least six possible variants which are further detailed in Biethahn and Nissen [1994]. A given parameter setting can be evaluated by executing the simulation. The resulting quality measure is then used by the optimisation component to determine better values for the decision variables of the simulation, based on the previous setting. It is obvious that only derivative-free optimisation methods are applicable here, since no analytical objective function exists, but rather simulation serves as a substitute evaluation component.

To implement a simulation model one can either use a general-purpose programming language like Pascal and C, or employ a more user-friendly simulation tool. For the purpose of optimisation only the first alternative seems reasonable at present. Since many solutions must be evaluated during the course of the optimisation, the computational requirements of each simulation should be kept as low as possible to avoid excessively long computer runs. This means that an efficient implementation of the simulation model is crucial for applications in practice. However, the attainable cost reduction or other advantages of a particularly good solution will frequently make it worthwile to use dedicated and powerful hardware for this purpose. Parallel systems, like a network of workstations or massively parallel computers can further reduce runtime-requirements of an optimisation with simulation. In our experiments with various simulation tools we have also encountered interface problems in coupling standard simulation tools with our individually developed and implemented optimisation modules.

Assessing the objective quality of solutions might pose a problem since information about the global optimum is usually not available. This should be treated in a pragmatic way, e.g. by comparing to historic data or the given situation of the simulated real system. The optimisation techique could also be run a couple of times with varying initialisations.

Particulary difficult is the optimsation of stochastic simulation models, since simulation results are subhect to stochastic perturbations. Therefore, it does generally not suffice to simulate each solution point only once, but one must find an acceptable way tto appreciate the stochastic nature of the underlying problem. We discuss this issue in the following section in the context of an inventory problem. The focus of this paper is not so much on the solution produced for this particular problem but rather on the general approach, as well as quality and robustness of the optimsation techniques employed. We build on thoughts first presented in Biethahn and Nissen [1994].

3   Stochastic Inventory Problem

The investigated optimisation problem is one of inventory management in a make-to-stock plant and more detailed discussed in Biethahn [1978]. It is a problem of moderate complexity that serves illustrative purposes here. Biethahn describes a capital-oriented one-product inventory model with two decision variables: order point *(s)* and order quantity *(q)*. A quantity of q is ordered whenever the item's inventory position (inventory on-hand + orders outstanding - demand backlog) is observed to have fallen to or below the level *s*. It is assumed that the item in question is continuously reviewed.

Starting with a given amount of capital (40.000 units) and an inventory level of 30 units, the aim is to maximise equity capital over a period of one year by setting *s* and *q* to optimal integer values. Demand quantity is stochastic and evenly distributed at random in the interval [1, 20]. When demand ocurred new demand will appear within one to five days according to the distribution given in figure 2. Replenishment times are (μ, σ)-normally distributed with $\mu = 20$ and $\sigma = 5$. Further details of the simulation model are given in figure 2. The model includes some simplifying assumptions, in particular the abstraction from stockout costs. For this reason, achievable differences w.r.t. the final level of equity capital are relatively moderate between different inventory policies (in the order of up to a few thousand units of capital). However, the resulting landscape of (substitute) objective function values is quite multimodal, making it hard to locate a global maximum.

To find an optimal *(s, q)*-policy the model is implemented as an event-driven simulation. In fact, we have re-implemented a model, originally developed by Biethahn on a mainframe, using standard 486-PCs. Pascal is used as the programming language for the model and all optimisation techniques. Compared to alternatives like C, this is, of course, not the most efficient programming language conceivable. However, it is sufficient for the purpose of demonstration.

The next question is how to account for the stochastic character of the simulation when determining good settings for order point and order quantity. Note that, due to the stochastic character of the simulation, different runs with the same decision

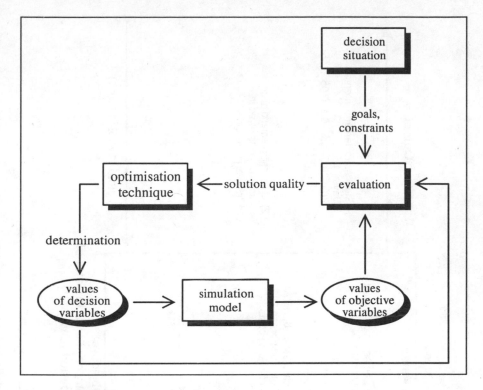

Fig. 1. Tuning decision variables of a simulation model [Biethahn and Nissen 1994]

values and initial solutions, but different random number seeds, will not lead to fully identical results. Thus, for a comparison of alternative parameter settings a substitute objective function must be constructed first. Biethahn [1978] systematically simulated equidistant points in a grid of *(s, q)*-policies and concluded that by taking the mean of 40 simulations/policy the resulting multimodal landscape of objective function values was approximately stable. However, 10 simulations/policy were sufficient to locate the relevant optima. With only one simulation/policy one would simply ignore the stochastic factors in the inventory model.

To investigate the influence of the number of simulations per solution on the final result under different optimisation techniques we conduct experiments with 1, 10 and 40 simulations per *(s, q)*-policy. With 40 and 10 simulations the mean is taken to be the 'true' objective function value as a basis for comparing different solutions. The final result of each optimisation is always evaluated with 40 simulations to allow for a more reliable estimate of the true performance of this particular *(s, q)*-policy.

244

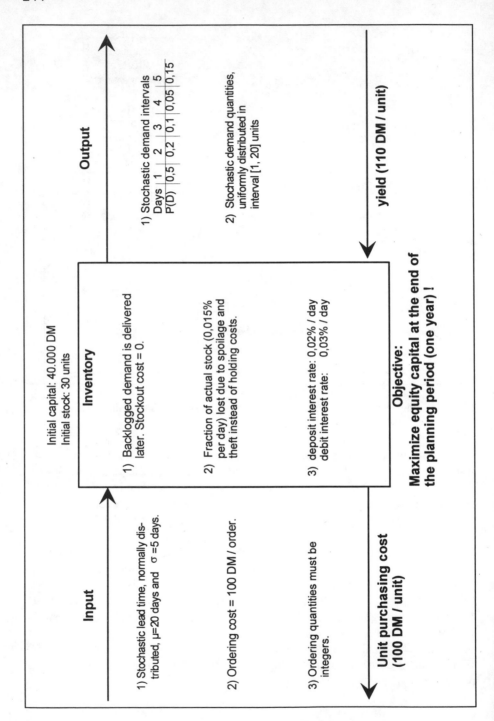

Fig. 2. Overview of the stochastic inventory model (simulation)

4 Three Optimisation Techniques

Since the substitute objective function is neither continuous nor differentiable only derivative-free optimisation methods are applicable. We use a GA as well as two conventional optimisation techniques. The GA-startpopulation includes all initial solutions taken individually as starting points for the two other methods. Results are based on five independent runs that vary only with respect to the random number seed.

The GA-implementation follows the pseudo-code given in the EA-tutorial in part I of this book, with the following specifications and extensions: A population size of 20 individuals is employed. Following common practice, we use Gray-code instead of standard binary code. 9 bits are used to code s and another 9 bits for q, allowing values between 0 and 511 for both decision variables. This results in a total of $2.6 \cdot 10^5$ conceivable (s, q)-policies. (This scope is also adopted for the other two methods.) The initial population (generation 0) is initialised with the (s, q)-policies $(20, 20)$; $(20, 150)$; $(150, 20)$; $(150, 150)$. The other 16 starting solutions of the GA are chosen at random. To determine mating partners for producing offspring, two individuals are randomly drawn from the parent generation and the one with higher fitness is kept. This procedure is then repeated to determine the second mating partner (deterministic binary tournament selection). Uniform crossover [Syswerda 1989] is applied with a probability $p_c = 0,8$. Mutation is implemented as bit inversion with a mutation probability per bit set to $p_m = 0.01$. The termination criterion for the GA is a predefined number of 25 generations leading to a total of 500 evaluated solutions (0.2% of the search space), not considering the initial solutions.

The two conventional optimisation techniques implemented are an alternating variable search (AVS) and a simplified gradient search (SGS). Their implementations are based on Biethahn [1978] who rates both methods as recommendable in the given context. The basic idea of AVS is to vary the variables individually in turn. Starting from an initial point in solution space the variable s is increased with a constant stepsize of 20 units of stock. If this is unsuccessful, decreasing s is tested. In case of success, the search proceeds in the chosen direction until failure. Then q is varied. Both variables are iteratively changed in turn until no further progress occurs. Then the steplength is halved (to an integer value), and the search continues as before. AVS terminates after a minimum steplength of 1 unit has been employed.

SGS proceeds in a similar way, but instead of varying only one variable at a time finds the direction of steepest ascent by changing s and/or q with predefined steplength. It then proceeds in this direction until failure, determines the steepest ascent anew and so on. When no further progress is achieved the steplength is halved. This procedure terminates after a minimum steplength of 1 unit. Both, AVS and SGS, employ identical steplengths and start from the same initial solutions.

5 Empirical Results and Implications

Empirical results for all three optimisation techniques tested are given in table 1 (40 simulations/solution) and table 2 (1 and 10 simulations/solution). The GA-results refer to the best individual ever discovered during the search. Note that the GA is designed in a way that the best solution does not necessarily survive forever. This ability to 'forget' has proven useful in overcoming local optima. In optimisation it is sensible, though, to always store the best solution disovered so far during one run in a separate 'golden cage', and update it whenever a better *(s, q)*-policy is discovered. This does not influence the GA search process, and must not be confused with an elitist approach, where usually the best solution is copied to the successor generation.

Interpreting table 1 first, one finds that the GA produces on average better results than SGS and particularly AVS. SGS proves to perform better than AVS but requires the evaluation of more trial solutions. However, the GA is even more time-consuming when 40 simulations/solution are performed.

Optimisation method (starting point)	Evaluated solutions (average)	Best run OF-value (s, q)-policy		Worst run OF-value (s,q)-policy		Average OF-value (5 runs)
AVS 20, 20	34,8	62743,83	(40, 200)	62108,35	(60, 142)	62379,52
20, 150	29,2	62867,42	(20, 220)	62410,74	(60, 170)	62590,01
150,20	40,0	62670,16	(30, 200)	62292,65	(70, 160)	62447,43
150, 150	29,0	62511,20	(50, 148)	60913,34	(180, 158)	61595,45
SGS 20, 20	81,4	62922,53	(20, 240)	62722,73	(20, 182)	62797,55
20, 150	61,4	62962,96	(0, 230)	62635,76	(10, 188)	62794,25
150,20	71,6	62931,90	(10, 200)	62527,79	(10, 162)	62737,56
150, 150	66,2	62990,04	(10, 290)	62133,62	(105, 185)	62603,79
GA	382,0	63109,03	(11, 245)	62984,45	(9, 241)	63034,79

Table 1. Empirical results using three different optimisation techniques to determine good settings for order point (s) and order quantity (q) in a stochastic inventory simulation. Each trial solution is evaluated with 40 simulations, taking the mean as fitness. (OF-value = objective function value)

The difference in solution quality between best and worst run is smaller for the population-based GA as compared to the point-based conventional optimisation methods. Moreover, in particular AVS shows a certain dependency of the final result on the initial solution. Thus, the GA is a more reliable optimiser than both SGS and AVS at the price of higher CPU-requirements. The recommended *(s,q)*-policy of the GA leads to a very small value ($\approx$ 10) for s and a rather high value ($\approx$ 250) for q. Figure 3 visualises the results regarding solution quality and reliability.

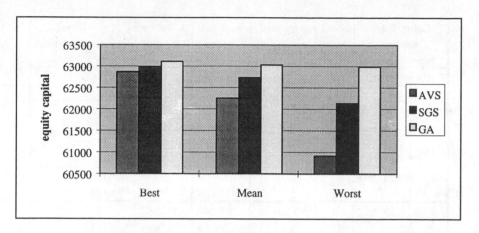

Fig. 3. Resulting values for equity capital at the end of the planning period (5 runs)

One should also point out that both conventional optimisation methods terminate once the minimum steplength has been reached, while the GA can, in principle, continue to improve the solution quality as long as resources are available. This makes GAs interesting, when computational requirements are not so important as opposed to solution quality.

Empirical results for 1 and 10 simulations/solution respectively are presented in table 2. An obvious finding is that the fewer evaluations one performs the higher the fitness of the final solution becomes. This is, however, only true before these final solutions are evaluated with 40 simulations to determine their 'real' quality. Then, it becomes clear that AVS and SGS produce rather bad results with only 1 simulation per (s,q)-policy. With 10 simulations the results are somewhat better but still strongly dependent on the initial solution. It is fair to say that for AVS and SGS simulating each trial solution 1 or 10 times is no reliable indicator for a truly good result after 40 simulations.

This may be explained as follows. With a point-based search, lucky evaluations of mediocre solutions manifest themselves and lead to a premature termination of the search process. With fewer simulations this effect becomes more pronounced. It appears that population-based approaches are not so easily misled. The GA concentrates on promising regions by exploiting the information contained in good solutions already discovered. One could say that the whole GA-population is involved in a learning process, storing information about the search space. At the same time, new search areas are continuously explored due to the stochastic element inherent in GA. To keep a proper balance between such exploitation and exploration is important for the success of a GA.

Figure 4 shows that the average results with 10 simulations/solution for the GA are roughly comparable to the two conventional methods, AVS and SGS, with 40 simulations/solution.

Optimisation method (starting point)		Sim./ point	Avg. total simulations	Best run OF-value	Worst run OF-value	Avg. OF-value after 40 simulations
AVS	20, 20	10	350,0	62845,14	62116,09	61967,24
		1	31,2	64921,53	62820,67	61550,57
	20, 150	10	252,0	62807,82	62713,28	62281,15
		1	27,8	65295,04	63815,71	62055,20
	150, 20	10	380,0	62992,19	62209,82	61999,85
		1	36,4	64217,25	62021,52	60497,36
	150, 150	10	290,0	62319,94	61260,45	61285,44
		1	25,2	63176,94	62599,56	61023,51
SGS	20, 20	10	772,0	63031,40	62100,92	62117,12
		1	65,8	65799,08	63288,81	61617,26
	20, 150	10	512,0	63057,51	62735,28	62434,35
		1	60,0	64515,64	63839,25	62018,25
	150, 20	10	676,0	62989,77	62312,86	62077,61
		1	66,2	64035,94	61637,51	60353,56
	150, 150	10	720,0	63096,47	61954,32	61893,34
		1	57,8	64133,95	63184,54	61124,84
GA		10	3560,0	63677,78	63420,48	62592,03
		1	320,0	65902,06	65441,03	62450,84

Table 2. Empirical results for 1 and 10 simulations/solution. The last column gives the average objective function value over 5 runs after evaluating each *final* solution with 40 simulations. This must not be confused with the data in table 1.

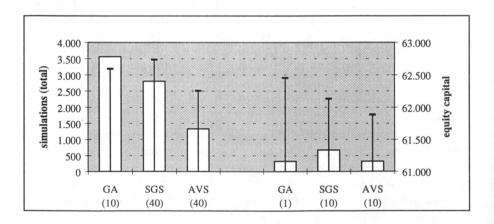

Fig. 4. Results regarding solution quality (vertical lines) and computational requirements (bars) for the different optimisation techniques when the number of simulations per solution is reduced from 40 to 10 and 1 respectively. The GA shows robustness.

The GA also produces good results even with only 1 simulation per trial solution. This robustness of the GA regarding stochastic perturbations in the evaluation function is in good agreement with earlier findings of Grefenstette and Fitzpatrick [1985]. They investigated an image registration problem where the evaluation of individual solutions was based on statistical sampling techniques. In essence, they also discovered a certain robustness of GAs with approximate evaluations, and concluded that candidate solutions need not be evaluated exactly.

A possible explanation for the GA-robustness in stochastic optimisation could be based on the similarity of parents and children as well as the cloud-like type of search in GAs. These factors seem to lead to an *implicit*, intensive evaluation of information about the search space contained in the population as a whole. This would then give the GA increased reliability as opposed to conventional point-based search techniques when only few evaluations per trial solution are performed. Experiments with other EA-variants [Nissen 1994] indicate similar effects for Evolution Strategy and Evolutionary Programming, which are also population-based search methods. This effect could be used in stochastic optimisation to alleviate the generally high CPU-requirements of EAs. However, the mentioned phenomenon requires further study before definite conclusions can be drawn.

Finally, we would like to point out that the chosen optimisation problem is of only moderate complexity to gain first experience. It remains an interesting field for further research to compare modern point-based heuristics like Simulated Annealing with EAs on more complex stochastic optimisation problems.

References

Biethahn, J. (1978): Optimierung und Simulation. Gabler, Wiesbaden

Biethahn, J.; Nissen, V. (1994): Combinations of Simulation and Evolutionary Algorithms in Management Science and Economics. Annals of OR 52:183-208

Grefenstette, J.J.; Fitzpatrick, J.M. (1985): Genetic Search with Approximate Function Evaluations. In: Grefenstette, J.J. (ed.): Proceedings of an International Conference on Genetic Algorithms and Their Applications. Erlbaum, Hillsdale/NJ

Nissen, V. (1994): Evolutionäre Algorithmen. Darstellung, Beispiele, betriebswirtschaft-liche Anwendungsmöglichkeiten. DUV, Wiesbaden

Syswerda, G. (1989): Uniform Crossover in Genetic Algorithms. In: Schaffer J.D. (ed.): Proceedings of the Third International Conference on Genetic Algorithms. Morgan-Kaufmann, San Mateo

Part Four
Applications in Financial Services

Genetic Algorithms and the Management of Exchange Rate Risk

Richard J. Bauer, Jr., Ph.D., CFA

School of Business and Administration, St. Mary's University, San Antonio, TX 78228-8607, USA

Abstract. Many financial market participants are affected by fluctuations in foreign exchange rates. This paper describes and tests a genetic algorithm approach to the problem of monthly currency allocation decisions. Since problem representation is often a significant issue in the application of evolutionary computation techniques, a major contribution of this paper is the description of how these types of decisions can be modeled using genetic algorithms.
The approach is applied to the problem of how to allocate assets between US dollars and German deutschemarks. The model is tested over the 1984-93 time period. The model assumes a fundamentalist perspective, using the base amounts and changes in 25 different US and German macroeconomics series as input data. The model examines a search space of trading rules with over 35 trillion possible combinations. The results show that the genetic algorithm approach can find interesting trading rules based on the fitness criteria, however, the results are inconclusive concerning the forecasting potential of these rules. Possible extensions of the basic methodology are described.

Keywords. Genetic algorithms, problem representation, exchange rates, genetic programming

1   Exchange Rate Forecasting

1.1   Introduction

There are only a few published applications of genetic algorithms to the world of finance (see Bauer [1992, 1994a, 1994b]). Research in this field is still in its infancy, even though genetic algorithms, as developed by Holland [1975], contains a vast literature. This may be due to the fact that while the basic mechanics are straightforward, visualizing how a given problem can be tackled with genetic algorithms is not always obvious.

The speed and efficiency of genetic algorithms make them ideal vehicles for exploring huge numbers of potential trading strategies. The purpose of this paper is to illustrate how genetic algorithms can be used to explore various exchange rate trading strategies. The focus of the paper will be on the problem representation and methodology, not the specific results.

1.2   The Exchange Rate Forecasting Problem

Participants in the foreign exchange market can be broadly classified as either hedgers or speculators. Importers and exporters, whose profits can be quickly reduced by unfavorable exchange rate fluctuations, have a natural motivation to hedge their exchange rate risk. Lenders, borrowers, and equity investors can also have the value of their financial transactions quickly changed by currency movements. Others try to outguess currency movements in hopes of swift speculative profit. All of these parties are either explicitly or implicitly managing their foreign exchange risk.

The ability to forecast exchange rates is obviously of great potential value. Many attempt it, but few succeed. Small improvements in forecasting accuracy can lead to large rewards. With so many players, it is difficult to get an edge on the rest of the crowd. This suggests that one's expectations regarding the successful development of forecasting models should be modest. However, even a small advantage can be lucrative.

Trading strategies can be broadly classified as either technical or fundamental. Technical strategies generally rely on past price and trading volume information to forecast future price movements. Fundamental strategies rely on economic relationships that affect underlying value. This paper will focus on strategies that are fundamental in nature.

The major economic theories affecting exchange rates are: interest rate parity theory, purchasing power parity theory, and the international Fisher effect theory. These theories are discussed in most international economics and international finance textbooks. These theoretical relationships revolve around interest rates differentials, inflation differentials, and the spot/forward rate relationship. Economic theory also suggests that the relative strengths of economies affects the value of currencies. Many economists think there is a strong linkage between money supply growth and inflation. For these reasons, this paper will focus primarily on the following economic variables: money supply, inflation, interest rates, and economic activity.

2   A Genetic Algorithm Approach

2.1   Problem Representation

Most research in genetic algorithms has been done using a fixed-length binary string problem representation. That approach will be used in this paper. This entails converting real-valued variables into a binary representation. This can be accomplished by converting a range of values into discrete intervals.

This approach will be illustrated using the 3-month US Treasury bill rate. Over the 1984-89 time period, end-of-the-month 3-month Treasury bill rates ranged from 5.18 percent to 10.49 percent. This range can be partitioned into eight intervals, that will be referred to as *range octiles*. If the difference between 10.49 and 5.18 is divided by 8, the result is 0.66375. Using this value, the range octiles can be formed as follows:

Range Octile	Range of Treasury Bill rates
1	5.18 - 5.84
2	5.84 - 6.51
3	6.51 - 7.17
4	7.17 - 7.84
5	7.84 - 8.50
6	8.50 - 9.16
7	9.16 - 9.83
8	9.83 - 10.49

Intuitively, it seems that the relative level of a particular macroeconomic variable would be important to financial market participants. For example, "high" interest rates might warrant certain investment actions. The relative level of a given macroeconomic variable will be identified in this paper using a *range code*. The range octiles that form the basis for the range codes were computed using the values for the relevant time series over the previous five year period. The following list shows the relationships between range codes and range octiles:

Range Code	Range Octiles
1	1
2	1, 2
3	1, 2, 3, 4
4	5, 6, 7, 8
5	7, 8
6	8
7	3, 4, 5, 6
8	2, 3, 4, 5, 6, 7

Using this scheme, range codes 5 and 6 could both refer to "high" interest rates. However, range code 6 captures rates in the highest octile of values, while range code 5 captures rates in the highest quartile (the two highest octiles). Some variables might be important for forecasting only when they are not at extreme highs or extreme lows. Range codes 7 and 8 allow for this possibility.

This paper will focus on developing trading rules for the monthly allocation of assets into either US dollars (US$) or German deutschemarks (DM). Therefore, the ultimate decision can be viewed as simply a binary signal to be"in" or "out" of US dollar assets. Trading rules can take many possible forms. A simple rule would be: If the *change* in the 3-month US Treasury Bill over the last month is greater than 0.5 percent, then invest in US dollar assets. A table of range octiles and range codes could be constructed for the *changes* in 3-month Treasury Bills similar to what was described above for the *level* of Treasury Bill rates. Assuming that a change of greater than 0.5 percent corresponds to a range code of 5 in this new table, then the first portion of this rule could be rephrased as"if the range code for the change in the 3-month US Treasury Bill rate over the last month equals 5, then invest in US dollar assets. If this condition is not met, then the funds would be invested in DM assets."

Simple rules can be combined in various ways to produce more complicated rules. The following basic logical operators form a logically complete set: AND, OR, and NOT. These operators can be combined with various logical conditions to represent virtually any possible trading rule. For example, a trading rule might be: if the range code for US M1 money supply growth is equal to 8 and the range code for the German M1 money supply growth is equal to 6, then invest in US dollar assets.

More complex rules can be represented in the form of a small tree. The term *functions* will be used to designate the AND, OR, and NOT operators. Each logical condition concerning the range code of a particular macroeconomic variable will be referred to as a *terminal*. The rule in the preceding paragraph contains one function and two terminals. The AND operator is the function and the two logical conditions of the rule that refer to US and German money supply changes are the terminals. In this paper, only terminals of this type, which are either logically true or logically false, will be used. Several functions and several terminals can be combined to form a small tree that represents a particular trading rule.

Consider the tree shown in Figure 2.1, consisting of three functions (labeled F1, F2, and F3) and four terminals (labeled T1, T2, T3, and T4). This structure is not large, but it is sufficient to represent some reasonably complex trading rules.

Rules of the described form can be represented as binary strings that can be manipulated by genetic algorithms. To simplify the representation, some minor additional constraints will be introduced. Referring to figure 1.1, function F1 will be allowed to be either the AND operator or the OR operator. Functions F2 and F3 can be AND, OR, or NOT. If functions F2 and F3 are the NOT operator, then they will have only one terminal associated with them. If they are either AND or OR, then they will have two terminals. The terminals will consist of a macroeconomic variable and a range code. Twenty-five different macroeconomic time series will be used. However, there will be five possible monthly change levels for each macroeconomic series. The base amount of the series will be referred to as having a change level of 0. Changes in the base amount of each series over the last 1, 3, 6, or 12 months will be referred to as monthly change levels of 1, 3, 6, or 12.. The range code will take on values from 1 to 8, as described earlier. Each terminal will be evaluated as logically true or logically false. As an example, a terminal could represent the answer to the question "Is the range code for the 6-month change in the German money supply equal to 8?" If this were true, then the German money supply would be increasing relatively quickly.

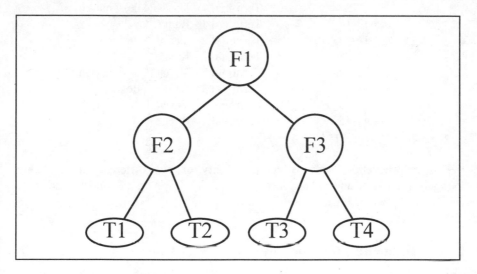

Figure 2.1. Tree of functions and terminals

The first function can be represented using one bit. The second and third functions, which can assume 3 values, require two bits. Two bits can assume patterns of 00, 01, 10, and 11. A pattern of 01 will represent the OR operator, while 10 and 11 will represent the AND and NOT operators. A string with a pattern of 00 will receive an arbitrarily low fitness value, which will cause these patterns to gradually be forced out of the population.

Terminals will require more bits for their representation. Since there are 25 macroeconomic series, with 5 variations each, a total of 125 combinations are possible. This requires seven bits, with patterns ranging from 0000000 to 1111111, to produce 128 possible patterns. Since only 125 patterns are needed, strings with the other 3 patterns will receive an arbitrarily low fitness value. Each variable will have an associated range code, with 8 possible values. Three bits will be sufficient to represent the range codes, leading to a total of ten bits per terminal.

Using this representation scheme, each possible rule tree of the form in Figure 2.1 can be represented by a 45-bit string as follows:

Bit Positions	Represent
1	Function 1 (AND or OR)
2-3	Function 2 (AND, OR, or NOT)
4-5	Function 3 (AND, OR, or NOT)
6-12	Terminal 1 - Variable designation
13-15	Terminal 1 - Range code
16-22	Terminal 2 - Variable designation
23-25	Terminal 2 - Range code
26-32	Terminal 3 - Variable designation
33-35	Terminal 3 - Range code
36-42	Terminal 4 - Variable designation
43-45	Terminal 4 - Range code

This representation leads to the possibility of two different strings being logically redundant and having identical fitness. However, this did not seem to present any practical difficulties.

2.2   Data and Methodology

The 25 macroeconomic series that were used are shown in Table 2.1. Data for the first twenty series in the list were obtained from the US Department of Commerce's Economic Bulletin Board. Data for the last five series were obtained from the Deutsche Bundesbank. Since the trading rules being examined were for monthly trading decisions, there is a problem regarding data availability due to the lag in publication for some of the series. For example, when considering a monthly allocation of currency assets for the month of November, some of the data might only be available through August. To allow for this, each time series was adjusted to control for its actual availability.

A simple genetic algorithm, with a population size of 100, was used. One-point crossover was used with a probability of 0.6. Mutation was performed with a probability of 0.001. election was performed using a simple ranking procedure. Each trial of the genetic algorithm was terminated after 300 generations or when population bias exceeded 95 percent. These settings are all described in Bauer [1994a].

Fitness is, in many ways, the heart of the genetic algorithm. For this application, each binary string corresponds to a specific foreign exchange monthly trading rule. A starting wealth, on January 1, 1984, of $1,000 was assumed. Each month during the 1984-89 testing period, the trading rule signaled whether the investor should keep these monetary assets denominated in US dollars or switch into deutschemarks. The fitness measure was the US dollar value of the assets at the end of the 5-year testing period. Interest was ignored in the calculation, which would understate the ending wealth that an investor could earn from each trading strategy. However, trading costs were also ignored, which overstates the ending wealth.

Number	Description
1	US, Index of stock prices
2	US, Money supply M2
3	US, Index of industrial production
4	US, Producer price index, finished goods
5	US, CPI for all urban consumers, all items
6	US, Money supply M1
7	US, Federal funds rate
8	US, Discount rate on new 91-day T-bills
9	US, Yield on new high-grade corporate bonds
10	US, Yield on long-term Treasury bonds
11	OECD, Industrial production
12	Japan, Industrial production
13	Germany, Industrial production
14	Japan, Consumer price index
15	Germany, Consumer price index
16	Japan, Stock prices
17	Germany, Stock prices
18	US, Exchange value of US dollar
19	Japan, Exchange rate per US dollar
20	Germany, Exchange rate per US dollar
21	Germany, Producer price index
22	Germany, Money stock M3 - change over last 6 months
23	Germany, Money stock M2 - change over last 6 months
24	Germany, Money stock M1 - change over last 6 months
25	Germany, Money market rate - 3 month funds

Table 2.1. Macroeconomic variables used in the tests

3 Results

3.1 Enumerative Search Results

For comparison purposes, an enumerative search of 2,000 (8 x 5 x 25 x 2) single variable trading rules was conducted. All 8 range code settings for the five variations of the 25 macroeconomic series were examined. In addition, both the positive and negative form of the rule were tested. For example, the rule that says "if the range code for the 1-month change in variable 3 is equal to 8, then invest in US dollar assets" was tested as well as the rule that says "if the range code for the 1-month change in variable 3 is NOT equal to 8, then invest in US dollar assets." Of the 2,000 trading rules examined, the 25 rules with the highest ending wealth are shown in Table 3.1.

	Variable	Monthly Change	Range Code		1984-88 Fitness	1989-90 Fitness	1992-93 Fitness
1	1	12	NOT	4	1992.66	1118.52	913.77
2	1	12		3	1992.66	1118.52	913.77
3	6	3		7	1967.34	941.11	1111.28
4	6	0		8	1911.41	887.51	946.27
5	6	0	NOT	6	1911.41	887.51	946.27
6	9	0		4	1890.46	1172.27	913.77
7	9	0	NOT	3	1890.46	1172.27	913.77
8	23	12	NOT	8	1889.54	1025.86	798.17
9	24	12		6	1877.93	1172.27	913.77
10	24	12		5	1877.93	1159.21	913.77
11	22	12	NOT	8	1867.82	1069.83	801.44
12	18	1		5	1865.90	1147.72	910.72
13	7	1		5	1859.53	1235.88	913.77
14	7	1	NOT	7	1859.53	1235.88	918.42
15	22	12		6	1841.87	1172.27	798.17
16	23	12		6	1841.87	1124.09	798.17
17	1	12		1	1811.53	1172.27	913.77
18	7	0	NOT	2	1798.01	1000.00	913.77
19	22	12	NOT	7	1797.56	1070.69	823.41
20	6	6	NOT	5	1789.64	1000.00	1089.87
21	8	1	NOT	8	1788.07	1225.27	919.92
22	8	1		6	1788.07	1225.27	910.72
23	12	12		6	1777.04	1225.27	913.77
24	10	12		4	1776.46	1194.17	919.38
25	10	12	NOT	3	1776.46	1194.17	919.38

Table 3.1. Enumerative Search Results

The ending wealth values for two additional holdout periods are also reported. The January 1, 1989 - December 31, 1990 period is the two year period immediately after the initial test period. When German reunification occurred in 1991, the money supply experienced a major shock. Due to this unusual event, the results for a second holdout period, January 1, 1992 - December 31, 1992 after reunification, are also reported.

During the January 1984 - December 1988 testing period, the DM appreciated substantially relative to the dollar. Therefore, one comparison value of interest is the ending wealth that would have resulted from converting dollars to DM at the beginning of the period, holding DM until the end of the period, and exchanging back to dollars at the end of the period. If this had been done, the ending value would have been $1,566. Similar values for the 1989-90 and 1992-93 period are $1,172 and $914, respectively. The ending value of less than $1,000 for the 1992-93 period reflects the depreciation of the DM following reunification. These three buy-and-hold strategies provide a basis for comparison with the active switching strategies under consideration.

The results from Table 3.1 show that all 25 of these strategies substantially outperformed the buy-and-hold alternative over the testing period. The first two rules in the table are mirror images of each other that represent identical strategies. The first rule says to stay invested in dollar assets whenever the 12-month change in US stock prices is not in range code 4, which encompasses range octiles of 5, 6, 7, and 8. If this variable is not in these range octiles then it must be in range octile 1, 2, 3, or 4, which would give it a range code of 3. Since the second rule dictates a range code of 3, the first two rules are exactly equivalent in meaning.

The results for the later holdout periods are mixed. Some of the rules, such as 13 and 14 continued to perform well in the 1989-90 holdout period. Others, such as 3, 4, and 5, performed poorly. Rules 6 and 7 had an ending wealth in the 1989-90 holdout period of $1,172, which equaled the buy-and-hold value. This performance should be viewed as good, since the decision to stay invested in DM assets over this time period was positive. The second holdout period of 1992-93 is after the reunification. Given the unusual nature of this shock, it is not surprising that many of the rules did not fare well in this new environment.

3.2   Genetic Algorithm Results

The genetic algorithm procedure begins using random initialization. Ideally, when the population converges, the optimal (based on the fitness measure being used) solution will have been found. However, in most cases only a near-optimal solution is found. One method to control for premature convergence to non-optimal solutions is to conduct multiple trials of the genetic algorithm. In this paper, 100 trials of the genetic algorithm were conducted. With the string representation used in this paper, there were over 35 trillion possible trading rules in the search space.

	F1	F2	F3	T1	T2	T3	T4	84-88 Fitness	89-90 Fitness	92-93 Fitness
1	OR	AND	AND	1/12/3	2/3/7	21/12/4	10/12/5	2388.05	1072.55	913.77
2	OR	AND	AND	1/12/3	2/3/7	21/12/4	10/12/5	2388.05	1072.55	913.77
3	OR	AND	AND	1/12/3	2/3/7	21/12/4	10/12/5	2388.05	1072.55	913.77
4	OR	AND	AND	1/12/3	2/3/7	21/12/4	10/12/5	2388.05	1072.55	913.77
5	OR	AND	AND	1/12/3	2/3/7	21/12/4	10/12/5	2388.05	1072.55	913.77
6	AND	OR	AND	9/12/4	22/12/6	6/3/7	11/12/4	2375.13	1023.36	913.77
7	AND	OR	AND	9/12/4	22/12/6	6/3/7	11/12/4	2375.13	1023.36	913.77
8	AND	OR	AND	9/12/4	24/12/6	6/3/7	11/12/4	2375.13	1023.36	913.77
9	AND	OR	AND	9/12/4	22/12/6	6/3/7	11/12/4	2375.13	1023.36	913.77
10	AND	OR	AND	9/12/4	22/12/6	6/3/7	11/12/4	2375.13	1023.36	913.77
11	AND	OR	OR	24/12/5	9/12/4	15/1/7	20/3/6	2370.51	1162.01	911.59
12	OR	AND	AND	12/3/4	6/3/7	19/1/5	16/6/4	2370.00	1071.22	1038.31
13	OR	AND	AND	12/3/4	6/3/7	19/1/5	16/6/4	2370.00	1071.22	1038.31
14	OR	AND	AND	12/3/4	6/3/7	19/1/5	16/6/4	2370.00	1071.22	1038.31
15	OR	AND	AND	12/3/4	6/3/7	19/1/5	16/6/4	2370.00	1071.22	1038.31
16	OR	AND	AND	12/3/4	6/3/7	19/1/5	16/6/4	2370.00	1071.22	1038.31
17	AND	OR	OR	16/1/1	1/12/3	17/0/3	2/3/7	2368.19	1159.21	913.77
18	AND	OR	OR	16/1/1	1/12/3	17/0/3	2/3/7	2368.19	1159.21	913.77
19	AND	OR	OR	16/1/1	1/12/3	17/0/3	2/3/7	2368.19	1159.21	913.77
20	AND	OR	OR	16/1/1	1/12/3	17/0/3	2/3/7	2368.19	1159.21	913.77
21	AND	OR	OR	16/1/1	1/12/3	17/0/3	2/3/7	2368.19	1159.21	913.77
22	OR	AND	AND	16/3/4	18/6/5	6/3/7	12/3/4	2360.93	1091.43	1026.74
23	OR	AND	AND	16/3/4	18/6/5	6/3/7	12/3/4	2360.93	1091.43	1026.74
24	OR	AND	AND	22/12/4	18/6/5	6/3/7	12/3/4	2360.93	1091.43	1055.68
25	OR	AND	AND	22/12/4	18/6/5	6/3/7	12/3/4	2360.93	1091.43	1055.68

Table 3.2. Genetic Algorithm Test Results

The rules with the 25 highest fitness values are reported in Table 3.2. Some rules appear more than once, since they may have been found in different trials. The four terminals are reported in a similar format, with the variable reported first, followed by the monthly change code and the range code. The first rule can be decomposed as follows:

If (the change in US stock prices over the past 12 months is in range code 3 AND the change in the US M2 money supply over the last 3 months is in range code 7) OR (the change in Germany's producer price index is in range code 4 AND the change in the US long-term Treasury Bond rate over the last 12 months is in range code 5) then invest in US$ assets. If not, invest in DM assets.

Several conclusions are warranted. First, the genetic algorithm did identify trading rules with fitness levels that were substantially greater than the best of the one variable rules examined using enumerative search. Second, the performance of these rules in subsequent periods was somewhat mixed. None of the rules outperformed the buy-and-hold DM strategy over the 1989-90 holdout period, although some did equal this result. In the 1992-93 period, some of the rules performed quite well, such as rule 12.

3.3 Suggestions for Future Research

There are many possible variations to the basic methodology used in this paper. A few of the many potential refinements are:

- Other macroeconomic variables could be substituted or added to the list used in this paper.
- Technical variables could be substituted or added.
- The fitness function could be altered. For example, later time periods could receive greater weighting.
- The genetic algorithm parameters, such as crossover probability, could be modified to prolong the search.

A major possible extension of this research would be to recast the problem into a genetic programming framework. The use of the terms functions and terminals in this paper was deliberate, since these terms are used in Koza [1992]. Clearly, evolutionary computation seems to offer great potential for trading applications.

References

Bauer, Jr., R.J.; Liepins, G.L. (1992): Genetic Algorithms and Computerized Trading Strategies. In: O'Leary, D.E.; Watkins, P.R. (eds.): Expert Systems in Finance. Elsevier Science, Amsterdam: 89-100.

Bauer, Jr., R.J. (1994a): Genetic Algorithms and Investment Strategies. John Wiley & Sons, New York.

Bauer, Jr., R.J. (1994b): An Introduction to Genetic Algorithms: A Mutual Fund Screening Example. Neurove$t Journal 4: 16-19.

Holland, J.H. (1975): Adaptation in Natural and Artificial Systems. University of Michigan Press, Ann Arbor.

Koza, J.R. (1992): Genetic Programming: On the Programming of Computers by Means of Natural Selection. MIT Press, Cambridge, MA.

Evolving Decision Support Models for Credit Control

Neil S. Ireson and Terence C. Fogarty

Faculty of Computer Studies and Mathematics,
University of the West of England,
Bristol,
England.

1 Introduction

With the introduction of computerised monitoring, collection and storage systems, many organisations have accumulated massive amounts of operational data. This has lead to the desire to exploit these repositories of information to improve the formation of successful current and future strategies. However, the extraction of management information is not easy, and few companies believe they are fully utilising its potential. Where any attempt is made, the predominant approach is to apply statistical analysis techniques to generate a model highlighting the prevalent trends and patterns which can be used to predicted future behaviours. The general flow and usage of this information is shown in Figure 1.

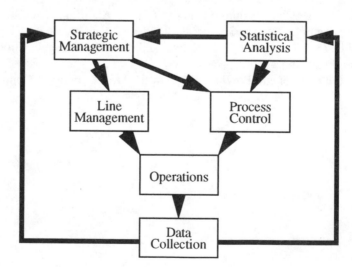

Figure 1. Management Control and Information Flow

This chapter describes an alternative Genetic Algorithm (GA) based decision support system for evolving Bayesian classifiers from a set of observed data. This was initially developed as part of the IDIOMS[1] project to demonstrate the use of novel techniques to extract useful information from large amounts of historic data. The system provides a Graphical User-Interface (GUI), described elsewhere [Gammack, et al. 1992], to facilitate interaction both with the GA parameters and with the decision model, allowing the incorporation of human expertise into the model generation and final decision process.

The model is evolved by searching the space of possible models using a GA. This iterative search process has a probabilistic focus on those parts of the decision space which tend to optimise the models' information content. In comparative tests the approach provided predictive accuracy comparable with current statistical methods, without the need for statistical expertise.

Section 2 introduces the credit control problem, discussing the general difficulties and the limitations of the current statistical approaches. Section 3 describes the salient feature of the IDIOMS decision model and how these interact with the GA search. The next sections describe the features of the GA; the genetic representation of the model (Section 4), model evaluation and selection (section 5) and the crossover and mutation operators (section 6). We conclude in section 7 with a brief discussion of experimental results and general advantages in using the techniques presented.

2   The Credit Control Problem

The most extensive application of data analysis techniques to aid in decision making has been in the financial industry, primarily in the area of credit control. Companies control credit using data gained from their customers, credit card bureaus and from their own operational systems and experts. They use this data to guide and support decisions throughout the life of a customers account; determining which applicants to accept, whether to increase the credit allowance, the amount of bad debt provision required, how to deal with an individual bad debtor, etc. The standard procedure is to use linear regression, logistic regression or discriminant analysis on a sample of past data to give a function which can be implemented as a scorecard [Thomas, et al. 1992]. A scorecard is constructed from the variables relating to the particular features of the bank/customer relationship, the values of each variable are partitioned into ranges (for continuous variables) and exclusive

---

1. IDIOMS (Intelligent Decision-making In On-line Management Systems) is a collaborative project involving the National Transputer Support Centre at Sheffield, Strand Software Technology Ltd., Bristol Transputer Centre and a high street bank. It is partially funded by the DTI under the Information Engineering Advanced Technology Program.

sets (for discrete variables). A score is assigned to each partition which determines the degree to which a customer having those values effects a linear goal value, e.g. likelihood of being a bad debtor. The construction of such scorecards is a time consuming task carried out by statisticians in consultation with business experts.

The successful extraction of information is dependent on a number of factors, the first and foremost of these is the data. To some degree this data will be incomplete, inconsistent and incorrect, which is due to the nature of the domain which is being represented and the data collection process. As the data only represents those variables which are observable and observed, some important information may be excluded. Also the variables which are included in the data set may be irrelevant or contain repeated information. It is important to have an understanding of the *quality* of the data as this will critically effect the process used in generating the model.

All modelling processes make assumptions about the data which impose limitations on the model and certain, possibly critical, features of the domain may not be represent due to the modelling constraints. Which ever approach is applied, care must be taken to ensure the information in the final model is summarised and presented in a form comprehensible to the particular target audience.

Consideration should be given to how the performance of the model will degrade over time as the information in the model becomes obsolete. As construction of a new model is not always feasible or desirable (due to the length and expense of the process) their should be some augmentation facility to maintain the models performance at an adequate level. The process must consider; a) identifying the elements which require altering, b) what alterations are required and c) when augmentation can no longer maintain the model within an acceptable limit.

2.1   Limitation of Statistical Techniques

The current statistical approaches are dominated by the use of linear regression, although other techniques are available they are: more complex to implement, tend to produce more complex models and the increase in prediction is not deemed sufficient to warrant there use. The efficacy of the current statistical approaches are constrained by a number of factors

• The data must be manipulated into a form suitable for analysis, which can involve certain ad hoc approaches, for example where the data contains mixed types (requiring the use of dummy variables) or missing values (where the entire example is removed or a default value assumed).
• The application of the techniques, and models developed as a result, assume linear variable relationships.
• The process used to generate the predictive model are incremental. The variables are partitioned into meaningful categories (also known as 'classings')

maximising some measure of category discrimination within a variable. The relationship between variable values in the context of the other variables in the model is not considered. The categories and related scores are fixed in a stepwise search which biases the model, dependent on the order in which the variables are fixed.

• The statistical nature of the decision models provide limited descriptive capabilities, especially as the target audience are unlikely to be statistically literate.

3   The Decision Model

The alternative approach, adopted in IDIOMS, to generating a model for decision support attempts to provide the benefits of both statistical and expert system/ machine learning techniques and overcomes some of their limitations. The decision model is a probabilistic constraint or inference network ([Pearl 1988] and [Neapolitan 1990]), in the form of a simple directed acyclic graph (DAG) or tree. The nodes represent the variables whose values are partitioned into discrete categories and the arcs represent the conditional probabilities, derived from the data, relating to these categories. This representation naturally handles mixed data types and missing values, has an explicit relationship between the results of the inference (class probability distribution) and the data, and provides a symbolic model of the decision domain which is amenable to interpretation.

A critical assumption in the model is that the branches of the tree are conditionally independent. In the diagram below, Figure 2, it is assumed that B is independent of C given A, that is, $P(B|A \cap C) = P(B|A)$. Within the model it is possible to consider the dependency between variables, such as D and E, by forming a *hidden node*, B.

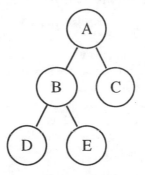

Figure 2. Inference Tree

In terms of the data, the independence assumption is obviously untrue, i.e. constraining the data to one variable's category is almost certain to effect the class distribution in all the other variable categories. In the evolution of the model, the effects of this assumption are considered either explicitly by excluding variables from the predictive set or joining predictors in bivariant groups, or implicitly in the construction of the variable categories. As the degree of covariance amongst the predictors increases the variable categorisation is increasingly dependent on its context, i.e. the model of which it forms a part. This both limits the effectiveness of the GA search process (due to the epistatis[1] in the chromosome representation) and the interpretation of the elements of the decision model in isolation.

A general problem with the use of the GA as an optimisation techniques is that it converges towards a single point in the decision space, although some success has been achieved using crowding and sharing schemes [Deb and Goldberg 1989]. Where the decision problem is dynamic, due to the changing environment and decision objectives, the model can soon become obsolete. This problem is partly considered by evolving more general models which are favoured by the optimisation function and search process, and by constraining the complexity of the model through the use of ad hoc limitations on the models parameters (e.g. number of categories in a variable, number of predictors in any group).

4 Representation

The genetic representation, or chromosome, relating to a probabilistic network is divided into sections, the first of these represents the network structure, defining which variables are selected and how they are to be combined. The remaining sections relate to the variable categorizations. There are two distinct types of category representations, for continuous and discrete variables, each type has different semantics and a different set of operators.

4.1 Predictor Selection and Combinations

Given a data set, each variable is allocated a unique identification (ID) number (e.g. AGE = 1, SEX = 2, INCOME = 3, OCCUPATION = 4, HOME = 5, CLASS = 6). The set of variables selected as predictors are represented as an ordered string of IDs. The predictive variable combinations are specified by contiguous variable IDs delimited and separated by a defined value (e.g. -1). The example in Figure 3a uses four out of the five possible predictors, SEX is ignored, two of those selected predictors, AGE and HOME, are combined as a joint predictor. Figure 3b shows how this genetic representation would appear as a constraint network.

$$\boxed{3}\boxed{-1}\boxed{1}\boxed{5}\boxed{-1}\boxed{4}$$

Figure 3a. Genetic representation of predictors and their combinations

---

1. Epistasis refers to the interaction between parts of the representation, i.e. the degree to which the contribution to fitness of one part depends upon the values of other parts.

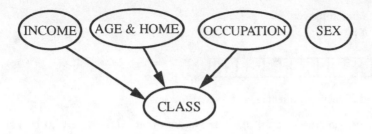

Figure 3b. Constraint network derived from the above representation

This first section of the chromosome acts as the control, determining the activation of the variable, whether the sections of the chromosome are switched 'on' or 'off', and the degree of variable interaction during translation of the genetic representation. Such control genes are also found in biological chromosomes, although there functions are more complex than those represented here.

4.2   Continuous Variable Categories

The genetic representation for the continuous variables specifies the upper boundaries of the category intervals. Thus, in the example below, Figure 4, the 'INCOME' variable has been partitioned into four categories:
C_1 = less than £9,000
C_2 = from £9,000 to £18,000
C_3 = form £18,000 to £35,000
C_4 = greater than £35,000

| 9,000 | 18,000 | 35,000 |

Figure 4. Genetic representation of continuous variable boundaries

It is worth noting that the continuous variable values are limited to a finite set defined by the training data. This ensures that the changes to the boundary values introduced by crossover and mutation will have a significant effect, i.e. change the probability matrix.

4.3   Discrete Variable Category

The genetic representation of discrete variables is similar to that of the variable selection and combinations except that all the values are included in the string. Discrete sets are represented as contiguous strings of values delimited and partitioned by a defined value (e.g. -1). In the example below, Figure 5, 'OCCUPATION' is partitioned into three sets:
C_1 = Unemployed or Student

C_2 = Retired or Employed
C_3 = Self-Employed

U	S	-1	R	E	-1	SE

Figure 5. Genetic representation of discrete variable sets

Note that proximate values in the representation are more likely to be copied together, thus sets once formed are likely to be preserved.

5 Fitness Function and Selection

The fitness of a given chromosome in the population, is calculated by constructing a probabilistic classifier from the representation and evaluating the prediction on a training set of data.

For each selected predictor combination a matrix is constructed where the columns relate to the classes, and the rows, on each of the other dimensions, relate to the predictive categories, i.e. numeric intervals or discrete sets. The number of dimensions in a matrix is dependent on the number of combined predictive variables. The figures below show the matrices derived from the examples (Figure 4 and Figure 5) above. Figure 6a shows the variables as two single predictor matrices, and Figure 6b shows them combined as a bivariant predictor matrix.

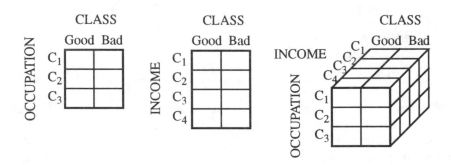

Figure 6a. Two Single Predictor Matrices   Figure 5a. A Two Predictor Matrix

The matrices are populated from the data, where each cell value is the co-occurrence count of the class and predictor categories. These co-occurrence matrices are then transformed into probability matrices by dividing the cell values by the column total. Thus the cell value becomes p(e|H), the probability of the *evidence* (variable category) given the *hypothesis* (class). With these probabilities and the class prior probabilities, p(H), (in effect the probability of the hypothesis given no evidence) it is then possible to calculate the probability of the hypothesis given the evidence called the posterior probability, p(H|e), for the classes using Bayes' Rule:

$$p(H|e) = \frac{p(H)p(e|H)}{p(e)}$$

The evidence, e, is the observed values for the predictive variables. These observations are assumed to be independent, that is, the value of one variable does not effect the values of any other. Given the assumption of independence the calculation of a class' posterior probability from the combined predictive evidence is simply the product of p(e|H) for all the evidence, multiplied by the prior probability for that class. The probability of the evidence, p(e) = $\sum$p(e|H)p(H) for all H, is the normalising constant and can be computed by requiring that $\sum$p(H|e) = 1

Once the probabilistic classifier has been constructed it is applied to the training set. For each record the predicted class is assumed to be the class with the highest probability. The result of the prediction is mapped onto a *confusion matrix*, where the rows and columns relate to the predicted and the actual or observed classes, respectively. From the confusion matrix a value representing the predictive power of the classifier on the training data can be calculated. The simplest is merely to divide the number of correct classifications by the total number of records. However, if the interaction between the classes is more complex, a payoff matrix can determine the benefit associated with a correct classification and the cost associated with an incorrect classification. Thus the fitness is given by:

$$\frac{MaximumPayoff}{\sum_i \sum_j cell_{ij} \times payoff_{ij}}$$

Where i and j are the actual and predicted class, respectively, $cell_{ij}$ is the number of records predicted as j whose actual class is i, and $payoff_{ij}$ is the payoff associated with this classification. This equation provides a fitness, between [0,1], where 1 is perfectly predictive.

Selection of the parental chromosomes is either directly proportional to fitness or based on rank. Due to the complex nature of the problem, the pressure to converge (i.e. the degree to which the probability of selection is dependent on fitness) is relatively low. Reducing the convergence pressure increases the exploration of the search space relative to the exploitation of the fittest members in the population.

6 Recombination (Crossover) and Mutation

The aim of the recombination operator is to combine good *building blocks* of two parent (source) chromosomes to form a new target (child) chromosome. The selection of the parents, guided by the fitness values, ensures that the parents are likely to possess relatively good building blocks in terms of the population. The crossover operator is constructed, as a complement to the genetic representation, such that. in disrupting the parents. it is likely to maintain the building blocks whilst being unbiased so as to freely explore the recombination possibilities. Three recombination operators are applied to the representation, depending on the chromosome section currently being copied. All three are based upon a uniform crossover [Syswerda 1989]. This was chosen as it provides the flexibility needed to deal with the complex, variable length representation.

The mutation operator is very secondary to the crossover operator in the search process. It is used to alter the representation, with a low probability, which means values which are not present in the initial population or which have been removed by crossover can be recovered. Most such alterations are deleterious to a chromosome's fitness.

Both operators ensure that the child chromosome is complete and consistent, i.e. defined limits are not exceeded, there is no duplication, etc.

6.1 Propagation of Predictor Selection and Combination

The order in which the variable values are copied from the parent to the child is determined by the predictor selection and combination representation. As the variable IDs are copied from the parental source to the child, the category values for the variable are also copied. After each value is copied there is a chance, defined by the *rate of crossover*, that the source will change from one parent to the other, this process is shown below. To ensure the values in the child's representation are legitimate, once a variable ID has been copied it will be ignored if encountered in the other parent, further the child can not possess a predictor combination which exceeds the user defined maximum limit. The process of copying continues until meeting the end of the current source parent's representation.

The following example, Figure 7, shows how two parental chromosome predictor representation are combined. The shaded positions on the parents show the source values.

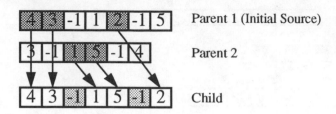

Parent 1 (Initial Source)

Parent 2

Child

Figure 7. Example of crossover of predictors and combinations

The effect of this crossover operator is that variable IDs which are proximate in the representation, such as those in the same combination, are more likely to be copied together. It is possible to vary the crossover rate to increase the likelihood of variable categorisation being copied from a single parent. Whilst this approach is more likely to preserve 'good' variable categories, it imposes a, possible detrimental, bias on the explorative search.

The mutation operator for the predictor selection and combination values either adds, deletes a variable ID from the predictor set, or moves one of the variable IDs between sets.

Although only the *active* variables (i.e. ones selected as predictors) are shown here, the representation includes all the variable IDs and also categorisations for those *inactive* variables. Both crossover and mutation are applied to the propagation of the values in the inactive parts of the representation. Such, *neutral* areas of the chromosome have no effect upon the fitness measure, and thus are open to undirected evolution, until they are "switch on" through crossover or mutation.

6.2 Propagation of Continuous Variable Categories

When copying the boundary values for a continuous variable, after each of the values is copied from the current source parent there is a probability that the parental source will change. Copying continues from the new parent at the next highest boundary value to the one previously copied. This process continues until the end of the current source parent's representation. If the number of boundaries in the child's representation exceeds the user defined limit, randomly selected boundaries are removed until the limit is reached.

The following example, Figure 8, shows how two parental chromosome continuous categorizations are combined. The shaded positions (loci) on the parents show the source values.

274

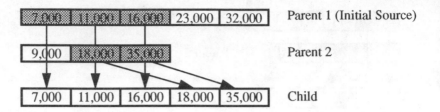

Figure 8. Example of crossover of continuous category boundaries

There are four different mutation operators for the continuous category boundary values:

- Creep: increments or decrements, by one, a randomly selected boundary value
- Jump: alters a randomly selected boundary to a value within the limits of the two contiguous boundaries, these may be the minimum or maximum values.
- Add: creates a random boundary value.
- Delete: removes a randomly selected boundary value.

6.3   Propagation of Discrete Variable Categories

In copying the set values for a discrete variable after each value is copied from the current source parent there is a probability that the parental source will change. Copying continues from the new parent at the first value not previously copied. This process continues until all the variable values have been copied. If the number of sets in the child's representation exceeds the user defined limit, randomly selected set delimiters are removed until the limit is reached.

The following example, Figure 9, shows how two parental chromosome discrete categorizations are combined. The shaded positions (loci) on the parents show the source values.

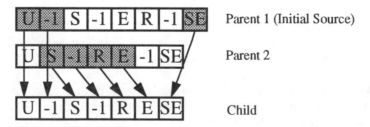

Figure 9. Example of crossover of discrete category sets

It is possible to alter crossover making it is more likely the crossover point will occur at a set separator. In effect, this is the same as having a uniform crossover rate and expanding number of values used to designate the separation point. This offers an approach similar to that used in evolutionary strategies [Hoffmeister and Back 1991] where the evolutionary parameters used in the genetic operators are subject to the evolutionary process. In the above representation the value of the separator could determine the likelihood of crossover (and mutation) in the following set. Thus 'good' sets would tend evolve a 'separator' value which reduced the likelihood of disruption.

The mutation operator for the discrete category set values moves one of the values from one set to another.

7   Results and Conclusion

In the development of the IDIOMS system a number of evaluations have been performed. In a comparisons with alternative machine learning algorithms [Fogarty and Ireson 1994] the GA produced significantly better performance. A detailed evaluation of the system is presently being carried out in conjunction with a bank, comparing the performance against current statistical techniques. In the initial tests the GA has produced the most predictive model for the evaluation problems [Ireson 1994].

The primary benefit from the approach involves exploiting an alternative to the standard statistical approaches to scorecard generation requiring a good deal of specialist expertise. This includes knowledge of the data and statistical techniques, to select and group the predictors, partition their values and determine the partitions' scores. This expertise is expensive and limited. The GA offers the advantage that the basic process is simple, yet powerful. With an understanding of the predictive model and its data requirements it is possible to construct a scorecard without the need for such specialist expertise. While the GA does require a few user defined parameters, their effects can be understood with minimal training.

The probabilistic network provides a goal directed model, summarizing the data, which can be used in the understanding of the domain which the data represents. The categories show the significant discrimination between the variable values, and by measuring the degree of constraint imposed by the node's values upon the class distribution (i.e. the information entropy of the matrices) the relative influence of the variables upon the class is shown. Applying Bayesian inference to determine the class posterior probability distribution, the most likely class, given the current state of information, can be inferred. This predictive model can be conceived as a scorecard with the probabilities in the matrices rows being equivalent to a scorecard's scores.

As new data becomes available the matrix probabilities can be updated, and by examining how the changing data is effecting the constraints, it is possible to determine whether and why the model is becoming less predictive. This can be used to indicate the changes in the environment being modelled by the data and when the model is ceasing to be an effective predictor in that environment.

Although, the approach provides a novel way to generate decision models, it in no way replaces the statistical approaches, which have been used in this field over the past thirty years and have a more sound theoretical basis, although, arguably, a similar ad hoc implementation. However, it does provide an alternative approach which is applicable in situations where the statistical approach is either not expedient or available (possible due to resource limitations). As these novel approaches become more widely used in this area and the understanding, algorithms and software improve they are likely to become a standard method of scorecard generation.

References

Deb, K.; Goldberg, D.E. (1989): An Investigation of Niche and Species Formulation in Genetic Function Optimization. ICGA 3: 42-50

Fogarty, T.C.; Ireson, N.S. (1994): Evolving Bayesian Classifiers for Credit Control - a Comparison with other Machine Learning Methods. IMA Journal of Mathematics Applied in Business and Industry 5:63-75

Gammack, J.; Fogarty, T.C.; Battle, S.; Ireson, N.S.; Cui, J. (1992): Human-centred Decision Support: the IDIOMS system. AI & Society 6: 345-66

Hoffmeister, F.; Back, T. (1991): Genetic Algorithms and Evolution-Strategies: Similarities and Differences. Parallel Problem Solving from Nature: 455-469

Ireson, N.S. (1994): Evolving a Classifier for the TSB Loan Application Data, UWE, Bristol

Neapolitan, R.E. (1990): Probabilistic Reasoning in Expert Systems. John Wiley & Sons

Pearl, J. (1988): Probabilistic Reasoning in Intelligent Systems. Morgan Kaufmann

Syswerda, G. (1989): Uniform Crossover in Genetic Algorithms. ICGA 3: 2-9

Thomas, L.C.; Crook, J.N.; Edelman, D.B. (1992): Credit Scoring and Credit Control. Oxford University Press

Genetic Classification Trees

Steven A. Vere

Bank of America, 2001 Clayton Road, Concord, CA 94520, USA
e-mail: vere@netcom.com

Abstract. The genetic processes of tree crossover and mutation, used by Koza in genetic programming, have been adapted and customized for classification tree evolution. Classification trees are ideal for genetic evolution because the fitness (error) contribution of each subtree is localized and independent of other disjoint subtrees. Consequently, good building "wedges" from parent trees can readily combine to produce superior offspring. Leaf decision analysis enables the system to concentrate crossover and mutation on replacing those subtrees which contribute the most error, instead of doing these operations randomly. Leaf analysis is also used to control automatic pruning of new trees, so that the average size of the trees grows only gradually with successive generations. All these features combine to produce a system which exhibits brisk convergence on classification problems. The system has been sucessfully applied to the prediction of prepayment rates for adjustable rate home mortgage loans.

Keywords. genetic algorithm, genetic programming, evolutionary algorithm, classification tree, decision tree, finance

1   Introduction

A number of schemes have previously been investigated for applying vector-representation genetic algorithms to the problem of generating a classifier by evolutionary processes [Wilson and Goldberg, 1989]. This paper introduces a new method for evolution of classification (or decision) systems using classification trees as the representation on which the evolutionary processes of tree crossover and mutation are applied [Koza, 1992]. Classification trees are a very natural representation for a classification system, and allow the application of several intuitively appealing customizations which will be shown to substantially improve system performance. This new method has been implemented in a system called GCT and successfully applied to two real-world financial problems, one of which will be discussed in detail in this paper. GCT is implemented in Lisp and runs on a 486 PC.

Classification trees (or decision trees) are particularly well suited for genetic evolution. In this paper the words decision and classification will be used interchangeably. Fig. 1 shows an example of a small classification tree of the kind

278

that might appear in the initial population in GCT for the financial problem from Section 6. Here "source" is a code designating where a loan originated, "points" means the fees payed to obtain the loan as a percentage of the loan amount, and "zip_code" is a two-digit U.S. postal code. Binary classification trees will be assumed throughout this paper, but the principles can be extended to general n-ary classification problems.

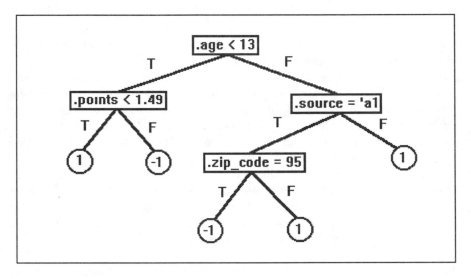

Fig. 1 A small classification tree

In classification problems, the natural fitness measure is the number of classification errors made by a particular tree on a training set. While computing the fitness, it is easy to determine for each leaf node a count of the number of times the decision at that leaf is right and wrong. Fig. 2 shows an abstract decision tree with right and wrong counts at the leaves. The first number is the right count; the second number is the wrong count. The total fitness rating of a classification tree is the sum of the wrong counts at the individual leaf nodes. The right counts will be used later.

Notice that for classification trees the fitness contribution of each subtree is precisely known. If tree crossover or mutation replaces a subtree, the fitness contribution of the remainder of the tree remains unchanged. This contrasts with general genetic programming where the fitness of a program is holistic, credit or blame is difficult to apportion among the subtrees, and even very fit programs may contain irrelevant code [Tackett, 1995]. It will be shown in a later section that subtree fitness can be used to simplify and prune classification trees of extraneous material. As a result, classification trees show brisk convergence when subjected to evolutionary operations. It has been possible to obtain good results on a 486 PC with small populations (70-100 trees) and large training sets (on the order of 10,000 instances).

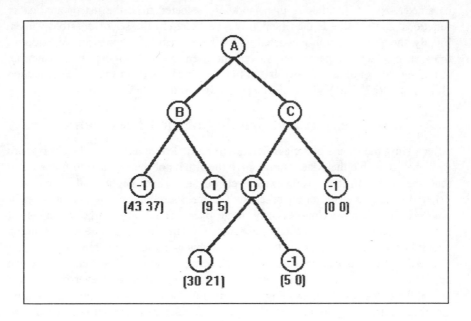

Fig. 2 Leaf counts for an abstract tree

2   Generation of the Initial Population of Classification Trees

The initial population of decision trees is generated randomly. To generate random decision trees, it is necessary to specify a list of the parameters to be tested, whether the parameter is symbolic or numerical, and the domain of the parameter. For symbolic parameters, a finite set of possible values of the parameter must be specified. For numerical parameters, a numerical interval must be specified. The classifications at the leaf nodes are also randomly selected from the classification set (1, -1). The depth of the initial trees ranges from 3 to 10, and is controlled by GCT input parameters.

For example, two of the decision parameters for the financial application are the age in months of a loan and the source, already described. Age is an integer parameter with values in an interval such as (0 72), and source is a symbolic parameter taking values from a set such as (a1 a2 b1 c1 d1 e1 e5). A list of possible functions for numerical and symbolic parameters also must be specified to the system. For symbolic parameters, the possible functions are usually the Lisp functions 'eq (identity) and 'member (set membership). For numerical parameters a reasonable set of functions is '< and 'eql (numerical equality). A test in a decision tree is generated by first randomly selecting a parameter from the parameter list. A function is then randomly selected from the list of applicable functions, and a value is then randomly selected from the set of possible values. Finally, the test is randomly negated with 50% probability. For example, suppose the system selects the parameter .source and then selects 'member as the function. A random subset of at least two but not all of the elements of the value set is then chosen, say '(a2 e5 c1), giving the test (member .source '(a2 e5 c1)).

3   Improvement and Pruning of the Classification Trees

After testing the fitness of a classification tree, the leaf counts described above are available to enable the system to improve the fitness of the tree and to prune it, so that the trees do not grow excessively in size and depth with successive generations of the evolutionary process. The tree "size" means the total number of nodes in the tree. Unnecessarily large trees can waste large amounts of computation time and memory resources. The improvement and pruning operations are performed as the trees of each new generation are created.

These leaf counts can be used in several ways: 1) to spot leaf decisions which should be inverted; 2) to prune off "dead" subtrees which are never reached for any of the instances in the training set; and 3) to focus crossover and mutation on subtrees contributing the most error, as will be discussed in Section 5. GCT also simplifies subtrees where all the leaves specify the same decision.

Fig. 3a shows a subtree in which the leaf count (5 200) indicates that the randomly generated decision should be inverted to -1, because it is wrong more often than right. Whenever the "wrong" count exceeds the "right" count, the decision should be inverted. Note that the fitness of the revised tree can be updated by a simple arithmetic computation, and does not have to be retested. The improvement in fitness is just the difference between the old wrong count and the new wrong count. The revised tree is shown in Fig. 3b.

This new tree illustrates another deficiency, however. Both leaves specify the same classification, -1. Any subtree in which the leaves all show the same classification can be pruned to a single leaf with that classification, reducing the size and depth of the tree. This operation transforms Fig. 3b into Fig. 4. This operation does not affect fitness, but for consistency the leaf counts for the new leaf can be set to the sum of the counts for the old leaves.

The pruning off of dead subtrees is motivated by Fig. 5a. The (0 0) leaf counts show that the subtree CGH is never visited at all for any of the training instances. This means that the test A serves no purpose and can be eliminated, along with the dead subtree CGH, to yield Fig. 5b. Again, this pruning operation does not affect fitness. Dead subtree elimination was found to be such a ruthless operation that in early generations it can cause the loss of a lot of potentially useful genetic "material." Consequently, in GCT dead subtree elimination is actually performed only on trees whose size exceeds a certain threshold, presently 20.

It is possible to extend the circumstances in which this third kind of transformation is applied. It may be desirable to set minimum cluster sizes for the classification tree. We may want to restructure any tree where the decision only applies to a small number of cases, because this may indicate idiosyncratic classification. This can be done by establishing two input parameters, min.P and min.N, representing respectively the minimum acceptable right counts at positive and negative leaves.

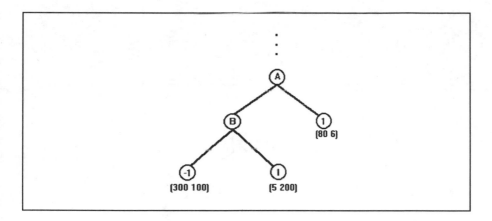

Fig. 3a. A subtree with a decision which can be improved

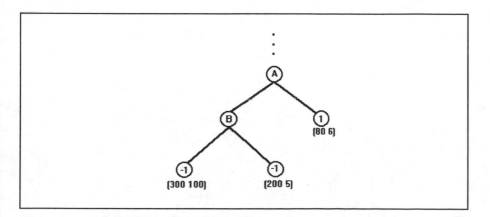

Fig. 3b. The same subtree with an inverted decision

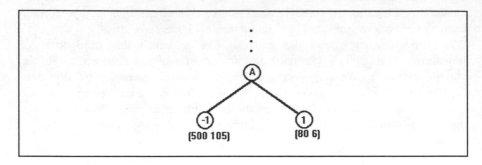

Fig. 4. The same subtree simplified

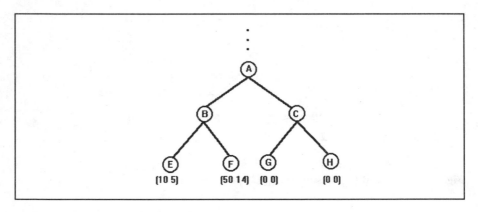

Fig. 5a. An example of a dead branch

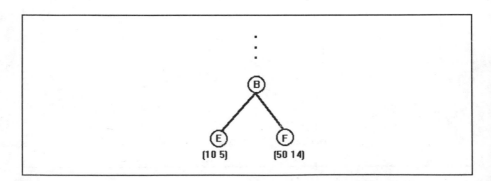

Fig. 5b. The same tree with the dead branch pruned out

If the counts at a leaf fail to meet these minimums, a subtree is pruned off just as in the case of (0 0) counts. The disadvantage is that it is not possible to quickly update the fitness. If it is necessary to prune back subtrees with nonzero clusters, the fitness of the tree changes in an unpredictable way and must be recalculated. The re-evaluation of fitness for the pruned tree incurs a nontrivial computation time penalty.

4   Extension to Weighted Error

When dealing with large real-world classification problems, it is often not possible to expect a perfect classification rule. Some instances are going to be misclassified. Up to this point, we have taken fitness to be the sum of the misclassification errors at each leaf node in the classification tree. This assumes that for a binary classification problem, false positives and false negatives are equally bad. This is not always true. The "cost" of a false positive may be very different from the cost of a false negative.

The GCT system has as an input parameter a false positive weight W. A third variable is then introduced at each leaf node, called the "blame," which is weighted error. If the classification is -1, the blame is equal to the error count. If the classification is 1, the blame is the error count multiplied by W, the false positive weight. With this extended system, the fitness is then the sum of the blame values at each leaf node. If W = 1, the GCT system will evolve classification rules that tend to generate roughly equal numbers of false positives and false negatives. For values of W greater than 1, the GCT system will favor classification rules that decrease the number of false positives at the expense of false negatives. For fractional values of W, the system will favor rules that generate more false positives and fewer false negatives. Negative values of W are not used. Thus the system can be tuned by adjusting W to generate classification rules with varying ratios of -1 to 1 decisions. Also, for purposes of focussing crossover and mutation, discussed in the next section, the blame values are used instead of the raw error to derive the insertion point probabilities. The use of a false positive weight is also very important in problems where the number of positive and negative instances is radically disproportionate. Without it, the system will converge on simple trees that nearly always select just one of the classifications.

The rule for inverting decisions at leaf nodes based on error counts is readily extended to the case where the error is weighted. Instead of selecting the decision that minimizes the error, the system should select the decision that minimizes the blame. For example suppose W = 10 and the leaf counts at a node with a -1 decision are (2 15). The blame value here is 15. However, if we invert the decision to 1, then the leaf counts become (15 2) and the blame is 20. Consequently, the system should NOT invert the decision here. If W > 1, we can expect to see some leaf counts where the decision is wrong more often than right.

5 Using Subtree Fitness to Focus Crossover and Mutation

Initially in the development of GCT, leaf counts were computed to facilitate the improvement and pruning of the classification trees. I then noticed that after some generations, most of the error is commonly contributed by just a few leaves. If tree crossover and mutation are done randomly, the chance of replacing a "bad" subtree becomes low, and the chance of replacing it with a better subtree even lower. In the same way, the chance of replacing a good, low error subtree with a poorer one is undesirably high. This suggested the idea of using the weighted error of a subtree to "focus" crossover and mutation on those subtrees which contribute the most error, to further improve the performance of the system.

Instead of doing crossover and mutation completely randomly, the probability of a subtree being replaced by these operations is made proportional to the error contribution of that subtree. For example, in Fig. 6 it can be seen that most of the error is contributed by leaf G. For a leaf node, the error is the weighted error at the leaf. For an interior node such as C, the error is taken to be the average (not the sum) of the error ratings of its subtrees. The procedure presently used in GCT is to square the error value for each node and then normalize the squared values into probabilities. Fig. 7 shows the probabilities that the various nodes of Fig. 6 will be selected for replacement by crossover or mutation. The net effect is that G is the most likely to be replaced (probability = .71), C has a moderate chance of replacement (.22), A (i.e. the whole tree) has a slight chance (.06), while replacement of B, D, E or F is very unlikely. In general, the bad parts of the classification trees in the population are continually bombarded with innovation, while the good parts of the trees tend to remain undisturbed.

The graph in Fig. 8 shows the impact on performance of the several procedures described above. These curves are taken from a fraud detection application. Details of this application cannot be discussed, due to the confidential nature of fraud detection. The results are for 30 minute runs with a population size of 70. Each run begins with the identical population of randomly generated trees. There are approximately 7000 instances in this problem set. The weighted error for the best tree from each generation is plotted as a function of generation. Each curve is for a single run on the same problem set. The top curve shows the results if no pruning or artificial limits on tree depth are imposed. The second curve shows the performance when only dead subtree pruning is performed. The third curve shows the results when decision inversion is also performed. For the bottom curve, error focussed crossover is added to the other enhancements. Note that the number of generations which can be achieved within the 30 minute time limit varies.

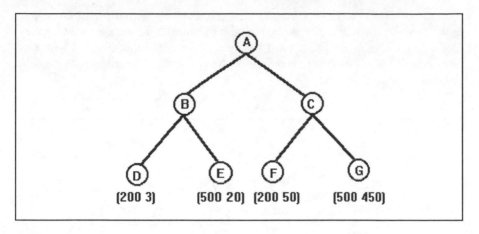

Fig. 6. One leaf contributes most of the error

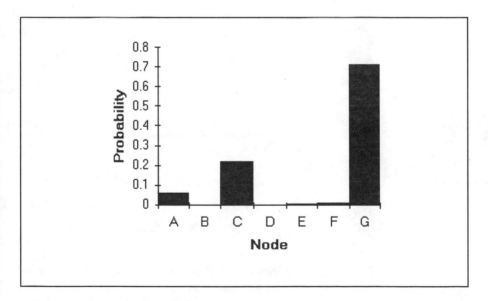

Fig. 7. Probability of subtree replacement

There is a natural extension to the error focussing procedure. We have concentrated our attention on only one of the two parents. One parent, the source, supplies a subtree to be inserted into the other parent, the destination, at a selected point. Error focussed crossover guides the selection of the destination point for the crossover, but still allows the source subtree to be randomly selected. The natural extension is to favor subtrees in the source parent with the least error, just as we favor insertion points in the destination parent with the most error. Contrary to expectation, in experiments that I have run, favoring source subtrees with low error actually degrades the convergence of the system in comparison with random selection of source subtrees.

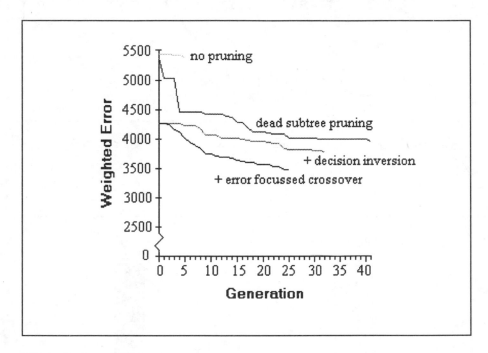

Fig. 8. Performance improvements

6   A Financial Application of Genetic Classification Trees

The GCT system has been successfully applied to two real-world financial problems. One is the fraud detection problem mentioned above. The other is the prediction of the prepayment of home mortgages, which will be discussed in detail in this section.

Individual home mortgage loans have a lifespan. The nominal period of a mortgage loan in the United States is typically 20 to 30 years, but the average lifespan of a loan is in fact only about seven years, due to "prepayment." People prepay a loan because they are selling their house for various reasons, or they may prepay if they decide to refinance the loan, to take advantage of lower interest rates. The financial return which a lender derives from a loan is a function of the actual lifespan of the loan. Financial institutions such as Bank of America need to be able to predict the lifespans of loans in order to set loan parameters so as to maximize profits. The situation is analogous to that of insurance companies, which need to predict the lifespans of people with life insurance policies.

The GCT system has been applied to the prediction of prepayments for one kind of adjustable-rate mortgage loan at Bank of America that I will call "Product M." A random sample of 1000 Product M loans was selected for the years 1989 through 1994. The available data consists of two kinds: static information about the loan and time-varying information. Examples of static parameters are the source (mentioned earlier), the loan origination fees ("points"), the ratio of loan amount to home value ("loan to value"), and the postal zip code. Examples of time-varying parameters are the loan ballance and the current interest rate. Prior to analysis by GCT, some straightforward preprocessing is done. This includes conversion to a two-digit zip code and the derivation of a "rate delta," which is the difference between the present interest rate on the loan and the prevailing interest rate on fixed-rate mortgages. For conceptual simplicity, the static data for a particular loan were replicated for each month that the loan is open and appended to the time-varying data, creating one instance vector for each month for each loan. This resulted in a total of approximately 20,000 instances, i.e. the average Product M loan had 20 months of time-varying data since the sample consisted of 1000 loans. Each month that each loan is open represents a "trial" in the probabilistic sense. Either the loan is prepayed in that month or it is not. Since the database specifies which loans were prepayed and when, each instance can be classified as either -1 (prepayed that month) or 1 (did not prepay that month).

Clearly in this kind of problem we cannot expect to find a perfect decision rule, but rather a rule that detects tendencies. Once GCT terminates, the best classification tree is further processed to replace the binary decisions (1, -1) at the leaf nodes with probabilities which are derived in an obvious way from the leaf counts. GCT was trained on 2/3 of the 20,000 instances in an overnight run of 15 hours. The resulting classification tree was then tested on the other 1/3 of the instances. Fig. 9 shows actual versus predicted prepayments for this test set for each year. The classification tree predicts a total of 174.3 prepayments over the six years, whereas the actual number of prepayments is 178.

GCT represents trees internally as nested Lisp "if" structures, which are then dynamically compiled into functions for efficient fitness evaluation. The syntax of these if statements is: (if <test> <true-clause> <false-clause>). Fig. 10 presents a short, 13 node example of the kind of classification tree generated by GCT for the loan prepayment problem. The values form is the Common Lisp method for returning multiple values from a function call. The values lines present leaf probabilities followed by a triple consisting of the right count, wrong count, and blame value. Note that the false positive weight W is 30 for this problem. These probability numbers represent the probability that the loan will be prepayed in a given month. The ".quarter" parameter is the quarter of the year in which the

288

prepayment decision is made. The actual tree which produced the results in Fig. 9 is much larger, with 53 nodes and a depth of 12.

The results in Fig. 9 were generated in the following way. "Bins" for each year are initialized to 0. Each test instance has a date field, e.g. Feb. 1994. The classification tree (now actually a probability tree) is applied to each instance in the test set and yields a probability value, e.g. 0.04521, which is added to the bin for that year. When all test instances have been processed, the bin total is the prediction for the year.

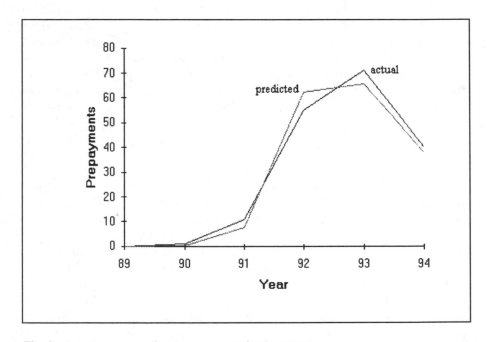

Fig. 9. Actual versus predicted prepayments for the test set

At the moment some borrower data, such as the borrower's age and marital status, are not yet available for input to the classification system. Adding this data to the input parameters is expected to further improve the performance. For example, borrowers over 70 years old are probably less likely to refinance their loans than younger people.

```
(if (not (< .rate.delta -1.37))
   (if (not (< .age 13))
      (if (not (member .source '(e1 a5 e2 a1 c1)))
         (if (eq .quarter '1)
            (if (eq .zip.code '97)
               (values 0.0 '(25 0 0))
               (values 0.04521 '(17 359 359)))
            (if (member .quarter '(2 3 1))
               (values 0.04943 '(44 846 846))
               (values 0.01201 '(411 5 150))))
         (values 0.01389 '(2768 39 1170)))
      (values 0.00351 '(5388 19 570)))
   (values 0.00278 '(3578 10 300)))
```

Fig. 10. A prepayment probability tree in Lisp form

7 Conclusion

The genetic programming operations of tree crossover and mutation have been extended and customized to advantage for the evolution of classification trees, using the notions of subtree visitation and subtree fitness contributions. It seems likely that these ideas could also produce performance improvements in general genetic programming in cases where conditional functions, such as if statements, are used in the trees. Unvisited subtrees could be pruned away and subtree fitness could be monitored in order to focus crossover and mutation activity, just as for classification trees. The main difference is that non-conditional subtrees, e.g. numerical expression subtrees, function as a unit with regard to visitation and error contribution. These ideas for improving the performance of genetic programming merit investigation.

References

Koza, John R. (1992): Genetic Programming. MIT Press
Tacket, Walter A. (1995): Mining the Genetic Program. IEEE Expert, to appear
Wilson, Stewart W.; Goldberg, David E. (1989): A Critical Review of Classifier Systems. Proc. Third Intl. Conference on Genetic Algorithms: 244-255.

A Model of Stock Market Participants

Michael de la Maza and Deniz Yuret

Numinous Noetics Group
Artificial Intelligence Laboratory
Massachusetts Institute of Technology
Cambridge, MA 02139
mdlm@ai.mit.edu, deniz@ai.mit.edu

Abstract. In this chapter we describe a stock market simulation in which stock market participants use genetic algorithms to gradually improve their trading strategies over time. A variety of experiments show that, under certain conditions, some market participants can make consistent profits over an extended period of time, a finding that might explain the success of some real-world money managers.

These experiments suggest a four parameter model of market participants. Each participant can be described along four dimensions: information set, constraint set, algorithm set, and model set. The information set captures what data the participant has access to (e.g., the participant has access to all historical price data). The constraint set describes under what restrictions the participant operates (e.g., the participant can borrow money at 1% above the prime rate). The algorithm set indicates what programs the participant can use (e.g., the participant is restricted to hill-climbing optimization algorithms). The model set specifies the language which the participant employs to describe its findings (e.g., the participant uses stochastic differential equations). This four parameter model explains the relative strengths and weaknesses of market participants. After describing the market participant model, we briefly turn to a critique of neural networks, which are the most widely used artificial intelligence tools for financial time series analysis.

We have applied some of the insights that we have gained from doing this and related research to our own trading accounts. We participated in the 1993 U.S. Investing Championships (options division) and finished with a 43.9% return over a period of four months. To leverage this success we have formed a money management firm, called Redfire Capital Management Group, that employs evolutionary algorithms to create fully automated trading strategies for bond, currency, and equity markets. Redfire Capital Management Group launched the first hedge fund that exclusively employs genetic algorithms to create computerized trading strategies on April 3, 1995.

Keywords. Simulation, genetic algorithm, futures markets

1   Motivation

At the turn of the century, Texas wildcatters would decide were to dig for oil by taking a pinch of sand from the ground and tasting it. Their methods were uninformed by any understanding of the causal processes that led to the formation of oil deposits. Everett Lee De Golyer, known as the Father of American Geophysics, was the first to introduce scientific methods into the oil discovery field on a wide scale. As a result, he became a multimillionaire in an age in which a million dollars was still a lot of money.

The money management industry today is similar to the oil industry at the turn of the century. Virtually all of the trillions of dollars invested in today's financial markets are managed by seat of the pants methods that are similar to digging for oil by tasting sand. However, in recent years a growing number of individuals and companies have dedicated themselves to applying the methods of science and engineering to the stock market. Those who have been successful in doing so have made fortunes and there are many more fortunes to be made.

In this chapter, we take another step in this direction by applying our understanding of genetic algorithms to the market. This chapter describes a simulation of a market in which individuals evolve trading strategies and compete against each other to maximize profits.

2   Justification

Why simulate instead of studying real markets? Simulations have several advantages over direct observation:

- The parameters of the simulation can be endlessly modified in order to provide greater understanding.

- Simulations are typically much faster than real markets, therefore many more experiments can be done.

- The investigator has very fine-grained control over the simulation.

However, there are some disadvantages associated with simulations:

- Care must be taken when carrying over the results of a simulation to real markets. They may not apply because all models make assumptions about real markets which may be incorrect.

- A simulation necessarily involves abstraction, and this abstraction may leave out some of the most important elements of the market. Of course, this would not occur intentionally but given the complex and little understood structure of the markets it may happen unintentionally.

- A trader who makes a million dollars in a simulation has not made a million dollars!

The simulation described here does not capture all of the subtleties and nuances of the market. Its implementation contains many simplifications and assumptions. Nevertheless, it gives insight into how some market participants may be able to consistently uncover profit-making opportunities.

This chapter begins by discussing the details of this simulation and three experiments with the simulation are described and analyzed. Based on the data from these experiments, we suggest a four parameter model of participants that we have found helpful in characterizing what are the relative advantages and disadvantages of a market participant. The chapter concludes with a brief criticism of the standard application of neural networks to financial time series analysis.

3 Simulation Details

Our market simulation consists of a series of days. A day contains four steps:

1. Each participant computes a fair price for a security. In our simulation, there is only one security in the entire market and each participant is forced to submit a bid during each day.

2. An equilibrium price, which balances the buyers and sellers, is computed from the fair prices submitted by each participant. The equilibrium price is the median of the fair prices.

3. Participants whose fair prices are above the equilibrium price buy at the equilibrium price, and participants whose fair prices are below the equilibrium price sell at the equilibrium price. Thus, for every security that is sold, a security is bought and so one participant's gain is another participant's loss. No transaction fees are charged. All traders buy or sell a single contract. They may not vary the trade size.

4. Participants improve their bidding strategies by using a genetic algorithm.

Each individual has a *visible strategy* which it uses to compute the fair price. In addition, each individual has a set of *invisible strategies* that cannot be directly perceived by other market participants. The visible strategy is the strategy that performed the best during the last day and it is updated every day.

The strategies that individuals can learn are very simple. They consist of a quadruple $< a, b, c, d >$ of four real numbers and the fair price is computed by the formula:

$$f(a, b, c, d) = a \cdot x + b \cdot y + c \cdot z + d$$

where x is the ten day moving average of the equilibrium prices; y is the last equilibrium price; and z is 1 if the last change in equilibrium prices is positive, -1 if it is negative, and 0 otherwise.

Suppose, for example, that the visible strategy of a market participant is $< 1, 2, 3, 4 >$ and that the ten day moving average is 12, the last equilibrium price is 11, and the last change in equilibrium prices is negative. Then, the fair price compute by this strategy is:

$$1 \cdot 12 + 2 \cdot 11 + 3 \cdot -1 + 4 = 35.$$

If there are four participants which submit fair prices of 33, 34, 35, and 36 then the equilibrium price is 34.5. The two participants who submitted fair prices below 34.5 sell the security at 34.5 and the two participants that submitted fair prices above 34.5 buy the security at 34.5.

The participants are forced to liquidate their holdings at the equilibrium price of the next round. So, if the equilibrium price is above 34.5, then the two participants who purchased the security at 34.5 will make money and the two participants who sold the security will lose money. On the other hand, if the equilibrium price is below 34.5 the two participants who sold the security at 34.5 will make money and the two participants who purchased the security will lose money.

The strategies maintained by each participant are modified and improved by a genetic algorithm [Holland 1975, Goldberg 1989] with traditional mutation and crossover operators. The mutation operator adds a number uniformly distributed between -.1 and .1 to a coefficient and the crossover operator is traditional single point crossover. The best strategies are selected and copied using standard proportional selection with a constant offset that ensures that all fitness values are positive [Michalewicz 1992]. The fitness values are calculated by subtracting the fair value computed by a strategy from the spot price on the next day.

4 Experiments

This section describes three experiments that we have done to explore various facets of our simulation. In all of the experiments, there are four participants who trade.

4.1 Effect of Noise

Some market pundits say that the market makes many unexplainable moves that will eventually wipe out all strategies. Separating the signal from this noise is thought to be one of the hardest problems facing all traders.

Can market participants still uncover good market strategies in the face of noise? That is the question that this experiment is designed to test. In this experiment, the ten day moving average, the last equilibrium price, and the sign of the last change are all replaced with random numbers between -5 and 5 and the equilibrium price is set to 1. Thus, the optimal strategy is <0, 0, 0, 1>, which reflects the decision to ignore the three noisy variables. We chose to add the noise directly to the input variables instead of to the output to make the simulation conceptually clearer.

A ten day moving average of the equilibrium prices is shown in Figure 1. As you can see, the equilibrium price slowly but surely moves towards 1, indicating that the participants are able, over time, to ignore the noise in the information provided to them.

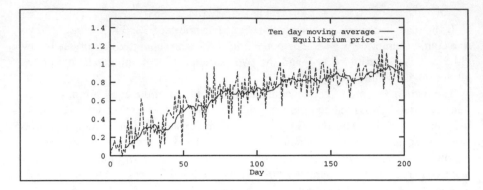

Figure 1. Equilibrium price as a function of time. The ten day moving average, the last equilibrium price, and the sign of the last change are all random numbers between -5 and 5.

4.2 Forced Liquidations

This experiment tests what effect forced liquidations have on profits. Market participants must sometimes liquidate their holdings for a variety of reasons - they get hit with lawsuits, they want to send their children to college, or they have substantial losses in real estate.

In this experiment, a participant, with probability .2, is forced to report a fair price that is one half of the fair price computed by its visible strategy. This gives market participants who do not have to liquidate their holdings the opportunity to make substantial profits. Figure 2 shows how the profit of the most profitable participant changes over time. Initially, the profit rises and then drops sharply, but it never reaches zero as the participants who do not have to liquidate take advantage of those who do.

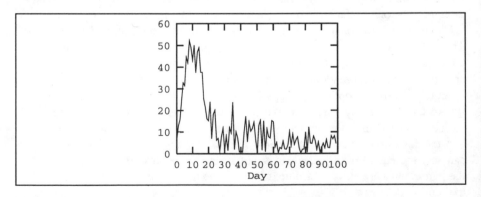

Figure 2. Profit of most profitable individual as a function of time. This data is averaged over ten runs of the simulation. Because participants are forced to liquidate their holdings with some probability, the profit does not approach 0.

In contrast, Figure 3 shows the profit in an experiment in which participants are not forced to liquidate. In this case, the profit quickly approaches zero as the participants lock in on optimal trading strategies.

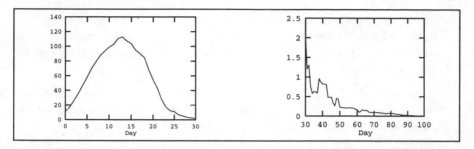

Figure 3. Profit of most profitable individual as a function of time. This data is averaged over ten runs of the simulation. The profit approaches 0 because the participants are able to learn optimal strategies.

4.3 Sharing Strategies

In our final experiment we studied what happens to profitability when the market participants share their visible strategies. After each day each participant's visible strategy is added to the list of strategies of all of the other participants. As shown in Figure 4 the profitability of the most profitable experiment drops sharply. This figure should be compared to Figure 3 which shows the profitability of the most profitable participant when no sharing occurs.

This experiment helps to explain why most of the results published in the field of stock market analysis are negative. Sharing profitable strategies really does reduce profitability for everyone.

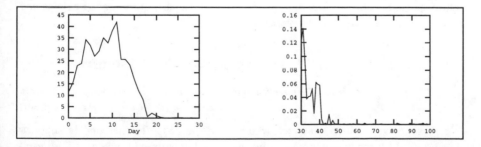

Figure 4. Profit of most profitable individual as a function of time. This data is averaged over ten runs of the simulation. Profit quickly approaches 0 because the participants are sharing their visible strategies.

5   Understanding Market Participants

As a result of these experiments we have arrived at a four parameter model of market participants. Each market participant can be characterized along these four dimensions:

- Constraint set. Is the participant beholden to shareholders or investors? Do profits have to be reported on a monthly, quarterly, or yearly basis? At what rate can the participant borrow capital? What securities and markets can the participant trade?

- Information set. Does the participant have access to end of day data, minute data, or tic data? Is information about order flow available? Does the participant have access to floor traders or market makers?

- Algorithm set. Does the participant use pencil and paper to explore the space of trading strategies? Backpropagation? Genetic algorithms? Dynamic hill climbing?

- Model set. Is the participant restricted to linear models? Can if-then rules, previous market scenarios, and stochastic differential equations all be employed to represent market knowledge?

At our own money management firm, Redfire Capital Management Group, we only trade markets in which we have a considerable advantage along two or more of these four dimensions.

6   Two Shortcomings of Neural Networks

Neural networks are the most widely used artificial intelligence method for financial time series analysis and thus they are the main competitors to the form of research explored in the previous sections of this chapter. In this section we describe two shortcomings of the standard neural network application. First, backpropagation search takes place in sum of squared errors space instead of risk-adjusted return space. Second, the standard neural network has difficulty ignoring noise and focusing in on discoverable regularities.

6.1   Sum of Squared Errors vs. Risk-Adjusted Return

> *My financial success stands in stark contrast with my ability to forecast events.*
> - George Soros [1994, p. 301]

We present two trading strategies which have the property that one is superior when sum of squared errors is the utility measure but is inferior when risk-adjusted return, as defined by the Sharpe ratio, is the utility measure. Because what matters to investment managers and their clients is risk-adjusted return, this suggests that the standard neural network application, which minimizes the sum of squared errors, should be retooled.

Sequence (input)	Next Element (output)	Strategy A		Strategy B	
		Prediction	Profit	Prediction	Profit
10,20,30	60	35	30	30	0
20,30,60	10	10	50	10	50
30,60,10	20	20	10	20	10
60,10,20	30	30	10	30	10
10,20,30	10	35	-20	30	0

Table 1. The five sequences in the time series 10,20,30,60,10,20,30,10. The neural network is asked to predict the next element in the sequence given the previous three elements. Strategy A is the prediction made by the strategy which minimizes the sum of squared errors. Strategy B is a strategy which has a higher sum of squared errors, but a lower Sharpe ratio, than strategy A, as shown in Table 2.

Consider the time series: 10, 20, 30, 60, 10, 20, 30, 10. This can be thought of as the price of a security on consecutive days. If the neural network is asked to predict the next element in this series given the three previous elements then there are a total of four unique input sequences and five input/output pairs, as shown in Table 1. This table shows two strategies, strategy A and strategy B, which produce the same output for three of the four input sequences, but differ on the only sequence which is not followed by a unique element (the first and last rows in Table 1). Strategy A is the optimal sum of squared errors strategy but strategy B has a better Sharpe ratio, as shown in Table 2. This comparison assumes that the strategy buys when the predicted value of the next element is greater than the last element of the sequence, sells when the predicted value of the next element is less than the last element of the sequence, and does not trade when these two values are the same. A constant amount is traded each time and the market is assumed to be frictionless.

	sum of squared errors	μ	σ	Sharpe ratio $\left(\dfrac{\mu}{\sigma}\right)$
Strategy A	1250	16	23.324	0.686
Strategy B	1300	14	18.547	0.755

Table 2. Comparison of strategy A and strategy B. Strategy A has a lower sum of squared errors, but strategy B has a better Sharpe ratio (the risk-free rate is assumed to be 0%).

A skeptic would argue that the flaw in this example is that a *forecasting* strategy should not be confused with a *trading* strategy. Such a skeptic would say that once the neural network has been trained to be a good *forecasting* strategy then some sort of post-processor should be added to the output to turn it into a good *trading* strategy. This appears to be a somewhat circuitous approach: Why search in the wrong space (sum of squared errors) and then repair, when the search can be done in the space of interest (risk-adjusted return)?

6.2   The Importance of Knowing What You Don't Know

The standard application of neural networks forces a prediction to be made for every input sequence. Because of this, the neural network must distribute its representational capacity across the entire time series, instead of being able to focus in on regions which have discoverable regularity. As a result, the neural network is sometimes incapable of uncovering simple regularities because its representational capacity is inappropriately employed.

This point is illustrated by the function shown in Figure 5(A) which has three segments: the first (points 0 to 49) and third (points 100 to 149) segments were generated by randomly choosing numbers between 0.25 and 0.75 and the second segment (points 50 to 99) is the line $y = x/100 - .25$. A wide variety of neural networks with varying numbers of hidden units (0, 2, 5, 10, 20, and 50), different learning rates (.01, .001, and .0001), and different inertia parameters (0, .1, .2, .3, .4, .5, .6, .7, .8, and .9) were trained to predict the value of point *n* given points *n-5* through *n-1*. The predictions made by one representative neural network are shown in Figure 5(B). The predictions made by the same neural network when trained only on the second segment of the function shown in Figure 5(A) are shown in Figure 5(C).

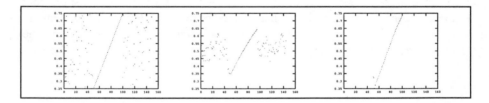

Figure 5. (A) Target function. The neural network is asked to predict the value of point *n* and is given as input the value of points *n-5* through *n-1*. The first 50 points are random numbers between 0.25 and 0.75 as are the last 50 points. The middle 50 points satisfy the linear equation $y = x/100 - .25$. (B) Output of a neural network with five hidden units trained on the target function. The inertia parameter was set to 0.9 and the learning rate was set to .001. The neural network was trained for one million epochs. This output graph is representative of the performance of many neural networks that we tested on this function. (C) Output of a neural network with five hidden units trained on the middle 50 points of the target function. The inertia parameter was set to 0.9 and the learning rate was set to .001. The network was trained for one million epochs. Compare to the middle 50 points in (B).

A comparison of these two graphs shows that the prediction of the middle segment is much more accurate in Figure 5(C) than in Figure 5(B). Why? Because part of the neural network's representational capacity has been spent trying to model the first and third segments, even though these segments do not have discoverable regularity. Importantly, the function in Figure 5(A) is extremely simple. The regularities in real financial time series are significantly more subtle and the ability to distinguish between the knowable and unknowable becomes significantly more important.

The underlying problem on which this example stands is the requirement that the standard neural network make a prediction at every data point: „don't know" is not an option. However, not only does the capability to say „don't know" free up representational capacity, but, as in the case of Figure 5(A) over the interval [0,49] and [100,149], it is sometimes the best possible model of the data given the representational capacity of the neural network. Many statistical methods, such as linear and multiple regression, share this shortcoming with the standard neural network application. As a result, these methods are, in effect, unable to say what human traders often do: „Current market conditions are beyond my comprehension, therefore I am not going to try to understand them." For the graph shown in Figure 5(A) this is *the* appropriate response for the first and third segments.

6.3   Possible Solutions

Our view is that the shortcomings discussed above are potential showstoppers which demand the full attention of those who are interested in applications of neural networks to financial time series analysis. In this section we speculate on ways of overcoming these limitations.

One way to address both problems is to change the search algorithm from back-propagation to simulated annealing [Kirkpatrick et. al. 1983, Ingber 1993], genetic algorithms [Holland 1975, Goldberg 1989], standard gradient descent, or any one of the many optimization methods which allow search over arbitrary utility functions. Adopting this solution would allow the direct implementation of risk-adjusted return as the utility function and the neural network would no longer be forced to make a prediction for every input. Under this scheme, the representation (or model) would still be sums of nested sigmoidal functions.

Finessing the data so that minimizing the sum of squared errors is equivalent to maximizing risk-adjusted return is another way to address the first shortcoming. Success in finding such a transformation would probably be helpful in finding solutions to other problems not associated with financial time series analysis.

A possible solution to the second problem has been explored by Jordan and Jacobs [1993]. They suggest creating a hierarchical mixture of neural networks so that each neural network can become an expert at identifying the regularities in one component of the data.

7 Related Work

Nottola, Leroy, and Davalo [1992] describe an artificial market system in which agents (called participants in this paper) learn rules that predict movements in price. Much of their paper describes different approaches to modeling markets, but they do discuss one experiment which compares the performance of agents with different learning strategies and they conclude that adaptive agents out-perform non-adapting ones.

LeBaron [1994] has developed a stock market simulation in which participants learn strategies using a genetic algorithm, as they do in this paper. The strategies of his market participants are encoded as bitstrings in which each bit corresponds to a boolean variable that is precomputed. His system features a mechanism for easily changing the risk aversion of individual participants. LeBaron [1993] notes that even if there are regularities in real market data that can be exploited, the data might contain so much noise that the regularities are barely perceptible.

There is substantial evidence that the currency futures market is not efficient [Thomas 1986, Cavanaugh 1987, Glassman 1987, Harpaz et. al. 1990]. As empirical evidents mounts against the view that markets are efficient, theoreticians will be forced to provide alternative explanations of the market's behavior. One of the most likely candidates for this is Simon's bounded rationality theory [Simon 1957, Simon 1982]. Sargent [1993, p. 4] explores markets in which the participants have bounded rationality and writes that „the bounded rationality program wants to make the agents in our models more like the econometricians who estimate and use them.“

We have not compared our genetic algorithm approach to neural network approaches because neural network training time is prohibitive.

8 Conclusion

We plan to extend the simulation described in this chapter in at least two ways. First, the algorithm and model sets of all of the participants in these experiments are the same - only the constraint sets and information sets change. For example, in one experiment the constraint set of participants includes forced liquidations while in other two experiments it does not. Likewise, in one experiment the participants have access to uncorrupted moving average information while in the other two they do not.

In the future we will pit participants with different algorithm sets and model sets against each other. Second, this simulation contains only one security and all of the participants are required to purchase or sell a security during every round. Our future market simulations will have multiple securities and the participants will have the option of not trading.

We have applied some of the insights that we have gained from doing this and related research to our own trading accounts. We participated in the 1993 U.S. Investing Championships (options division) and finished fifth with a 43.9% return over a period of four months. To leverage this success we have formed a money management firm, called Redfire Capital Management Group, that employs artificial intelligence methods, including simulations similar to the ones described here, to create fully automated trading strategies for interest rate, currency, and equity markets. We trust that other market aficionados will find these simulations equally helpful.

Acknowledgments

Thanks to Steve Baron, Tom Berghage, Prof. Joerg Biethahn, Jim Hutchinson, Michael Jones, and Dr. Volker Nissen. Some of the neural network simulations were performed on the Cray C90 at the Pittsburgh Supercomputing Center. This paper describes research done at the Artificial Intelligence Laboratory of the Massachusetts Institute of Technology. Support for the laboratory's artificial intelligence research is provided in part by the Advanced Research Projects Agency of the Department of Defense under Office of Naval Research contract N00014-92-J-4097 and by the National Science Foundation under grant number MIP-9001651.

References

Cavanaugh, K. (1987): Price dynamics in foreign currency futures markets. Journal of International Money and Finance 6 (3): 295-314

Freedman, D. (1987): Enter the market merlins. Forbes ASAP

Glassman, D. (1987): The efficiency of foreign exchange futures markets in turbulent and non-turbulent periods. The Journal of Futures Markets 7 (3): 245-267

Goldberg, D. (1989): Genetic Algorithms in Search, Optimization and Machine Learning. Addison-Wesley, Reading, MA

Harpaz, G.; Krull, S.; Yagil, J. (1990): The efficiency of the U.S. dollar index futures market. The Journal of Futures Markets 10 (5): 469-479

Holland, J.H. (1975): Adaptation in Natural and Artificial Systems. University of Michigan Press, Ann Arbor

Ingber, L. (1993): Simulated annealing: Practice versus theory. Mathematical and Computer Modeling 18 (11): 29-57

Jordan, M.I.; Jacobs, R.A. (1993): Hierarchical mixtures of experts and the EM algorithm. Technical Report 1440, Artificial Intelligence Laboratory, Massachusetts Institute of Technology, Cambridge, MA

Kirkpatrick, S.; Gelatt Jr., C.D.; Vecchi, M.P. (1983): Optimization by simulated annealing. Science 220: 671-680

LeBaron, B. (1994): An artificial stock market. MIT AI vision seminar colloquium

Michalewicz, Z. (1992): Genetic Algorithms + Data Structures = Evolution Programs. Springer, Berlin

Nottola, C.; Leroy, F., Davalo, F. (1992): Dynamics of artificial markets: Speculative markets and emerging 'common sense' knowledge. In: Towards a Practice of Autonomous Systems: Proceedings of the First European Conference on Artificial Life: 185-194

Sargent, T.J. (1993): Bounded Rationality in Macroeconomics. Clarendon Press, Oxford

Simon, H. (1957): Models of Man: Social and Rational; Mathematical Essays on Rational Human Behavior in Society Setting. John Wiley, New York

Simon, H. (1982): Models of Bounded Rationality. MIT Press, Cambridge, MA

Soros, G. (1994): The Alchemy of Finance: Reading the Mind of the Market. John Wiley & Sons, New York

Thomas, L. (1986): Random walk profits in currency futures trading. The Journal of Futures Markets 6 (1): 109-125

Part Five
Applications in Traffic Management

Using Evolutionary Programming to Control Metering Rates on Freeway Ramps

John R. McDonnell, David B. Fogel[1], Craig R. Rindt[2], Wilfred W. Recker[2], Lawrence J. Fogel[1]

[1] Natural Selection, Inc., La Jolla, CA
[2] Institute of Transportation Studies, U.C. Irvine

Abstract. A rule-based strategy is proposed for freeway ramp metering control. The rule-based controller determines ramp discharge rates based on upstream, downstream, and adjacent freeway occupancy levels. The use of a rule-base is advantageous because it can be implemented in real-time via a look-up table and because knowledge from traffic control engineers can be directly incorporated into the control strategy. Evolutionary programming is used to adapt rule thresholds so that this general procedure can be applied to any freeway configuration. A rule set is presented that operates on sensed occupancy rates. Evolutionary optimization of these sensor occupancy rate thresholds is described. The proposed method is then evaluated using INTRAS, a sophisticated traffic simulation program, on a uniform freeway segment. The results demonstrate that evolutionary programming is a viable approach to achieving ramp metering control strategies that can alleviate both recurrent and nonrecurrent freeway congestion. The presented study focuses on ramp meter control which, by itself, is effective only over a narrow regime of traffic flow conditions. Consideration is not given to ramp queues, surface street congestions, or traffic diversion.

Keywords. Evolutionary programming, traffic control, ramp metering

1   Introduction

Ramp control has long been considered an effective way to reduce freeway congestion [Newman et al. 1969] and its implementation via ramp metering (i.e., regulating the rate at which cars enter a freeway) has become commonplace on many of America's roadways. Robinson and Doctor [1989] cite several benefits to ramp metering in a nationwide case study: (1) a decrease in the number of accidents, (2) an increase in the average freeway speed, and (3) reduced travel times in light of suburban growth. Much of the current research in this area has focused on elaborate ramp control strategies that can use information from a centralized traffic coordination control facility. But "the biggest gain is going from no control to the simplest forms of control; increasing sophistication quickly runs into diminishing returns" [Newman et al. 1969]. What is needed is a robust, real-time ramp metering strategy that is simple to implement and able to alleviate both recurring and nonrecurring congestion based on available freeway sensor information.

An effective freeway metering system must be responsive to the mainline and ramp demands, as well as be responsive to the conditions of the global traffic network [Chang et al. 1994]. Thus ramp control meters should be sensor-driven as opposed to relying on fixed-time metering rates that are set based on recurring traffic demands. Should an incident occur, preset metering rates may not adequately reflect traffic flow onto a freeway with diminished capacity. Similarly, in the event that mainline freeway demand is unusually light, preset fixed-time metering rates may unnecessarily limit ramp flow. Robinson and Doctor [1989] speculated that traffic-responsive metering should yield traffic flows that are five to 10 percent greater than flows resulting from the usage of fixed-time metering.

Determining globally optimal, responsive control strategies for traffic networks is a challenging endeavor. Many approaches for real-time ramp metering have been developed, but to date no single method has proven "adequate for real-time freeway control and operations. Hence, it is still a challenging task to develop more effective real-time control strategies" [Chang et al. 1994]. The current study offers a rule-based system that acts on freeway occupancy information for determining ramp-metering rates. The advantages of a rule-based system include its ability to respond in real-time to a variety of traffic states, including nonrecurrent congestion, and also its ease of implementation. The disadvantage of a rule-based system is that the heuristics must be quantified for purposes of implementation (i.e., they must be made specific for the case at hand) and are geometry dependent (i.e., the appropriate set of heuristics for one section of freeway may not be the same as another due to the physical properties of the freeway, such as onramp and offramp spacings, demand rates, curvature, and incline). The approach taken here is to use a set of ramp metering rules which are conditioned on the traffic state, and adjust the transition boundaries between these rules using evolutionary programming (EP). The proposed approach is evaluated using the Integrated Traffic Simulation (INTRAS) model [Wicks and Lieberman 1980] on selected case studies.

This study offers a preliminary investigation into how evolutionary search may be applied to the nonlinear problem of traffic control. Although a crisp rule-based controller is selected, other types of control (e.g., fuzzy logic) may provide equally good, or perhaps superior, candidate control strategies which can benefit from the application of evolutionary programming. The present study concerns only the optimization of freeway ramp metering rates to maximize total freeway throughput (vehicle count). It does not consider the effects that the ramp control strategy has on the arterial surface streets. For purposes of simplification, the focus is on global optimization of the ramp metering control strategy for a uniform short freeway segment. The following sections outline the evolutionary programming search algorithm and its application to a rule-based ramp metering control strategy. INTRAS simulation results are then presented for the uniform short freeway segment.

2   Background on Evolutionary Programming

Evolutionary programming [Fogel et al. 1966] is a general optimization technique that emulates Darwinian evolution. It maintains a population of candidate solutions that undergo random mutation and selection, and iteratively converges on optimal solutions to the task at hand [Fogel 1995]. An initial population of solutions (parents) is typically chosen at random from the space of potential solutions. These parents are randomly altered to create offspring. The form of mutation generally follows from the representation of the solution, but for real-valued parameter optimization problems mutation is often implemented by adding a multi-variate zero mean Gaussian random variable to each parent. All parents and offspring compete for survival based on their fitness in light of a functional describing the worth of any potential solution. Selection is typically made a probabilistic function of each solution's fitness, in that those solutions with greater fitness (or lower cost) have a higher probability of surviving. Figure 1 outlines the general form of the evolutionary procedure.

More specifically, the following six-step procedure is employed:

1. Form an initial population $\mathbf{P} = [\mathbf{x}_0, \mathbf{x}_1, \mathbf{x}_2, ..., \mathbf{x}_{N-1}]$ of size N by randomly initializing each n-dimensional solution vector $\mathbf{x}_i$. A user-specified search domain $\mathbf{x}_i \in [x_{min}, x_{max}]^n$ may be imposed.

2. Assign a cost to each element $\mathbf{x}_i$ in the population, $i = 0, ..., N-1$, based on the associated objective function $J_i = F(\mathbf{x}_i)$, where $F:R^n \to R$.

3. Generate offspring $[\mathbf{x}_N, ..., \mathbf{x}_{2N-1}]$ from $[\mathbf{x}_0, ..., \mathbf{x}_N]$ by mutating each $x_{ij}, i = 1, ..., N-1, j = 1, ..., n$, with a random perturbation:

$$\delta x_{ij} \sim N(0, \alpha_{ij}J_i + \beta_{ij})$$

such that $x_{i+N,j} = x_{ij} + \delta x_{ij}$.

4. Assign a cost to each offspring $\mathbf{x}_i$ in the population, $i = N, ..., 2N-1$, based on the associated objective function value.

5. Index the population in descending order based on the number of wins generated from a stochastic competition across all solutions, $i = 1, ..., 2N-1$. Wins are generated by randomly selecting q other members in the population and incrementing the number of wins by one if $J_i < J_k$ (minimization), where k is the randomly selected opponent.

6. If the available time has expired, halt; else return to step 3.

Typical implementations of evolutionary programming use relatively large population sizes (e.g., > 500) in conjunction with a large number of generations, yielding an optimization process that occurs over many function evaluations. For the traffic control study presented here, each function evaluation is a single run of INTRAS, which requires about one minute on a Sparc10. Thus a small population of 10 parents over a short run of 100 generations requires 1000 INTRAS function evaluations and 16.67 hours. But the inherently parallel nature of evolutionary programming can be taken advantage of by using a network of such workstations. Much of the initial research in this study was conducted on such a network at the Institute for

```
evolutionary programming procedure
begin
k=0
initialize parent population P(k)
evaluate P(k)
do {
        generate offspring O(k) from P(k)
        evaluate O(k)
        select P(k+1) from {P(k) ∪ O(k)}
        k=k+1
} while (terminate condition not met)
end
```

Figure 1. The general form of the evolutionary programming procedure. An initial parent population is evaluated and offspring are randomly generated from each parent. These offspring are then evaluated and selection determines which solutions to maintain as parents for the next generation. The procedure is iterative and continues until some predetermined halting condition is met.

Transportation Studies, University of California, Irvine. As the CPU time required to modify the ramp metering strategies (i.e., generate offspring) was insignificant relative to the INTRAS run times, only the INTRAS runs themselves were executed in parallel. This parallel implementation is shown in Figure 2.

3   Ramp-Metering Control Rules

The most commonly used sensor-based ramp metering controller is based on the demand-capacity algorithm. Demand-capacity ramp control adjusts the ramp metering rates based on the difference between downstream capacity and the sum of mainline and ramp demands. This difference is used in determining the number of vehicles per hour (vph) that should be allowed onto the freeway. For example, if mainline demand is 4800 vph and downstream capacity is 6000 vph, then a metering period of $T = 3$ seconds, or 1200 vph, is the maximum discharge rate that ensures capacity is not exceeded. Jacobsen et al. [1989] present a centralized implementation of this technique for system-wide traffic-responsive control.

In contrast to a system-wide demand-capacity type of metering system, a rule-based system is proposed that operates on both feedback information from the downstream freeway sensors and feedforward information from the upstream freeway sensors. If the upstream freeway sensors indicate an approaching high mainline volume, the ramp meter can reduce the discharge rate so that the downstream capacity is not exceeded. Similarly, high occupancy rates from downstream freeway sensors may also warrant a reduction in the ramp discharge rate. A simple example of this is given in Figure 3, which shows upstream, adjacent, and downstream sensor stations. Table 1 provides a list of rules which correspond to the sensors and middle onramp meter of Figure 3.

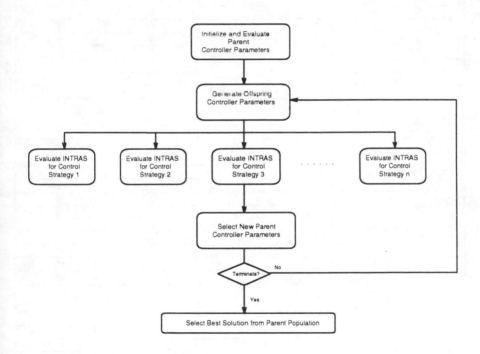

Figure 2. Parallel implementation of evolutionary programming for evaluating ramp metering control strategies. INTRAS was evaluated in parallel over a network of workstations at the Institute for Transportation Studies, U.C. Irvine.

Table 1. The rules for mapping sensor occupancy ranges to metering rates. The occupancy categories are defined as low (L), medium (M), and high (H). The headway levels are defined as low (L), medium-low (ML), medium (M), medium-high (MH), and high (H). These headway levels are arbitrarily assigned in Table 2. "x" is a wild card or "don't care" condition. Each of the sensor stations (i-1, i, i+1) are assigned as shown in Figure 3. Note that rule 28 supersedes rules 1, 10, and 19. The rationale behind using rule 28 is that, should an upstream incident cause low occupancies on the downstream links, then traffic should be let on at a higher rate. Discrimination between a wave of high occupancy traffic and an incident yields a more appropriate implementation of this diversionary tactic. NM refers to no metering.

	Sensor Occupancy Percentages			Headway
Rule	sensor i-1	sensor i	sensor i+1	meter i
1	L	L	L	L
2	L	L	M	L
3	L	L	H	M
4	L	M	L	ML
5	L	M	M	M
6	L	M	H	MH
7	L	H	L	H
8	L	H	M	H
9	L	H	H	H
10	M	L	L	L
11	M	L	M	ML
12	M	L	H	M
13	M	M	L	ML
14	M	M	M	M
15	M	M	H	MH
16	M	H	L	H
17	M	H	M	H
18	M	H	H	H
19	H	L	L	ML
20	H	L	M	M
21	H	L	H	M
22	H	M	L	M
23	H	M	M	MH
24	H	M	H	H
25	H	H	L	H
26	H	H	M	H
27	H	H	H	H
28	x	L	L	NM

The average occupancies of each sensor station are converted to linguistic variables according to the linear mapping shown in Figure 4. The linguistic variable conditions assigned to the average occupancy rates of the suite of sensor stations are then converted to a meter rate using rules such as IF (conditions C_{i-1} and C_i and

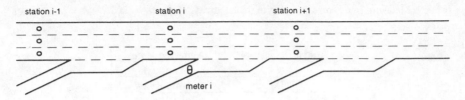

Figure 3. A simple freeway segment that uses the rules given in Table 1 to determine the headway at meter 1. Table 1 implements the rules according to the average occupancy conditions at each sensor station.

C_{i+1}) THEN (headway = H_i). The metering rates in Table 1 were arbitrarily quantified according to the values given in Table 2. Fifteen seconds has been identified as a "practical minimum discharge rate" [Robinson and Doctor 1989]; drivers will not wait beyond this time period and this results in a "significant increase in violations." Banks [1994], however, presents a case study where ramp meter limits preclude an adequate range for the ramp controller to respond to the varying mainline demands, indicating the upper limit assumption of Robinson and Doctor [1989] may not be sufficient for highly congested conditions. The maximum discharge rate advocated by Robinson and Doctor [1989] is about 900 vph, or a meter rate of four seconds. Thus the three-second meter rate given in Table 2 might need to be adjusted upward to four seconds to more accurately reflect meter limitations in future studies.

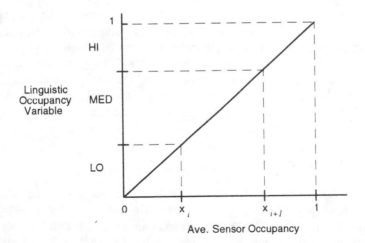

Figure 4. The sensor occupancy to linguistic occupancy variable mapping. The threshold values, x_i and x_{i+1}, are determined using evolutionary programming.

Table 2. Metering rates corresponding to the headway levels given in Table 1.

Linguistic variable	Metering Rate (seconds)
NM	no-metering
L	3
ML	6
M	9
MH	12
H	15

The proposed rule-based system fits well with the ramp meter supervisory block (RMSB) [Bullock and Henderson 1994]. Unlike the RMSB, which uses upstream volumes and downstream occupancies, headways are determined based on the average occupancies at the upstream and downstream sensor stations as shown in Figure 5. Upstream volumes may be used in lieu of occupancy information given high confidence level in the historical volume-occupancy relationships and how one desires to take advantage of this information in the rule-based controller.

Similar to demand-capacity control, the proposed rule-based system is intuitive to the traffic control engineer, easy to implement, and offers real-time performance. It must be tuned for the particular geometries and traffic conditions on which it is implemented because thresholds that divide the occupancy categories for regions of interest are traditionally determined from historical data and can vary from region to region. For example, Chen et al. [1990] indicate that seven categories of occupancy have been defined for the San Francisco-Oakland Bay Bridge, with heavy congestion occurring above 20% occupancy. But traffic flow in Los Angeles has been considered heavily congested for occupancies greater than 18% [Breiman 1974]. As indicated in Table 1, only three distinct categories of occupancy, low (L), medium (M), and high (H), are assumed here. The occupancy thresholds that discriminate between categories of occupancy as shown in Figure 4 are determined using evolutionary programming.

4   Methods and Materials

The measure of effectiveness (MOE) was taken to be the total number of vehicles exiting the system (following Chang et al. [1994]). The freeway system used in this study is shown in Figure 6 with three onramps and four sensor stations. The location of an incident, when it was simulated, is indicated downstream from sensor station 4. One-mile spacings were used between each ramp with the sensor locations halfway in between. One-mile freeway segments existed upstream of the first onramp and downstream of the last onramp. The incident was located roughly 100 meters downstream of sensor station 4.

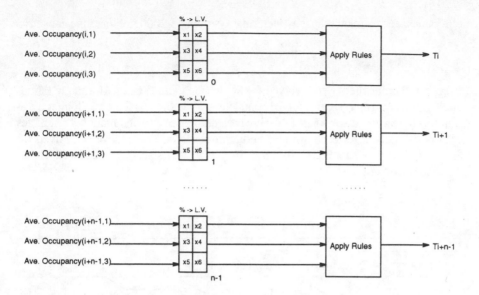

Figure 5. The transformation from average occupancy rates at each sensor station to corresponding ramp metering levels. L.V. designates the linguistic variables as shown in Figure 4. The evolutionary search vector for $n = 3$ (used in this study) can be written as $\mathbf{x} = [x_1, ..., x_{18}]$.

Three different scenarios were investigated using the proposed approach:

Scenario I: High freeway and ramp demand (142% capacity) with no incident.
Scenario II: Moderate freeway and ramp demand (86% capacity) with an incident.
Scenario III: High freeway and ramp demand (100-136% capacity) with an incident.

Ramp metering can be of benefit only within the window of freeway operations where the maximum and minimum metering rates do not allow traffic to violate freeway or ramp capacity limits. The demand volumes for each simulation scenario were selected to ensure that ramp metering would have an effect on traffic flow conditions. Scenario I tested the ability of the ramp metering algorithm to reduce ramp flow in the presence of high mainline demand. Scenario II tested the ability of the control algorithm to respond to an incident that creates a bottleneck during the run. Scenario III combined the high mainline demand of Scenario I with the incident of Scenario II to evaluate traffic responsive metering for high volumes.

Comparisons were made between the best evolved rules and no ramp control, the optimal uniformly-applied fixed-time metering (i.e., all meters set to the same rate) found for that scenario, the rule-based procedure implemented with arbitrary threshold values, and demand-capacity metering assuming a 2000 vph per lane capacity.

5 Results

Rule-based controllers were evolved for Scenarios I and II using 10-minute (simulated) INTRAS runs. These evolved controllers were then evaluated on longer duration INTRAS runs as shown in Table 3, which compares the total number of vehicles exiting the system for each of the different controllers. The controller evolved for Scenario II was also applied to Scenario III to evaluate its performance under higher demand traffic conditions.

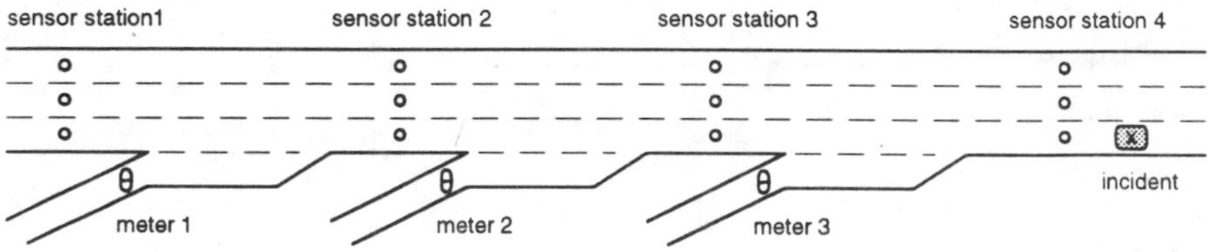

Figure 6. The uniform freeway segment used.

Table 3. Total freeway throughput in number of vehicles for each scenario: Scenarios I and III had 30-minute run-times, while Scenario II had a 40-minute run time.

Control Strategy	Scenario I High Demand No Incident	Scenario II Moderate Demand + Incident	Scenario III High Demand + Incident
No-metering	2641	2732	2349
Uniform fixed-time	3012	2779	2454
Demand-capacity	2952	2755	2161
Rule base	2976	2833	2459
Evolved rule base	3045	2975	2496

5.1 Scenario I: High Mainline and Ramp Demand

This scenario incorporated a mainline demand of 5800 and no initial ramp demand. At 10 seconds into the 10-minute simulation, the ramp demand changed to 900 vph at each ramp. This prevented the metering control strategy from having to alleviate any previous congestion condition. The 10-minute duration may not have been sufficiently long to thoroughly evaluate any control strategy due to the variability of INTRAS as a function of the initial seed value to its random number generator. This is best shown in Figure 7, which depicts the mean value of the MOE (total number of vehicles exiting the system) and the 5σ limits about the mean (where σ is taken as the sample standard deviations) from 30 random trials. 5σ was chosen to have a lower bound of 96% (i.e., > 95%) deviation about the mean under the nonparametric Tchebycheff inequality. The uniformly applied fixed-time metering of $T = 12$ seconds yielded the best mean value of $\mu = 1039$ vehicles with a standard deviation $\sigma = 28.4$ over the 30-run ensemble. The solution evolved for a single seed yielded a mean value of $\mu = 1045$ vehicles with a standard deviation of $\sigma = 28.2$ over the same ensemble. There is no statistical difference between the evolved solution and the solutions from the fixed-time values of $T = 12$ to 16 seconds. A fixed-time value of $T = 12$ corresponds to a freeway capacity of 6700 vph. Although this exceeds the expected capacity of 6000 vph, there are 1000'-long auxiliary lanes at each onramp, which may account for some of the added volume.

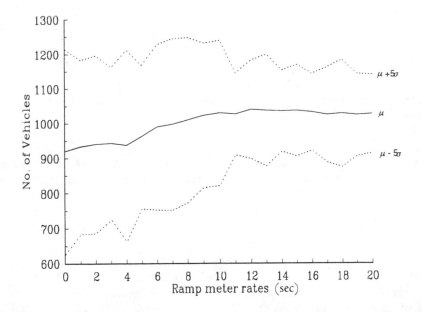

Figure 7. Variability in the total throughput (number of vehicles) over 30 10-minute INTRAS runs for different fixed-time ramp meter rates ($T = 0, ..., 20$ seconds). A zero ramp meter rate corresponds to the no-metering condition. 5σ was chosen to have a lower bound of 96% deviation about the mean under the nonparametric Tchebycheff inequality. The scenario was fixed for all 30 runs.

316

Figure 8 shows the evolutionary learning that occurred using five parents and 200 generations, and yielded an MOE of 1142 vehicles, or a 7% improvement over fixed-time metering for the same INTRAS random seed value. An improvement is also seen by adapting the rule-based occupancy thresholds as opposed to using preset thresholds of 0.05 for the low-medium and 0.2 for the medium-high settings. Since a 10-minute INTRAS run may not have been long enough to ascertain performance capabilities, the simulated run-time was increased to 30 minutes, with the first sub-interval increased to 60 seconds and the second subinterval increased to 29 minutes, to better investigate the behavior of the evolved rule-based metering strategy. Table 3 provides a summary of the final results for each of the different techniques.

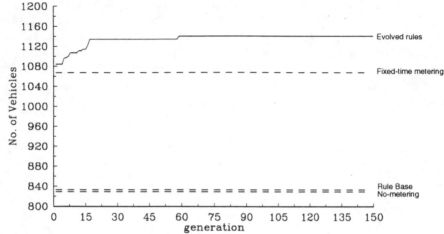

Figure 8. Evolving a solution for Scenario I: high mainline (5800 vph) and ramp (900 vph) demand. The evolved rule-based control strategy outperforms fixed-time metering, rule-based metering, and no-metering.

Figure 9 compares the MOEs of each of the ramp control methods relative to no-metering. No-metering was better than all other methods at six minutes into the run, but by nine minutes, no-metering became and remained the worst approach. For Scenario I, ramp metering was expected to outperform the no-metering case due to the high ramp demands. It was not expected that the evolved solution would necessarily perform better than the fixed-time case. The average metering times for the evolved rule-base controlled ramp meters (i.e., the time between allowing two cars to enter the freeway from the onramp) over the course of the simulation were 11.2, 11.7, and 14.1 seconds, respectively. When these average meter settings were rounded to the nearest fixed-time values of 11, 12, and 14 seconds, respectively, an MOE of 3178 total vehicles resulted. This MOE is 4.4% better than the evolved solution and 5.5% better than uniformly applied fixed-time metering. Although these results suggest that evolutionary programming can refine a fixed-time solution, the improvement observed by adjusting the fixed-time meter rates also suggests that perhaps more INTRAS function evaluations would be required to discover optimal control strategies either by using a larger population size, more generations, or a combination of both.

Table 4 lists the final network (combined freeway and ramps) statistics for Scenario I. The demand-capacity control strategy yields better results in all categories except total vehicle throughput (the MOE). Further investigation revealed that the demand-capacity controller yielded lower upstream freeway densities and higher speeds, but downstream freeway densities were higher and resulted in increased congestion which in turn reduced the number of vehicles exiting the system. The MOEs for the evolved rule-based controller and the uniform fixed-time controller were virtually the same for this particular run. Figures 10 and 11 indicate the average occupancy values and ramp metering rates, respectively, for each of the four sensor stations over the course of the 30-minute INTRAS run.

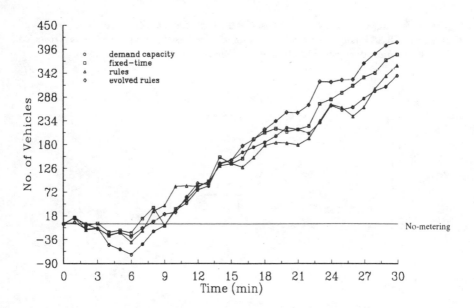

Figure 9. Cumulative throughput increase (in number of vehicles) over the 30-minute INTRAS simulation for each ramp control strategy relative to no-metering for Scenario I. After nine minutes, all of the ramp control strategies yielded a higher vehicle exit count than the no-metering controller.

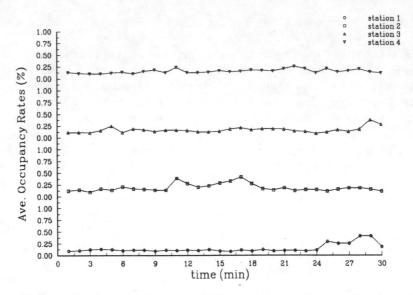

Figure 10. Average occupancy values at each of the four sensor stations over the course of the 30-minute INTRAS run for Scenario I under evolved rule-based control. The y-axis is rescaled to show the average occupancy levels at each of the sensor stations in one graph.

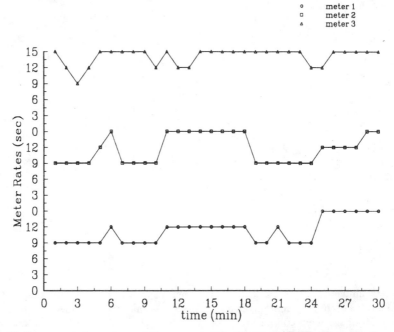

Figure 11. Ramp metering rates over the course of the 30-minute INTRAS run for Scenario I using the evolved rule-based control. The y-axis is rescaled to show the metering levels at each of the meters in one graph.

Table 4. A comparison of the controllers using the total number of vehicle-miles, vehicle-minutes, average speed, and average delay over the whole network (combined freeway and ramps) for test Scenario I: high demand and no incident.

Control Strategy	Vehicle-miles	Vehicle-minutes	Speed (mph)	Delay (min/mile)
No-metering	9458.97	28379.62	20.00	2.25
Uniform fixed-time, T=12	11806.13	16596.11	42.68	0.65
Demand-capacity	11837.75	15107.23	47.01	0.53
Rule base	11811.84	18342.36	38.64	0.80
Evolved rule base	11786.85	16651.17	42.47	0.66

5.2 Scenario II: Moderate Mainline and Ramp Demand

This scenario incorporated demands of 2500 vph on the mainline freeway and 900 vph at each of the ramps. A control strategy was evolved for a 10-minute INTRAS run where an incident occurred at two minutes and was cleared at seven minutes. The evolutionary programming optimization is shown in Figure 12, where the evolved solution yielded an MOE that is 9.9% better than the best uniform fixed-time controller of T = 4 seconds.

A 40-minute INTRAS run was used to evaluate the longer term behavior of this solution. At five minutes into the 40-minute run, an incident was made to occur on the number three lane, approximately 100 meters downstream from sensor station 4. The incident lasted for 15 minutes before being cleared. There was sufficient capacity to accommodate the estimated 5200 vph that would have entered the system if no incident had occurred. But when the incident occurred, the freeway went from an operating capacity of about 87% to a congested condition of 130% capacity if anything less than T = 4 second fixed-time metering was employed. For the short (10 minute) and long (40 minute) runs, a fixed-time metering rate of T = 4 seconds proved best for this scenario. Even though a fixed-time metering rate of T = 4 seconds yielded the same estimated 900 vph demand into the system as no-metering, note that ramp metering breaks up vehicle platoons by allowing only a single vehicle onto the freeway at a time.

Figure 13 shows that the no-metering strategy provides better performance than fixed-time (T = 4), demand-capacity, the rule-based, and the evolved rule-based controllers during the incident (5 to 20 minutes). But after the incident, both the rule-based and evolved rule-based controllers allowed for a higher number of vehicles to exit from the bottleneck region created by the incident. The densities and

320

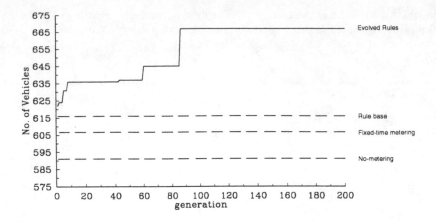

Figure 12. Evolving a solution for Scenario II: moderate mainline (2500 vph) and high ramp (900 vph) demand. The evolved rule-based control strategy outperformed uniformly applied fixed-time metering (T = 4), rule-based metering, and no-metering.

speeds on the link immediately upstream of the bottleneck were plotted for the duration of the run, as shown in Figure 14 and 15. Figure 14 shows that the upstream link densities for both the rule-based and evolved rule-based are lower than for the other control methods. Similarly, Figure 15 reveals that the vehicle speeds generated by the rule-based and evolved rule-based controllers were better than for the other techniques. The slightly higher speeds combined with the lower densities upstream from the bottleneck allowed for faster clearing after the incident and resulted in greater traffic throughput. For peak period operation where traffic demand is greater than freeway capacity, the "peak period is dictated by the specified demand and it is not affected by the type of control used. However, the post-peak period depends on the control" [Chen et al. 1974]. This observation appears to apply to Scenario II, where the peak period occurred during the incident and the post-peak period was the clearing time after the incident.

Figure 16 shows the average occupancy rates at each sensor station for the evolved rule-based solution. Sensor station 4 had fairly high occupancy rates during the course of the incident, but it required over 10 minutes for the effects of the incident to be observed at sensor station 3, one-mile upstream from sensor station 4. The metering rates for the evolved rule-based ramp controller are shown in Figure 17 and correspond with the observed average occupancy readings of Figure 16. Figure 17 also shows the need for propagating the sensory information further upstream so that meter 1 could react to the incident, instead of relying on sensor stations 1 and 2, which remained relatively low during the course of the incident. The average meter rates for this run, rounded to the nearest second, were T = 3, 4, and 11 seconds, respectively. An MOE of 2836 vehicles resulted when this fixed-time strategy was implemented indicating that, for this case, traffic-responsive metering was better than using a fixed-time controller.

Table 5 summarizes the network statistics for each of the control strategies evaluated on this scenario. To fairly assess the demand-capacity algorithm, an incident detection routine should have been implemented so that the demand-capacity controller could have used a reduced capacity in its calculations for determining meter rates. For this scenario, the rule-base with 0.05 and 0.15 thresholds and the evolved rule-based controllers yielded the best MOEs and were the only controllers with average vehicle speeds above 30 mph.

5.3   Scenario III: High Mainline/Ramp Demand with Incident

This scenario combined the high ramp and mainline freeway demands of Scenario I with the incident of Scenario II. Two subintervals were used to step up the demands. The first subinterval constituted the initial three minutes of the simulation with a mainline freeway demand of 4500 vph and ramp demands of 500 vph. The second

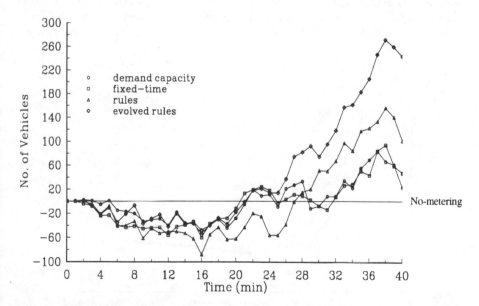

Figure 13. Cumulative throughput increase (in number of vehicles) over the 40-minute INTRAS simulation for each ramp control strategy relative to no-metering for Scenario II. During the incident, from five to 20 minutes, no-metering performed best. As the incident was cleared, the other strategies performed better than no-metering. Both the rule-base and evolved rule-based controllers performed better than the other methods because they had lower density levels in the link upstream from the bottleneck caused by the incident.

322

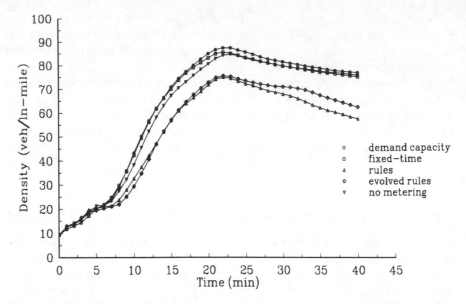

Figure 14. Densities in the link upstream from the bottleneck caused by the incident in Scenario II. The incident started at five minutes and lasted until 20 minutes. Both the rule-base and evolved rule-based controllers allowed fewer vehicles onto the congested freeway resulting in lower density levels in the link upstream from the bottleneck caused by the incident.

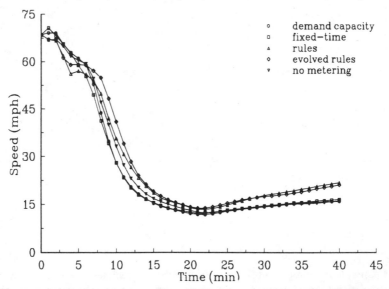

Figure 15. Vehicle speeds at the bottleneck caused by the incident in Scenario II. The incident started at five minutes and lasted until 20 minutes. Both the rule-based and evolved rule-based controllers allowed faster clearing as they had lower density levels in the link upstream from the bottleneck caused by the incident.

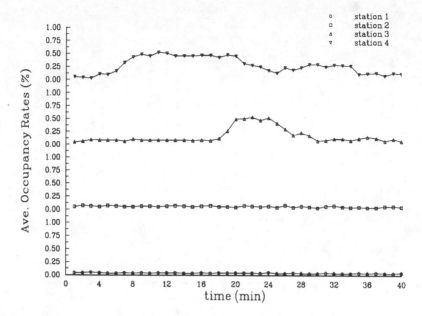

Figure 16. Average sensor occupancies at each station for Scenario II under evolved rule-based control. The incident started at five minutes and lasted until 20 minutes. Note that the average occupancy levels at station 4 reveal a congested traffic condition. It took over 10 minutes for the traffic to back up to sensor station 3. Sensor stations 1 and 2 do not indicate the presence of a congestion.

subinterval used a mainline freeway demand of 5500 vph and ramp demands of 900 vph. An incident occurred at five minutes and lasted for 10 minutes before being cleared. A new rule-based controller was not evolved for this case. Instead, the same threshold parameters evolved for Scenario II were used again for this scenario. This was done in order to assess the robustness of the solution evolved for Scenario II.

Table 3 summarizes the final MOE value and Figure 18 shows the cumulative increase in total traffic throughput over the course of the run. A uniformly applied, fixed-time metering rate of $T = 8$ seconds performed best for this scenario. The no-metering control strategy appeared best both during and as the incident was cleared. Six minutes after the incident was cleared, the rule-based, evolved rule-based, and fixed-time control strategies all performed better than the no-metering strategy. The demand-capacity technique might have benefited from an incident detection capability so as to reduce the assumed capacity levels after an incident occurred. Without such capability, demand-capacity operation yielded the poorest performance for this scenario. Table 6 shows that the other network statistics were also best for the evolved rule-based controller. While the increase over the best uniformly applied fixed-time metering controller was relatively small, the results indicate that the controller evolved for Scenario II could be applied to a similar situation in the presence of increased demand.

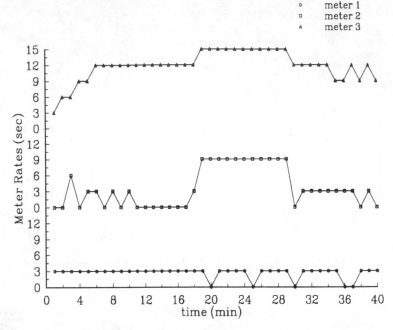

Figure 17. Ramp metering rates for Scenario II under evolved rule-based control. The incident started at five minutes and lasted until 20 minutes. Note the correlation between this figure and the previous figure. Meter 2 did not respond until traffic backed up to sensor station 3. Meter 1 did not reduce its discharge rate at all, indicating the need to expand the number of sensor stations that provide information to each meter.

Table 5. A comparison of the controllers using the total number of vehicle-miles, vehicle-minutes, average speed, and average delay over the whole network (combined freeway and ramps) for test Scenario II: moderate demand with an incident.

Control Strategy	Vehicle-miles	Vehicle-minutes	Speed (mph)	Delay (min/mile)
No-metering	9203.23	25087.88	22.01	1.97
Uniform fixed-time (T=12sec)	9377.78	23489.14	23.95	1.75
Demand-capacity	9305.70	25116.30	22.23	1.94
Rule base	9641.26	15139.16	38.21	0.82
Evolved rules	9973.03	15887.57	37.66	0.84

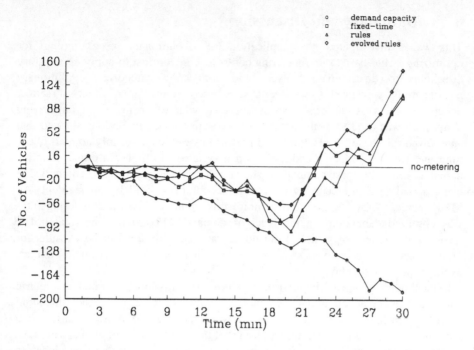

Figure 18. Cumulative throughput increase (in number of vehicles) over the 30-minute INTRAS simulation for each ramp control strategy relative to no-metering for Scenario III. During the incident, from five to 15 minutes, no-metering generally performed best. As the incident cleared, the other strategies performed poorly relatively to no-metering as the peak period demand precluded reduced congestion levels until six minutes after the incident started to clear. The traffic-responsive demand-capacity algorithm is not well suited to this type of scenario unless it can also detect the occurrence of an incident and lower the allowable link capacities.

Table 6. A comparison of the controllers using the total number of vehicle-miles, vehicle-minutes, average speed, and average delay over the entire network (combined freeway and ramps) for test Scenario III: high demand with incident.

Control Strategy	Vehicle-miles	Vehicle-minutes	Speed (mph)	Delay (min/mile)
No-metering	8318.89	31846.87	15.67	3.08
Uniform fixed-time	9321.01	25527.76	21.91	1.99
Demand-Capacity	7830.46	32549.83	14.45	3.41
Rule base	9677.66	23512.30	24.70	1.68
Evolved rules	9813.16	23162.51	25.42	1.61

6   Summary and Discussion

This work investigated the application of evolutionary programming for optimizing a rule-based ramp metering controller. In contrast to applying arbitrary thresholds to discriminate between the congestion categories, evolutionary programming was used to evolve a rule-based controller in light of sensor occupancy rates. A uniform freeway segment with recurring and nonrecurring congestion was used to evaluate the proposed approach. Simulations showed that an evolved rule-based controller could perform as well as uniformly applied fixed-time metering for reducing congestion on a system with high ramp and mainline demand. Similarly, these simulations showed that an evolved rule-based controller can respond to a nonrecurring congestion condition caused by an incident. An MOE increase of 1.5% to 7% over uniformly applied fixed-time metering rates was observed depending on the level of demand. Maximizing the total traffic throughput (number of vehicles) did not always yield the overall best results for other measures of effectiveness such as total vehicle-miles, total vehicle-minutes, average speed, and delay.

Even though geometry invariance was not explicitly demonstrated, geometric variability can be accommodated by evolving higher or lower occupancy threshold levels for each meter. In effect, this allows a meter to be more sensitive to a particular sensor station. It is not required that the sensors be contiguous. The most pertinent sensors, for any ramp, can be used regardless of their physical location relative to the onramp.

The current study demonstrates that the proposed evolutionary procedure has real potential as a nonparametric, real-time ramp metering control algorithm. Moreover, evolutionary programming can be applied to any ramp metering control algorithm. A rule-based controller, as proposed here, may not be the optimal type of controller for this task. But such a controller does have many attractive features, including (1) real-time performance, (2) simple implementation, and (3) the potential to take advantage of the traffic engineerÕs knowledge. Although the presented study is limited in terms of freeway dynamics, the proposed rule-based controller can also take advantage of more complex arterial-freeway interaction by specifying rules that implement diversionary control which diverts traffic around an incident. This would probably require the development of a more sophisticated rule base for mapping occupancies to ramp meter rates. An appropriately complex rule-base may also require higher resolution of the occupancy levels and thus more categories of congestion.

Acknowledgments

The authors thank V. Nissen for encouraging our participation and for his patience.

References

Banks, J.H. (1993): Effect of Response Limitations on Traffic-Responsive Ramp Metering. 72nd Annual Meeting of the Transportation Review Board

Breiman, L. (1974): A Case Study Ñ LAAFSCP. Urban Freeway Surveillance and Control Short Course. Technology Service Corporation, Bethesda/MD

Bullock, D.; Hendrickson, C. (1994): Roadway Traffic Control Software. In: IEEE Trans. on Control Systems Technology 2: 255-264

Chang, G.-L.; Wu, J., Cohen, S.L. (1994): An Integrated Real-Time Metering Model for Non-recurrent Congestion: Framework and Preliminary Results. 73rd Annual Meeting of the Transportation Research Board, Paper no. 940569

Chen, L.; May, A.D.; Auslander, D.M. (1990): Freeway Ramp Control Using Fuzzy Set Theory for Inexact Reasoning. Transportation Research-A 24A: 15-25

Chen, C.-I.; Cruz, J.B.; Paquet, J.G. (1974): Entrance Ramp Control for Travel-Rate Maximization in Expressways. Transportation Research 8: 503-580

Fogel, D.B. (1995): Evolutionary Computation: Toward a New Philosophy of Machine Intelligence. IEEE Press, Piscataway/NJ

Fogel, L.J.; Owens, A.J.; Walsh, M.J. (1966): Artificial Intelligence through Simulated Evolution. John Wiley/NY

Hadi, M.A.; Wallace, C.E. (1993): A Hybrid Genetic Algorithm to Optimize Signal Phasing and Timing. 72nd Annual Meeting of the Transportation Review Board

Jacobson, L.N.; Henry, K.C.; Mehyar, O. (1989): Real-Time Metering Algorithm for Centralized Control. Transportation Research Record Vol 1232: Urban Traffic Systems and Operations. Transportation Research Board, National Research Council: 17-26

Newman, L.; Dunnet, A.; Meis, G.J. (1969): Freeway Ramp Control Ñ What It Can and Cannot Do. Traffic Engineering, June: 14-21

Pooran, F.J.; Sumner, R.; Lieu, H.C.; Chen, H. (1994): Development of System Operating Strategies for Ramp Metering and Traffic Signal Coordination. 73rd Annual Meeting of the Transportation Research Board

Robinson, J.; Doctor, M. (1989): Ramp Metering: Does it Really Work? ITE 1989 Compendium of Technical Papers: 503-508

Wicks, D.A.; Lieberman, E.B. (1980): Development and Testing of INTRAS, A Microscopic Freeway Simulation Model. Vol. 1, Report No. FHWA/RD-80/106, KLD Associates, Inc., Huntington/NY

Application of Genetic Algorithms for Solving Problems Related to Free Routing for Aircraft

Ingrid Gerdes

Institute of Flight Guidance, Department Traffic Systems Analysis, German Aerospace Research Establishment, Lilienthalplatz 7, 38108 Braunschweig, Germany

Abstract. This paper describes a special genetic algorithm for the creation of flight routes for aircraft in the airspace. A detailed description of the problem and the implemented algorithm is presented together with a test of two mutation types for a special gene. Furthermore, the results of several experiments with a randomly generated flight scenario and a real traffic scenario are lined out. In sum, the paper shows the initial stages of finding a solution to decrease the delay of aircraft and to use the airspace more efficiently.

Keywords. Free-routing, genetic algorithm, air-traffic-management

1   Introduction

Presently, the air traffic control systems in many countries have to cope with rising traffic congestion and, therefore, with an increasing delay. One reason is the growing air traffic over the last years (approximately 4.5 % per year). The other reason is the airspace structure with overloaded control sectors and prescribed standard flight routes (ATS-Routes). Each sector has its own limited number of aircraft (A/C) which can be handled and every aircraft normally uses a standard route (normally not the direct link) between start and destination airport (figure 1). In case of aircraft on different routes this reduces the number of points where conflicts may occur to the crossing points of routes. Therefore, talking about congested airspace means talking about congested standard routes. The limited number of aircraft which can be controlled for each sector or on each route is responsible for the increasing delay. Such a situation is very problematic for those aircraft which have missed the scheduled time slot for departure or which are not planned in advance because the airspace is nearly occupied by aircraft, which are already scheduled. Improvements are necessary for a better use of the airspace surrounding the prescribed routes.

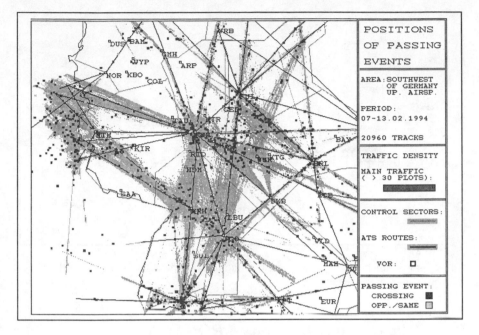

Fig. 1. Air space structure over Southern Germany with sectors, standard flight routes (ATS-Routes) and main traffic areas [Schmitz 1994].

A possible solution for raising the airspace capacity could be giving up these standard routes. This strategy is called 'Free-Routing', which includes the permission to fly in any direction on any level at any time if the controller allocates such a route. This would lead to the following advantages:

—   The whole airspace would be usable for air traffic.
—   Flight routes would be shorter than nowadays.
—   It would be easier to find new slots or a new route if the time of departure has changed.
—   The delay would decrease.
—   Noise and pollution would be uniformly distributed.

But the introduction of free routing will lead to a major disadvantage. It will be nearly impossible for airspace controllers to detect conflicts between aircraft in advance. Because there are no longer fixed points where conflicts can occur, a system is needed which is able to assist the controllers in developing routes between start and destination points in such a way that conflicts with other aircraft are avoided.

A proposal how to find the best routes without conflicts is presented by the tool ROGENA (free ROuting with GENetic Algorithms [Gerdes 1994]). This paper gives a short description about the present state of ROGENA.

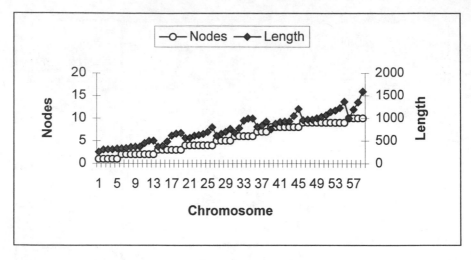

Fig. 2. Graph which shows for each route of the initial population the length of the routes and the number of way points.

2 The Genetic Algorithm of ROGENA

2.1 Characteristics of the Application Domain

When comparing the problem of finding short and conflict free routes for aircraft to the well known Travelling Salesman Problem (TSP) a number of substantial differences can be found. The most important difference is the number of way-points for a route. For the TSP the number of nodes is fixed but for the aircraft routes it is better to work with a variable number of nodes (cities) because it is not possible to estimate the number of necessary nodes for the shortest route in advance.

But the usage of a variable number of points leads to another problem. In the initial generation of the genetic algorithm routes with a high number of nodes are normally longer than those with a small number of nodes because the routes of the initial population are created randomly (figure 2). During the ongoing optimisation process long routes will be eliminated due to low quality. Therefore, there will be a loss of routes with higher numbers of nodes. If the optimal route has many nodes it will be necessary to prevent the loss of multi-node-routes or to re-introduce them in the population.

Another difference to the TSP which makes the problem of free-routing much more complicated is the necessity to avoid certain areas in the airspace. These regions may be caused by the existence of military areas in the airspace. They are assumed as fixed obstacles independent of time. Moreover; the airspace is filled with a high number of moving obstacles, e.g. other aircraft, which have already entered the airspace. Therefore, the conflict probability depends on the time when an aircraft arrives at a specific point of the airspace.

2.2 Formalisation of the Problem

For the formalisation of free routing with genetic algorithms it is necessary to code a certain part of the airspace. For the following experiments an area of 200 x 200 nautical miles (NM) was covered by a grid of 80 x 80 squares of size 2.5 x 2.5 NM and 6561 numbered grid nodes. This area corresponds to a geographical part of northern Germany. On the basis of this grid it is possible to define a route as a sequence of nodes (so-called way points). Flying a route now means moving on the links between the neighbouring nodes. With this definition the actual position of the aircraft is not necessarily a grid node.

Normally within a genetic algorithm the mutation operator is applied to all genes and the crossover operator to all chromosomes with a certain probability, but the principle idea of the algorithm of ROGENA is based on the modGA of Michalewicz [1992], where special groups of chromosomes are selected for crossover and mutation. However, problem specific modifications of the modGA have to be included for a significant improvement in performance. The resulting genetic algorithm avoids the problem of premature convergence which is frequently caused by the dominance of particularly fit individuals (super individuals) in the selection phase.

The size of the population is set to 60 chromosomes (or routes). The information is integer-coded as a chromosome of length eleven with way points (way points are integer numbers) in the first ten genes which are available for the definition of the route. The information in the last gene is the number of actually used way points which ranges from one to ten. Like in biological chromosomes, the unused information is not lost but stored in case that it would be needed.

Theoretically it is possible to get a solution using all ten genes of the chromosome. But several runs with the GA with such a high number of way points have shown very bad results. Because it is necessary to arrange ten points straight on a line instead of one or two, it has taken more than 600 generations for a population of 40 chromosomes just to get the diagonal between the upper right and the lower left corner of the grid, without paying attention to any obstacle or other moving aircraft.

By using integers for representing information it is easy to code the node numbers and handle the genetic operators. Applying a crossover operator to two individuals then means an exchange of way points (subroutes) between two chromosomes in a very simple way. During mutation it is possible to change the content of a gene directly to a new way point.

2.3 Evaluation

The main factors influencing the quality of a flight route are the length of the route and the number of conflicts with other already moving aircraft.

Therefore, the following formula was taken as the evaluation function to be minimized:

> eval(chromosome) = (length of route)*(1 + 0.2 * (number of conflicts with other aircraft))

There where two reasons for including the number of conflicts in this formula.

1. Routes with conflicts will not be automatically removed from the population. With this evaluation function short routes with a low number of conflicts have the chance to change under crossover or mutation to good routes without conflicts.
2. The inclusion allows a better handling of local optima. If, for instance, there exists a local optimum surrounded by routes with conflicts, there is now a good chance to jump over such a barrier of conflicts out of the local optimum.

2.4 Selection

The implemented GA is based on the modGA. The principle idea of the selection procedure of this algorithm is to divide the population of chromosomes in three different groups after each generation:

1. Unchanged chromosomes,
2. chromosomes, which will undergo crossover, and
3. chromosomes, which will undergo mutation.

The selection process is primarily based on the fitness of the chromosomes (roulette wheel) and the selection procedure will be 'stochastic sampling with replacement' [Goldberg 1989]. All groups will consist of twenty routes (chromosomes).

For the first group, five of the twenty routes are <u>not</u> selected with stochastic sampling with replacement. Instead, four of these five routes are the best four routes of the population. The fifth selected route is the best one with a number of way points that exceeds the number of way points of the already selected four other routes. The idea is to prevent a complete loss of routes with higher numbers of way points (see section 2.1). All selected routes of this group have to be different to preserve the diversity within the population. They will be passed to the next generation without any changes.

For the second group, the selection of identical routes is not forbidden because they will change under the influence of the crossover operator to probably different routes. The same is true for the third group, where the routes will undergo mutation.

2.5   Crossover

Depending on the 'Number of Used Way Points' (NWP) in the eleventh position of the chromosome two different types of crossover are applied. If at least one of the affected chromosomes uses more than two way points then two-point crossover is applied. Otherwise the operator must be one-point crossover because it is not possible to use the usually more effective two-point crossover for a chromosome of a length less than three [Eshelmann 1989]. The crossover points are selected randomly within the part of the chromosome with the used genes.

2.6   Mutation

Two different types of mutation are used. Each of them is applied with a probability of 0.5 to a chromosome of the mutation group. Only one gene of each chromosome is randomly selected for mutation. We use:
- Non-Bounded-Mutation: The allel of a selected gene can change to any other way point with the same probability.
- One-Bounded-Mutation: The content of a gene can only change to one of the eight neighbouring way points (nodes on the grid). Each of these points has the same probability to be selected.

The first type is very important in the initial phase of a simulation run for searching the space of solutions or for situations where the best found solution lies in a local optimum and it is necessary to jump out with a big step.

The second type makes the optimisation process much faster in situations where better solutions can be found in the surrounding of a given solution. This is of great importance especially in the end phase of the optimisation process.

At the beginning of the evolution process the routes with many way points are very long and, therefore, lead to bad evaluation values. To prevent the loss of individuals with many way points a mutation operator for the eleventh gene indicating the number of way points has to be introduced. Two types of mutation have been tested (see section 4.2):
- random mutation, and
- increase by one ('+1').

It must be mentioned that the coding of a route is not unique. It is possible to code the same route e.g. with two or with three points where, for instance, in the latter case the second point could lie on the link between the others. Losing the individuals with low numbers of way points means an increse in terms of the average number of way points per route. However, this case would not endanger the quality of solutions in the GA-population. Because of the results of the test the mutation type '+1' was chosen for ROGENA.

334

3 The Algorithm of ROGENA

ROGENA is a program which is driven by a flight schedule. This schedule contains a number of flights with the following information:
- time when the aircraft enters the system.
- x- and y-coordinate of the start-point.
- x- and y-coordinate of the destination-point.
- speed of the aircraft.
- type of flight (level between 1 and 6).

The first type level (1) stands, for instance, for aircraft like the B747 with a high speed and a high number of passengers. Aircraft with a high type level like 6 are, for instance, small general aviation aircraft.

A position update of aircraft which have already entered the system is made every 10 seconds of flight time. Distances between aircraft are calculated on the basis of the actual positions.

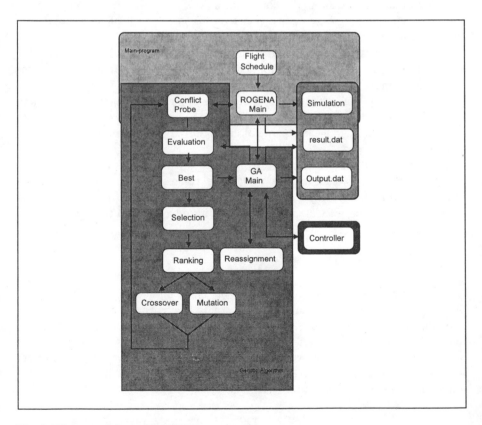

Fig. 3. Diagram of the tool ROGENA

If a new aircraft A enters the system (see figure 3) the following process is executed:

The direct link between start- and destination point is checked for conflicts (Conflict Probe). If there are none, aircraft A is handed over to the simulation part of ROGENA, which is responsible for the calculation of the aircraft positions and the animation. Otherwise the genetic algorithm is started (GA-Main). First, a randomly generated population is created and evaluated (Evaluation). Then the best chromosome is shown to the controller, and he has the possibility to accept or reject this route (Best). In case of rejection a new generation is created until the controller accepts a route. If no good route can be found, the controller has the possibility to reassign a new route to an already moving aircraft B, which has conflicts with the actual aircraft A (Reassignment). In this case the selected aircraft B is removed from the system until a new route for aircraft A is found. Then the genetic algorithm starts again and creates a new route for the removed aircraft B.

Figure 4 displays the main screen of ROGENA showing the airspace of northern Germany. Here the routes are indicated as dark lines and the aircraft as circles, where the size of the circles is half of the prescribed minimum distance between aircraft in the airspace. The German border is shown as a grey line.

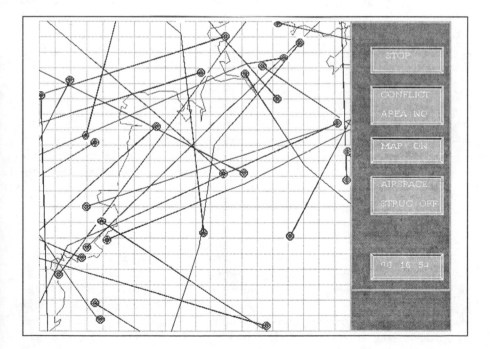

Fig. 4. Main screen of ROGENA with a solved test example.

4 Results

4.1 Results for a Real Traffic Scenario and a Randomly-Generated Scenario Simulated with ROGENA

In this section the results of two different experiments with ROGENA are described.

The first experiment (scenario 1) was carried out with three randomly created flight schedules. Each flight schedule includes twenty flights with a time interval of thirty seconds between the starting times. The randomly-generated speed ranges from three-hundred to six-hundred knots (NM per hour). For this scenario a comparison between the length of the direct routes ignoring possible conflicts and the conflict-free routes generated by ROGENA was made.

Scenario 2 is composed of real aircraft trajectories which were extracted from radar data from the north of Germany. These data were collected for a EUROCONTROL study of vertical separation between aircraft [Schmitz 1994]. Each of the three flight schedules contained the data of a special flight level. Starting time for each aircraft was the actual time when the aircraft crossed the border of the grid or had reached the actual flight level, respectively. Start and destination points were the positions where the aircraft had entered and left the grid. The speed was average speed on the route as far as the flight was conducted within the actual flight level. The comparison was made between the measured length of the radar tracks and the routes generated by ROGENA.

For both types of scenarios no reassignment was necessary, e.g. there were no unsolvable conflicts within all scenarios.

Number of Conflicts	Route Length (Sum)		ROGENA in % of Direct	Average Increase (NM) per Conflict
	Direct	ROGENA		
7	3734.47	3742.17	100.21	1.10
3	3240.99	3244.05	100.09	1.02
3	3152.96	3158.41	100.17	1.82

Table 1. Scenario 1. Comparison between the length of direct links between start and destination points with conflicts and the length of routes created with ROGENA.

A comparison between the length of the direct routes and the ROGENA routes (table 1) shows that the requirement to avoid conflicts does not increase the length of the route dramatically in spite of the high number of moving aircraft. The average loss per conflict is 1.24 NM but this value must be seen in connection with the sum of the route lengths. The average length of the ROGENA routes in percent of the direct routes is 100.16 %. It can be said that all aircraft are able to fly a route which is about as short as the direct route. If ROGENA could handle more aircraft in a given sector than the controllers are actually able to handle without any support, the delay for every aircraft caused by the avoidance of conflicts would be small compared to the increased number of handled aircraft.

Number of		Route Length (Sum)		ROGENA in	Average Decrease
A/C	Conflicts	Traffic	ROGENA	% of Traffic	(NM) per Conflict
12	0	834.43	820.29	98.31	1.18
22	2	1647.70	1602.07	97.31	2.02
31	2	1747.24	1714.00	98.10	1.07

Table 2. Scenario 2. Comparison between the length of standard routes and the more direct routes generated by ROGENA. Traffic: Real traffic scenario.

The results in table 2 which represent scenario 2 with real traffic show only a small number of conflicts. Again, the 'Number of Conflicts' stands for conflict situations in case of using the direct links between start and destination points. There are no conflicts when using the standard routes and the routes of ROGENA. The routes for ROGENA are shorter than for the standard routes. This confirms the assumption that free-routing works well and would not lead to a high number of conflicts. The gain is caused by using the more direct routes of ROGENA. However, we have the highest gain in scenarios with more conflicts.

4.2   Mutation of 'Number of Way Points'

As mentioned before (section 2.6) two types of mutation have been tested for the number of way points:
−   random mutation, and
−   increase by one ('+1').
As test case a scenario with twenty flights was chosen and 6 runs of ROGENA were conducted for each type of mutation. The results of these tests are given in table 3. The table contains the results for all flights, where the direct route between start and destination point leads to conflicts with other already moving aircraft. The 'Number of A/C' means the number of the actual aircraft (A/C) in the sequence of arriving airplanes within the flight schedule of this scenario. For each flight with a conflict on the direct route two-hundred generations of the genetic algorithm part of ROGENA are carried out. The main goal of this first experiment was to check the algorithm's ability to re-introduce higher numbers of way points. Therefore, the most important results in table 3 are the values of the average number of way points. It can easily be observed that '+1' leads to better results for each flight within 200 generations than the random mutation does. All flights where the average number of way points for 'random mutation' is lower than for '+1' have an average length, which is equal to or larger than the corresponding value for '+1'. Therefore, as mutation type for the eleventh gene (indicating the number of way points) the '+1'-mutation was selected for all further simulations.

Direct Length	Number of A/C	Type '+1'		Type Random	
		Ø NWP	Ø Length	Ø NWP	Ø Length
242.44	7	2	242.74	2	242.74
210.16	9	1	210.44	1	210.44
119.34	10	1.83	120.42	1.16	120.70
211.56	12	1.16	211.57	1	211.57
188.17	15	1.83	188.20	1.5	188.21
207.00	16	1.66	208.83	1	208.93
186.37	20	2.33	191.11	2	194.50
	Ø Value	1.68	196.18	1.38	196.72

Table 3. Comparison between mutation types '+1' and 'Random'. A/C=aircraft. NWP=Number of Way Points.

4.3 Comparison Between the Results of Hill-Climbing / Simulated Annealing and ROGENA

As examples for other optimisation algorithms hill-climbing and simulated annealing were selected. All simulations were carried out with a flight schedule of forty flights and an average of seventeen conflicts. For all algorithms six simulation runs were carried out. To make hill-climbing and simulated annealing comparable to the implementation of the genetic algorithm forty different starting routes for each conflict were selected for both algorithms. The size of the starting route set was selected in this way, because only forty of sixty routes of the population of ROGENA undergo mutation and crossover. For each of these different starting routes two hundred optimisation steps were conducted. For each step one way point of the route was randomly selected and then changed to one of the neighbouring eight way points. If this lead to an improvement, then the old way point was replaced by the new one, else, in case of hill-climbing, it was not replaced. Simulated annealing has, dependent on the number of already accepted deteriorations, a certain probability to accept the less good route. The results of hill-climbing and simulated annealing were compared with the results of the ROGENA algorithm explained before.

First tests demonstrated that for hill-climbing and simulated annealing it would also be necessary to allow for a mutation of the number of way points. Because each set of simulations of these two algorithms involves forty different starting routes, there will otherwise be on average only four routes with the correct number of way points for the design of the optimal route.

The results of the tests are shown in table 4. The column 'Distance Ratio of Type to Direct' shows the value of the ratio of the length of the conflict-free routes created by ROGENA / hill-climbing / simulated annealing to the length of the direct link between start and destination point. The other columns show the average increase in the route length per aircraft and per conflict.

Table 4 shows that the values for hill-climbing in column three and four are more than four times higher than the results for the genetic algorithm and 2.5 times the results of simulated annealing. Furthermore, one of the simulation runs with hill-climbing was not able to solve all conflicts. Therefore, the value for hill-climbing is obtained by averaging the data of five simulation runs.

Type	Distance Ratio of Type to Direct	Average Increase (NM) per Aircraft	Average Increase (NM) per Conflict
Hill-climbing	1.02230	3.47	8.49
Simulated Annealing	1.00897	1.39	3.28
ROGENA	1.00504	0.78	1.75

Table 4. Comparison between hill-climbing, simulated annealing and the genetic algorithm of ROGENA.

4.4 Comparison between Different Parameter Sets for ROGENA

Three different settings of strategy parameters were tested:
- ROGENA30: 30 unchanged chromosomes, 16 chromosomes in the crossover-group, 14 chromosomes in the mutation-group.
- ROGENA20: 20 unchanged chromosomes, 20 chromosomes in the crossover-group, 20 chromosomes in the mutation-group.
- ROGENA10: 10 unchanged chromosomes, 26 chromosomes in the crossover-group, 24 chromosomes in the mutation-group.

ROGENA20 corresponds to the genetic algorithm which was explained in section two. The same flight schedule as for section 4.3 was used. For each type six simulation runs were conducted with 200 generations per conflict within the genetic algorithm part of ROGENA. The results for these tests can be found in table 5. The meaning of the columns is the same as in table 4.

Type	Distance Ratio of Type to Direct	Average Increase (NM) per Aircraft	Average Increase (NM) per Conflict
ROGENA30	1.00515	0.80	1.80
ROGENA20	1.00504	0.78	1.75
ROGENA10	1.00515	0.80	1.81

Table 5. Results for simulations runs of ROGENA with different parameter sets. Direct: direct link between start and destination point.

Obviously, ROGENA20 produces the best results. The results for the different parameter sets are very similar. Therefore, it can be assumed, that ROGENA with the tested sets of parameters is very stable, where on the one hand enough information (routes) of previous generations is stored (unchanged chromosomes) and, on the other hand, enough new routes are created and tested (mutation- and crossover-groups).

5   Conclusions

A forecast of the future air traffic demand shows a further increase of aircraft movements at the rate of 4.5 % per year. This will make it necessary to find new strategies for the usage of airspace and to develop new tools which are able to reduce the controller work load. A comparison between the length of all prescribed standard routes in Germany and the length of the direct links between the airports in Germany has shown a potential for reduction of approximately 16 % by giving up the standard routes.

In order to get a tool which is applicable to the real air traffic control system more details have to be investigated including the possibility to climb and descend to other levels, the flight behaviour of aircraft (e.g. curve radius), and the connection between adjoining sector (how to hand over aircraft).

Since ROGENA has to take into account the navigation accuracy with which an aircraft is able to fly the assigned route, the equipment of the aircraft is very important.

Finally, additional theoretical analysis of ROGENA will be carried out, including the influence of crossover and mutation operators.

References

De Jong, K.A. (1975): An Analysis of the Behaviour of a Class of Genetic Adaptive Systems. University of Michigan, Doctoral Dissertation, Michigan

Eshelmann, L.J.; Caruana, R.A.; Schaffer, J.D. (1989): Biases in the Crossover Landscape. In: Schaffer, J. (ed.): Third International Conference on Genetic Algorithms. Morgan Kaufmann, San Mateo/CA: 10-19

Gerdes, I.S. (1994): Application of Genetic Algorithms to the Problem of Free-Routing of Aircraft. IEEE : ICEC'94, IEEE Service Center, Orlando, Vol. II: 536-541

Goldberg, D.E. (1989): Genetic Algorithms in Search, Optimization, and Machine Learning. Addison Wesley, Reading/MA

Michalewicz, Z. (1992): Genetic Algorithms + Data Structures = Evolution Programs. Springer Verlag, Berlin

Schmitz. R.; Hurraß, K. (1994): Bestimmung der Passing Frequencies auf benachbarten Flugflächen im oberen Luftraum der Bundesrepublik. DLR Braunschweig, Institut für Flugführung, IB 112-94/38, Braunschweig

Soucek, B. and IRIS Group (1992): Dynamic, Genetic, and Chaotic Programming. Wiley, New York

Whitley, D. (1993): A Genetic Algorithm Tutorial. Colorado State University, Department of Computer Science, Technical Report CS-93-103, Colorado

Genetic Algorithm with Redundancies for the Vehicle Scheduling Problem

Flavio Baita[1], Francesco Mason[1], Carlo Poloni[2] and Walter Ukovich[3]

[1] Department of Mathematics and Computer Science, University of Venice, Italy

[2] (corresponding author) Department of Energetics, 34100 University of Trieste, Italy

[3] Department of Electrical Engineering, 34100 University of Trieste, Italy

Abstract. A real vehicle scheduling problem concerning the urban public transportation system of the city of Mestre (Venice) has been approached by Genetic Algorithm enhanced using redundancies. Redundant alleles fix the string at cross-over positions in order to improve solution feasibility. The scheduling problem has been studied both as a single and as a multiple objective optimisation problem. A significant reduction of resources as compared to the currently used solution has been achieved.

Keywords. Genetic Algorithms, mass transportation, multi-objective, redundancy, vehicle scheduling

1 Introduction

This paper is concerned with an application of Genetic Algorithms (GA) to a real problem of Vehicle Scheduling. The problem was proposed by the Mass Transportation Company of Venice (ACTV), which operates the public transportation system of the city of Mestre. The ordinary daily duty consists of more than 2.500 trips, performed by over 200 buses.

The Vehicle Scheduling Problem (VSP) consists in the assignment of a fleet of vehicles to a set of trips in such a way as to optimise a defined objective function. The VSP is a classical optimisation problem, widely studied in the literature, for which different solution algorithms exist.

However, GA seems to have some unique features in real-life applications. Actually, the algorithm gives a set of good solutions, instead of an unique one: these solutions can later be evaluated by the decision maker in order to select the most suitable one for implementation. Moreover, a multi-criteria optimisation can be handled in a very natural way by a GA, whereas traditional algorithms are typically single-objective.

2   Statement of the Problem

2.1   Problem Description

The VSP consists in the assignment of vehicles to time-tabled trips in such a way that each trip is carried out by one vehicle, a given set of constraints is satisfied, and a cost function is minimised.

The problem input is a set of trips, each one defined by the starting and ending times and the corresponding terminals. The objective consists in minimising: 1) the number of vehicles; 2) the operational costs related to deadheading trips[1]; 3) both the above objectives [Bertossi et al., 1987].

Three real-world constraints commonly determine the form of vehicle scheduling problems: 1) a constraint on the length of time during which a vehicle may stay in service before returning to the depot for servicing or refuelling; 2) the restriction that certain tasks can only be performed by certain vehicle types; 3) the presence of multiple depots where vehicles may be housed [Bodin et al., 1983].

The next section describes the formulation of the basic problem (the unconstrained case).

2.2   Problem Formulation

The input of the problem is a set of trips, each one characterised by a start location SL_i and time ST_i, an end location EL_i and time ET_i. For any pair of terminal locations L_1 and L_2, $TM(L_1, L_2)$ is the time needed to travel from L_1 to L_2.

The problem may be represented by means of a network like the one of Fig. 2.1[2]. The node set N consists in as many nodes as trips plus two more nodes, both representing the depot (starting (node S) and ending (node T) terminal). The arc set A is obtained by inserting an arc (solid arrows) from node i to node j if it is feasible for a single vehicle to perform both tasks, i.e. if $ST_j - ET_i > TM(L_1, L_2)$. Furthermore, an arc (dotted arrows) is inserted from S to each node and from each node to T: these arcs represent the trips from and to the depot. Each path from S to T through this network is a feasible schedule for a single vehicle.

The solution to the VSP is a set of disjoint (S, T)-paths that cover all nodes. If a cost is associated with each arc (i,j) A, the covering problem may be formulated as a minimum cost flow problem as follows:

---

[1] The expression "deadheading trip" indicates an idle transfer, i.e. between two different terminal locations of two subsequent trips without carrying passengers. These trips generate operational costs: gas, driver etc. with no corresponding service.

[2] To simplify the graphical representation, in Fig. 2.1 we assume that each trip has the same start and end locations. The start and end times are given within the node representing the trip.

$$\min \sum_{(i,j)\in A} c_{ij}\, x_{ij}$$

s.t.

(1) $\displaystyle\sum_{i:(i,j)\in A} x_{ij} - \sum_{i:(j,i)\in A} x_{ji} = 0, \ \forall j \in N - \{S,T\}$

(2) $\displaystyle\sum_{i:(i,j)\in A} x_{ij} = 1, \ \forall j \in N - \{S,T\}$

(3) $x_{ij} \in \{0,1\}, \ \forall (i,j) \in A$

The variable x_{ij} is interpreted in this way:

$$x_{ij} = \begin{cases} 1 \text{ if some vehicle traverses arc } (i, j) \\ 0 \text{ othervise} \end{cases}$$

Constraints (1) are the standard conservation flow constraints; constraints (2) guarantee that exactly one path (one vehicle) will pass through each intermediate node (trip). Vehicle operating costs c_{ij} may be assumed as a linear function of vehicle mileage and travel time and a fixed capital cost may be associated with each vehicle used.

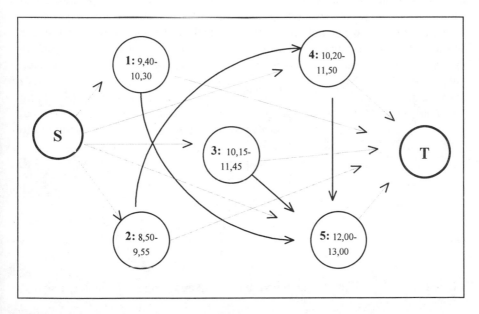

Fig. 2.1. Unconstrained Vehicle Scheduling Problem

For constrained cases similar formulations exist, with suitable modifications to account for different constraints.

2.3   Solution Approaches

The mathematical programming problem formulated in section 2.2 is easily seen to be a minimum cost flow problem and, therefore, it can be efficiently solved[3]. Another approach to solve the covering problem by means of an efficient algorithm consists in transforming it in an assignment problem on an appropriate graph.

While the unconstrained case is "*easy*[4]", efficient algorithms are not known for other cases, and so it is necessary to resort to heuristics or approximate procedures to obtain near-optimal solutions in lieu of seeking optimal solutions. Bodin et al., [1983] describe some heuristic procedures for constrained vehicle scheduling problems (length of path restrictions, multiple vehicle types, multiple depots); other approximated methods are described in [Carpaneto et al. 1988].

Traditional methods are typically single-objective, while the GA approach is well suited to a multi-objective optimisation, as explained below.

3   GA for VSP

3.1   Description and Coding

The GA developed for the VSP presents some features that make it different from traditional GA. It adopts the most natural way of representing a bus schedule as shown in Tab. 3.1: each allele represents a vehicle and the position of the allele represents the trip assigned to the corresponding vehicle.

Trips	Vehicles
1	1
2	1
3	2
4	1
5	2
6	2

Tab. 3.1.

In the example, vehicle 1 is assigned to trips 1,2 and 4, and vehicle 2 is assigned to trips 3, 5 and 6.

---

[3] The use of this formulation to solve VSP was first suggested by Dantzig and Fulkerson [1954].

[4] We say that a problem is *easy* when we know an *efficient* algorithm to solve it exactly, where an algorithm is efficient if it solves the problem in a polynomial time: see [Garey and Johnson, 1979].

An integer representation has been preferred to a (more classic) binary one. However, the main problem that arises in treating these strings is related to the compatibility among trips assigned to the same vehicle. Even if this constraint is satisfied at the beginning, it might not be maintained after the cross-over action. In similar situations, Nakano et al. [1991] have applied repairing mechanisms that are based on the search of the nearest - in terms of Hamming distance - feasible individual. Here a completely different approach is adopted. The structure of the individual is characterised by multiple alleles. As shown in Tab. 3.2, an individual is represented by a matrix (not by a single vector), where the first column contains the dominant alleles. Following columns contain the redundant genes that are used to fix incompatibilities, as explained below.

Trips	Vehicles		
1	2	1	3
2	3	2	3
3	2	1	1
4	1	2	3
5	3	2	1
6	3	3	2

↑
Dominant alleles

Tab. 3.2.

In the single objective optimisation (see 3.3), the fitness value of each individual i is calculated by means of the following expression: $f_i = \dfrac{1}{NV_i \cdot NI_i}$, where NV_i is the number of vehicles, and NI_i the number of incompatibilities[5] of the corresponding solution; in this way the costs related to deadheading trips are not considered. These costs are faced in the multiple objective optimisation: the fitness function takes a vector form, as described in 3.4 .

3.1.1 Redundant Genes

In each generation, when an individual is evaluated, and the algorithm discovers that in the solution a trip assigned to a vehicle is incompatible with another trip assigned to the same vehicle, it tries to bypass this problem using a redundant allele instead of the dominant one. In other terms, it assigns the trip to another

---

[5] More precisely, it is the total number of incompatibilities found between the trips assigned to each vehicle of the solution.

vehicle (under the condition that the trip is compatible with other trips of the new vehicle). This can be made by a cycle that tests all redundant alleles until a feasible assignment is found: in this case the value of the dominant gene is swapped with the feasible redundant one. So the redundant one becomes dominant and vice versa; this situation is permanent after the reproduction. Only if none of the redundant values allows to fix the incompatibility during the evaluation, the fitness is penalised by the incompatibility.

3.2   Selection Methods and Genetic Operators

Three selection methods have been adopted: roulette wheel selection[6] with linear scaling, deterministic tournament selection with two individuals in each tournament [Goldberg, 1989], and local geographic selection, described in section 3.2.1.

3.2.1   Local Geographic Selection, Crossover and Mutation

While traditional selection schemata allow to select an individual within the whole population, local geographic selection is based on the idea that the population has a particular spatial structure. It is divided in *demes* or semi-isolated sub-populations, with relatively thorough gene mixing within the same deme, but restricted gene flow between different demes. One way in which demes can be created in a continuous population and environment is *isolation by distance*: the probability that two individuals mate is a fast-declining function of their geographical distance [Collins et al., 1991].

To simulate this schema, individuals are placed on a toroidal grid with one individual per grid location. Selection takes place locally on this grid. Each individual competes with its nearby neighbours. Specifically, an individual finds his mate during a *random walk* starting from his location: the individual with the best fitness value is selected. Local selection has been mainly adopted because of its applicability to multi-objective optimisation. It represents, in fact, a *niching* technique, whose aim is to maintain a useful form of diversity in the population [Harik, 1994]. In this sense, it is an alternative to the *fitness sharing* techniques [Goldberg, 1989]. Local selection has been preferred to the use of sharing techniques as it should naturally create niches without the need of problem-dependent parameter tuning.

As for the crossover, a two-point crossover operator has been used to improve GA's search, as suggested by Booker [1987].

Finally, the mutation operator acts by randomly changing the value of a gene (including redundant alleles).

---

[6] The roulette wheel selection has been applied only to the case of the single-objective algorithm, while the other methods have been applied to the multi-objective algorithm too.

3.3 Single Objective Optimisation

As a first approach, a GA has been applied to unconstrained VSP with the purpose of finding the minimum number of vehicles that cover all the trips.

After some trial runs to identify appropriate parameter settings, the following parameters have been fixed: cross-over rate = 0.8; mutation rate = 0.05.

There have not been significant differences among the three selection schemata adopted: modified roulette wheel selection with linear scaling at each generation, tournament selection and local selection. The last selection schema, developed expressly for the multi objective approach, has turned out to be well applicable also to this kind of optimisation.

The algorithm has been applied to the whole set of over 2,500 trips, taking advantage from the nature of data, which permits to divide the problem in sub-problems adopting two criteria: type of vehicle and time-interval. There are in fact two types of vehicle, whose trips are not overlapping. Moreover, three different time-intervals may be identified during the day, with different passengers quantities. In particular, the peak time (from 6.30 a.m. to 8.30 a.m.) was analysed separately.

3.4 Multiple Objective Optimisation

The most interesting application consists of a multiple objective approach: the objectives of minimising the number of vehicles and the number of deadheading trips are simultaneously considered.

Instead of combining the two objectives in a scalar fitness function, each individual is evaluated by means of a vector function, i. e. the value related to each objective is explicitly and separately considered. In [Horn et al., 1993], the multi-attribute optimisation is carried on by the use of a modified tournament selection scheme and fitness sharing techniques, while in this approach the sub-population construction is secured by the use of the local selection for reproduction based on crossover operator. Tournament selection, which operates among all the sub-populations and assures a (low) mixing of genes between the demes, is maintained as a complement to the local one.

Selection schemata that have been used (local and tournament selection), are based on a set of comparisons between two individuals[7]; the winner is the individual that *dominates* the other one. The meaning of the dominance relation is the following: an individual dominates another one if all its fitness values are not worse, and at least one of them is strictly better. If neither individual dominates the other, one of them is randomly selected.

After some preliminary numerical experiments, it was decided to reproduce 85% of the population by means of cross-over based on local selection and the

---

[7] Roulette wheel selection, instead, is based on the assignment of a probability of selection proportionate to the individual's (scalar) fitness value.

remaining by means of tournament selection; a part of these last individuals (5% of total population) is reproduced by mutation. Empirical results are given in section 4.2.

4   Numerical Results

4.1   Single Objective Optimisation

4.1.1   Parameter Setting

First, we considered only a small subproblem problem with 86 trips and a limited time period.

Some preliminary experiments revealed that 200 was a good choice for population size. Tab. 4.1 shows the results obtained in a series of 5 runs[8] performed in order to assess the effect of the number of redundant alleles on algorithm's performance, analysed by means of the fitness value of the best individual after 50 generations, using roulette wheel selection schema. Fig. 4.1 shows the trend of the average of the five runs. It can be noted that the number of redundant alleles first heavily affects the quality of the obtained solution, then a stabilisation is reached with 16 to 64 redundant alleles for each gene[9].

	Number of redundant genes						
	1	2	4	8	16	32	64
Run	Fitness value (%[10])						
1	11,77	28,54	40,02	66,65	100	100	100
2	15,37	20,71	40,02	100	100	100	100
3	14,33	22,22	0,00862	66,65	100	100	100
4	15,37	22,22	66,65	66,65	100	100	100
5	11,77	28,54	40,02	66,65	100	100	100
Aver.	13,75	24,42	47,33	73,31	100	100	100

Tab. 4.1. Results with different numbers of redundant genes

The results obtained with different selection operators are shown in Tab. 4.2 and Fig. 4.2, which report the best fitness values in a population of 200 individuals after 50 generations with 4 redundant alleles for each gene. It can be seen that all the methods are almost equivalent, even if tournament selection seems to perform a little better.

---

[8] Five different seeds for the random number generator have been used.

[9] The question pops up whether redundant alleles over the 16th are ever used during a run. However the question requires additional investigation.

[10] Fitness values are transformed to the range 0%-100%, where 100% is the best known solution.

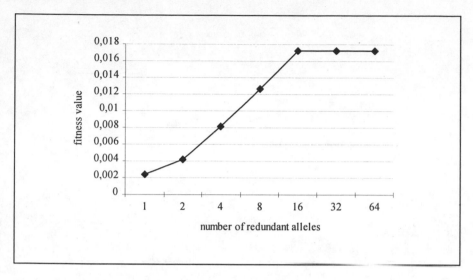

Fig. 4.1. Average trends with different numbers of redundant alleles

Although the above values for the algorithm parameters are strictly valid only for the small problem, they have been used to set the parameters for the main problem as follows:

- the initial population size is about equal to the number of one individual's genes;
- an acceptable level for the number of redundant genes is in the range from 1/10 to 1/5 of the number of genes;
- tournament and local selection are preferred.

	Selection schema		
	Roul. Wheel	Tournament	Local
Runs	Fitness value (%)		
1	40.02	50	50
2	40.02	66.65	66.65
3	50	50	66.65
4	66.65	100	50
5	40.02	100	66.65
Average	47,33	73.31	59.98

Tab. 4.2. Results with different selection methods

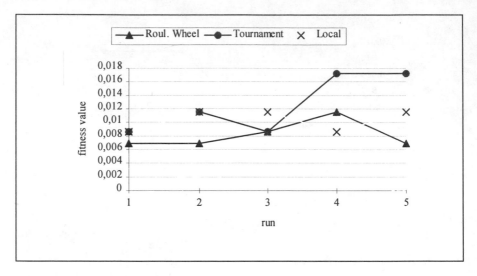

Fig. 4.2. Results with different selection methods

4.1.2 Main Problem

The results for the real problem are summarised in Tab. 4.3, which shows the number of vehicles necessary to cover the trips in the six sub-problems (two types of vehicles and three time intervals). The total number of vehicles (189) is substantially smaller than the number of vehicles actually used in the solution adopted by the company[11] (202).

	Type A vehicles		Type B vehicles		
TIME INT.	Trips	Vehicles	Trips	Vehicles	TOT.
1	86	30	110	47	77
2	194	84	243	104	188
3	734	52	1157	58	116
TOTAL	1014	85	1510	104	189

Tab. 4.3. Results for the real problem

---

[11] This solution is obtained by means of a dedicated software, developed by the bus company programmers. The program output is still not a feasible solution and requires heavy manual adjustments. At present, company is studying the practical applicability of our solutions.

4.2   Multiple Objective Optimisation

The algorithm has been applied to the peak-hour sub-problem (corresponding to the second time-interval, as mentioned in section 3.3) to test a significant case without unnecessarily overloading the system. A useful way to analyse the results of the algorithm is the study of the population's evolution in the two dimensional plane of the objectives. Fig. 4.3 shows 500 individuals iterated for 2000 generations. Plotted is the *number of vehicles* versus the *number of deadheading trips* .

Since there are just two different objectives, it should be noted that the Pareto frontier is very limited and consists of only two points. Nevertheless, the algorithm allows, with respect to the same problem and single objective optimisation, to obtain a solution with the same number of vehicles, but with a much reduced number of deadheading trips (28 for the multi-objective case and 52 in the single objective case).

4.3   Computational Data

All the computations where performed on a DEC Alfa AXP 7000/610 at the computing centre of the University of Trieste. Typical cpu-times for the problems faced are summarised in Tab. 4.5.

	prob.	n° ind.	n° redund.	n° genes	n° gener.	CPU [min]
	1	100	16	86	500	5
single-obj	2	200	100	194	500	20
	3	100	100	1014	500	87
multi-obj	1	100	16	86	500	8
	2	200	100	194	500	31

Tab. 4.4. Computational data

5   Conclusions

The vehicle scheduling problem concerning the urban public transportation system of the city of Mestre (Venice) has been successfully solved using Genetic Algorithm with redundancies.

352

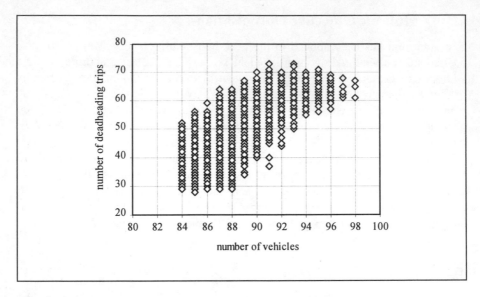

Fig 4.3. Computed individuals in the multi objective optimisation

Even though such a problem could be efficiently approached using traditional algorithms, two main features of the method have been pointed out:

- the method is very flexible and could in principle be extended to hard problems like multi depot or other more constrained cases.
- the algorithm provides several feasible solutions that can later be evaluated by the decision maker on a different basis.

Finally, it has been proved that a multi objective optimisation can be performed with a single run with comparable cpu time as needed for a single objective optimisation.

Acknowledgements

This research takes place in the PFT2 project, supported by the CNR[12] under contacts CO94.01472.74 and CO93.01855. We gratefully acknowledge the company management and programmers for their useful contribution to this study.

References

Bertossi, A.A.; Carraresi, P.; Gallo, G. (1987): On Some Matching Problems Arising in Vehicle Scheduling Models. Network 17: 271-281

Bodin, L.; Golden, B.; Assad, A.; Ball, M. (1993): Routing and Scheduling of Vehicles and Crew-The State of the Art. Computers and Operations Research: 63-211

---

[12] The CNR is the Italian National Research Centre.

Booker, L. (1987): Improving Search in Genetic Algorithms. In: Davis, L. (ed.): Genetic Algorithms and Simulated Annealing. Morgan Kaufmann Publishers, Los Altos: 61-73

Carpaneto, G.; Dell'Amico, M.; Fischetti, M.; Toth, P. (1988): Algoritmi Euristici per il Multiple Depot Vehicle Scheduling Problem con veicoli diversi. Atti delle Giornate AIRO, Pisa, Italy

Collins, R.J.; Jefferson, D.R. (1991): Selection in Massively Parallel Genetic Algorithms. In: Forrest, S. (ed.): Proceedings of The Fourth International Conference on Genetic Algorithms. San Diego: 249-256

Dantzig, G.; Fulkerson, D. (1954): Minimising the number of tankers to meet a fixed schedule. Naval Res. Logistics Quart. 1: 217-222

Garey, M.R.; Johnson, D.S. (1979): Computers and intractability. A guide to the theory of NP-completeness. "A Series of Books in the Mathematical Sciences". W. H. Freeman and Company, San Francisco

Goldberg, D.E. (1989): Genetic Algorithms in Search. Optimisation and Machine Learning. Addison-Wesley, Reading/Mass.

Harik, G. (1994): Finding Multiple Solutions in Problems of Bounded Difficulty. (IlliGAL Report n. 94002), University of Illinois at Urbana-Champaign, Illinois Genetic Algorithm Laboratory, Urbana

Horn, J.; Nafpliotis, N. (1993): Multiobjective Optimisation Using the Niched Pareto Genetic Algorithm. (IlliGAL Report n. 93005), University of Illinois at Urbana-Champaign, Illinois Genetic Algorithm Laboratory, Urbana

Nakano, R.; Yamada, T. (1991): Conventional Genetic Algorithm for Job Shop Prolems. In: Forrest, S. (ed.): Proceedings of The Fourth International Conference on Genetic Algorithms. San Diego: 474-479

Part Six
Planning in Education

Course Scheduling by Genetic Algorithms

Werner Junginger

Institut für Informatik, Universität der Bundeswehr Hamburg,
Holstenhofweg 85, D-22043 Hamburg, Germany
e-mail: w_ju@unibw-hamburg.de

Abstract. This paper is concerned with constructing timetables by computer. This problem has been investigated for about 35 years by different methods, however, no totally satisfying procedure for its solution has been found until today. As a new approach, an evolutionary algorithm will be applied to a special timetable problem which arises in German Gymnasien (high schools): the problem of assigning courses to periods. The paper describes the algorithm and reports on results achieved with it. These results suggest ideas for further research.

Keywords. timetabling, scheduling, genetic algorithm

1   Introduction

Constructing timetables is a very hard and time consuming task which has to be performed at schools and universities again and again. Constructing timetables by computer, therefore, has been investigated for about 35 years (cf. [Junginger 1982] and [Ferland 1992] for some overviews). However, no totally satisfying method for timetabling has been found until today. This is not surprising, because according to a result of Even et. al. [1976] a simplified version of a timetable problem is already NP-complete. So, several methods have been investigated, often heuristics, with more or less success.

Evolutionary algorithms constitute a class of methods by which for a lot of combinatorial problems good results have been achieved in the last years [Michalewicz 1992]. Thus, it is promising to apply these methods also to the combinatorial problems which arise in timetabling. One such approach is the application of a genetic algorithm to a class-teacher timetabling problem in Italy (Colorni et. al. [1991]). Another timetabling problem will be investigated in this paper: the problem of assigning courses to periods, which has to be performed in the upper classes of German Gymnasien (high schools). This problem is defined in section 2. A genetic algorithm to solve this problem has been developed and successfully tested. This algorithm is described in sections 3 and 4. Section 5 reports on the results. Concluding remarks are given in section 6.

2 The Problem of Course Scheduling

In the upper classes of German Gymnasien (high schools) the teaching subjects are offered as courses. The courses may vary in duration. Each pupil has to choose some of these courses. Then, a timetable for all courses has to be found such that each course is scheduled in full length and no student has to attend two courses at the same time.

To state this problem exactly, denote

C   the set of courses
S   the set of pupils (we shall call them students)
P   the set of periods in which the courses are to be given

Additionally, we are given two functions:

$d: C \rightarrow N$ where $d(c)$ is the duration (in periods) of course $c \in C$,

$w: S \rightarrow 2^C$ where $w(s)$ denotes all courses that student $s \in S$ has chosen.

The periods P represent the school hours in which the courses are given, e.g. 35 hours a week. The duration $d(c)$ of a course c expresses the number of school hours (periods) required for it. Thus, c must be assigned to $d(c)$ different periods. These periods do not need to be consecutive.

Then, the problem of course scheduling (considered in this paper) can be stated as:

Find an assignment $C \rightarrow P$ such that

a) each $c \in C$ is assigned to exactly $d(c)$ different periods, and
b) for each $s \in S$ all courses $w(s)$ are assigned to different periods.

Each such assignment yields a valid timetable.

As an example, consider 8 courses, 6 students, and 5 time periods. Then, we have

a set of time periods $P = \{ p_1 , p_2 , p_3 , p_4 , p_5 \}$
a set of courses $C = \{ c_1 , c_2 , c_3 , c_4 , c_5 , c_6 , c_7 , c_8 \}$
with length $d(c_i)$:   3   3   2   2   2   2   2   2
and a set of students $S = \{ s_1 , s_2 , s_3 , s_4 , s_5 , s_6 \}$

Each student has chosen 2 courses according to

$w(s_1) = \{ c_1 , c_5 \}$ $w(s_2) = \{ c_1 , c_6 \}$
$w(s_3) = \{ c_2 , c_3 \}$ $w(s_4) = \{ c_2 , c_4 \}$
$w(s_5) = \{ c_1 , c_8 \}$ $w(s_6) = \{ c_2 , c_7 \}$

It is not very difficult to find a solution in this special case. One possibility can be seen in table 1. Here, each course is assigned according to its length, and no student has to attend two courses simultaneously.

period 1 :	c_1	c_2				
period 2 :	c_1	c_2				
period 3 :	c_1	c_2				
period 4 :	c_3	c_4	c_5	c_6	c_7	c_8
period 5 :	c_3	c_4	c_5	c_6	c_7	c_8

Table 1. Valid timetable for the example of section 2

3 The Structure of the Genetic Algorithm

To solve this problem, a genetic algorithm has been developed. For this, first an appropriate *representation* of a solution of the problem must be defined. This can be done easily and adequately by using a zero-one matrix (x_{pc}) in which the rows signify the periods and the columns signify the courses. Then $x_{pc} = 1$, if course c is assigned to period p , and 0 otherwise. For example, the matrix in table 2 corresponds to the timetable of table 1.

			c_1	c_2	c_3	c_4	c_5	c_6	c_7	c_8
period	1:		1	1	0	0	0	0	0	0
period	2:		1	1	0	0	0	0	0	0
period	3:		1	1	0	0	0	0	0	0
period	4:		0	0	1	1	1	1	1	1
period	5:		0	0	1	1	1	1	1	1

Table 2. Representation of the timetable of table 1 as a 0-1 matrix

The genetic algorithm proceeds as usual with some variations. Table 3 gives an outline of it. First, an *initial population* of n individuals is created, where n is a user-defined parameter. These individuals are generated by randomly producing zero-one matrices as representations of solutions. However, in doing this, an aspect of feasibility is taken into account such that each individual contains exactly d(c) ones in column c . So, each course in any individual just takes place as often as required.

Then, the r most fit individuals are selected ($r \le n$ is a user-defined parameter) and used to create new individuals (offspring) by genetic operators like crossover and mutation. Details about these genetic operators and their use as well as about the fitness function will be given in section 4. After this, some individuals of the current population (parents) will be replaced by offspring (children) in order to yield a new population. This *reproduction* is repeated until a valid timetable is found or some other termination condition (e.g. a limit for the iteration number) is met.

---

generate an initial population of size n
repeat
        reproduction:
            select the r most fit individuals
            create r offspring from them using genetic operators
            build a new population by replacing individuals by offspring
until   termination criterion holds

Table 3. Outline of the genetic algorithm

This procedure is a variation of the ususal basic scheme of genetic algorithms. It is also known as *steady-state reproduction* [Davis 1991] or as *modified genetic algorithm* [Michalewicz 1992]. As this can be performed in different ways, two versions have been implemented and investigated:

Version 1 of reproduction:

Select the r most fit individuals and create r children. Then replace the r least fit individuals of the current population by these r children. This yields the next population.

Version 2 of reproduction:

Select the r most fit individuals and create r children. Add these children to the current population. Select from this set the n most fit individuals. This yields the next population.

4   Details about the Genetic Algorithm

Due to the way they are generated, all individuals of the initial population are already feasible concerning the number of periods each course is assigned to. However, it is not guaranteed that each student does not attend two courses at the same time. Consider, for example, the timetable given in table 4 with regard to the example in section 2.

		c_1	c_2	c_3	c_4	c_5	c_6	c_7	c_8
period	1:	1	1	0	0	1	0	0	0
period	2:	0	1	1	0	1	1	0	1
period	3:	1	1	0	0	0	0	0	0
period	4:	1	0	0	1	0	1	1	0
period	5:	0	0	1	1	0	0	1	1

Table 4. Example of a nonoptimal timetable

This timetable contains in period 1 a clash for student s_1 because he has chosen the courses c_1 and c_5 and both courses are assigned to this period. Additionally, period 2 contains a clash for s_3 whose choice is $w(s_3) = \{ c_2 , c_3 \}$. Therefore, as an appropriate *fitness function,* the number of clashes for all students is summarized. Then, a high function value corresponds to a bad solution, and an individual that corresponds to a valid timetable has a fitness value of zero.

In our algorithm *crossover* is performed in a similar way as the usual one-point crossover. Given two zero-one matrices as individuals for crossover, a column number *pos* (before the last column) is chosen at random. Then all columns after column *pos* are exchanged between these two matrices. Consider as an example table 5, where in the upper half two individuals are given (with additional rows denoting the courses). If *pos* is equal to 3, then the result of crossover can be seen at the bottom. This kind of crossover corresponds to the classical one-point crossover of zero-one strings when each component of the strings is being replaced by a column. It maintains also the feasibility of the individuals concerning the number of ones in a column, because whole valid columns are exchanged.

The fitness of the children produced by crossover can be better than their parent's fitness, as the example in table 5 demonstrates. However, this is not guaranteed. The same is true for mutation, the other genetic operation. *Mutation* is also performed analogeous to the usual procedure. A column of a zero-one matrix is chosen at random. Then both a one and a zero element in this column is chosen at random and both are exchanged. This yields a new individual for which feasibility concerning the number of ones in a column is preserved again. Table 6 contains an example: The matrix on the left side is mutated in column 5; this yields the matrix to the right (the changed elements are marked by circles).

parents:

c_1	c_2	c_3		c_4	c_5	c_6	c_7	c_8
1	1	0	|	0	0	0	0	0
1	1	1	|	1	1	1	1	1
1	1	1	|	1	1	1	1	1
0	0	0	|	0	0	0	0	0
0	0	0	|	0	0	0	0	0

fitness value 12

c_1	c_2	c_3		c_4	c_5	c_6	c_7	c_8
0	0	0	|	0	0	0	0	0
0	0	0	|	0	0	0	0	0
1	1	0	|	0	0	0	0	0
1	1	1	|	1	1	1	1	1
1	1	1	|	1	1	1	1	1

fitness value 12

children:

c_1	c_2	c_3		c_4	c_5	c_6	c_7	c_8
1	1	0	|	0	0	0	0	0
1	1	1	|	0	0	0	0	0
1	1	1	|	0	0	0	0	0
0	0	0	|	1	1	1	1	1
0	0	0	|	1	1	1	1	1

fitness value 2

c_1	c_2	c_3		c_4	c_5	c_6	c_7	c_8
0	0	0	|	0	0	0	0	0
0	0	0	|	1	1	1	1	1
1	1	0	|	1	1	1	1	1
1	1	1	|	0	0	0	0	0
1	1	1	|	0	0	0	0	0

fitness value 7

Table 5. Example of crossover

c_1	c_2	c_3	c_4	c_5	c_6	c_7	c_8
1	1	0	0	(1)	0	0	0
0	1	1	0	1	1	0	1
1	1	0	0	0	0	0	0
1	0	0	1	0	1	1	0
0	0	1	1	(0)	0	1	1

c_1	c_2	c_3	c_4	c_5	c_6	c_7	c_8
1	1	0	0	(0)	0	0	0
0	1	1	0	1	1	0	1
1	1	0	0	0	0	0	0
1	0	0	1	0	1	1	0
0	0	1	1	(1)	0	1	1

Table 6. Example of mutation

The *use of crossover and mutation* is, as usual, controlled by a crossover probability *pcross* and a mutation rate *pmut* . Two different approaches have been implemented. Tables 7 and 8 contain more details about them.

```
dofor    each of the r selected individuals
         generate a random (float) number pc from the range [0,1]
         if  pc < pcross  then
             the individual will become a candidate for crossover
             resp.
             perform crossover, if there is already another candidate for this
         else
             dofor    each column of the individual
                      generate a random (float) number pm from the range [0,1]
                      if  pm < pmut  then
                          mutate this column
                      endif
             enddo
         endif
enddo
```

Table 7. Use of crossover and mutation, first approach: Both crossover and mutation depend on probabilitiy parameters

(1)   First approach:

Crossover and mutation, both depending on probabilitiy parameters.

For each of the r selected individuals, a random (float) number pc is generated from the range [0,1]. Then, an individual will become a candidate for crossover (and if there is already a candidate, crossover will be performed) if $pc < pcross$. Otherwise, for each column of the individual, another random (float) number pm is generated, and a column is mutated if $pm < pmut$.

(2)   Second approach:

Crossover depending on pcross, with mutation otherwise.

For each of the r chosen individuals, a random (float) number pc is generated from the range [0,1]. Then, an individual will become a candidate for crossover (and if there is already a candidate, crossover will be performed) if $pc < pcross$. Otherwise, a column of the individual is chosen at random and mutated.

Additionaly, a third approach can be derived from the other approaches :

(3)   *Mutation only.*

This can be derived either from (1) or from (2) by setting $pcross = 0$. In this case, no crossover can occur. Then only mutations will be performed. As can be derived from tests, it is advisable to combine this approach with (2) in order to get a suitable mutation rate.

---

dofor   each of the *r* selected individuals
    generate a random (float) number *pc* from the range [0,1]
    if *pc < pcross* **then**
        the individual will become a candidate for crossover
        resp.
        perform crossover, if there is already another candidate for this
    else
        chose a column of the individual at random
        and mutate this column
    endif
enddo

Table 8. Use of crossover and mutation, second approach: Only crossover depends on a probability parameter

Note, that in this algorithm an individual is either used for crossover or it may be mutated. This is different to the common practice where an individual may be mutated independently of crossover [Michalewicz 1992].

5   Results

The algorithm has been implemented in the programming language C and tested on a number of examples. At first, the example given in section 2 was used to test the principal usability of this algorithm for determining course schedules. It succeeded in finding a valid solution, however, depending on the right setting of the parameters. Table 9 contains some of the results. The parameters *n*, *r*, *pcross*, and *pmut* have been described in sections 3 and 4. A value of 1 for *pmut* means a use of crossover and mutation according to approach (2) as described in section 4, otherwise according to (1). The last column contains the number of iterations which were needed to find a valid solution (fitness value 0), both for a processing according to version 1 of reproduction and to version 2. The computational effort of evaluating the fitness is equal in both versions: in each iteration the fitness of *n+r* individuals has to be calculated.

For each setting of *n, r, pcross*, and *pmut* given in table 9 a valid solution was found. Both versions of reproduction succeeded after a small number of iterations. The results do not permit to give preference to one of these versions. However, something else is notable: the significance of mutation for this kind of problem. Usually, for *pmut* = 1 an optimal solution was found with fewer iterations than for other values of *pmut*. A setting of *pmut* = 1 guarantees a mutation of an individual if it is not used for crossover (whereas e.g. *pmut* < 0.2 does not guarantee this). Additionally, it is interesting to note that a relatively small value of *n* = 4 (last line) is sufficient to find a valid solution, and in this case only mutations have been used (*pcross* = 0).

n	r	pcross	pmut	Iterations (Version 1 / 2)
20	13	0.45	0.2	38 / 21
20	13	0.45	1	18 / 25
20	13	0.6	1	12 / 11
10	6	0.45	0.1	61 / 61
10	6	0.45	0.15	69 / 49
10	6	0.45	1	47 / 26
4	2	0	1	26 / 27

Table 9. Example with 8 courses, 6 students, and 5 periods

Finally note, that in this case approximately the same number of iterations was needed as in an instance with a much greater population of $n = 20$ and $r = 13$ (row 2). The reason for this may be the good quality of a first population for this example (fitness value 5 and 6, resp., in both cases). As mutation is very efficient for this problem, only a few iterations are necessary to find a valid solution in both cases.

It is also possible to find valid solutions in larger examples. This may be demonstrated by table 10. Here, 15 courses are given (5 of length 5 and 10 of length 3) and 25 students, each of them having choosen a varying number of courses (between 3 and 5, mostly one or two of them having length 5). It can be shown that for this example at least 19 periods are necessary to build a valid timetable. So, it was demanded to generate timetables with exactly 19 periods. As table 10 demonstrates, different settings of the parameters are successful.

n	r	pcross	pmut	valid solutions version 1	version 2
16	10	0.25	0.1	3 of 10 tests (400-637)	2 of 10 tests (423-530)
16	10	0	1	7 of 10 tests (230-1138)	4 of 10 tests (234-452)
10	6	0	1	3 of 10 tests (310-744)	4 of 10 tests (278-675)

Table 10. Example with 15 courses, 25 students, and 19 periods

In the last columns of table 10 the result is to be read as follows: For each setting of the parameters 10 tests with different sequences of random numbers have been performed. The last two columns indicate how many of them succeeded in producing a valid timetable, both by reproduction version 1 and 2. The numbers in brackets below give the least and the maximum number of iterations that was required to find such a timetable. If no valid solution was found, the fitness of the best soultion was usually 1 or 2, and a first such solution was usually found after 300-500 iterations.

As can be seen from table 10, both version 1 and 2 proved to be approximately equally good. However, in other cases version 2 can be better than version 1. This may be demonstrated by table 11. In this example, 6 courses of length 5 and 16 courses of length 3 are given. Then, 60 students are incorporated and each of them has to choose 2 courses of length 5 and 3 courses of length 3.

n	r	pcross	pmut	valid solutions	
				version 1	version 2
16	11	0	1	0 of 10 tests [fitness: 9-53]	3 of 10 tests (1121-1861)
18	13	0	1	1 of 10 tests (1619)	5 of 10 tests (1189-1806)
18	13	0.3	1	0 of 10 tests [fitness: 14-54]	0 of 10 tests [fitness: 14-61]

Table 11. Example with 22 courses, 60 students, and 19 periods

It can be shown that for this problem a valid timetable requires at least 19 periods, so this was forced. In this case, the performance of version 2 proves to be better than that of version 1. (Table 11 is to be read in the same way as table 10. Additionally, for those cases in which no valid timetable could be found, the domain of the fitness of the best solutions found after 2000 iterations is given in square brackets.)

Note, that a valid solution has been found by using mutations only and without crossover. To test the influence of the crossover rate, the examples of table 10 and 11 have also been tested with larger values of $pcross$, e.g. $pcross = 0.65$. However, usually the results were less good than under the settings of table 10 and 11.

The convergence of this algorithm is typical for genetic algorithms: Usually, the fitness of the initial population is rather bad. In the example of table 10 this value lies between about 45 and 90. Thereafter, it will quickly improve at the beginning and rather slowly in subsequent iterations. In some cases the algorithm converges to a valid solution whereas in other cases it seems to converge to a suboptimum. In such a case the best fitness value does not reach zero.

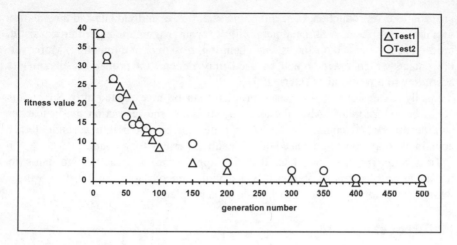

Fig. 1 Behaviour of convergence

Figure 1 shows as an example the behaviour of two tests presented in Table 10. The circles and the triangles, resp., represent the fitness values of the best individuals in each generation. One of these tests (triangle) reaches a valid solution in generation 304, whereas the other circle maintains a fitness value of 1 from generation 350 on.

Another result is notable. Genetic algorithms depend on random numbers. Usually, these numbers are produced by algorithms generating pseudo random numbers. In the algorithm presented here we use a random number generator of Chang et al [1994]. As usual, depending on a parameter *seed*, different sequences of random numbers are generated. It was observed that the behavior of the genetic algorithm also depends on this sequence of random numbers. This becomes apperent in table 10 and 11. Here, with the same setting of *n, r, pcross,* and *pmut* several tests were performed with different values of *seed*. As pointed out in the tables, some of these tests succeeded in finding a valid solution, others did not. This may be caused by different ways of the search process depending on *seed*.

6   Concluding Remarks

The results produced by this kind of algorithm show that genetic algorithms can be successfully applied to timetabling problems treated here. Coloni et. al.´s investigations [1991] confirm this for a different kind of timetabling problem. In both investigations, the results are similar insofar as it cannot be guaranteed to find an optimal solution without any clashes concerning the restrictions.

In this case, a suboptimum might have been found. This is a well known problem in designing genetic algorithms: How to find an appropriate design of the algorithm such that it will not converge to a suboptimum. In our algorithm, therefore, it is worth-while to invest additional research efforts in modifying the procedure of reproduction, concerning the selection of individuals and the creation of a new population. Additional possibilities for improving the algorithm consist in modifying the genetic operators, e.g. changing crossover and mutation. Moreover, the choice which operator will be used may depend on probability parameters according to a proposal of Davis [1991].

Finally, extensions of the treated problem can be investigated also. So, rooms could be incorporated. Also, the teaching staff and the restriction that a teacher cannot attend two courses at the same time can be taken into account. Other constraints may concern the need of consecutive periods for a course.

To summarize, we can state, that the application of genetic algorithms to timetable problems is an approach which yields encouraging results. It is worthwhile to also apply them to other kinds of this problem.

References

Chang, P.-L.; Hwang, S.-N.; Kao, Ch. (1994): Some good Multipiers for Random Number Generator for 16-Bit Microcomputers. Computers Ops. Res. 21: 199-204

Colorni, A.; Dorigo, M.; Maniezzo, V. (1991): Gli algoritmi genetici e il problema dell'orario. Ricera Operativa 60: 5-31

Davis, L. (1991): Handbook of Genetic Algorithms. Van Norstrand Reinhold, New York

Even, S.; Itai, A.; Shamir, A. (1976): On the Complexity of Timetable and Multicommodity Flow Problems. SIAM J. Comput. 5: 691-703

Ferland, J.A.; Lavoie, A. (1992): Exchanges Procedures for Timetabling Problems. Discr. Appl. Mathematics 35: 237-252

Junginger, W. (1982): Zum aktuellen Stand der automatischen Stundenplanerstellung. Angewandte Informatik 24: 20-25

Michalewicz, Z. (1992): Genetic Algorithms + Data Structure = Evolution Programs. Springer, Berlin

Appendix

About the Authors

Flavio Baita graduated in Business Administration. Currently he works for the Department of Applied Mathematics and Computer Science at the University of Venice. His research areas are computer science themes and combinatorial optimisation.

Richard J. Bauer, Jr. is Associate Dean and Associate Professor of the School of Business and Administration at St. Mary's University in San Antonio, Texas, USA. He is author of *Genetic Algorithms and Investment Strategies*, published by John Wiley & Sons in 1994, and several other articles concerning expert systems and computerised trading applications. Bauer is a Chartered Financial Analyst and Secretary of the San Antonio Society of Financial Analysts. He earned his Ph.D. in Finance at Texas Tech University and also has a B.S. in Physics, M.S. in Physics, and M.S. in Economics from Baylor University. He is a member of the American Finance Association, Financial Management Association, Southern Finance Association, and Southwestern Finance Association.

Christian Bierwirth studied Mathematics and Philosophy at the Universities of Hamburg and Heidelberg, Germany. From 1988 to 1992 he was an assistant of Prof. Dr. Siegmar Stoeppler at the University of Bremen. In 1992 he published a doctoral dissertation on *Flowshop Scheduling with parallel Genetic Algorithms*. Since 1993 he has worked as a lecturer for Operations Research and Business Informatics at the chair of Logistics of Prof. Dr. H. Kopfer, Bremen.

Jörg Biethahn is currently Professor of Operations Research and Business Informatics at the Georg-August-University of Göttingen, Germany. After studying Mathematics and Business Administration he received the Ph.D. in Business Sciences in 1972. From 1973 to 1979 he was Assistant Professor at the University of Frankfurt/M. before becoming Full Professor of Business Adminstration with focus on Business Informatics at the Universities of Bochum and, later, Duisburg. In 1984 he became Full Professor and head of the local computer center at Göttingen. The University of Hefei, China, elected him Visiting Professor in 1988. Prof. Biethahn has published articles and several books on holistic information management, simulation, CASE, linear programming and other themes. His current research interests include computer-based training, expert systems, softcomputing and controlling.

Royce Bowden is an Assistant Professor of Industrial Engineering at Mississippi State University, USA. He received his Ph.D. degree in Industrial Engineering from Mississippi State University. His research interests include artifcial intelligence applications to manufacturing control problems and the application of computer simulation to the analysis of manufacturing systems.

Rob A.C.M. Broekmeulen is a research scientist at the Agrotechnological Research Institute, Wageningen, The Netherlands. He received his degree in Agricultural Sciences at the Wageningen Agricultural University. His research interests include operations research themes like decision support systems, combinatorial optimisation and simulation. Current research projects are concerned with logistic problems in the postharvest chain of agricultural products. He currently works on his doctoral thesis with Prof. Dr. E.H.L. Aarts from Eindhoven University of Technology as his advisor.

Stanley Bullington is an Associate Professor of Industrial Engineering at Mississippi State University, USA. He received his Ph.D. degree in Industrial Engineering from Auburn University. His research interests include operations planning and scheduling, and quality management.

Lee G. Cooper is Professor at the Anderson School, UCLA, USA, since 1969. His methods for studying market structure and market response have been published in Management Science, Marketing Science, the Journal of Marketing Research, Psychometrika, Behavioral Science, the Journal of Consumer Research, and Applied Stochastic Models and Data Analysis. His 1988 book on Market-Share Analysis (with Masao Nakanishi) won the „Excellent Publication Award" from the Japanese Society of Commercial Sciences - the first book published outside Japan to be honored.

Markus Ettl studied Computer Science at the University of Erlangen, Germany, where he received the Engineering degree in 1990. He is currently pursuing a doctoral degree at the University of Erlangen-Nürnberg in the group of Prof. Dr. Ulrich Herzog. His research interests include queueing networks, performance evaluation, and application of stochastic approximation and optimisation techniques, with emphasis on modeling and analysis of telecommunications and manufacturing systems.

Emanuel Falkenauer holds an M.Sc. in Computer Science and a Ph.D. in Applied Sciences, both from the Free University of Brussels (ULB), Belgium. Since 1989 he has been with the Department of Industrial Management and Automation of CRIF (Research Centre of the Belgian Metalworking Industry), where he is involved in research and development in the fields of optimisation of industrial operations and collision-free path planning of redundant robots, with a special emphasis on the use of genetic algorithms in these fields. He has authored and coauthored more than twenty articles on the subjects. His research interests include genetic algorithms and combinatorial optimisation in general, machine learning and artificial intelligence in general, complexity theory, and formal systems.

Bogdan Filipic received diploma, masters and doctoral degrees in Computer Science from the University of Ljubljana, Slovenia, in 1983, 1989 and 1993, respectively. From 1983 to 1984 he worked at the LTH Computer Center, Skofja Loka. In 1985 he joined the Computer Science Department of the Jozef Stefan Institute in Ljubljana as a research assistant. He is currently a researcher at the Artificial Intelligence Laboratory of the Jozef Stefan Institute, and at the Faculty of Mechanical Engineering, University of Ljubljana. He has participated in several research and applied projects in the area of automated knowledge synthesis and expert systems. Recently, he has worked on genetic algorithms and their applications in engineering and resource management. He is a member of the IEEE Computer Society and Slovenian Artificial Intelligence Society.

Terry Fogarty has been at UWE, Bristol, England, since 1986 first as a Ph.D. student, then a lecturer and now a principal lecturer. He did his Ph.D. from 1986-89 using the genetic algorithm to optimise rules for controlling combustion in multiple burner installations with British Steel plc. He went on to lead a large project from 1990-92 using the genetic algorithm to optimise Bayesian Classifiers for credit control applications with TSB Bank Ltd. Current projects are on sugar beet presses optimisation, coevolving communicating rule-based control systems, optimising combustion in a multiple burner boiler, evolving machine vision for surface inspection and evolving gate for a wall climbing robot. He has published widely in journals, books and conferences and is on the editorial board of the Evolutionary Computation Journal and the programme committees for the International Conferences on Genetic Algorithms and Parallel Problem Solving from Nature.

David B. Fogel received the Ph.D. in Engineering Sciences (Systems Science) from the University of California at San Diego, USA. He is currently chief scientist of Natural Selection, Inc. Dr. Fogel has numerous journal and conference publications in evolutionary algorithms, and is the author of *Evolutionary Computation: Toward a New Philosophy of Machine Intelligence*, published by IEEE Press, 1995.

Lawrence J. Fogel received the Ph.D. in Engineering from the University of California at Los Angeles, USA. He is currently president of Natural Selection, Inc. Dr. Fogel was co-author of *Artificial Intelligence through Simulated Evolution*, published by John Wiley, 1966. He was technical chairman of the Third Annual Conference on Evolutionary Programming (1994) and will serve as general chairman of the Fifth Annual Conference on Evolutionary Programming (1996) in San Diego.

Ingrid Gerdes received a masters degree in Mathematics with subsidiary subject Business Management in 1989 from the Technical University of Braunschweig, Germany. Since 1990 she has worked as a scientist for the German Aerospace Research Center, Institute for Flight Guidance, where she has been involved as a staff member and leader in various projects such as the capacity enhancement of Frankfurt airport. She is also a teacher in mathematics for the education of mathematical-technical assistants.

Arlindo Gómes is a lecturer at the Computer Science Department of the Federal University of Espirito Santo, Brazil. His research interests include mathematical and heuristic programming oriented to solve combinatorial optimisation problems. He received his masters degree (1983) and his Dr.Sc. (1986) in Systems Engineering and Computing at the Federal University of Rio the Janeiro.

Neil Ireson is a Ph.D. student at the UWE, Bristol, England, where he has worked as a researcher on various projects since 1990. His research interests include applying genetic algorithms to knowledge discovery in databases and specifically the evolution of ecosystems in the context of classifiers. He received his B.A. in Management Studies from Liverpool John Moores University and his M.Sc. in Artificial Intelligence from Cranfield Institute of Technology.

Yoko Ishino received his B.A. degree in 1987 from the University of Tokyo, Japan. Since then, she has been employed at LION corporation. She is also currently a graduate student at GSSM, the University of Tsukuba. Her research interests include marketing sciences and genetic algorithm-based machine learning.

Werner Junginger is Professor for Applied Computer Science/Business Informatics at the University of the German Forces, Hamburg. Having graduated in Mathematics in 1965 he received the Ph.D. from the University of Stuttgart in 1970. From 1971 to 1979 he was Assistant Professor at the Computer Science Department of the University of Stuttgart. Afterwards, he became Associate Professor and Full Professor (1981) in Hamburg. His research interests include computer-aided timetabling, personnel scheduling, genetic algorithms, computerised OR-methods in business, and software engineering.

Herbert Kopfer studied Mathematics at the Technical University of Darmstadt from 1972 to 1978. From 1978 to 1982 he worked as a software engineer in industry, and from 1982 to 1991 as an assistant at the Universities of Bremen, Dortmund and Berlin (FU). In 1985 he received his Ph.D. from the Department of Computer Science of the University of Bremen, and in 1991 he finished his *Habilitation* at the Department of Economics of the Free University of Berlin. He had a professorship for Business Informatics at the University of Siegen from 1990 to 1992. Since 1992 he has been a Professor for Logistics at the University of Bremen.

Matthias Krause is a graduate student of Business Administration at the University of Göttingen, Germany, Department of Business Informatics. In his diploma thesis, supervised by Dr. V. Nissen, he worked on evolutionary algorithms in facility layout.

Robert Marks. After graduating in Engineering from the University of Melbourne, he studied at M.I.T. and the University of Cambridge before completing a doctorate in Economics at Stanford University. Since 1978 he has lectured at the Australian Graduate School of Management, where his research interests are the use of game theory and machine learning in the analysis of strategic behaviour, energy and environmental policy, drug policy, and the economics of the world oil market. He has recently been a visitor to Stanford University and the Santa Fe Institute.

Francesco Mason is currently Professor of Operations Research at the Faculty of Economics at the University of Venice. Being author of about 40 publications, he is mainly interested in combinatorial optimisation applied to transport organisation problems.

Michael de la Maza is a cofounder of Redfire Capital Management Group, Cambridge/MA, USA, a money management firm which employs evolutionary algorithms to create fully automated trading strategies for bond, currency, and equity markets. He has a graduate degree from the Artificial Intelligence Laboratory at the Massachusetts Institute of Technology.

John McDonnell is a principal engineer at the Navy NCCOSC, RDT&E Division, USA, where he is involved with teleoperated and autonomous robotic programs, virtual environments and neural networks for pattern recognition. He also serves as an Adjunct Professor to the San Diego State University Mechanical Engineering Department where he teaches courses in simulation, optimisation, and controls. He is also the current president of the Evolutionary Programming Society (1995-1996).

David Midgley. After graduating in Physics, he completed his doctorate in Marketing at the University of Bradford, Australia. A foundation faculty member at the Australian Graduate School of Management, he has written widely in new product marketing and the process of marketing innovation, marketing strategy, and export planning.

Ricardo Muñoz is a student in the sixth year of Informatic Engineering at the Santiago University of Chile.

Volker Nissen is Assistant Professor of Operations Research and Business Informatics at the University of Göttingen, Germany. After studying Business Administration and Economics at the Universities of Nuremberg and Manchester, he graduated with distinction in 1991. Then he held a research position in an interdisciplinary institution at Göttingen University, also studying Cognitive Psychology. He received the Ph.D. in Business Sciences (Business Informatics) from the University of Göttingen in 1994. Dr. Nissen has published many papers on evolutionary algorithms, with a focus on management applications. He is author of *Evolutionäre Algorithmen. Darstellung, Beispiele, betriebswirtschaftliche Anwendungsmöglichkeiten.*, published by DUV Verlag, 1994. Dr. Nissen is on the programme committee of the IEEE Int. Conference on Evolutionary Computing 1995 in Perth, Australia. He also leads the softcomputing research group at Göttingen which is part of the European EvoNet of Excellence in Evolutionary Computation.

Victor Parada Daza is a lecturer at the Informatic Engineering Department at the Santiago University of Chile. His research interests include artificial intelligence and heuristic programming oriented to solve combinatorial optimisation problems. He is a Chemical Engineer and received his masters degree in Industrial Engineering from the Catholic University of Rio de Janeiro in 1986. In 1989, he received his Dr.Sc. degree in Systems Engineering and Computer Science from the Federal University of Rio the Janeiro.

Carlo Poloni is a Research Assistant of Machinery Design in the Department of Energetics at the University of Trieste, Italy. His present main interests involve the study and application of algorithms for fluid dynamic and multi disciplinary design and optimisation and in this field he has implemented and developed GA tecniques. Carlo Poloni co-authored about 20 papers, some of which appeared in international journals like Journal of Wind Engineering and Industrial Aerodynamics, and Review of Scientific Instruments.

Wilfred Recker is currently Professor of Civil Engineering and Director of the Institute of Transportation Studies, University of California, Irvine, USA. He was educated at the Carnegie Institute of Technology of Carnegie-Mellon University where he was awarded the Ph.D. degree in Civil Engineering. Dr. Recker is active as a university educator, researcher, and administrator. He has authored over seventy research articles and served as principal investigator on many research projects in both transportation and applied mechanics. His initial research efforts were directed toward the development of solution techniques for complex problems in elasto-dynamics. The major portion of his research endeavors, however, have been focused on travel demand models, disaggregate modeling methodologies and transportation systems analysis. He currently heads the California Advanced Transportation Management Systems (ATMS) Testbed Research Program.

Craig Rindt is a graduate student researcher for the Institute of Transportation Studies at the University of California, Irvine, USA, where he has worked on various research projects for the past two years. Mr. Rindt received a B.S. in Civil Engineering at UCI and is currently working towards a Ph.D. in Transportation Systems Engineering. His areas of research include operations research, traffic control, and traffic simulation models.

Ivo Rixen studied Business and Management Science from 1985 to 1990 at the University of Bremen, Germany. In 1992 he became an assistant of Prof. Dr. Siegmar Stoeppler at the Institute for Production and Computer Science in Bremen. Since 1993 he has worked as a doctoral student at the Chair of Logistics of Prof. Dr. Herbert Kopfer. His research interests include production planning and heuristic optimisation. In his doctoral thesis he develops genetic algorithms for production scheduling.

Markus Schwehm studied Mathematics at TU Karlsruhe and TU München, Germany, and received his diploma degree in 1988. Afterwards he did civil service at the Gesellschaft für Strahlen und Umweltforschung (GSF), Munich, working on visualisation, pattern recognition and neural networks. He currently works at the chair of Prof. Dr. Ulrich Herzog at the University of Erlangen-Nürnberg in the group on massively parallel architectures and algorithms. He writes his doctoral thesis about massively parallel genetic algorithms.

Takao Terano received his BA degree in 1976, M.A. degree in 1978, both from the University of Tokyo, Japan, and became Doctor of Engineering in 1991 at the Tokyo Institute of Technology. Between 1978 and 1989, he was research scientist at the Central Research Institute of the Electric Power Industry. He is currently Associate Professor at the Graduate School of Systems Management (GSSM), the University of Tsukuba, Tokyo. His research interests include genetic algorithms, case-based reasoning, knowledge acquisition, machine learning, and distributed artificial intelligence. He is a member of the editorial board of various AI-related academic societies in Japan and a member of IEEE and AAAI.

Walter Ukovich is Associate Professor of Operations Research in the Department of Electrical Engineering, Electronics and Computer Science at the University of Trieste, Italy. He also teaches Operations Research for Engineering students at the University of Udine, Italy. His present research interests include planning, management and operations problems in different application areas, such as logistics, transportation, and public services. Prof. Ukovich co-authored about 100 papers, some of which appeared in international journals such as Operations Research, Journal of Optimisation Theory and Applications, International Journal of Production Economics, SIAM Journal on Algebraic and Discrete Methods, European Journal of Operational Research.

Steven Vere obtained a Ph.D. in Computer Science from the University of California at Los Angeles, USA, in 1970. He has done research in artificial intelligence for the past 20 years in the areas of machine learning, temporal planning, and integrated agents. He has held academic and research positions at the University of Illinois at Chicago, the Jet Propulsion Laboratory, and an aerospace corporation research laboratory. He is the author of the article on Planning in the Encyclopedia of Artificial Intelligence. His integrated agent, Homer, was featured in the Scientific American magazine in 1991, and was rated the top integrated agent in the field. Since 1993 Dr. Vere has been a member of the AI applications group at Bank of America.

Kazuyuki Yoshinaga received his B.A. degree in 1988 from Waseda University, Japan. He is currently Lecturer at Kurume-Shinai Women's College. He is also a graduate student at GSSM, the University of Tsukuba. His research interests include machine learning, reinforcement learning, and genetic algorithms.

Deniz Yuret is a cofounder of Redfire Capital Management Group, Cambridge/MA, USA, a money management firm which employs evolutionary algorithms to create fully automated trading strategies for bond, currency, and equity markets. He has a graduate degree from the Artificial Intelligence Laboratory at the Massachusetts Institute of Technology.

Springer-Verlag
and the Environment

We at Springer-Verlag firmly believe that an international science publisher has a special obligation to the environment, and our corporate policies consistently reflect this conviction.

We also expect our business partners – paper mills, printers, packaging manufacturers, etc. – to commit themselves to using environmentally friendly materials and production processes.

The paper in this book is made from low- or no-chlorine pulp and is acid free, in conformance with international standards for paper permanency.